The American Polity

The American Polity

A Social and Cultural Interpretation

WILLIAM C. MITCHELL

UNIVERSITY OF OREGON

New York: THE FREE PRESS OF GLENCOE
London: MACMILLAN NEW YORK

To My Wife, Joyce

Preface

This volume is an *interpretative essay* on American politics as viewed in the early 1960's. And while the book is expected to be of some value to all persons interested in American politics, it is primarily intended for advanced students. In the language of economics, this book might be described as "intermediate theory." That is, it is suitable for advanced undergraduates and beginning graduate students or for those persons who have already given some thought on how better to understand the American political system.

The book is guided by an explicit conceptual framework derived mostly from the sociological work of Talcott Parsons. Two objectives have dominated my thinking and writing: first, to illustrate the potentialities of "structural-functional" analysis with regard to the study of political systems; and, secondly, to synthesize a considerable amount of heterogeneous data—both institutional and behavioral—on American politics so that we might have a more integrated and complete view of our nation's political life.

I have chosen to use the "structural-functional" approach largely because it seems to offer the best possibilities for eventually developing a general theory of American politics and, indeed, of political systems. At best, most "theories" of American politics are partial, dealing with limited questions on parties, elections, and interest groups. The emphasis has been placed upon conflict in allocative processes and outcomes. The conceptual scheme employed in this book is based on the assumption that polities, like social systems, consist of many types of action or processes. Conflict and allocation, although very crucial aspects, are still only part of the total story. The reader, therefore, will find a variety of processes and materials in the following pages that may appear neither political nor politically relevant. I hope that the discussions will convince him to the contrary. Among the questions raised are the following:

1. How is the polity integrated?
2. How are societal goals determined and achieved?
3. How is the polity maintained through time?
4. How are values and costs allocated?
5. Who gets what from the system?

Admittedly, these inquiries are hardly unique or unconventional; various political philosophers and scientists have attempted to find or provide answers to them in different ways, at different times, and in various places. Yet, as suggested above, scholars have tended to identify political science with the analysis of only one or two of these questions. Answers of a sort may have been provided for the remaining questions, but this is usually done indirectly, and the answers must often be inferred. I have attempted to deal with all these questions. No doubt the effort is ambitious and falls far short of realization. But as we live in total systems, and cannot escape their workings, it behooves us to make at least a periodic attempt to understand the whole enterprise. To be sure, we shall not attain a very high level of scientific reliability or validity when dealing with a macroscopic system of the size and complexity of the American; but the quest for some understanding has its payoffs in the excitement it engenders. I hope that students who may come across this book will perhaps find some hint of the pleasure I have had in trying to be systematic about political behavior.

In attempting to provide answers to the problems raised, I have sought to use whatever data and theories seemed relevant and "authoritative" to me. The results, no doubt, are mixed. In some areas the data is extensive, reliable, and valid; in others, it is scanty, questionable, and indirect. And, of course, my own acquaintance with so vast an array of materials is bound to be uneven. My colleagues will remind me, and quite properly so, of my omissions, errors of commission, and misinterpretations. But since this is an interpretative essay and not a scientific treatise, I hope they will recognize the differences when it comes to criticism.

While the inquiries that guide this essay were derived, primarily, from the writings of Talcott Parsons on the social system, it would be foolish and inaccurate to say that I have not been the recipient of much from my colleagues in political science as well as other sociologists. As the footnotes will surely indicate, I have relied heavily on the work of Gabriel Almond, Robert Dahl, David Easton, E. Pendleton Herring, V. O. Key, Jr., Robert Lane, Seymour Martin Lipset, C. Wright Mills, E. E. Schattschneider, and David Truman. Indeed, no one can write at length about American politics without incurring a debt to them. I want to express my indebtedness to them for making this book an easier and more interesting one to write. Yet, it is still true that this book would not have taken the form it has without my having read Parsons.

I wish also to acknowledge a number of other persons and institutions for the help they have tendered me in the preparation of the book. Heinz Eulau, the Political Science Editor of The Free Press, was exceedingly kind and helpful in his role as editor. The same must also be said of Martin Kessler of The Free Press, who had to perform his tasks under very trying conditions. I want, too, to thank the Department of Political Science at the University of Oregon for its financial assistance in the preparation of the manuscript, and two of its secretaries for their superb work on the various drafts: Mrs. Pat Meyers and Mrs. Eugenia Koburger. The unsung leg-men of the book were Rafigul Choudhury, Carl Praktish, Stephen Wasby, and William Wroth, all energetic and imaginative graduate students.

Finally, I want to express my appreciation to two rather special people in my life: Doug Price and my wife, Joyce. To the former, I owe getting started on the project. The book is dedicated to my wife as a token of my love. She tried very hard to make this a better book; had she succeeded more than she did, her name would appear on the cover.

While the above-mentioned individuals did their best to help me, they must not be associated with the shortcomings of the book; I do not look forward to hearing about them, but I do accept the responsibility.

WILLIAM C. MITCHELL

Eugene, Oregon
January, 1962

Contents

Contents

Part Six   Political Processes: The Allocation of Values and Costs

Part Seven   Political Change

Part One

A Conceptual Framework

THE purpose of Part One and Chapter 1 is simple: to elaborate a schema for the interpretation of American politics that will be as inclusive and economical as possible. Such an effort, of necessity, entails a good deal of purely abstract, logical manipulation of concepts. For many readers such efforts will probably be thought to be rather arid, and, no doubt, many such schemes are precisely that. Accordingly, one could read this volume without reference to the first chapter. Yet, the functions of conceptual frameworks are of such importance that to do so would produce a less rewarding understanding of what the author is attempting.

Conceptual schemes sensitize the reader to the organization of the work by making him aware of the questions being asked, the methods employed to answer them, and the concepts and categories used to convey the answers. These are useful things to know before delving into the subject-matter, the data, the generalizations, and theories. In one sense, moreover, it is quite impossible to avoid conceptualizing. One does ask questions, and produces answers in some sort of order. Is it not better then to proceed in the most logical and economical manner? Is it not better to make one's terms and assumptions as explicit as possible? Indeed, the writer does think it worth the effort, and hopes that the reader will share in this belief upon laying down this book.

1

The Polity and Society

The present chapter is intended to provide a framework of analysis for the empirical data we will develop in subsequent chapters on the American political system. Consequently, we shall be more concerned with the elaboration of the scheme of concepts and basic ideas that underlie our conception of the political process than with detailed facts. The reader therefore must prepare himself to accept and reason in a purely abstract manner. Should he master the frame of analysis in this chapter, he will be that much better prepared to understand and appreciate the materials of succeeding chapters.

A conceptual scheme or framework is an essential tool in all scientific investigation for it provides the elementary concepts, assumptions, ideas, and directives that guide the selection and interpretation of facts. Of course, there are always a variety of schemes to be used in any investigation. The one a person employs depends upon a number of factors including his own personality and the requirements of the subject matter. We shall not concern ourselves with this problem, however, since, while relevant, it would take us far afield. We simply announce that the framework to be developed here is usually termed "structural-functional" analysis, and will proceed to elaborate upon it in some detail.[1]

THE SOCIAL SYSTEM

Social systems have been variously defined, but all definitions have contained the notion that the system is made up of two or more variables or components that are functionally interdependent, so that to affect a change in one of these variables is to produce a change or set of changes

3

in all of the remaining ones.[2] Thus, in a physical system such as a container of gas: if one produces a change in the heat of the container, concomitant changes will take place in the volume and pressure of the gas within the chamber. This will occur through the changing of the rate of movement of the gas molecules. A similar set of changes may be shown in the case of an economic system. Suppose a perfectly competitive market: should a change occur in the price of a good, there will be changes in the amount suppliers are willing to offer at the new price and, similarly, changes in the demand schedule or the amounts that consumers are willing to purchase at the new price.

The above illustrations are of comparatively simple systems. When we speak of a social system we may also picture some rather simple ones, as in the case of the market. But when we deal with a society as a social system, we are confronted with the most complex system known to man, for it is made up of literally an infinite number of variables. Difficulties are much greater, therefore, in understanding the functioning of these variables. Inevitably, prediction and control of so many variables are also vastly more difficult. Nevertheless, the job of the social scientist is to attempt to simplify this complex phenomena by the imposition of conceptual frameworks so that the more crucial variables may be pointed out and relationships established among them. A number of social scientists have devised means that enable us to gain greater understanding of human action. Among them is Talcott Parsons.[3] It is his approach, primarily, that we will now develop and employ in our analysis of American politics.

A social system, including that of a society—the largest and most general type of social system—consists of *two or more persons* who are engaged in a *patterned* or structured form of *relationship or interaction,* and who are guided by sets of *values and norms* generally called *roles.* It must also be noted that the interaction is *relatively persistent;* a chance meeting of strangers on a street cannot be considered as a social system. From these properties it is also easily seen that a social system has certain *boundaries,* that is, it is possible to determine who is or is not a member of the system. The last property of a system—all systems—is implied in the other properties of "patterned-interaction," "boundaries," and persistence: that is, the system tends to establish an *equilibrium* or balance of the forces that tend both to integrate and disintegrate. These are the elements of a social system, and therefore the variables we will use in analyzing the United States and its politics. But these are not the only things we wish to know about social systems. Systems, if they are to maintain their equilibrium and persist through time, must cope successfully with a number of problems presented by their own structure and environment. However, it is with but one of the problems of social systems that we are primarily concerned.

According to Parsons, social systems are confronted by four problems, which involve their very survival.[4] While the solutions to these problems are greatly varied in actual societies, solutions must be attempted if the society is to survive. These universal problems include the following:

1. Adaptation to the environment.
2. Mobilization of resources to meet system goals.
3. Integration of the members.
4. Maintenance of the value and normative system and tension-management.

These four problems tend to be handled by different subsystems or sets of structures and processes, each becoming more differentiated as society becomes more complex. Each subsystem thus may be said to be functionally specialized with respect to the solution or meeting of one of these four problems.

In the case of the first problem (adaptation to the environment) or production of wealth, the subsystem most concerned is the economic. Of primary interest here is the problem of mobilizing societal resources for system goals, and it centrally concerns the political action of the society. The polity, then, is the subsystem most involved in the problems of goal-attainment.[5] The other functional problems require still other systems, such as the social control system that deals with the integration of society, and the socialization system that handles the maintenance of societal values and norms. See Figure 1-1 showing the four problems and the systems most concerned with their handling.

In Figure 1-1 each of the capital letters symbolizes the functional problem toward which the subsystem is oriented: thus, *A* stands for adaptation; *G,* goal attainment; *L,* maintenance of values and tension-

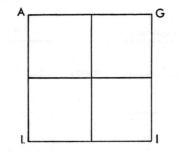

Figure 1-1. The Social System and Its Four Functional Problems.

management; and *I,* integration. Each cell symbolizes its appropriate subsystem. While we will have need to refer to all of these systems throughout the book, our prime interest of course, is, in the *G* cell, or the polity.

It must be apparent that, if a social system is so structured as to have a number of subsystems, various relationships are to be expected among these subunits. Just as one can find a set of relationships among the elements or parts of a physical system, such as a gasoline engine, so one will find various relationships in social systems. These relationships may best be thought of as *exchanges* of something from each of the systems to each of the others. In the terms of engineering and economics, these exchanges may be denoted as *inputs* and *outputs*. In the case of physical systems, the inputs and outputs are generally concrete, substantive things that can easily be seen, or at least imagined and measured. In the case of social systems, however, these exchanges are seldom so concrete; although they may be as in the case of money, or income and goods, that circulate in the economic system. Even in the case of the polity, we may note the highly visible output of laws. But most of the exchanges among the subsystems of a society are of a symbolic nature. While this may be a difficult conception for literal-minded students, it is one that is important to grasp. For although symbolic exchanges are less concrete they are no less significant. Moreover, in many cases, these exchanges can be operationalized, that is, we can provide quantitative indicators. Prestige, for example, may be symbolized or indicated by money and various forms of deference among men.

Perhaps we can gain a better picture of these matters of relationships among systems if we single out the polity from the remainder of society, showing through the use of a diagram the various input-output exchanges.[6] In Figure 1-2 the reader will find the polity pictured along with the various inputs and outputs.

As Figure 1-2 suggests, the inputs to the polity from other subsystems

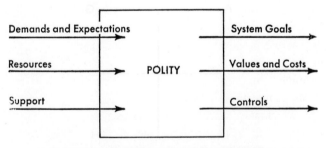

Figure 1-2.   Input-Output Exchanges of the Polity.

in society consist of various demands, resources, and support for elements of the polity. On the output side, the polity furnishes decisions and other actions concerning, first, the goals to be pursued by collective effort, secondly, the means of implementing those goals, and thirdly, the distribution of values and costs. The job of the polity, in short, is to transform the inputs into effective decisions or actions on the output side. How the political system in the United States achieves this set of tasks constitutes Parts Four and Five of the book.

FUNCTIONS OF THE POLITY

Here we will consider the contributions made by the polity to the survival and successful functioning of the more inclusive social system. In brief, the polity performs at least four major functions:

1. The authoritative specification of system goals.
2. The authoritative mobilization of resources to implement goals.
3. The integration of the system.
4. The allocation of values and costs.

At various times each of these functions has been stressed by various writers. Seldom, however, have all four functions been recognized simultaneously. Perhaps one reason why one or two have been stressed at the expense of the others stems from the fact that at certain times in individual societies one of these functions has appeared more crucial than at others. During times of stress, as in international relations, for example, the emphasis may well be placed upon integration; the same may be so in periods of rebellion or revolution. During times of peace, on the other hand, the emphasis may be upon the domestic allocation of values and costs. In the case of the United States, emphasis has historically been placed upon this latter function.

Authoritative Specification of Societal Goals

Societies are constituted by individuals playing a variety of roles, and while most of the goals pursued in a society are those of separate individuals, there are, nevertheless, collective goals, which are sought by individuals as a group or as a society. Note that we speak of goals as being determined by individuals, not by society as a mystical entity. Still, it is also important to note that societal goals, regardless of the processes by which they were selected, or originated and acted upon, are originated and acted upon in the name of the society. It is from this identification that they derive their authoritative character.

Indeed, it is doubtful whether a society could escape having system goals and continue to survive. In the first instance, many of these goals are related to the desire to survive as a society. Self-defense therefore is one of the more likely collective goals. But it is not the only one. In the industrial societies of the West, a great many other goals beyond that of mere survival have been enacted as the official goals of these societies. They have included social welfare of various types, plus economic protection, management of valued resources, education, and protection of the consumer, the worker, and the businessman.

But regardless of the particular goals found in society, it is imperative that some means be regarded as authoritative for their selection if not for their origination. A large and rapidly changing society may be expected to be confronted with demands for all sorts of goals, which in many cases are likely to be in conflict. Thus some means must be used for their final determination or selection for most societies do not have sufficient resources to provide for all of them to be met in full. In other words, most societies, if not all, are faced with a situation or environment of scarce resources, at least in some respects. Should goals not be reconciled, the alternative would appear to be chaos, disintegration, or even civil war.

Once the determination of system goals has been made, however, there still remains the problem of allocating the values and costs involved in attaining them. Thus, a society may decide through its polity to attain and maintain full employment as an end. But the problem of allocation still remains both at the level of values, namely, who is to have how much of the national income derived from full employment and the allocation of the costs entailed by the policy or goal of full employment. It is to these problems and functions that we now turn.

Authoritative Allocation of Values and Costs

We normally think that the function of allocation is performed by the economic system. Yet it is manifest that the political system also performs the same function whenever it decides, for example, who is to derive a certain value or benefit and who is to pay for that value. Indeed, it would often seem that the polity is beginning to perform the allocation function with as much frequency as the economy. Certainly this is the case in socialistic societies where the polity makes major economic calculations and decisions. But since the free market, which in capitalist societies prices goods and services and allocates income and resources, is simply non-existent, the same functions must therefore be performed by some other structure and persons: this structure is the polity, and the persons are the politicians and administrators.

Even the societies that depend upon a free economy to perform distributive functions with respect to economic values cannot rely solely upon the economy. Here, too, the polity serves, if only indirectly, to allocate through provision of the rules of the game by which the economy operates. The consequences of these rules are distributive, for they affect if not determine "who gets what, when, and how." While it is apparent that the polity does serve to allocate values and costs, it is still not so apparent why this should be the case.

Problems of allocation or distribution arise because, or whenever a society has an imbalance of demands over supplies, or, in other words, whenever the society is required to distribute scarce or limited values. More people want more of a certain value than there are supplies to satisfy all. The problems of allocation, then, consist of two distinct phases: first, deciding the principles or rules by which the allocation is to proceed; secondly, allocating the scarce resources once rules have been established. Some form of conflict is likely to accompany each of these processes, for no society has ever completely agreed upon the rules, and certainly no society has ever been completely satisfied with the process of distribution even though the general rules are approved. That some people will not receive all they would prefer guarantees dissension.

Just as a society must devise ways of allocating values, so it must also devise means of allocating costs, for scarce values cannot be provided for without some cost. Indeed, a scarce value without a cost is a contradiction in terms—a fact that appears to be more widely understood in the marketplace than in politics. But if the polity is to provide all the expected services, costs are bound to be entailed, and sooner or later someone must pay them. Consequently, just as a struggle is likely to occur over the distribution of values, so it is likely to ensue over the allocation of costs. In fact, the struggle over costs often may be more intense and involve more persons and groups than does the struggle over goals and values. Witness the hue and cry whenever a tax measure comes before a legislative assembly. There are good reasons, of course, why such a struggle should be intense. Governmental actions that promise a value, or an increase in one, to one group do not automatically and immediately adversely affect all others; but, an action that proposes to impose or increase taxes or costs on a group for which they receive no benefit, or at least no tangible one in the immediate period, is easily understood and therefore resented and opposed. For cost is a taking away of values or resources from a group or a person, an action that few can accept without objection, particularly when the benefits may go to a group whom one dislikes, Moreover, the allocation of costs in the polity, to a greater extent than the economy, is done not through the free play of abstract forces, but through the authoritative actions of officials who may be more easily identifiable, and are frequently thought of as, incompetent, dishonest, or impersonal. Thus, the political action of allocation is often less appreciated than the economic action of allocation, and, one might add, probably less well understood.

We should not conclude from our discussion, however, that the economy and the polity are the only rationing, distributive, or allocative systems in society; there are others, including the stratification system. Nevertheless, there does appear to be a functional specificity about each of these allocation structures and processes. The economy, for example, specializes in distributing *wealth* and *income;* the polity, in *power;* while the social stratification system deals primarily in *prestige.* Yet none of these structures or systems allocates a single "commodity" for, as we have seen, the polity may allocate money costs just as does the economy. And, to be sure, the stratification system also aids in the allocation of wealth and income in that a person may be born into a certain class and thereby be allocated a share of the goods and services of society for which he is not responsible. Nevertheless, each of these structures does tend to specialize in a single commodity, and each may utilize quite different principles for the allocation. Thus, in the United States, allocation in the economy is conducted on the rule that men are presumed unequal and earn their own way; while in the polity we proceed on the basis that all men are equal and therefore have but a single share and vote. No matter how much income a person may have, he presumably has but one vote. Of course, this same person may exercise greater power than is implied by one vote because of his economic-social status, but the formal governmental structure does not provide for this to be the case. Of course, while the man's power is informal, it is no less real. What we are here concerned with, then, is both the formal rule by which the allocation is partially determined and with the actual process where all men are not in fact equal and some get more than others. Indeed, the ideals of allocation and the realities are seldom the same. Thus, the whole history of social philosophy has been concerned with the problem of justice, which usually means a dispute over the principles by which wealth, power, and prestige *should* be allocated among men. We shall not enter that debate, but simply describe and explain how allocation takes place in the United States.

Authoritative Mobilization of Resources

Although decisions may be made on societal goals, and the allocation of values and costs thereby decided, the polity cannot be said to be effective until it can implement these decisions by calling upon and acquiring resources. In short, polities require resources to operate just as do economies. All who have ever paid the government taxes, fees, services, or provided materials know about the "authoritative mobilization of resources" from personal experience. Modern polities and governments require enormous supplies of time, energy, and materials to perform their expected tasks, all of which the citizens must provide or acquire from other systems. Much of the action of a government revolves around the processes of acquiring these resources and then combining them in new forms so as to carry out goals. How polities proceed to mobilize available resources has been the subject of much research in political science and public administration. In Part Five we will learn how the American polity carries out this process of mobilization. For the moment this much may be said: polities employ a vast and imaginative array of controls ranging from the direct to the most indirect; from the simple to the highly complex; and from the coercive to the voluntary. Not even democracies are exempt from the use of controls to mobilize resources. The great difference, of course, stems from the preference of democracies for limiting the number of controls, and for preferring those that are less coercive, and voluntarily agreed upon. But they are controls, nevertheless. And with increasing demands being made upon governments for resources, these controls may also be expected to increase. All of which leads us into the problem of integrating the society.

Integration of Society

One of the oldest recognized functions of governments is that of integrating the members of society. No one would seriously contend, however, that the government or, more widely, the polity, is the only integrating structure in society. In fact, it may not even be the most important, and certainly is not in the United States. We need not detail the integrative structures and processes except to say that they include both formal and informal processes of socialization and social control. Of these processes, governments rely heavily upon formal social controls to secure the support or cooperation of their citizens. Other agencies—the family, church, and school, plus many other private organizations—may play a less dramatic, but certainly a more significant, role.

Where societal goals are formalized, however, the political system, through the officials and offices of government, uses both rewards and penalties to coordinate the actions of its people. In effect, the implementation of goals is dependent upon the capacity to integrate services and resources. The most dramatic illustration of the power of government to do this usually occurs during a war when cohesion is a prime requisite of effective action. In totalitarian societies, of course, which pursue more collective goals than do the democracies, this drama of total mobilization of resources and support is an everyday occurrence.

Even in a democracy, however, integration is an imperative, especially as the determination of goals and the allocation of values and costs are likely to produce considerable conflict. After goals have been determined, and values and costs assessed, dissidents, admittedly, are to be expected. Yet, although not everyone will be satisfied with the results, the goals must be fulfilled if the victorious are not also to become disaffected. Thus, the government must have available a capacity to integrate the population into a coordinated group in order to fulfill the goals decided upon.

THE INTERNAL STRUCTURE OF THE POLITY

Political scientists have long been concerned with the internal structures of the political system, or at least of one type, the state. As this concern is a necessary one in the analysis of political behavior and its consequences, it will also be a major concern of ours.

When we study the structure of a social system, we are attempting to describe and explain the relationships of the component parts.[7] In the case of social systems, the parts consist, as we have stated above, of roles or sets of norms governing the relationships. But in the analysis of politics we are particularly interested in one aspect of these arrangements or relationships: that aspect is *power*. We thus want to concentrate upon those features of the role or normative structure that affect the capacities of the members of the system to control one another, as well as the capacity of the system itself to control the members.

Interest in power or capacity to control is a focal point in political science because of the functions of the political system. The functions, it will be recalled, are to determine societal goals, mobilize resources, allocate values and costs, and, finally, to integrate the polity. For a great many reasons, then, members of the society are interested in the decisions of the polity with respect to these functions, and want to have some control over these decisions. How these decisions are made, which demands will be enacted into societal goals, and who will receive the benefits and pay the costs—all are vitally affected by the normative structure of the political system. Nor are the final results determined solely by the rules or norms, for there are many other exogenous variables of similar significance. No analysis of the politics of any social system can be grasped, however, without a detailed knowledge of the role structure of the polity.

Consequently, a number of interesting and vital questions can and must be posed regarding structures. To understand how the functions of the polity are met, we thus must find answers to the following questions:

1. Is the polity functionally specialized?
2. To what extent is the internal structure differentiated? Along what lines?
3. How visible is the power structure?
4. How open is the structure? In terms of the circulation of power-holders? In terms of the accessibility to demands? What are the bases of access?
5. How concentrated or diffused is the power structure?
6. How are authoritative roles acquired and controlled?
7. How are norms enforced?
8. What effects does structure have on goal-attainment, allocation, tension-management, and integration?

The above queries are but a few of the more general lines of inquiry that necessitate consideration. In the chapters that follow we will attempt to provide answers with respect to the American polity.

INPUTS TO THE POLITY

The first input we shall consider is that of *demands and expectations* on the part of the members of the society for favorable decisions from the polity. The demands may include almost any concern of the members, whether considered as individuals or in groups. Thus, the range of demands might include a tariff, a new street, a law specifying loyalty, a minimum wage, or legal recognition of a union.

Needless to say, the demands of one member of society or group are not demands upon the polity, but demands made through the political system upon other members of the society. Demands, in fact, may be best thought of as originating outside of the polity and handled within it. In America, most demands appear to originate around the economic needs and aspirations of the citizens, although there is no aspect of social life that has not become a problem for the polity.

Demands and Expectations

In considering the functioning of a polity, it is important to know certain characteristics of the demand schedule. We need to know, for example, what is demanded; how much; by whom; from whom; the intensity of the demand; and how such demands are handled. The amount and intensity of the conflict that normally results from a demand being made is conditioned by these six sets of facts. Generally speaking, we can probably say that the less some value is demanded in terms of quantity and intensity, given the supply, the less conflict will result and the more likely a favorable decision to the demander or consumer will ensue. In addition, we might assume that the time during which the conflict is waged or the decision made will also be shorter. Equilibrium, in short, can be more quickly established. These propositions, of course, would be hypotheses for empirical testing. We will examine what evidence there is on such questions in subsequent chapters.

If the input of demand is to be a useful category in our analysis, it will be necessary to operationalize it, or to provide indicators that will not only identify the variable, but provide indices for its measurement. Fortunately, political demands can be so identified and measured. In the case of the United States, moreover, we can locate demands easily and quickly. Among the indicators of demands are the following:

1. The number of bills introduced into the legislatures.
2. The proliferation of interest groups.
3. The number of group resolutions.
4. The demands expressed in newspapers and other media of communication.
5. The size of the governmental budgets.
6. The numerical size of the government or number of employees.
7. Work-loads of the officials.

The above constitute some of the more direct and useful indices of political demands being made or fulfilled. Others may be direct or indirect. In addition to the above, which deal only with the number of demands, there are means available for classifying and measuring the type of demands, their individual scope, the number of persons affected by them, and the costs of meeting these demands. Likewise, it is possible, although undoubtedly more difficult, to construct indices of the intensity by which demands are made upon society and the polity. In the discussion of demands in Part Six we will use a number of these indices for characterizing the present state of the demand input in the United States. We will also advance a number of propositions concerning relationships among sources of demand, type of demand, number, intensity, and their probable fates. In other words, we will attempt to predict the outcome of different demands under varying conditions of American politics.

Thus far we have considered the most active and perhaps rational form of political action, namely, the making of demands on the political process for favorable decisions. Demands do not, however, exhaust the possibilities of political actions. In fact, they may well be preceded by a more frequent type of belief we can call "expectations." By this term is meant that rather amorphous group of beliefs that citizens have regarding what the government ought to do and the way its officials and other citizens ought to, or probably will, behave. This set of beliefs tends to remain passive, simply forming the background of the more active demands. In the United States, for example, citizens tend to expect that the government will minimize the use of coercion, that it will pursue the public interest, and that public officials will not beat the citizens. Any of these generalized expectations may, of course, become an active demand under the appropriate conditions. In other societies, such as the Mexican, the citizenry tend to expect that the government will not be honest, that the officials will be self-interested and corrupt, and that violence will be a part of the polity. But whatever the range and content of expectations, and despite their somewhat amorphous character, they still are subject to empirical analysis so that we can determine what they are, their distribution, intensity, and significance.

Resources

If the demands of the members of the society are to be met, a supply of resources must be available. We are speaking in this instance of both material and nonmaterial resources. Examples of the former include such obvious items as money, time, labor, and natural resources; while the latter include prestige, safety, freedom, and well-being. These various resources, or, "values" in the words of Harold Lasswell, are the objects of demand, and command varying prices depending upon the available supply and demand.

In the United States, the supply of material resources has been more than adequate in most instances to fulfill a great range of the demands. The nation has been fortunate in having a large land mass with plentiful natural resources and power to develop them. It is important to realize how significant this fact of plenty or abundance has been in the evolution of political action. Because we have been so fortunate, the struggle for values has been less intense and prolonged than in countries where the resources are more limited. For it is precisely those demands that are frustrated or unfulfilled that are likely to lead to greater tension in the system. In such instances, the adequacy of the society and the polity itself are likely to be challenged. Conversely, where demands can be met in reasonable amounts and within reasonable time, expectations are less likely to be frustrated,

and support for the society and polity maintained. Political action therefore becomes less prolonged and intense, and the stability of the regime
is protected.

Support

The third input from society to the polity consists of the support that
members of that society are willing to give the polity, whether through
compulsion, as a result of rational decision, or through simple habit and
even indifference. Indeed, it is difficult to imagine a society that could
long cohere without being able to secure or depend upon the support,
cooperation, or compliance of its members.

Support is not an undifferentiated action. It may take various forms
and degrees, and have different objects. It would seem useful, in fact, to
think of support in terms of the objects for which it is given or extracted.
Thus, we can conceive of these objects in the form of a hierarchy of levels
ranging from the most generalized political values to the specific leaders
and public policies in the government. The objects of support consist of the
political values the polity presumably attempts to honor and realize, the
polity itself (structures), the laws that govern society, the leaders and
other personnel who operate the polity and government, and the policies
being pursued by specific governments. Theoretically, we ought to be
able to measure the extent and intensity of support at each level or for
each object in the hierarchy. We ought also to be able to identify who
supports what, how much, and with what consequences. Practically, however, this is an extremely difficult task and little has been done regarding
it. Nevertheless, we can still usefully conceive of the political system in
this manner, and make limited or qualified assertions about the various
facets or questions we have just raised. In the not too distant future, we
should be able to see considerable methodological advances and applications to these concerns. And at such time we will be able to devise indices
of support and construct profiles of conflict and agreement in all political
systems. When these things come to pass, our understanding of the role
of conflict and support in different types of polities will be so improved
that we will be able to make accurate predictions about the extent and type
of conflicts which various systems can handle. Conversely, we shall also
be able to specify what levels of support are required for a viable system.

While we cannot produce validated propositions about the amount of
support a society and polity require at each of the levels, it would seem
apparent, from common sense, that societies can tolerate a great deal of
conflict or disagreement. At the same time, it should also be apparent that
the amount must differ at each level, with the least amount at the highest,

and the most at the lowest level. A society can tolerate, indeed benefit, from conflict at certain levels, provided consensus is affirmed at some other, particularly the next higher ones. This, in fact, seems to be the case in the more stable democracies. In the United States, for example, we have more conflict at the lower levels of personnel and policies. But in doing so we and the politicians always reaffirm the higher levels of dedication to law and obedience, insisting that our polity is the best created under the sun, and that American values are superior. In this connection it is interesting to note that contending politicians just prior to and immediately after an election and after the most rigorous of campaigns will always moderate their tone and publicly reaffirm their loyalties to the higher levels of the system. At such times agreement on fundamentals is always stressed. The continued existence of the system is paramount.

The means by which support is generated at each level are many and varied. We need mention but a few. In the first instance, the polity depends upon the socialization of citizens at the very earliest ages. Here the family, the school, and the churches are of great significance, for they are the groups that mould the future citizens and inculcate notions of patriotism and authority. Witness the daily pledging of allegiance in the schools, or the activities of the Boy Scouts. The example of the teacher, the minister, and the parents in their relations with the symbols of the polity become crucial elements in this socialization process. So are the patriotic holidays and symbols in which children and adults are constantly reminded of their roles as citizens. Each of these actions and symbols serves to build in a loyalty, a predisposition to act in favor of the state. Thus, part of a person's conscience includes political loyalties. The abject confessions of political prisoners in communistic countries are frequently thought of as coerced. And no doubt many are. But in many instances the prisoner confesses out of honesty and loyalty, for he fears that he has done his state wrong, just as Socrates refused to escape his tormentors when he was offered the opportunity, aware of the evil of the accuser, yet upholding the system itself. Americans who have been temporarily disloyal have also been known to make the same abject confessions. And, not infrequently, they also have become "superpatriots" after the experience.

The socialization process is not, of course, the only means by which support and resources are elicited by the government. A whole series of inducements including both rewards and sanctions are available to all governments. Of the rewards offered, the government may propose monetary ones such as salaries, tax reductions and rebates, subsidy payments, tariffs, and the like. Less tangible are the rewards of power or participation in decision-making, consultation in programs affecting one, social status through appointments, and other forms of recognition, as in the rewarding of a medal.

Of the negative type of inducement, governments may use their power to command performances. The sanctions of law, including the ultimate one of death, make up an entire range of penalties for attaining compliance. In the United States, however, the emphasis is upon the rewards rather than sanctions, although the latter must not be underestimated. Regardless of the type of inducement, it is safe to say that the American government, because of the value and normative systems, does encounter difficulties in mobilizing support and resources at the levels of policies and personnel. In subsequent chapters (Part Three) we shall attempt to explain in greater detail the sources or reasons for this difficulty. The costs of mobilization are likewise higher than in many other countries. Costs, here, includes the psychic as well as material.

OUTPUTS OF THE POLITY

We have already stated in our discussion of the functions of the polity that the specification of system goals, the mobilization of resources, allocation of costs and values, and integration of the society are the major contributions of the polity to the larger social system. Implicit in these functions, then, are the outputs. Stated most generally, the output is power or the capacity of the system to realize these functions. Stated concretely, the power generated by the polity takes the form of decisions or policies and actions respecting each of the functions. Thus, in Figure 1-2 we noted two types of decisions, those specifying goals and those pertaining to the means by which these goals are implemented or resources (widely understood) are mobilized. Although the authoritative form of these decisions is what is commonly termed law, we should also add policies, that is, statements about goals and means that are not necessarily enacted into formal law, but constitute the general direction a government intends to or, in fact, does take. Policies thus might be thought of as informal directives.

The output of power from the polity is meant to influence the inputs of demands, resources, and support; but perhaps the major impact is upon resources and support. The government requires each of these inputs in order to implement its decisions. One might therefore speak of it as Schumpeter did of the economy, namely, as a "circular flow" of decisions and action instead of income and goods.

In the previous section on inputs we mentioned the fact that the government, and more widely the political system, had to pay a price or costs in the form of various inducements to secure support and resources. Consequently, the mobilization process is an economic as well as a political and psychological problem. From this point of view output of the polity may be considered as the price that the polity is willing to pay in order to acquire the needed inputs. How much a government is willing to pay depends upon a number of conditions including the value of goal, the demands being made upon the government, the resistance of the holders or suppliers of support and resources, and the nature of the problem facing the polity. During a war or a depression, for example, the threshold of action may be very low.

EQUILIBRIUM OF THE SYSTEM

The system of action that we have termed the polity is a complex one in all societies, and particularly so in the United States. Furthermore, it is a system deeply enmeshed in relationships of a conflicting or competitive order. This must be so for the demands that are made upon the system are made against scarce resources; not everyone can have his demands or expectations completely fulfilled. It is therefore a useful question to ask how the system manages to persist.

The answer, if there be but one, revolves around the idea of equilibrium, an old idea in history but not one used with much skill in political science. Unless a political system is to end in chaos, it must arrive at some state in which most of the members feel reasonably satisfied with their positions and the results of the system's actions. In the struggle to have demands met, however, some members or perhaps all may fail to get all they would like. Yet, they do not revolt. Thus a state is reached that may be loosely described as one of equilibrium. More precisely, we might say that a state of equilibrium has been attained in the system whenever the expectations of the members have been met. In still other language we might say that an equilibrium has been attained whenever members of the system have nothing else to gain by further exchanges with one another. In short, each member has maximized or better "satisficed" his expectations within the range of alternatives provided by the situation. No polity, of course, is ever in a perfect state of equilibrium, and certainly not one of complete rest. Indeed, there will always be some who feel deprived with the results of a particular exchange or with the system that makes the exchange possible. We do however think of polities and societies as attaining various degrees of stability even though the notion itself cannot be easily quantified. There are several indicators of a common sense type available for measuring the stability of systems, which we shall utilize in assessing the state of America. For the moment, however, we need simply point to the number of civil wars and rebellions as one indicator. And, in considering the demand input, we can easily determine the type of demand as a reflection of satisfaction or deprivation. Subsequent chapters will deal with the problem more fully.

POLITICAL CHANGE

Our discussion of equilibrium in the political system and, indeed, in the use of the word "system" itself must not be construed to mean that societies and polities do not undergo change. One of the more apparent facts of politics is that change is persistent and ubiquitous. But the fact that change is a fact does not mean that systems analysis is useless, nor does it mean that change defies empirical explanation. Political change can be understood in systems theory.

When we analyze change we are interested in knowing a number of things about it, including its magnitude, its sources, its tempo, the order, if any, and some of the consequences both for society and the polity. And while we cannot present here a full-blown and accepted theory of change, we can offer some important considerations that should enable us to better understand change per se as well as political change in the United States.

Perhaps the first question that our analysis of the political system raises concerns types of changes. Logically, it would seem that but two types are possible: changes of the system itself; and changes of persons within the system. The first type is illustrated whenever a society changes the structure of its political system as did Germany, for example, in the early 1930's, changing from a democratic to a totalitarian polity, or as did Russia in 1917, changing from a monarchy to a communist dictatorship. In both these instances, the change was total, that is, from one system to an entirely different one, different in its power structure, its ideologies, symbols, and authority. The magnitude of change, however, need not be so complete. Indeed, partial changes are more likely in societies that are reasonably stable. Thus, the system may be partially changed in some one or a few of its elements or components. The power structure may be changed, ideologies revised, symbols abandoned and new ones developed, or the bases of authority changed to new ones. Note, for example, the relatively peaceful displacement of the king as a power-holder in Britain. Or, in the United States itself, where the declining power of the Congress and the increased power of the President has amounted to a change in the actual if not the formal system.

While we have suggested something of the nature of change in terms of its scope and objects, the illustrations have been of system changes. There is also another type—that of changes of personnel in the system rather than the system itself. A good illustration of this may be found in the elections of democracies when some officials are replaced by new ones. No changes have been made in the structure of the polity, but they have been made of those who are to fulfill the offices and devise societal policies. While such alterations in themselves are not structural, they may eventually lead to structural revisions.

But regardless of the type of change, either of the structure or of the operating personnel, the sources of these changes may be either within or without the polity and society. A polity may be changed by its members, for example, without influences being felt from the environment, as in societies that are relatively isolated, if such changes are to be made at all. And, more likely than not, an internal source of change will be related to changes of personnel rather than to that of the system. That does not, however, exclude internal structural variations. In a world in which few societies are isolated, such as today, changes of political systems are likely to be influenced in some way by factors outside of their immediate control. Not only may military conquest impose a new structure, but influences may stem from the challenges posed by other nations, or by the diffusion of new ideologies such as Marxism from abroad. Whatever their impact on the various inputs we have described—demands, resources, and support—changes in one or more of these variables will produce varying responses of or in the polity.

The tempo of political change ranges from the revolutionary and violent to the barely perceptible and peaceful. In point of fact, the rate of change is hardly constant: sometimes it may be exceedingly rapid; at still others, slow and passive. Even the periods of rapid change, as historians have repeatedly demonstrated, have their long, slow, almost unnoticed buildups, during which the forces that finally erupt are fashioned and interwoven into a set of conditions favorable to some final, swift, and thoroughgoing change. A revolution establishing a dictatorship or a democracy is hardly ever an event of the moment. Conditions such as deprivation have probably been long in existence; not until leadership and the failures of society are correlated does the final overthrow become possible.

For the most part, the rate of change in a political system is not likely to be very rapid. The forces of the status quo and the frequent apathy of men, in addition to the capacities of most systems to meet minimal needs of societies, are usually powerful enough to forestall change or to keep down its rate. Thus, while revolutions are numerous and dramatic forms of political action, they are hardly the most prevalent type nor are they typical. For change is generally slow, indirect, imperceptible, undramatic, and difficult to assess in terms of consequences—a fact that makes political analysis much harder. But even where change does occur we can still make meaningful statements about it. And if we cannot always explain rates in general theoretical terms, we can explain individual instances.

The problem of the sequence of changes is by far the most difficult one we have encountered. As yet we have only developed alternative theories, none of which can be said to be widely accepted. The difficulty stems from the fact that history does not provide us with a single determinate course of development. We simply cannot say, although many famous theorists have so argued, that societies or polities go through a determinate set of stages. About all that does seem possible is the description and explanation of particular courses of particular systems. What may be conceivable is a theory that accounts for ranges of alternatives available to a society whenever it does undergo change. That is, in political systems that are consistent on a value and normative basis, certain types of social structure are likely to have but limited variations or alternatives. Other types of political structures would not be consistent and presumably could not be established nor long persist. Either the society or the polity would be forced to adjust in the direction of the other. This we assume because of an apparent tendency toward consistency in value and normative systems. But as evidence on these matters is extremely limited, the above propositions are really hypotheses, still in need of rigorous testing.

POLITICAL CULTURE:
BELIEFS, SYMBOLS, AND AUTHORITY

No society could possibly be understood without a knowledge of its culture: that is, the sum total of artifacts, belief systems, and symbols prevalent in that society which shape the behavior of its members. In understanding the polity, however, it is not essential to know all of the culture, for not all of it is directly relevant to political action. Thus, we need not know the content of science to understand the political behavior of the society, although science, as is art, is a part of the sum total of culture. For while both science and art may at times become politically relevant, we need only have knowledge of certain aspects of the culture that are constantly associated with political action. Those aspects or portions of the culture of a society that are important in this respect may be termed the *political culture*. They operate on and through the three inputs to the polity, but particularly on demands, expectations, and support. We may further refine our conception of political culture by indicating its major components. These include the belief system of the society, symbols of power and authority, and the conceptions of authority that predominate.

A belief system may best be thought of as a set of ideas about the organization of society, particularly with respect to what are thought to be ideal relationships and their defense. Included in such a system is of course a set of values and norms: the former specifying what is considered to be good or valuable or worth striving for; the latter, referring to preferred conduct or prescriptions of behavior. In total, beliefs really constitute a way of perceiving and evaluating the world. And in every society there will be one or more sets of such beliefs, although in the stable ones the tendency is for one to dominate, that is, more people will believe in it than in some other. The beliefs that dominate may be expected to constitute a defense of the society and in particular of the political system as a just one. As such it acts as protector of the status quo. Those who would prefer another system must therefore deal with the ideology, for it contains the defense, or the rationalizations of the polity. But since political beliefs are inculcated in the members of that society from childhood on, it is not easy to redefine or challenge them. Indeed they will continue to be held long after they have ceased to be operative in daily political life, for we do not so much devise our beliefs by reference to reality as we define reality by our beliefs.

Beliefs themselves are not the only elements of a political culture that tend to support the system; there are also symbolic systems that appeal or are based for the most part on the affective or emotional and esthetic needs of man. Among the foremost employers of such symbols are political systems, although they are hardly the only ones. As Charles E. Merriam put it:

> From the beginning the power situations have been woven about with garlands to cover the sadder aspects of the incidence of authority. Many of the most attractive symbolisms designed by human creative and artistic skill have had for their object figures of the political world, around which they have draped their decorations. No other relationship has supplied more moving imagery for mankind than these political personalities and situations.[9]

Merriam continued by stating that the political system has taken over more days of the calendar than any other system excepting the church; that it has the largest proportion of the land and has endowed places with power symbols and names; that its buildings are more impressive than any save the church; and that it rivals all groups in its use of music.[10]

These are but a few illustrations of the association between the political system and symbolism. Indeed, the analysis of the symbolic elements of a polity must be an important part of the analysis of the polity, for symbols and symbolism are not only products of the system, but conditioning factors as well. We cannot understand patriotism or loyalty, and the general level of support given a system, unless we include the elements of symbolism in the explanation. Further we must understand that political symbols, like the ideological elements, are not things apart from political action and the role structure of the polity, but vital, integral aspects of the roles and the actual behavior. A Fourth of July military parade is not an isolated occurrence in the background of politics. It is a politically relevant action in its own right, a part of the daily functioning of the political system. Thus, we shall so treat symbolism in this book.

A third element in the political culture, and one closely allied with the ideological, is that of authority. Indeed, we might well regard it as a part of the dominant system of beliefs in a political system and society, for the attitudes that pertain to authority are hardly confined to politics alone. Nevertheless, we will separate authority from belief systems for analytical purposes in order to focus attention upon its extreme importance.

By authority will be meant *legitimate power*. Of course, what the members of a particular system regard as legitimate exercise of power varies greatly among human groups. But, there is always some notion of what constitutes legitimacy. Accordingly, the bases on which it is founded also vary greatly. In our analysis we shall employ the types of authority created by Max Weber in his justly famous analysis.[11] No claim is being made that Weber's typology is the only one conceivable, but no one has yet come up with a better one.

In brief, Weber claimed that authority could be based on three different grounds, that is, three different types of reasons for obeying or ruling could be found in society. The types of authority were called, first, rational-legal; secondly, traditional; and, thirdly, charismatic. The first type was said to be found whenever both parties to the authoritative relationship accept it because rational or legal rules define the relationship or the right of one to specify the behavior of the other. Traditional authority, on the other hand, was said to depend on reference to the historical or traditional practices governing such relationships. In such cases rational rules are simply irrelevant, for what is to be done is what has always been done. The third type of authority, charismatic, refers neither to rationality nor to custom, but to the presumed qualities of the person giving the commands in the situation. He is obeyed if the subordinate believes the ruler to be possessed of "grace" or some kind of superhuman attributes. In each of these instances, then, the relationship between the ruler and the ruled is defined by a different set of norms. As Weber said, each is an "ideal type," found not in pure form in any empirical situation, but in varying combinations and degrees in all societies. The combination or ratio is the important consideration as we shall see when discussing authority in America (Chapter 5).

STRUCTURE AND PROCESSES: A FINAL NOTE

Thus far we have provided a kind of cross-section of society and the political system, a photograph of motion arrested at an instance of time. However, social and political systems are not motionless entities; on the contrary, they are generally engaged in highly complex and incessant movements. In the final analysis, then, we must understand this movement. To do so, however, requires us to have some knowledge of the various components of the system and their interrelationships at some given moment of time. We have stopped the system in order to determine what these parts are and how they mesh with one another. We have done so because it is easier in this way to visualize the complexities than when they are in motion. But once we have learned to visualize the society and polity at rest, we must go on to see how the system functions in operation.

When we speak of the polity in motion, we mean the various processes that take place in transforming the three inputs of demand, resources, and support into the outputs of system goals and means of implementation. We will attempt to show how demands originate and how they interact and which ones become politicized and acted upon; how resources are mobilized to implement demands and systems goals; and who supports what elements in the society and political system. Finally, we will attempt to show how all these inputs are combined through the political structures and processes. In the process of doing these things, we will also explain the allocation of values and costs or "who gets what, when, and how." We will explain, too, how the American political system manages to handle all the conflict with which it is presented as well as that generated within the system. While all these processes are complex and difficult to analyze, we shall make the attempt knowing full well that each cannot be fully described or accounted for, content to simplify and reduce them to essentials. That, of course, is all that any study can hope to achieve.

Part Two

The American Environment
and Political Structure

Wε now take up the more empirical aspects of our endeavor. The focus of this, Part Two, is the setting of the political system and structural properties of that system. Accordingly, we begin with a brief description and interpretation of the physical and social environments of the polity. The assumption is that the inputs from the remainder of society depend to a significant degree on what is to be received from these other sectors or subsystems such as the economy, social stratification, and the various socialization institutions. Crucial properties will be noted and illustrative hypotheses advanced concerning relationships among subsystems and the inputs to the polity. Many of these hypotheses will be treated at greater length in subsequent chapters.

In addition to sketching the general environment of politics, we will get a bit closer to the political scientist's traditional interests in the power structure by considering its properties and the actual distribution of power. In the process we will identify political roles and the people who play them. In short, we will deal with many of the "raw materials," as Schattschneider has called them, of American politics. And while the analysis—to use an overworked word—is somewhat static, it is a necessary step to get at the dynamics that will be dealt with in Parts Four, Five, and Six.

2

Environment
Social and Physical Elements

Political systems function within environments constituted of still other social and political systems. Perhaps equally as important, although less directly, is the physical, for it is that that ultimately provides the basis of social existence.[1] The environment is particularly significant, for its elements affect by setting limits on the inputs that social and political systems receive. The number of demands, their type, intensity, scope, and source all depend upon the social and physical setting of the polity. Likewise, the various types and amounts of resources in the first instance are determined by the physical environment and secondly by the state of economic and social development. So too, the support that is fed into the polity is conditioned by the environment, particularly the social. Yet even the physical is important, for it affects support through the impact of physical distance on group cohesion. With these elementary remarks we will now discuss the social and physical environment of the American political system. Our problem: to select for emphasis the more significant properties of both, and to relate them to the political structure and the inputs of demand, support, and resources.

THE PHYSICAL ENVIRONMENT

The United States of America is unique in many respects, and certainly one of its uniquenesses has to do with the physical setting. In the first place, America is an enormous land mass, far larger, for example, than any single European nation-state. In the second place, this very size has been accompanied by great diversity of conditions: mountainous areas; plains; deserts; swamps; hot and humid sections; cold and dry regions; fertile and unproductive lands. Likewise, this great land mass has been blessed with huge reserves of raw materials of almost all types, but particularly with the basic resources of iron, coal, and in the early years, water power. For all practical purposes, the United States has been a self-sufficient nation; only a few of the more esoteric resources needed in modern industry have been in short supply. In addition, the country is well irrigated by great river chains. And, of course, these same waterways provided a cheap and easy form of transportation in the days before the railroads and trucks. From a political perspective it is equally important to remember that this large, bountiful nation was for a long while isolated from the rest of the world by two great oceans. The importance of this fact cannot be overestimated, but it also must be understood in conjunction with the above properties.[2]

Each of these properties or characteristics of the physical environment has had some bearing upon the inputs to the polity. Our plentiful supplies of raw materials, for example, have a direct association with the resources input.[3] Throughout American history the political system has been able, for the most part, to mobilize physical resources in sufficient quantities to meet the demands made upon it. Thus, during World War II, this nation had no difficulty comparable to others in providing the materials of warfare; the United States, in fact, supplied not only itself, but vast quantities of war goods to its allies as well. Even after the war, the demands for foreign aid were easily taken care of in terms of supplies if not always in attitude. On the domestic scene, these vast amounts of resources have made it possible to satisfy most demands of the population. In fact, the nation at times has even suffered from affluence as in the current agricultural situation where huge surpluses are being accumulated each year. Partly because material resources have been generally plentiful, the character of American politics is radically different from many other nations. Here, we have the politics of affluence rather than that of automatic scarcity. Therefore political problems of distribution are less divisive and crucial. Indeed, problems of distribution, while becoming more important in politics, are still relatively low-pressured because we employ so many private or nonpolitical institutions for handling them. The economy, for example, is still more crucial in the distribution of income than is the government. Likewise, prestige is allocated by a social stratification system, which is not solely based upon political power. These statements are not meant to imply that the polity is unimportant; it is highly significant and in some ways becoming more so. Traditionally, however, the American polity has not been the major allocative system in the society.

In considering the demand input, we again can appreciate the influence of physical factors in politics. The type as well as quantities of demands made through the polity are vitally affected by the environment. During the nineteenth century, one of the chief demands made, primarily, was for governmental assistance in the development of the land mass and its resources. Moreover, policies tended to reflect these demands as the government took an active hand in the building of the railroads, for example, and in the construction and improvement of other types of transportation. Then, too, the government aided immensely in the development of the frontier by making land cheap and available in addition to providing law enforcement and protection from the Indians. Large subsidies or legal encouragements have been and continue to be provided for the development of all sorts of resources as in mining, air transportation, and agriculture. There is even direct governmental development of resources as with the TVA, and municipal power plants.

Demands for certain types of governmental policies have also been greatly affected by the fact that America has been an isolated nation. Thus, the demand to refrain from foreign affairs has long been a dominant feature of American politics. Geographical isolation has helped to create psychological and political isolation as well. For a long while, Americans could see little sense in international participation, for they were a self-sufficient country. This isolation also contributed to a certain sense of superiority and narrow-mindedness, manifested in intolerance toward deviant political ideas and movements on the domestic scene, and ignorance of the foreign fields. In short, Americans wanted to be left alone and they could easily afford such a luxury. An interesting facet or indication of the isolationist approach is the fact that one veterans' association terms itself Veterans of *Foreign* Wars. The plea of George Washington to stay out of foreign entanglements has long been a favorite demand in the United States and a powerful plea among the politicians.

The fact of isolation has also had its effect upon the support input. Indeed, the fanaticism of American patriotism for our society and its way of life has been remarked upon by almost all foreign observers from de Tocqueville to the present.[4] And while we can only speculate on the relationship of support and physical environment, it does seem plausible that the high levels of support which Americans give their political system might be conditioned by the success of the society and polity in meeting the demands from its plentiful resources. A society not having such resources in relation to its demands might well be one in which new demands would be made to significantly change the system. In the United States few such demands have been seriously made; fewer still have been widely accepted or enacted.

It might also be contended that, had the United States not been isolated as it has during the greater part of its history, many other demands might have been made upon the polity and resources. A prime demand which has been moderated is that of the need for defense forces and expenditures. The United States has neither had to maintain large standing armies, nor expensive defense installations along its boundaries. The current debates over defense matters are thus quite new political problems for Americans. In addition to the economic and political aspects, this same isolation has enabled Americans to be somewhat more antimilitaristic than, say, Europeans. Not only have we been less willing to serve in armies, but we have also given no high social status to our officers and services. Only recently, now that their functions are more important, has their status also risen and more able persons entered the armed services or interested themselves in military matters.

Finally, it may be argued that isolation and the availability of resources to meet demands has also enabled this country to maintain and operate a governmental system that under more trying conditions could not possibly have met its demands. Indeed, the American system, one of the most complicated known to man, requires unique conditions for it to function well; these conditions related, in part, to the physical environment have been favorable. Demands, especially those resulting from the hostilities of other countries, have been small while the resources have been large. As a result, a cumbersome structure has been able to handle these demands in sufficient time and with sufficient effectiveness to be honored, and therefore support has been maintained at a high level. An equilibrium among the inputs and outputs has been generally maintained for long periods of time.

THE SOCIAL STRUCTURE

The political process takes place not only within a geographical setting, but within a social setting or structure as well. And while for analytical purposes and convenience we separate the political system from the social structure, one, in fact, merges into and influences the other constantly and profoundly. The present section is intended to offer a summary statement of the most characteristic features of the American social structure. We are very fortunate in this undertaking, for sociologists have been most industrious and successful in researching American society. The findings presented here have been selected from a vast accumulation of studies. Needless to say, we will not include all of it, but only that which appears most relevant to the understanding of political behavior.

Our selection of materials is based upon the considerations set forth in Chapter 1, where we said that societies consist of populations occupying a definite land area, whose members interact with one another through various role structures or subsystems organized around specific functional problems. These functional problems and subsystems, it will be recalled, number four, including the economy, the polity, the pattern-maintenance system (family, schools, and church), and finally, the integrative subsystem. In describing the American society we will choose our facts as they relate to each of the three subsystems other than the polity. Thus, we shall provide brief characterizations of the economy, and the integrative and the pattern-maintenance systems. Each of these subsystems we have maintained is engaged in certain exchanges with each of the others. Our ultimate concern, of course, is with the exchanges to the polity. We might refresh our memories of the social structure and boundary exchanges by referring to Figure 2-1.

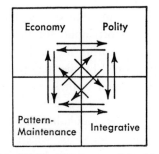

Figure 2-1. The Social System and Its Subsystems.

If we are to describe the inputs into the polity from each of the other subsystems, it is imperative to know something about the nature of each as well as their particular characteristics in the American case. The remainder of this chapter is thus devoted to spelling out these matters. In some cases, their significance will be immediately perceived; in other instances, the reader will not discover the full importance of the data until some subsequent chapters. We will begin the analysis with some comments about the general properties of American society, and then deal individually with each of the subsystems.

THE SOCIAL ENVIRONMENT

Not only is the United States a large country, geographically, but it is also a *large* country in population. In fact, with its nearly 183 million persons, it is the fourth most populous nation in the world. The political significance of this fact is apparent: the problems of self-government over such a vast territory and huge population are bound to be very considerable in terms of types of problems as well as their magnitudes. Consequently, a formal structure of government developed under earlier conditions has since had to be adapted to fit the conditions of quite a different time and society.

While population size itself is of some importance in politics, its significance is made greater when we have some idea of the characteristics or composition of the population. Certainly the *heterogeneity* of the membership is among the more salient characteristics. Whether it is the most diverse of the world's population is difficult to say, but it may well be. In any case, the United States does have sharp ethnic, racial, religious, and occupational differences, with further distinctions of education, income, and class. And each of these social cleavages offers possible sources of political cleavage. Indeed, it is entirely conceivable that it is precisely such differences that become the basis for different or competing demands on the polity. It is conceivable too that such distinctions also may become a source of strain at the support input, for the loyalties of some of the minority groups—particularly during the early years of assimilation into the society—might be questioned by the majority members. On the other hand, as we shall show in Chapter 9, these same sources of difference and conflict may contain the seeds of integration, or lessening of the conflict. Nevertheless, this heterogeneous population has been the source of many tensions in American society, many of which have eventually become politicized or are in the process of so becoming. As each immigrant group, for example, came to America, it had to endure a long period of gradual and frequently violent assimilation until its right to be recognized as a full-fledged American group could be attained.[5] Some commentators have estimated that it has generally taken a century for each group to be accepted in the sense of winning political offices in larger constituencies than merely in that of the group.[6] Political action itself, however, has often been a means of winning assimilation by improving the group's socio-economic conditions and by providing opportunities for the group leaders to become leaders in the larger community, opportunities that are not always available in business and the professions.

Thus, whatever the contributions of these diverse groups to American society, it is still a fact that the very diversity of the population has posed a considerable number of political problems at each level of input to the polity. Demands have increased in variety, number, and intensity. Furthermore, the demands upon the polity in terms of being able to mobilize the support of such a diverse collection of people have also been increased. For in order to attain group support, recognition has had to be given to their leaders, resulting in the phenomena of "balancing the ticket," an important consideration in the selection of party candidates. Few other countries have had to "balance their tickets" in the same sense that American parties must at each election.

A third characteristic of the population is that it is predominantly *urban*, a very different state from the time of the Revolution. Today, approximately 64 per cent of the people live in towns of 2,500 or more, while at the turn of the century about three-fifths of the population lived on farms or in rural communities of fewer than 2,500 inhabitants. By 1930, some 56 per cent of the population was classified as urban in the Census reports. Now, over 70 per cent of the urbanites live in metropolitan areas of over 50,000 population.[7]

A population that is predominantly urban may be expected to pose not only more political problems but problems of a different order than would a society of rural inhabitants. Furthermore, we might expect that the belief systems of people living under these radically different conditions will also differ. A political system functioning in a rural America could be rather simple, or, on the other hand, complex, and yet solve the problems with which it was presented, because the problems or demands themselves were relatively simple. Such conditions, in fact, posed fewer demands. Today, however, a large population living in urban situations is confronted with enormous responsibilities. A trivial example illustrates the difference: while traffic lights are hardly required in rural areas with few people and automobiles, the highly congested areas of the modern city literally force a traffic system and police control upon the people. The growing industrialization and urbanization of America has, in short, forced the political system to become more important in determining a greater range of behavior.

In addition to becoming an urban society, the American population has also become *highly mobile,* that is, Americans tend to move about the country a great deal. At present, the movements are taking place in all directions, although the most recent ones have tended to be from the farm to the city, from the East and North to the South and the West. In the nineteenth century the movements were generally and simply from one frontier to another, or from the East to the West. Unlike Europeans, few Americans live in but one place for their entire lives. Indeed, it is not uncommon to have lived in a dozen different and widely scattered areas in the course of a lifetime. While the political significance of this has not been generally stated, it would appear that a highly mobile population as distinct from a static one would make governing somewhat more difficult. Fewer persons today, for example, have long cultivated local loyalties to support local governments.[8] Moreover, close interpersonal relationships so vital in providing the basis for self-government are less frequent. Simply keeping records of a fast-moving population is a problem for most officials. On the other hand, these great movements of people have tended to ease certain national problems because they have enabled Americans to transcend regional and local ties that were predominant among most people during the early years of the Republic. The mobilization of support for national goals has thus become easier as a result of the nationalizing effect of movement.

Among other population factors worth noting is the fact that our numbers have continued to *increase,* and at high rates, ranging from 36.4 per cent during the early nineteenth century to 18.5 per cent during the last decade. Even the lowest rate of increase—during the Great Depression—was 7.2 per cent.[9] Between 1900 and 1960 we have much more than doubled: having gone from about 76 million to almost 180 million persons. We can gain a better and quicker appreciation of this increase, plus a picture of the changing rural-urban ratio, by viewing Figure 2-2.

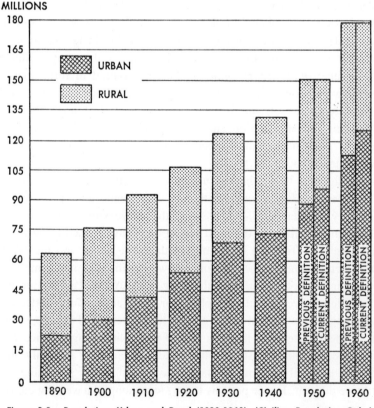

Figure 2-2. Population, Urban and Rural (1890-1960). (Civilian Population Only.)

Among the consequences of this increasing population is that of providing for a larger number of demands. Of course, a growing population is also an advantage in that human resources such as labor and skills too are thereby increased. From a political perspective, however, a growing population means political problems such as the need for more administrators, the need for more representatives, and shifts in the power potentials of various regions and in urban-rural power ratios. For while the country is primarily urban, the rural areas, because of formal structural features in our government, have continued to receive a disproportionate share of representation in many offices, particularly in the state legislatures.[10] Thus, the increase and shifting of our people has produced extraordinarily difficult and persistent problems of the relationship of political structures to the location and nature of its membership.

THE ECONOMY

Since Plato and Aristotle through Karl Marx on into the present time, the significance of the economic system for a society and its politics has been recognized and given varying amounts of importance. We need not be economic determinists to accept the fact that economies are of enormous significance in any realistic political analysis. On the other hand, it must also be recognized that economic action is influenced in turn by ideas and ideals of other than an economic nature. Thus, some great studies have shown us that religious ideas can have a profound impact upon economic behavior.[11] And, with the examples of totalitarian societies about us, we should now realize that political power can make of an economy almost anything the rulers choose to make of it. To those who are critics of socialism and government planning, it should also be readily apparent that politics can dominate economic relationships. In the United States, the relationship of economy and polity is a close and reciprocal one as our conceptual framework has already suggested. But since we are to deal with the economy as a part of the polity's environment, we will restrict ourselves here to a consideration of the economic system's influence on political action. Our concern, then, will be with the output of the economy to the polity, or as an input to the polity from the economy, that input which is one of resources for the polity. In the following pages we will attempt to characterize that input and the structure of our economy insofar as it is relevant to our subject matter.[12]

By way of introduction, the following characteristics seem important:

1. The American economy is predominantly a private enterprise and market economy.

2. It is a mass-production system.

3. The corporation is the major economic unit of enterprise.

4. The economy is subject to wide fluctuations.

5. On the whole the system has worked well, producing the highest material standard of living in history.

While the government plays a crucial role in regulating many of the conditions under which the economy functions, and, in fact, also owns and operates many enterprises of its own, it is still appropriate to describe the American economy as a privately owned and operated system. Most of the capital goods and productive processes are the property of private persons and groups who in turn make the vast majority of decisions as to how economic processes are to be conducted. Consequently, what their decisions are and how they are made are crucial determinants of the level and distribution of national income, employment, and the distribution of goods and services. As we shall note below, the fact that the economy is based upon literally millions of private decisions has had much to do with its cyclical behavior and demands for increasing governmental controls. That the United States has had a long tradition of private enterprise has also affected politics in still another way, namely, the powerful appeal of private enterprise and property in the struggles of politics. One of the two major parties in fact—the Republican—has come to be identified with the property holders and their interests to a greater extent than the Democratic. Yet the Democratic Party itself has never abandoned its own belief in the superiority of the private enterprise system. Indeed, the claim of the Democratic Party—at least of the liberal elements—is that they can make that system work better than the Republicans. Regardless of the validity of the claims, both parties do support the free economy.

In addition to being a private enterprise economy, it is also one that is based on mass production. Goods are produced using a minute division of labor in highly mechanized factories for a mass market. Thus, both production and the product itself are equally standardized, so that consumers tend to use the same products or types over and over again. Likewise, prices too are highly standardized. Yet inevitably in a mass production system, the quality of the goods is reduced, as the product must be adapted to the productive apparatus and not vice versa. In such a market saleability quite naturally becomes the ruling criteria, left not to chance but to the rational controls of the seller who attempts to shape the tastes and behavior of the consumers. Thus, the mass production system has created a huge sales force and advertising industry to control demand.

The character of mass production has created in turn an entire series of problems for the political system. Among these problems are those dealing with the work situation of the laborers, the distribution of costs and rewards in the economy, and the power of economic organizations to control not only their own position in the economy but also public policies. Not only does the work situation of the laborer involve more than wages and hours, but status, meaning, and purpose in life are also crucial. Mass production, however, has tended to depersonalize and make meaningless the activities of workers as, indeed, of most men concerned with the operation,[13] a problem of meaning that has led to discontent, unionization, and political action on the part of workers, managers, and owners. Increasingly, these groups have looked to the political system not only for solutions of their conflicts but also for authoritative decisions on the economic allocation of costs and rewards. Governmental agencies and politicians have been required, for example, to settle many labor-management disputes. In this area, the future would seem to promise still more governmental action.

Mass production, privately directed, is accomplished primarily through the device of corporations, the dominant form of economic organization in the United States. A legal creation, it therefore depends for its existence, in a formal sense, upon the polity, which may or may not allow a group of persons to incorporate. At the present time, there are approximately 700,000 firms organized as corporations. And while it is estimated that nearly 3.5 million unincorporated firms do business, they are generally rather small and do not exercise the same power as do the smaller number of larger corporations. Over 50 per cent of the national income earned each year comes from these large corporations, while only 30 per cent results from the activities of the unincorporated units. Other indices of the position of the corporation can be found in the number of persons they employ: about two-thirds of the working force. Likewise, the corporations account for about half of the total production of the economy and pay about 75 per cent of all the salaries and wages earned in private industry.[14]

As many observers have noted, the change from the old, small, individually-owned and managed firm to that of the giant corporation is one of the most significant in American history. A society in which production is carried on by large-scale manufacturing and distribution will very likely pose quite different political problems than one of individual entrepreneurs and partnerships. Interestingly, some still cling to the old economic belief system in a nostalgic sort of way, but act as though it will never be returned. In short, the new structure of the economy poses new problems in the integration of society and in the distribution of values, including that of power.

As might be expected in an economy in which millions of people make their own decisions, coordination is not easily attained. As a result the economy does not perform evenly, but rather in uneven ways. In other words, we have experienced alternating periods of depression and prosperity, however defined. A fluctuating economy obviously creates societal problems. Demands for governmental intervention to control the fluctuations and the consequences have always increased markedly during every downturn in employment and production. And these demands have not always emanated from the workers and unions; employers and corporations themselves also want their own markets and income increased and stabilized. Indeed, a rapidly fluctuating economy creates a tremendous demand for security, a demand to reduce the fluctuations in frequency and severity. Consequently, political action has been increasingly resorted to for protection. Just so, governmental regulation now pervades most of the crucial and many not so crucial segments of the economic system.

Our last concern with the economy again involves its performance. For while the economy has performed erratically, it has also brought, perhaps, the highest living standard in the world, if not for all time. The annual incomes that Americans derive from their economic system are the highest known. Our productivity has increased many times more than the increase in population. Since World War II, for example, we have seen an annual growth trend of about 4 per cent.[15] Today, it has been estimated that 60 per cent of the American families have incomes between $3,000 and $10,000. In 1947 about 25 per cent of the families had incomes of over $5,000 per year. In 1959 this number had increased to 54 per cent. Some of these facts are reported in Table 2-1.

But while the standards of living afforded by the American society and environment have been laudatory, there have always been a certain number of families who have not shared in the good fortunes. In 1959, for example, about 2.4 per cent of the families, or some 8 million families, earned less than $2,000 annually, this in a time of considerable inflation. Many of these people are old, incapacitated, or members of various minority groups whose opportunities are thereby artificially reduced. Their needs are always a demand in the political process.

We have now concluded our brief survey of the economic subsystem and suggested some of its properties and effects on the polity. We will now consider another subsystem, that of social control, with special emphasis on stratification.

Table 2-1—Families and Unattached Individuals and Family Personal Income, by Before-Tax Income Level (1944-1959). (Numbers in thousands; income in millions of dollars. Not adjusted to include Alaska and Hawaii. For distinction between personal income and money income, see Historical Statistics, Colonial Times to 1957, series G 1-28).

INCOME LEVEL (before income taxes)	FAMILIES AND UNATTACHED INDIVIDUALS					AGGREGATE BEFORE-TAX FAMILY PERSONAL INCOME			
	1944	1950	1955	1958	1959	1950	1955	1958	1959
Total	40,880	48,890	52,170	54,620	55,300	217,262	294,239	343,265	365,567
Under $2,000	12,460	11,325	8,241	7,912	7,622	13,276	9,326	8,970	8,612
$2,000 to $2,999	8,762	8,091	5,917	5,687	5,431	20,273	14,871	14,286	13,621
$3,000 to $3,999	7,723	8,586	7,339	6,415	6,049	29,983	25,815	22,458	21,212
$4,000 to $4,999	4,535	7,054	7,328	6,755	6,319	31,533	33,021	30,404	28,443
$5,000 to $5,999	2,515	4,694	6,321	5,955	6,100	25,603	34,648	32,638	33,520
$6,000 to $7,499	2,259	3,836	6,925	7,451	7,523	25,578	46,311	49,843	50,456
$7,500 to $9,999	1,385	2,758	5,203	6,975	7,642	23,364	44,468	60,034	65,862
$10,000 to $14,999	707	1,536	3,068	4,855	5,605	18,310	36,915	58,124	67,327
$15,000 and over	534	1,010	1,828	2,615	3,009	29,342	48,864	66,508	76,514
Per cent									
Total	100.0	100.0	100.0	100.0	100.0	100.0	100.0	100.0	100.0
Under $2,000	30.5	23.2	15.8	14.5	13.8	6.1	3.2	2.6	2.4
$2,000 to $2,999	21.4	16.6	11.3	10.4	9.8	9.3	5.1	4.2	3.7
$3,000 to $3,999	18.9	17.6	14.1	11.7	11.0	13.8	8.8	6.5	5.8
$4,000 to $4,999	11.1	14.4	14.0	12.4	11.4	14.5	11.2	8.9	7.8
$5,000 to $5,999	6.2	9.6	12.1	10.9	11.0	11.8	11.8	9.5	9.2
$6,000 to $7,499	5.5	7.9	13.3	13.6	13.6	11.8	15.8	14.5	13.8
$7,500 to $9,999	3.4	5.6	10.0	12.8	13.8	10.8	15.1	17.5	18.0
$10,000 to $14,999	1.7	3.1	5.9	8.9	10.1	8.4	12.5	16.9	18.4
$15,000 and over	1.3	2.0	3.5	4.8	5.5	13.5	16.5	19.4	20.9

Source: Department of Commerce, Office of Business Economics; Survey of Current Business, April 1961.

SOCIAL CONTROL AND SOCIAL STRATIFICATION

An important characteristic of all societies, and therefore an element in the environment of the polity, is the system by which the members of that society are stratified into classes, strata, castes, or whatever other rankings the particular society employs.[16] By stratification is meant the ranking of members in terms of some value system. Generally, men are ranked according to a number of values or criteria, but most often these are restricted to *power, wealth,* and *prestige.* One may be placed in different ranks according to each of these standards, although there often appears to be a tendency toward a convergence of them, so that one who ranks high in power will probably also tend to rank high with respect to wealth and prestige. But there is no necessary one-to-one correspondence among the rankings. This, we shall soon see, is the case in the United States.

Although the ranking of men in some form of hierarchy is inevitable, the basis of the ranking as stated above may vary. Further, the ranking of members of a society may be done by two quite different groups of persons with the result that the rankings may not be the same. In the first place, ranking may be done by someone from outside of the immediate situation, for example, by a sociological investigator. On the other hand, the ranking may be done by the members of the society themselves. Sociologists, who may study stratification from both perspectives, often derive quite different results about the same society as a consequence. We will not enter the methodological problems nor debate which is the better approach. Rather, we shall arbitrarily use the rankings of the members of the society as our chief source of data, but also employ the objective criteria of the outsider. Of interest to us then are both the subjective evaluations of the American people, in addition to the more objective standards of differentiation such as income levels. Both sets of information are needed to understand certain crucial aspects of the political system.

Broadly speaking, the American society is characterized by an *open class system.* That is, the population is ranked according to classes with different incomes, life-styles, job opportunities, educational attainments, prestige, power, and attitudes. But it is equally important to realize that this class system is a relatively open one. Thus, while the rewards of American life are differentially distributed among classes, it is also possible for Americans to move from one class to another or more during the course of a single lifetime or at least during two or more generations. To be sure, there are serious limitations on the number of persons and families who can move at any given time, and on the extent of their movement, but as compared to many societies America is a land of opportunity.[17] A poor man like Lincoln can become President, just as a poor immigrant such as Andrew Carnegie can become an industrial giant and multi-millionaire.

To be more accurate, we really have not one class system, but *countless* such systems, and each individual is a member of more than one of them. A citizen thus may be ranked rather high, in terms of power, prestige, or wealth, in his small home town, but be accorded a low ranking whenever he acts within the social classes of a larger city. Or, one may be considered powerful and prestigious in local politics, but have no such power or prestige on the state or national levels. Different persons do the evaluating in each status system, and in some cases, no doubt, also employ sharply different standards. Thus, prestige in the academic world does not mean prestige in the worlds of business and politics. The American, then, possesses a variety of statuses, the exact number depending on the number of status systems to which he belongs. Yet, it is entirely conceivable that most persons tend to have their prestige rankings all fall within a narrow range of variation. There will be some consistency in the various ratings for the simple reason that most of our reference groups or status systems are themselves of the same class. One is not likely, for example, to belong simultaneously to a trade union and the American Medical Association. Working men have as their reference group working-men's lodges, clubs, and other organizations that are composed of other working men; likewise, middle-class and upper-class persons associate with others of the same general statuses.

The basis or standards by which evaluating is done in the United States are several, including income, blood lineage, power, and others. But the major focal point in most evaluating is done from the basis of *achievement* as centered in an *occupation*.[18] Most Americans are less interested in knowing a person's family tree than they are in knowing what his job is. Frequently we inquire into a stranger's job before anything else, on the assumption that we will be better able to identify his rank in society. In short, we treat men differently according to their position in the division of labor. Needless to say, other standards of judgment are also applied by various groups. The "Boston Brahmins," for example, are primarily concerned with family history and connections. The same may also be noted among the old aristocracy of the South. In such instances, lineage counts for more than money or occupation. The predominant standard in the United States, however, remains that of occupational success.

Another notable characteristic of our stratification system is that no readily visible symbols have been stabilized as *the* exclusive symbols of high or low status. In Europe, on the other hand, the symbols of rank are clear-cut and quite visible or noticeable. Dress, speech, mannerisms, and the like are reduced to a fine art as symbols. There is little mistaking a man's position or rank in society as there is in the United States. Here, business tycoons may have very similar patterns of dress to working men, talk like them, and practice the same forms of courtesy or lack thereof. Or, in reverse, some members of the middle class may act and appear as do the upper classes. There is, then, no ready, rigidly defined set of status symbols; such symbols do exist, but they are more easily acquired in the United States than in traditional societies. Mass production is partly responsible for this state of affairs. Silk stockings, as Schumpeter noted, were once the possession of the aristocratic ladies; today, they are worn by almost all women, including the charwoman.[19] In a similar vein, our political leaders reflect the class situation in the United States by denying its existence altogether, and acting in the generally accepted ways as to dress, speech, and other forms of behavior.

We must now consider a distinctly American phenomenon that befuddles many Europeans, particularly those of a Marxist persuasion—that of the American perception of class. The Europeans and Marxists, specifically, find it difficult to comprehend that Americans do not share their same intense class consciousness.

The American liberal belief system postulates a belief not only in the essential equality of man before the law and under God, but also tends to believe that this equality is a good thing and that our society provides the necessary conditions for its realization. The notion of class, therefore, is somewhat repugnant to most Americans. In fact, many even deny that classes exist, or minimize their significance. A famous poll conducted during the depression (1940) by *Fortune* Magazine learned that when Americans were asked whether they belonged to the upper, middle, or lower classes, they tended to assign themselves to the middle class. In fact, 80 per cent responded in this manner. Other, more sophisticated studies, by sociologists, suggest that while the *Fortune* poll had grave shortcomings, the general proposition—that a very large number of Americans consider themselves as middle class—is true.[20] Even more striking is the fact that Americans like to believe that success and failure, as defined by Americans, is a product of individual and not social or class effort, advantages, or obstacles. To be sure, we do like to rank power, prestige, and wealth, but we do so not according to class categories. This is consistent, of course, with the highly individualistic and achievement orientation of our liberal belief system.

The importance of the stratification system for the polity can be made clear in the same manner as we have used to suggest the significance of other elements in society, that is, through tracing the impact of stratification on the three inputs to the polity. We will thus begin with some hypotheses about the relationship of stratification to political *expectations* and *demands*.

Common sense seems to suggest that different classes or other groups in the stratification system have different expectations, and make different demands upon one another and the polity. In the case of this country, as already indicated, differences between classes may be considerable with respect to such matters as income and style of life, but much less so with respect to certain other items such as the general belief systems. With these considerations, we can hypothesize that all the different strata tend to hold in common similar expectations of political performance and similar general political beliefs such as the belief in democracy, majority rule, checks and balances, federalism, or the structure of our polity and government. As will be pointed out in Chapter 5, political beliefs, including both the cognitive and evaluative elements, are widely shared regardless of class.

But if expectations are fairly similar, regardless of class membership, there still may be differences of interest and thereby differences with regard to the goals that society ought to pursue and the means of their implementation. At these levels citizens may demand different goals, and advocate various means. Thus, the working class may demand recognition of unions and press for social security, low-cost housing, or a higher minimum wage. Contrariwise, the higher income groups may work for a high interest rate, lower income taxes, or regulation of trade unions. Thus, we see the possibilities of competing demands upon the polity.

Generally speaking, we may maintain that the upper classes tend to resist the liberal economic demands of the lower classes. What seems to have happened in America is that the lower classes have been making more of the explicit demands upon the upper classes because the latter has had more control over the society, and is therefore the major target for attack. In this struggle, the middle class has tended to assume an ambivalent role: now making or supporting the demands of the workers; now lending support to the upper classes; and often splitting its support in both directions.[21] These struggles, however, have not been of the type prognosticated by Marx, but rather of interest struggles as described by such scholars as Arthur F. Bentley [22] and David Truman.[23] Nor has the struggle over demands been that of massive, well disciplined, highly conscious classes doing battle. It has been rather a struggle over interest among smaller groups, many from the same class but without immediate common interests, and certainly without self-consciousness as a class or discipline. We have witnessed, then, a political struggle in which demands are primarily based upon interest, none of which are entirely class-bound. Indeed, one union may politically fight another; one business fight another business; or one agricultural group fight another.

There are other indicators of differences of demands stemming from stratification factors. We have solid information on the voting behavior of citizens, for example, which shows that the various strata of the society tend to vote in different directions.[24] Thus, whereas the higher income groups have a pronounced affinity for the Republican party, the lower one goes in the income scale, the greater the appeal of the Democratic party. In terms of demands, this means differences as to who should hold public office and which policies, or goals, and means should be employed. Voting patterns, in other words, may be used as an indicator of the demand schedule or input.

The relationships of stratification and the *resources input* ought to be reasonably apparent. Here we must be concerned with such matters as who controls the resources, and how and how much are contributed by the different groups and persons making up the stratification order. Having noted that the concept of "resources" ought to include both human and nonhuman objects, we are immediately made aware, with respect to the nonhuman resources, of the bases from which governmental revenues come. Since governments must gain access to fiscal resources in order to perform their functions, and since these must come from the society, *who* bears *what* burdens thus becomes a very important problem of politicians and the polity. As might be expected, the amounts paid by the different groups in our society vary both in terms of absolute figures and proportions. Chapter 16 will present some interesting data on just such problems.

The impact of stratification on the matter of support is quite unclear, partially because the concept readily lends itself to a normative judgment, and partially because little research has been directed toward the problem-area. However, a few hypotheses do suggest themselves. For example, a number of studies have clearly indicated that the several classes participate in varying degrees and ways in the political system.[25] The higher one goes in the class system, the more probable it is that citizens will engage in more varieties of participation, and with greater frequency. One type of participation in which this generalization has been constantly demonstrated is voting. Another such generalization is that the middle and upper classes provide more of our political leaders, especially in the higher ranking offices. The point here, however, is not to compile an inventory of such statements,[26] but to illustrate the possible relationships between stratification and the polity. Evidence on these and other generalizations will be advanced in Chapters 14 and 16.

PATTERN MAINTENANCE: SOCIALIZATION AGENCIES

Here we are concerned with those structures and processes in American society that serve to maintain the political value system through their influence over political motivations. For the most part, we shall center attention upon the socialization agencies and their actions. Among these structures or agencies we must include the family, church, and school. To be sure, each provides other services to society, but the secular focal point of their contributions is that of preparing the young, primarily, to participate as useful members of the community. In the process of doing this, citizens are moulded, just as are civic and political attitudes, and beliefs about power, authority, rights, and duties. Indeed, we cannot understand how the American polity functions without some knowledge as to its relationship to the socialization process. While this is a reciprocal relationship, our concern at this point is with the influence of the family, church, and school on the political system.

The Family

The American family structure is an interesting one, far more unique than is commonly thought.[27] And it is this uniqueness that has had political consequences. In the first place, the American family is a *small nuclear* structure, consisting of one set of parents and their children— usually not more than two or three—living in isolation from other members of the extended kinship group. The parents are likely to define their own relationships in *informal* terms, permitting something more in the nature of a "partnership," "comradeship," and "love," rather than a patriarchy as exists in more traditional societies. In a situation such as this, it is highly unlikely that the child seeing his parents treat one another as equals will develop notions of hierarchy, order, or well-defined statuses. Indeed, he is more likely to develop democratic views of equality, and mutual participation in joint ventures. He is even likely, as he grows older, to learn something about bargaining and coalition-building, not only as he observes his parents, but attempts himself to shape their decisions concerning his role and its rewards. In the normal American family, the child likewise learns to question authority, including that of his parents. How often have we all heard the child *demand* to know *why* he must do a certain thing. And how often have we witnessed and perhaps participated in situations in which the child has refused to obey, and won. This kind of early experience cannot but influence the way in which the child will later behave with respect to authority figures and symbols in the polity, including the elective officials, administrators, and policemen. The actions of officials, it is thought, may be criticized, and, in any case, they must be rationalized in terms of legal-rational authority. The family is a prime agent in inculcating these orientations in members of the society.

Thus far, we have noted that the child acquires various attitudes and beliefs as a result of his direct participation in the politics of his family. But the child also receives attitudes and beliefs about the politics of the community, the state, and the nation from his parents and perhaps older brothers and sisters. Hearing his parents discuss or comment or emote upon these more abstract and distant persons and events, the child learns certain views that form a basis for his own later participation as a citizen. Among the matters he will pick up are notions on the extent and type of participation in which a citizen should engage; some conception of his rights as an American; his duties as a citizen; heroes and devils in American history; party preferences; and a way or style of thinking about politics. Thus, whether a person thinks about politics as a serious matter for either intellectual comprehension or moralistic preaching, or whether politics is thought of as beyond understanding and control, may be partially dependent on his family environment.

In the United States the child is likely to learn the liberal belief system with respect to the preceding items. As the content of this belief system will be dealt with in Chapter 5, it is unnecessary to detail it at this point. But it, too, is given expression in the content and manner of expectations and demands brought to bear on the political system.

Schools and Formal Education

While the role of the school system in society would seem apparent, its political significance has as yet been only sporadically recognized.[28] Schools not only train men to be skilled artisans, technicians and professional persons, or good members of society, but they also make *citizens* of them as well. Done most often and dramatically during the early childhood and teenage periods, it may well continue into adulthood under such programs as that of adult education. Our chief concern, however, is with the earlier years of training.

The educational system of our society is generally characterized as *free, secular, public,* and *decentralized.* That is, the American educational system is mostly concerned with teaching secular matters, administered by public officials for public purposes and on a localized basis. These characteristics, of course, are quite consistent with—indeed, reflections of—the dominant liberal belief system. To be sure, one will find parochial schools, nationally administered and controlled institutions such as the service academies, and privately owned and operated schools, but they are atypical. One does not often find students attending class in uniform, reading the same books, or meeting the same requirements. Whether on the primary, secondary, or university levels, curriculum and administration differ greatly throughout the nation. In these respects, the American system of education is remarkably different from that found in most other countries of the world.

Schools play a significant role in the socialization process if for no other reason than so large a percentage of Americans go to school. In fact, it is a general requirement that a certain number of years be spent in schools or that the student attend until a certain age, usually sixteen, depending on the state. Thus, the child may be expected to be under school influence for at least ten or eleven years at his most impressionable age. Free public education has long been a hallmark of the American society primarily because—and again this is a reflection of the liberal creed— education not only is considered to be a good thing for the individual and society, but because everyone is believed to be potentially capable of being educated. Admittedly, doubters may be found concerning both of these beliefs, but they are not so numerous nor so powerful as those who are optimistic about man's intelligence. Accordingly, we have extended education, or at least a minimum amount, to almost every segment of the population. Our literacy rate therefore is quite high—97 per cent—although still lower than some European nations. As Seymour Martin Lipset has noted, a high literacy rate is a necessary although not sufficient condition for democracy to develop and maintain itself.[29] Americans possess this necessary condition.

The secular outlook of Americans finds its expression in the schools in terms of control and curriculum. Most of our school system is administered and controlled not by church men but by local and state officials. This powerful insistence on secular control stems from the belief system and political attitudes that church and state ought and indeed must be kept separate. Church schools are not prohibited, but the government certainly does not encourage them verbally or financially. In many areas of the country, in fact, considerable tension has arisen and become political because of church attempts, particularly those of the Catholic Church, to extend its influence over the young through education. Along with secular control is secular dominance in the subject matter taught at all levels of training. Primary emphasis is placed upon the acquisition of skills, preparation for a job, and citizenship, rather than upon religious instruction. The chief concern is to equip the student with the necessary orientation and skills to participate in a highly secular, materialistic environment. In short, what is taught are "reading, writing, arithmetic," some social skills, and an appreciation, if not always an understanding, of being an American citizen. Thus, American history, literature, numbers, and civics are given a prominent place in the student's education. Indeed, in most schools, including many state universities, courses in civics, American government, or history are requirements. Since World War II, an increasing value has also been placed upon the social skills of getting along harmoniously, while the older disciplines of the mind have been devalued. That a democracy, functioning under the conditions in America, should stress these interpersonal values and skills, however, is not surprising; equality, personal liberty, and opportunity are all fundamental values in our belief system.

What is taught, how it is taught, and by whom are all important considerations in the socialization of American citizens. We have just indicated that much attention is devoted to the inculcation of civic virtues, a respect for and knowledge of American history, and, of course, some of the basic tools for the operation of democratic institutions. But how are these matters taught?

The pedagogy of a nation is an important reflection, creator, and sustainer of national values and norms. In the school room, consequently, the example of the teacher is as crucial to the development of the child as is the father in the home. And in American schoolrooms, the teacher is likely to conduct *her* classes (75 per cent of the primary and secondary teachers being women), in a democratic and highly informal manner or style. Students are treated as individuals with unique personalities, problems, interests, and skills, not as disembodied minds unencumbered with personal troubles and aspirations. In this same connection, there is a strong tendency to be more concerned with the slow and less able student than with the bright ones. Thus, the level of achievement is likely to be lower than in aristocratic or autocratic societies where attention is devoted to the better-advantaged. The teacher is not likely to employ discipline of a harsh nature, and, in fact, may be prohibited from doing so by state law. Students are to be treated with greater consideration as befits our notion and ideal of the free citizen. They are asked their opinions, and debate or argue with their teachers, an almost unheard of practice in European societies, including the democratic. In other words, the teacher bases work and appeal on some kind of rational authority, even though the level of discourse in mass education is likely to diminish in the process. According to the American ethic, the teacher must persuade the student, not coerce him. The very appearance of the teacher is also a reflection of the belief system; in the United States the teacher is likely to be, as noted above, a woman, and, moreover, a young woman who behaves in a pleasant and cheerful manner. She is not expected to frighten the children, but to lead them, and try to build their curiosity and direct it into useful directions. Should she fail it is generally thought to be her responsibility rather than the child's or the parents'. School, then, is a very permissive social system in its own right. Not only do students learn citizenship from books, but, perhaps equally important, they learn the American variety from practice, as in student government, and from their relationships with the faculty and one another.

Interestingly, however, American students, including the college ones, are not encouraged to participate in the politics of the nation. To be sure, student politics, confined to the school or campus, are encouraged and success is highly regarded among parents and students. But actual serious participation in national politics, including those of the state and local communities, is not so encouraged. Of course, there have been periods in American history, as during the 1930's, when such involvement was widespread and honored. More recent decades and many previous ones, however, have seen other views and activities as more desirable. Indeed, American students seem most different from foreign students in their apolitical or antipolitical attitudes. Profound intellectual or emotional involvement is felt to be abnormal. Likewise, American students have never had the power of their compatriots in foreign lands where the student movements not only discuss politics, but live it by rioting and revolutions. This past decade, for example, has seen student movements in South Korea and Turkey topple governments. The American student, however, is expected by his parents to live on a campus, learn a profession or job, and have a good time. Consequently, politics plays a small role in his life—a life of political isolation that for many of them is apt to carry over into their adult years as citizens.

The socialization process in the schools, like the process everywhere, is somewhat less perfect than many citizens would prefer. Many students do not learn all they are expected to learn nor do they learn what their parents may want for them. In fact, while the school system, particularly on the lower levels, tends to support the status quo, the colleges and universities tend to question societal values and other beliefs with greater consistency and vigor. The college student, then, is encouraged to develop a skeptical mind, one that does not take societal issues for granted. And while it is not likely that the higher levels of education question the American democracy to the point of destruction, they do expose the student to more doubts than at any other time in his life. On the whole, however, the universities, like the primary and secondary schools, implement the American belief system and deepen loyalties rather than weaken them. Few teachers are Fascists or Communists, and few question democracy; but, undoubtedly, some do question the means employed in its operations.

The Churches and Religion

The role of religion and religious organizations such as the church may seem somewhat less apparent in the development of political beliefs and attitudes than those of the family and school. Nothing, however, could be further from the truth. Indeed, the churches and religious beliefs are of crucial importance in the political life of every society.

Religious beliefs are fundamental with everyone for they are basic beliefs about the very meaning of life and death. And, as such, they are likely to be highly stable and tenaciously held views. Because they are so crucial and important in the lives of men, they are also bound to have a strong influence over the ways in which these same men will view the secular world about them, including the political. A man who has fundamental beliefs about his obligations to God is also likely to transfer some of his beliefs about his obligations to secular authorities and particularly to government. Much of the history of religion, in fact, is the history of church and secular conflicts, of political and religious doctrines battling one another. Much of church and religious history, however, is also an account of accommodation to each sphere's power and a mutual exchange of advantages. In short, the church and most religions have had a very great influence over the amount and intensity of *support* which their members or adherents have been willing to accord the state. They have also been able to shape the sort of *expectations* and *demands* that their members, as individuals and as interest groups, make upon the political system. Thus, the existence of religions and religious organizations vitally affects the inputs that the polity receives from the rest of society. And, finally, religious expectations and demands, plus support, affect the outputs of decisions the polity produces. Some of these decisions are obviously directed at or related to the position and welfare of religion; as such the religious organizations attempt to control or determine them.

But before we may deal with the role of religious organizations in shaping the political motivations and behavior of citizens, we must first arrive at some understanding of the religious situation in the United States. The basic fact is that we have a formal or legal separation of church and state, that is, there is no formal or legally prescribed state church to which all Americans are expected to pay homage. Religious beliefs are expected to be individual matters, or more accurately, family matters, and not the concern of government. As such, religious freedom is the ideal if not always the fact. While there are over 250 religious organizations in the United States, the dominant beliefs and affiliations are Protestant. Of the esti-mated 104 million church members in the United States, approximately 60 million are Protestant, while some 36 million are Catholic.[30] The Jews number about 5.5 million, while the remaining 3 million plus, or 2 per cent, belong to other denominations and cults. Some 70 million persons, then, are not members of any church; this, of course, includes persons under twenty-one.

Thus, while large numbers of Americans are claimed by the churches as members, the percentage of the total population who are so claimed is not more than 60 per cent. And many of these persons, as every minister, priest, and rabbi knows, are nominal. Yet, the fact of nominal or non-membership percentage cannot be interpreted to mean that such persons are not religious. Nor can it mean that they have not been subject to the influence of religious beliefs and the churches. Many adults have had re-ligious training as children and this training does not easily disappear.

Consequently, a knowledge of the numbers of church members and religious denominations is not sufficient to determine the effects of such matters on political behavior. To do so it is also necessary to know the content or general characteristics of the belief system. As pointed out above, the Protestant religion is the dominant one, with respect to church affiliations. In terms of beliefs Protestantism has, in America, tended to stress the free-willing individual, the perfectability of man, mastery of the external world, and individual moral responsibility. These, of course, are not the only beliefs, nor are they adhered to by all Protestants, nor with equal intensity. But they are reasonably accurate generalizations of the Protestant social position. In everyday behavior these same beliefs are likely to find many adherents among Jews and Catholics as well. Further, it should be noted that these beliefs are quite at variance in some regards to early Christian doctrine that pictured a rather sombre world. Indeed, these same present-day Protestant beliefs are often more akin to many elements of the liberal doctrines that we will discuss in Chapter 5. Both tend to reflect the materialistic, optimistic, and secular orientations of American life, and both tend to reinforce one another. Thus, American religious beliefs, including the Catholic and Jewish, have taken a highly secular approach to life. In other words, religious beliefs have also been affected by other belief systems and by social-economic conditions. Religion, in short, has been influenced as well as influencing.

An official doctrine of the Catholic Church, for example, is that one's loyalty to the Church is expected to be greater than that to the state. In the United States, however, the Catholic Church has qualified this doctrine to the point where the Church, in effect, has become subordinate to state obligations. Indeed, the Church has shown remarkable powers of adjustment to political situations throughout history. Protestantism, likewise, has so adapted itself that some commentators believe that religious beliefs today are no longer the serious doctrinal matters they were once assumed to be. All this is reflected in the prevalent notion that, "It isn't important which church you attend, just so long as you go." Obviously, this means that specific beliefs do not count, which in turn suggests a considerable amount of tolerance for those who do not believe deeply. Doctrinal tolerance, then, might well be a product of simply not caring one way or the other. It should come as no surprise, then, that Americans tend to derive social values from church affiliation rather than moral guidance and an intellectual orientation toward life. Ministers no longer preach "hell and brimstone" as they once did, but offer guidance and counseling services. Religious beliefs in the United States, then, have not been static. Nor does the fact that dogmas are less important today mean that religious beliefs have no implications for politics; they do.

Among other practices of the churches has been a pronounced tendency to avoid involvement in partisan politics and elections. Ministers ordinarily neither assume party positions nor propagate them; there are exceptions, but they merely tend to prove the rule. And when there are exceptions, as in the presidential elections of 1896, 1928, and 1960, a further fact about the relationship of politics and religion is suggested; namely, that Protestantism is the dominant religion and that presidential candidates who are not Protestants are likely to find it rather difficult to win such an election. Catholics, Jews, and agnostics have and do hold office, but only one Catholic has ever been elected President. Studies of the religious affiliations of certain public officials have strongly suggested that:

> Protestant denominations with congregations of high social status (Congregational, Presbyterian, Episcopal, Unitarian) possess about twice the number of Representatives and Senators they would have if Congressmen were completely representative in their religions. The Methodists, Lutherans, and Baptists have about the "right" number. On the other hand, Roman Catholics have only one-half to one-third and Jews one-sixth the number of Congressmen they should have if the Congress is to be a religious cross-section of the nation.[31]

Other studies have shown that voters tend to prefer to vote for persons sharing their own religious convictions and affiliations. Consequently, religion is an important element in the making of political decisions such as voting. It is also significant in the broader sense of shaping or conditioning the support that religious belief allows for political authorities. A few words need to be said on this point.

Generally speaking, it may be held that the various religions and churches in the United States encourage loyalty to the American value system, the polity, obedience of the laws, and respect for the officials of the government. Far from being conspicuous critics, in fact, the churches are more likely to be zealous patriots, as are many today in their struggle against communism. Indeed, no church has failed to support the government in any war in which the United States has been engaged. Even where support for American policies and institutions has not been vocal, the consequence of church refusals to be openly critical would seem to suggest support of the status quo. In terms of policy preferences, of course, it can be stated unequivocally that the higher prestige Protestant churches tend to support the more conservative views of the Republican party. This is in accord with the attitudes and beliefs of the membership who are generally of the upper classes.

But perhaps even more important is the fact that religion, while it has sometimes advocated rebellion in other times and lands, has tended to teach the necessity and desirability of obedience to duly constituted authorities. The virtues of patience, kindness, and forebearance, for example, which most religions preach are more apt to result in support for the "powers that be" than in rebellion. Moreover, religions are conservative even should religious people be occasionally radical. Thus, while American churches usually remain aloof from political action, except on those issues having an immediate impact on their positions, the consequence of aloofness has been that of lending support to the existing order and policies. In the process of organizational separation of spheres, members learn not to criticize, but to accept. Their ambivalent beliefs toward political authorities are thus reinforced. On the other hand, the gentle virtues that are taught stand in sharp contrast to political action. Politicians responsible for action in highly competitive situations are seldom in a position to act pious or to honor other tenets of religions. Thus, the religious person is put in a difficult spot of having to obey authorities whom he finds difficult to admire. How he resolves these dilemmas may vary, but normally it results in support for the institutions of government, and criticism for specific officials and persons or groups.

There is one other aspect of religion that has political relevance, and that is related to the political practices and institutions within the churches themselves. In the United States, the churches tend to use political structures and practices similar to those of the secular political system. That is, the churches—like the polity—tend to operate according to democratic principles, employing such practices as decentralized power, voting, or laity control, and bargaining. To be sure, hierarchies do exist, as in the Catholic Church and in some Protestant churches, but the over-all tendency is to emulate the secular polity.[32] As a result, we note that citizens receive training and practice in self-government, both in the church and in the polity. It would thus seem that the agencies of socialization—the family, school, and church—all reinforce one another and the polity with similar practices. What a citizen learns from one system is likely to be confirmed and applicable in the others. Although not all these agencies are perfectly nor continuously consistent with one another in principles or practices, there is a strong tendency for them to be so. And while none are as democratic as abstract ideals would have them, the push is in that direction. Each must proclaim, at least in public, that it is a democratic organization and institution.

From the point of view of most religions in the United States, politics is a necessary evil, and citizenship is construed largely in terms of duty— moral duty. Patriotism is strongly advocated, but it is based rather upon love for country than upon respect for actual political processes. The good Christian thus remains "above politics" instead of engaging in it. Consequently, churches encourage neither the young or old to consider politics as a career, although religious norms of service often do lead one to ultimate public professions. The role of the good Christian and the church is to set an example, and to judge in highly abstract moralistic tones. The churches, in these approaches to politics, resemble the normal family and school teachings. There are to be sure, variations on these themes. Indeed, the position of many religious groups as minorities or divergent faiths often leads them to political activism in order to defend or represent the group.[33]

3

The Structure of the Polity

Here, we are interested in those more durable relationships that exist among the units constituting the polity. We are concerned with determining the major properties of the system of roles as a whole.[1] For just as generalizations can be established concerning the structure of physical and biological entities, so generalizations can be made about social and political systems.

We emphasize generalization deliberately, because we wish to avoid the cataloguing of miscellaneous facts—important as they may be—substituting instead a set of concepts that will permit comparability and generality. Only by employing a more inclusive set of concepts are we able to compare and thereby to point up both similarities and differences with other structures. To be sure, the richness of detail is thereby sacrificed, but, for our purposes, the cost does not seem prohibitive. We will thus forego such statements as "Senators serve terms of six years," and try to attain generalizations of the order, "The polity is a differentiated, formalized, decentralized, and highly visible system." In the language of Georg Simmel, we will deal in *forms* rather than the *contents* of political relationships.[2]

The reason for dealing with structure ought to be apparent; it simply seems impossible to understand political processes and their outcomes without knowing the immediate environment of the action. Structure is that immediate environment. And it is within the political structures that integration, tension-management, goal-attainment, and adaptation all take place. When we have even a minimal knowledge of the properties of the polity we thus are better prepared to understand and predict how these processes will work, and what their range of outcomes are likely to be under various circumstances.

One last word of introductory comment: the relationships we will be discussing are, of course, power and authority relationships. Yet, many of our generalizations will not sound as though they concern power, at least in any direct sense. This is so because our chief concern in this chapter is to state over-all properties, only one of which is concerned with the traditional problem of the distribution of power. Because this problem is so crucial and difficult to resolve, a separate and entire chapter (Chapter 4) will be devoted to its analysis.

STRUCTURAL PROPERTIES

It is best perhaps to begin with a summary outline of the major structural features of the polity. They are listed in brief form for convenience and in the order of the presentation:

1. A sharply differentiated subsystem.
2. Enormous size of the polity.
3. Sharply differentiated roles.
4. Highly formalized.
5. High degree of visibility.
6. Highly complex system.
7. Multiplicity of access points.
8. Institutionalized competition for leadership roles.
9. A highly stable structure.

A Sharply Differentiated Subsystem

As compared to a primitive or traditional society, the United States is a sharply differentiated social system in which major functional problems tend to be handled by specialized organizations, persons, and roles. Thus, the problem of goal-attainment has become a peculiar one and a function of the political system. It is quite possible to see this division of labor in everyday life where some persons make a living at politics or some aspect thereof. But whether specific persons make careers of politics or administration is still less significant than the fact that political roles are distinct from other roles in society. Contrast this with what A. R. Radcliffe-Brown has to say about African polities:

> In Africa it is often hardly possible to separate, even in thought, political office from ritual or religious office. Thus in some African societies it may be said that the king is the executive head, the legislator, the supreme judge, the commander-in-chief of the army, the chief priest or supreme

head, and even perhaps the principal capitalist of the whole community. But, it is erroneous to think of him as combining in himself a number of distinct offices. There is a single office, that of king, and its various duties and activities, and its rights, prerogatives, and privileges, make up a single unified whole.[3]

Not having grown out of a traditional or primitive society, however, the United States has from its earliest days been subject to internal differentiation. From the beginning of the Republic, political action has been that of a relatively specialized set of actions. The original Constitution, itself, created a system of political relationships that attempted to separate politics from other activities, such as religious and economic. And, of course, the Founding Fathers regarded government as a rational instrument in which to operate in a limited sphere, for highly pragmatic goals. Such limited-purpose instruments are, of course, central to specialization. As the years have passed, the American polity has seemed to become even more differentiated as a system, with greater numbers of men making their livelihoods from politics. Likewise, the activity of governing itself is separated from other spheres of activity. State capitals, for example, have generally been isolated from the major centers of population. Just so, the buildings in which governmental activities are conducted are specialized buildings used for no other purposes than that of the political. And, of course, one frequently hears Americans speak of "keeping politics" out of some other phase of life. In short, they believe in keeping politics a "functionally-differentiated" process.

The fact that the polity is distinct from other subsystems, such as the economy, means that the norms which specify behavior and the behavior itself tend to take on distinct characteristics. This is especially true in the United States, in part because of extreme specialization, but also because of the higher value placed on nonpolitical behavior. The economy, for example, is concerned with the production and distribution of goods and services, while the polity is involved in goal-attainment efforts for society. The economy is primarily sustained by a profit-motive or "self-orientation," while the polity is supposed to be "collectivity-oriented," or in search of the "public interest." And even while the political system is far more rational in its orientation than traditional polities, still much greater range is given to "affectivity" or "expressive" behavior in our political life than in economic activities. Nonrational elements thus play a much more crucial role in political than economic behavior. These few observations should suffice to indicate the extent of functional differentiation in this country's politics.

Enormous Size of the Polity

In terms of the number of persons and groups who are members of the political system, the American, with its 182 million population, must be considered as a very sizable system, indeed. Whether Americans participate actively in the sense of voting, running for office, or otherwise making their demands known, they are all *members* of the political system. They are all subject to its directives, appeals, and burdens. Not that America is the world's largest society. Nor does it have the largest polity in the sense just defined. The Soviet Union, China, and India all have much larger populations. But the American is still large, proportionately speaking. Further, in terms of the total number of people who actively participate in decision-making, the American polity is the largest in the world. Moreover, as a democracy—a system in which the mass of men are expected to share in decision-making—the United States is the largest political system in history. We can gain some appreciation of this size by noting the number of qualified voters in 1956 alone: then, 100,200,000 Americans were legally able to vote. For purposes of comparison, we might look at the total electorates of a few other democracies. Table 2-2 [4] can give some perspective to the matter.

Table 2-2—Total Electorates of Some Western Democracies.

Country	Total Electorate
United Kingdom (1959)	35,080,000
Metropolitan France (1956)	26,772,000
Germany (1957)	35,403,000
Canada (1957)	8,902,000
Sweden (1956)	4,887,000
United States (1956)	100,200,000

Still another indicator of the size of the polity is to be found in the numbers of officials occupying official roles or offices in the government. As of 1957 the situation was as follows: there were 525,386 elective public officials of whom 514,000 were local; 10,852 state; and 533 national.[5] To these figures must now be added the officials of the newest states of Alaska and Hawaii. In addition to elected officials, there are many more civil servants. In fact, at the present time civil servants total nearly 2½ million persons.[6] In addition there are the appointive officials at all levels of government. While authoritative numbers are difficult to acquire, a reasonable estimate would suggest that the President appoints about 1,200 such officials in Washington, alone.

A fact not often considered in assessing the size of the political system has to do with the geographic area it covers. Again, the size of the land area is striking. The United States government rules over an area of approximately 3,628,130 square miles, including the newer states of Alaska—the largest of the fifty—and the Hawaiian Islands. This area, including only those people who are American citizens, does not apply to other areas that have the status of territories or are in other states of "dependence" on the United States. To govern by democratic means over so vast a territory is obviously no inconsiderable task. Indeed, many of the problems of ruling are conditioned by spatial considerations, as Madison noted in the Federalist Papers. And while his observations are less applicable today, because of developments in the technology of communications, the matter of area is still not to be ignored.

Functionally Differentiated Roles

Just as the polity is sharply differentiated from other subsystems in society, so the internal structure of the polity is marked by an advanced degree of differentiation of function and role. We have tried and succeeded to an amazing degree in creating a highly complicated political division of labor to parallel the economic system. Thus, while the separation of powers and federalism were adopted because the Founding Fathers believed they would aid thereby in the prevention of tyranny, they also created an extensive division of labor. Some positions and persons were expected to be concerned with legislating, some with administering, some with adjudicating, and some with executing. According to the Constitution, as well as the various state constitutions, it was possible to completely separate these roles and functions; thus, the elaborate attempt to define powers, duties, rights, and perquisites. This formal elaboration of roles extends even to the populace in terms of rights of citizens, duties of voting, and so forth. It was also anticipated that a real division of labor could be instituted. Accordingly, federalism provided a basis for dividing the tasks of government into local, state, and federal, with each sphere to be sharply distinguished from the others.

Although the above remarks relate to the formal structure of the polity, functional specialization has set in elsewhere as well. In addition to the 525,000 elective public officials, each engaged in fairly distinct tasks, there has been a multiplication of specialized interest groups. Each is characterized by a distinct set of goals and pattern of behavior, and performs a specialized set of functions for the system. And, as Gabriel Almond pointed out in his typology of political systems,[7] each one of these groups as well as the officials tends to be autonomous. The role of the political parties also has become highly specialized and distinct from other roles such as those of the interest groups. Even the diffused role and functions of the citizen take on internal differentiation as he becomes variously a taxpayer, a party worker, or a voter. As the polity generally operates according to a distinct set of rules or norms, so, too, do the roles of each member or occupant.

Although so extreme a specialization of political roles is probably unique to the United States, the other Western democracies themselves are far along the same continuum. Conversely, Almond tells us that totalitarian polities have a certain "shapelessness" or "functional instability," meaning that roles are not clearly and sharply distinguished from one another.[8] Lucian W. Pye writes that in "non-Western" political systems "it is the rare association that represents a limited and functionally specific interest." [9] There is in such societies a kind of "structureless" situation. Certainly, there is little in the way of functional differentiation of the political process.

A number of consequences flow from the kind and extent of role structure that we have built. While we will not—at this time—indicate many of them, it is worth while to note that, having created this complex division of labor, we are faced with the problem of integrating or coordinating its many specialist-oriented members. Collective action, swiftly arrived at, is not characteristic of the American polity. The system operates to minimize cooperation, retard action, support the status quo, make leadership difficult, and often to encourage apathy and cynicism among the citizenry. In addition to these general consequences, the extreme division of labor has, ironically, stimulated the development of all sorts of devices to overcome its consequences. Thus does Robert Merton explain the rise and functions of such informal groups as the "big city machine," bosses, and corruption.[10] And, one may also attribute the development of such devices as interstate compacts, grants-in-aid, associations of public officials, and indeed the party system as responses to the extreme fragmentation of power and authority. The division of labor, then, has had a variety of consequences, not all of which the Founding Fathers could have anticipated, nor would approve.

Formalized Role Structure

We have not left our political system very many chances to develop in a "hit or miss" style. In fact, the effort has been to define the structure as precisely as possible through legally specified terms. In a sense we are a nation of lawyers. We tend to want to stipulate as many actions as possible in the form of law—written law. Thus, we have all sorts of constitutions and probably more laws on the books than any other nation in the world. "There ought to be a law" summarizes the response of the American mind when faced with a problem or injustice.

With respect to the structure of the polity, Americans have tried to define every office and role of the system in legal terms. Qualifications for office, terms of office, duties and responsibilities, salaries, relationships, powers, rights: all are specified in minute detail in constitutions and statutes. No action can be taken without a lawyer advising the official on his sphere of operation. Because of the highly formalized role structure, constant awareness of limits on action is posed for every incumbent of office. Of course, a formalized situation does enable predictability of behavior. We know, for example, what sorts of action each official can take with much greater assurance than do the citizens of an autocratic or even non-Western society. On the other hand, the formalization of rules also tends to stabilize them and make reform difficult. At the same time, however, it also makes rulers conscious of their limitations in action or exercise of power. Whatever the variety of reasons for formalization and its consequences, the fact remains that we do have a highly formalized political system. And no realistic analysis can dismiss the importance of formal rules in shaping American political behavior. In totalitarian socie- ties, such rules may also exist in great numbers, but there, however, functions sometimes amount to little more than window-dressing.

Highly Visible Structure

The mere fact that the role structure of the American polity is so highly differentiated and formalized also makes this structure a highly "visible" one, that is, the total structure and each role are readily ob- servable.[11] This is not the case in many societies such as the tribal where it is almost impossible to distinguish the polity from other structures such as kinship. Even among Western industrialized nations the polity is char- acterized by varying degrees of visibility. The British political system, for example, is hardly as clear and visible as the American. There, a great many traditional practices have so concealed the roles that understanding the functioning of the system is not easy.

In the United States, the practice of writing the role structure down in the form of legal documents tends to make the political system itself more clear than it might otherwise be. Of course, the complexities of legal jargon and the accumulation of court decisions and informal processes also work in the opposite direction; nevertheless, the polity is clearly separated as a social subsystem and defined as such. Thus, those who wish to ob- serve and understand the politics of the United States can do so with far greater ease than can the student of totalitarian societies where most of the decision-making is done in secrecy and where political decisions may cover many more aspects of social life. Indeed, some commentators on American ways, notably Edward Shils, have claimed that we have, among other fetishes, a compulsive need to publicize everything, especially in politics.[12] Whether this is so may be debatable, but it is readily apparent that Americans do make and demand that their politics be made as public as possible. Thus, the many demands made, and generally accepted, that city council meetings be open to the public, that Congressional Committee hearings not be held in private, that Congressional sessions be held open to the public, that the President and other executive officers subject themselves to press conferences, that newspapermen be given access to governmental information, and so on. In short, publicity is held to be a major way of achieving responsiveness and responsibility in government. "No society," says Edward Shils, "has ever been so extensively exposed to public scrutiny as the United States in the twentieth century." [13]

Multiplicity of Access Points

When we say that a system has access points, we mean that those who make the decisions in that system are available to being influenced in their decisions by others, particularly by the ordinary citizen. In totalitarian societies, of course, the decision-makers, as in all autocratic systems, are isolated to a considerable extent from the influences of the citizen. The autocratic polity, in fact, does not make formal provision for the citizen to participate in decision-making. In our terms, there are simply few access points open to him.

The American polity and government, however, are characterized by an enormous number of such points, many, but not all of which, are provided for in the formal structure of the government. As David Truman puts it:

> Key decision points may be explicitly established by the formal legal framework of the government, or they may lie in the gaps and interstices of the formal structure, protected by custom or by semi-obscurity. One key point may be at the President's elbow as he writes his message on the state of the union; another may be in a smokefilled room at a nominating convention; and a third may be in a legislative committee chairman's coat pocket, into which it is desired to slip a bill to prevent its being considered by the Congress. . . .[14]

This multiplicity of access to points of decision guarantees that the citizen who fails at one point to get a successful hearing for his demands may turn to still another where officials or politicians may act on his demands. An illustration seems in order. Persons who get into trouble with the Immigration Service, for example, and are ordered deported, may and generally do call for assistance by pursuing their case through the entire judicial system to the Supreme Court. Should this fail they will probably also call upon their Congressman and Senator to prevail upon the Immigration officials, or to introduce bills in Congress to allow them to remain in the country. And, finally, these same members of Congress may request executive action from the President to prevent the "injustice." In many cases, these proceedings take several years. Likewise, a citizen or interest group pressing a demand may contact the government at all decision levels from the local through the state to the national.

These many points of access provide not only opportunities for persons to be heard, but also defense points for those who wish to resist demands. To be sure, the complexity of the system, in addition to freedom of access in many places, also tends to place obstacles in the paths of those who desire change. But, we shall have more to say on this in subsequent chapters; here, we simply make the observation.

Institutionalized Competition for Leadership Roles

No political system is without some form of competition for possession of the formal leadership roles or for influence over those who occupy these roles. What distinguishes various systems is whether the competition itself has been *institutionalized* or *legitimized,* and the particular forms the competition assumes within the more general framework of norms. A dictatorship, for example, may have a great deal of competition taking place at several levels, including the highest. But the competition is not institutionalized in the sense of its being regularly provided for and governed by norms. Indeed, opposition is regarded as illegitimate and subversive.

While competition for leadership roles in America is conducted in several ways, all are ultimately based upon the formal electoral system by which the final or periodic selection of leaders is determined. Those who wish to hold elective public office must, as the expression has it, "run for office," and to win in most instances they must attain a plurality of the votes cast in the election. Normally because of the two-party system, this means a majority.

The competitive process is said to be *institutionalized* in that it takes place under a reasonably stable, well-recognized, and accepted set of norms or rules, and the opposition is regarded as legitimate. The norms governing the electoral process range from the highly formalized or legal to the rather ill-defined and loosely enforced norms of campaigning. In any case, a candidate who has not complied with the legal obligations of filing for nomination or winning the nomination and the general election by the prescribed margin cannot realistically or legitimately lay claim to a public office. In addition, the state, through its officials, must recognize and confirm the results of the election. And, finally, the candidate usually must take an oath of office. But, of course, this is hardly the end of the competition. In one sense of the word, it is only the beginning, for the office holder must continue to compete with other members of the government as well as with defeated and potential rivals. In effect, the process of competition is not something apart from the actual governing process. Between selecting public office and the decisions that governors are expected to make runs a tenuous thread of connection. Thus, a new member of an important office is expected to "make a record for himself." And his rivals can be expected to search constantly for weak points in the actions of the incumbent, and to publicize them insofar as that is possible.

Competition in the polity, as in the economy, is seldom perfect. Not only can varying degrees of power or monopoly be found, but, from the point of view of the citizen and the aspiring politician, the "market" itself has restrictions on the freedom of entry into political competition. Machine control over nomination, the high cost of campaigning (which may be regarded as the equivalent of the investment cost in the economy), unequal access to the means of communication, and unfair practices on the part of competitors, such as gerrymandering, are but a few of the elements of an imperfect competitive model of the polity. Needless to say, even violence or threats of force have played a role in the course of American elections. By and large, however, political competition has been peaceful, if rather noisy and vulgar at times. On the other hand, there have been all too many situations, according to some critics of American democracy, in which competition did *not* take place, either over societal goals or the means. And this not because of monopolistic elements, but because of the simple fact of indifference to the results of an election. Some voters, for example, have been convinced that the political campaigns they witness are sham battles. Whether this is true and to what extent it is an empirical question must be determined by reference to the facts of specific cases. Yet, note that the *norm* by which such a judgment is made is still that of the competitive model. In any case, public office is an *achieved status* and not an ascribed one, although elements of ascription have been known to operate on an informal basis within the competitive framework set by the electoral process. The informal requirement of residence in a constituency, for example, may be regarded as an element of ascription. Likewise, the possession of a certain family name may be of considerable importance to a candidate. Not everyone, then, can participate equally in the competition. Ideally, however, it is expected to be equal between those eligible to compete.

Highly Complex Structure

In discussing the functional differentiation of roles and subsystems in the polity, we were suggesting, in effect, that the polity is highly complex. Indeed, in many ways the American system may well be the most complex in the world, if not in history.

By complexity we mean that not only are there many roles but many ways in which they are interrelated. In the first instance, as described before, the American political system consists of an enormous number of roles and subsystems, each functioning at several different levels of the system. A very minimal listing of these roles would have to include the citizen, voter, executive, administrator, legislator, judge, police, interest group, and political party. With tens of millions of persons playing these multiple roles, one can immediately sense the complexity.

One indicator of this intricacy is found in the constitutions that attempt to define each of these subsystems and their relationships. And we have not one constitution, but many: a national Constitution, fifty state constitutions, and countless charters regulating the local governments in each state. While the national Constitution is remarkable for its brevity, this is hardly the case with the state constitutions or the local charters. Alfred de Grazia [15] informs us that the shortest one, that of Vermont, is about 2,000 words longer with its 8,419 words than the national Constitution. Louisiana has the dubious distinction of having the longest, with 184,053 words. On an average, the states have constitutions with about 27,000 words, or four times the number in the federal Constitution. The mere length of these documents means not only that political behavior is closely specified, but that as many contingencies are provided for as possible. This being the case, the structure of action must inevitably be highly organized and complex.

Another indicator of the complexity is to be found in the number and incredible variety of governmental units affecting the behavior of Americans. According to one authoritative count, over 100,000 such units exist and function.[16] Table 2-3 [17] conveys a notion of the various types and their numbers.

While there has been a sizable reduction in the number of governmental units during the past two decades, most of the change has taken place as a result of the consolidation of school districts. During the period described in Table 2-3, school districts decreased by some 53 per cent, but

Table 2-3—Number of Local Governments in the United States, by Type.

	NUMBER OF UNITS		CHANGE IN NUMBER
TYPE OF GOVERNMENT	1942	1957	1942 to 1957
Total	155,116	102,328	—52,788
Federal Government	1	1	—
States	48	50	+2
Counties	3,050	3,047	—3
Municipalities	16,220	17,183	+963
Townships and Towns	18,919	17,198	—1,721
School Districts	108,579	50,446	—58,133
Special Districts	8,299	14,405	+6,106

during the same period, various other countertrends increased the number of nonschool special districts by 74 per cent.

The situation confronting the ordinary citizens in a single metropolitan area is almost unbelievable. In 1951, for example, the metropolitan district of St. Louis contained 5 counties, 18 townships, more than 100 municipalities, at least 425 school districts, and 21 special districts, or more than 560 separate governmental units.[18] To be sure, most citizens are not continuously subject to each or even a large number of these "governments," but each is periodically affected by many. In any case, a person who had incurred some difficulty would have a complicated task in determining who to see and what to do in resolving it.

Nor does Table 2-3 exhaust the possibilities or convey a complete picture of this complex structure. Many of the various types of governmental units mentioned are in themselves highly complex. We may note but one case, that of municipalities. City governments are not all of the same order. Reducing their differences to even the smallest number of categories, we find at least four major types with many variations. The same may be said of the state and national units. Figure 2-3,[19] in greatly simplified fashion, provides an elementary understanding of the situation.

These rather simple figures and indicators of structure ought to be sufficient to suggest the intricacy of American politics and government. Just as each of the previously mentioned structural properties of the polity has a set of consequences (both anticipated and unanticipated), so the simple fact of complexity has its consequences. These, however, we will leave to Parts Four and Five, where we will analyze consequences resulting from the total interaction of the American polity.

Stability of the System

Even the slightest familiarity with the American political system is sufficient to suggest that it has undergone many changes during the past

Table 2-4—The Non-Western and the American Political Processes.

The Non-Western Processes	The American
1. Political sphere is not sharply differentiated from the social and personal.	1. Sharply differentiated.
2. Political parties tend to take on world views and represent a way of life.	2. Highly pragmatic.
3. Characterized by a prevalence of cliques.	3. More impersonal, rationalized political organization.
4. Leadership has a high degree of freedom.	4. Action restricted by functional specialization.
5. Opposition and aspiring elites tend to appear as revolutionary movements.	5. Opposition is legitimized.
6. Lack of integration.	6. Highly integrated at value level.
7. High rate of recruitment of new elements to political roles.	7. Stabilized rates.
8. Sharp differences in political orientations of the generations.	8. Remarkable continuity.
9. Little consensus on ends and means.	9. High level of agreement.
10. Intensity and breadth of political discussion has little relationship to political decision-making.	10. Political talk is pragmatic.
11. High degree of substitutability of rules.	11. Functional specificity of roles.
12. Relatively few explicitly organized interest groups with functionally specific roles.	12. High number of such groups.
13. Leadership must appeal to an undifferentiated public.	13. Many publics and spokesmen.
14. Unstructured character of the process encourages leaders to adopt more clearly defined positions on foreign than domestic issues.	14. Domestic politics is more structured than the foreign affairs.
15. The affective or expressive aspect tends to override the problem-solving.	15. Instrumental aspect plays a more prominent role than in non-Western process.
16. Charismatic leaders tend to prevail.	16. Relatively colorless leaders predominate.
17. Operates largely without the benefit of political "brokers."	17. Countless political "brokers."

4

The Distribution of Power

One of the central characteristics of any political system is its distribution of power. Indeed, because the question is so crucial, controversial, and fascinating, we have decided to devote an entire chapter to the matter.[1] The reader, however, should be aware of the fact that the distribution of power is only one of the properties of the polity. This being so, the present chapter must be regarded as a continuation of the previous one, not simply as another and unrelated aspect—fascinating as it might be— of the American political scene.

Having oriented our interpretation in terms of the "structural-functional" framework, in which the concept "role" is prominent, it might be wise to refresh our memories on the relationship of the role concept with that of power, the focus of this chapter. As said earlier, the unit of analysis in polities, as in social systems, is the role or sets of norms that define, specify, or condition political behavior. These roles both prescribe and proscribe behavior. They range greatly in their contents, in the degree of precision, explicitness, complexity, universality, and means of enforcement. While most behavior is normatively conditioned, the political scientist is not interested in behavior per se; rather, he is interested in certain types and in certain aspects of still other behavior. What distinguishes the political science orientation, then, is its concern for that behavior which has to do with the realization of societal goals. It is this behavior that we call political, or that may be called power.

When we talk about power we mean the capacity to set and realize system or, in our case, societal goals. He who can determine which goals are to be attained can very likely also realize his own goals in the process. Such a person or group will be said to have power; he who cannot do these things has none. Quite obviously it is not a question of either/or, but one of various gradations. The problem thus confronting us is one of determining who has how much power. In other words we want to know the actual distribution of power among the people who fill the role structure of the polity. Further, we want eventually to determine, if we can, whose values are realized in America and who pays the costs of maintaining the system. Knowing the power structure is one way of getting to that knowledge. For power may be considered a kind of intervening variable between persons and the outcomes of the allocation struggles. For research purposes, of course, it may also be viewed as the dependent variable that needs to be explained. It is in the latter sense that we will discuss power in this chapter.

One of the reasons why an inquiry into the pattern of power distribution is even raised stems from the fact that the actual distribution does not always seem to be in accord with the ideal prescriptions of the role structure as found in our belief system, the Constitution, and other documents. If the ideal model were realized in fact we would not have to ask questions about actual distribution. But as personal experiences and the weight of research have suggested a discrepancy between ideal and reality, we thus must inquire into who has power. To do this we will begin with a summary statement of the American ideal model that is most commonly shared as our base point. We will then point up some of the discrepancies, and turn to a consideration of two well-known efforts to portray the "real" power structure. Each will be summarized and criticized. Finally, we will attempt to synthesize that which is relevant, reliable, and valid from each of these models.

We will begin with a consideration of the idealistic view mentioned above. For convenience' sake it will be termed the "Popular Rule" model.

POPULAR RULE MODEL

The model we are about to discuss is not so much a description of the actual power structure as it is an *ideal* or prescription of how power ought to be distributed and politics conducted. Yet, there are many Americans who would like to believe that what ought to be is already a fact. Fourth of July orators are just as fond of portraying American democracy in these idealistic terms as are the writers of children's civics texts.

We will summarize this model as though it consisted of a series of normative statements or prescriptions meant to indicate the conditions required of a well-functioning democracy in the United States.[2] Many of these statements or prescriptions have been left ambiguous and broad because that is the way in which most of them have been handled throughout our national history. Yet, these beliefs are a part of our heritage regarding the operations of our democracy. The model of popular rule can be easily and concisely summarized in the form of a series of short propositions. They are as follows:

1. Each citizen will have one vote.
2. Each citizen will behave rationally.
3. Each citizen will be highly motivated, politically.
4. Each citizen will have access to vital information.
5. Each citizen will have freedom of access to decision-making centers.
6. Each citizen will have freedom to communicate.
7. Each citizen will have freedom of choice among alternative policies and officials.
8. Each citizen will pursue the public interest.
9. Each citizen will participate fully and continuously.
10. Decisions will be made by majority rule.

The objective of the popular rule model is to ensure that each and every citizen will participate with equal power in the deliberations of government, and that each will derive more or less equal values and share more or less equally in the maintenance of the system. The ideal image is one consisting of a society composed of individuals, rather than of groups and classes, and one that is motivated by public rather than self-interest. Not only is such a society expected to have little conflict, but what little it does have is expected to be readily handled or resolved through rational argumentation among well-intentioned citizens and with decision by majority rule. It is assumed rather than stated that the types of political problems which will arise are of a kind that lend themselves to relatively simple and quick solutions. In other words, it is viewed as a simple society with a government performing little more than the most elementary functions that self-reliant citizens cannot do for themselves. Under this system, liberty and participation in decision-making are maximized, while tyranny and the costs of government are minimized. Perhaps the closest that Americans have ever come to the attainment of this ideal was in the town-meetings of some of the New England communities.

But if this is the ideal, what are the realities of American democracy? Are the prescriptions of the model realistic ones? Can the model be said to be an accurate picture of what goes on in the United States? Let us consider each of the prescriptions in the order listed, and finally judge the entire model and its assumptions as a whole.

The Popular Rule Model: A Critique

According to the model, each citizen is to have one vote in decision-making, whether that decision be over candidates or policies. And, in a purely legal sense, each qualified adult in the United States does have one vote and one only. But the legalities of the situation are quite misleading when we weigh the actual power possessed by each citizen. In the first place, entire groups of the population are prohibited from voting both by legal and illegal means, even though they may have the qualifications that entitle them to vote under most conditions.[3] The Negro race, for example, is only the most prominent case of a group not allowed to vote in one entire section of the country. To be sure, they are now voting in increasing numbers, but historically they have not been able to do so. Many other qualified voters cannot qualify in a specific election because of local legal requirements, such as residence in a given area for a specified length of time. But the most pervasive instance of inequality in voting is found in the imbalance that results from the apportionment and districting practices of state legislatures.[4] Gerrymandering and failure to reapportion and re-district as population changes have, in fact, resulted in huge disparities in the voting power of millions of Americans.

In the first place each state—at the national level, regardless of population—has or elects the same number of senators: two. Thus, in 1950, New York with a population of nearly 15 million had the same number of senators as did Nevada with a total population of only 160,000. In the House of Representatives unequal representation is just as marked. Each state gets approximately the number of representatives it should by the standard of population; in 1950, the standard was one Congressman per 350,000 persons. But while each state does have the right to apportion and district their quota, it is at this point that the equality of representation principle has been ignored. The state legislatures do the districting, and they have a strong tendency to do so in ways that will benefit the majority party. As a result, one finds situations such as the following: in Illinois, one Congressional district had 112,000 people, while another had as many as 914,000; in Ohio the districts ranged from a low of 163,500 to a high of 698,000.[5] Disparities of this order are unusual neither at the national nor the state levels. It is quite clear, therefore, that the ideal of one man, one vote, has not been attained, nor is soon likely to be.

The second proposition in the model states that citizens will act rationally, that is, that they will relate political means to political ends. A prescription of this type naturally assumes many things, some of which constitute other propositions in the model. Above all, however, it assumes that men have the capacity to consider public matters rationally. Yet we need only to invoke the psychological studies to see that, while every man may have the capacity to act somewhat rationally about some things, he also has nonrational and irrational forces within him that severely restrict the possibilities of rational action.[6] Some of these limiting factors may be biological or acquired, but many are social and yet just as restrictive. The model overestimates the capacity of man to rise above his interests and his ability to be objective when he is impelled by motives of which he is unaware, or misunderstands. There are, of course, other limiting factors, but since they constitute a part of the model we will take them up as we proceed to each prescription.

A high degree of political motivation is assumed to be needed and desirable. Consequently, every citizen must be willing to take time from his more private concerns, and devote it to public matters. It is further assumed that the society will give support to the motive and, in a sense, reward it, thereby keeping motivation high in the citizenry. That such a widespread motive does exist with such overriding strength is most doubtful. Indeed, the evidence is contrary to the hope. Relatively few citizens desire to participate continuously in political life. Studies of voting and various other forms of participation, in fact, have suggested that relatively few of the total population even take political action seriously.[7] Nor does American culture effectively reward direct and continuous political action. Encouragements to sustain high motivation are neither extensive nor impressive.

The fourth prescription of the model is that each citizen has access to the required or needed information to act rationally and in the public interest. But while there is an avalanche of information concerning politics, much of it is not useful for political decision-making, and that which is, is hardly accessible to all. Some people cannot afford to acquire it, for information has costs (both material and psychological), and still others cannot hope to master that which is free.[8] Nor can any citizen in twentieth-century America devote all the time necessary to acquiring and evaluating the information that the model seems to demand. These reasons, perhaps, may suggest why the information levels of the citizenry are so low (see Chapter 7). In short, Americans do not possess the needed information to act rationally except under the most limited circumstances. The model rests on the assumption, of course, that government will be simple in structure and functioning, and that the problems confronting the society will also be simple, immediate, and meaningful to the ordinary citizen. The problems assumed by the model are not those of the complex, technical, and indirect type posed by international politics and economic systems of the present day world.[9]

In order to make equal participation and power possible, a fifth condition is regarded as necessary, namely, that the citizen have access to decision-making centers such as elections, public officials, and their meetings. Nothing is to be secret or concealed, and no one is to be denied access by violence or other controls. We are all aware of the fact, however, that public officials are not always personally available, and the higher their rank, the less so. We are also aware of the fact that many decisions are made in secret at all levels of government, from the caucuses of local committeemen, to the President and the National Security Council. Just so, many Congressional hearings and committee meetings are executive, that is, secret. While some of these denials of access are legal, many are not. In any case, the ordinary citizen does not have equal access to decision-makers and decision-making. As a result, he cannot have equal influence over the outcomes of the political process. Those who do have more access are likely, of course, to have greater influence and power.

The right to communicate freely with other citizens is the sixth condition of the model. Indeed, democracy would hardly be conceivable without such a prerequisite. For while a citizen might have a vote, be rational, have information, be highly motivated, and have access to decision-making centers, he would not be able to realize any of his values and goals should he not have freedom to communicate his expectations, demands, and thoughts. Yet while this is true, most of us recognize that, in fact, considerable restraints upon freedom of expression do exist in the country, running from the subtle social constraints to official or legal limitations on one's rights to express himself in public. Certain expressions, moreover, are taboo, while, under special conditions, others are not permissible. Religious beliefs, ideas of what is politically moral, prevailing local and national prejudices—all serve to repress the expression of many alternative types of demands, through the electoral and policy process. In addition to these limitations, many others stem from the organization of the means of communication, including the high costs of maintaining newspapers and radio and television stations. Few citizens, indeed, can afford to hire time or space in these media, and those who can have an advantage in their power to spread their own views and persuade others.

Freedom of choice constitutes the seventh condition of the popular rule model. Of what value is freedom if there are no alternatives from which to select policies and candidates? Yet, for many Americans, few if any continuous meaningful alternatives exist in either of these areas. Many elections go uncontested at the state and local levels.[10] And even where opposition candidates do appear, there is little guarantee that alternative policies will thereby be offered to the citizen. Countless commentators have noted that our party system tends to dampen differences and emphasize common approaches to public issues. Even where there are differences, they are often neither very marked nor meaningful as alternatives. Also, it is clear that certain types of alternatives are effectively prohibited from consideration. Socialism, and parties of radical dissent, as well as extreme right wing policies and candidates, are seldom given a serious hearing or made available as possible alternatives to existing leaders and public policies. Admittedly, a sizable third party may appear at times with programs and persons quite opposed to the major parties, but they have little chance in the electoral process beyond a few localities. Thus, in most political situations, the citizen is left with a narrow range or set of alternatives, if with any, except, perhaps, on more or less technical issues in local community affairs. There the alternatives *may* be several and clear-cut regarding such matters as fluoridation and expansion of the school system, increases in the pay of firemen, and the like. But these are seldom the big and dramatic issues of either state or national politics.

Earlier, we said that one of the preconditions of democracy in the popular rule model was that the citizen be motivated to participate; we did not, however, specify the objective of the motivation and participation. Generally, the objective is phrased as one of realizing the *public interest*.[11] The citizen is expected to seek not his own self-interest, but the greater interest of all. Just what this public interest consists of, however, is generally disputed by the contestants, nor has a method been devised by which the ordinary citizen might ascertain the public's interest in any given situation. Yet it does seem certain that whenever an individual's private interest manifestly diverges from some of the more obvious ones of the nation, the latter is expected to be paramount. But in daily political life the public interest surely is not so readily apparent. Not only is there no scientific means for determining it, but few of us would accept mystical or divine ordinations on the part of self-styled prophets. And, finally, even if we did know what was in the best interests of the country, there is no guarantee that citizens would always willingly surrender private ones that might conflict. What evidence there is, in fact, suggests the opposite conclusion. To be sure, some citizens would sacrifice, but hardly all or most would do so voluntarily on all occasions.

One of the more cherished exhortations in our public life is to participate frequently, if not continuously, in politics, and to do so in many ways. Yet the percentage of citizens who engage in direct forms of political action meant to influence public policies is exceedingly small.[12] In Chapter 7, we will quote some studies as to the extent of various modes of participation. Here, it is sufficient to mention that the findings are disheartening if activity is the goal, as it most certainly is in the popular rule model. If one does not take part in politics, it seems hard to believe that he can mobilize the same power as the person who does. Indeed, those who can and do devote their energies and other resources to political life cannot help but exercise more influence than those who do not. And since so many do not, a few will influence the course of events, policies, and men.

All political systems require some means whereby decisions can be made to terminate issues or conflicts. In the popular rule model the system is a simple rule: majority rule, or 50 per cent plus one.[13] With each member of the system entitled to an equal share or a single vote, there really is no logical alternative to majority vote. The problem in real life, however, is that relatively few issues are ever presented so that votes may be taken and majorities created. At best, we hold elections to select officials at periodic and predetermined times. But these elections do not often occur at the precise moment of the origins of an issue. Indeed most decisions are made between elections, and the voters, in any direct sense,[14] do not participate. Representatives may vote and follow majority sentiment, but there is no guarantee of this. In the Congress, for example, minorities have various means of subverting majorities, in addition to which the President can veto the actions of up to two-thirds of the Congress. And, as pointed out above, majorities may be meaningless if they are constructed of coalitions of minority groups who are overrepresented in many offices of the government. Finally, the model fails to consider the role of bureaucrats who make many of the decisions in daily governmental matters. What they decide may have little correspondence to what a majority of the people would prefer if consulted.

It should be quite apparent from the above discussion that the popular rule model has little to commend it as a *description* or *explanation* of politics or of the power structure of the country. At best, the model is an ideal that has played a significant normative role and one that may be useful in maintaining democracy. But it may also have some unsatisfactory consequences. The model—as an ideal—creating expectations too high for mortals, may, in so doing, lead to inevitable disappointment or frustration. Just as an ideal confronted by contrasting reality is likely to be dealt a severe blow, so, too, the man who entertains such a vision and sees it shattered. Apparently, then, political role structures cannot be understood completely in terms of the basic and most generalized normative ideals, however widely held. For while it may be a strong motivating force for political waves of indignation and reform, it obviously accounts neither for all aspects of role performance nor for the actual structure of power.

PLURALISTIC GROUP MODEL

Around the turn of the twentieth century, a political scientist-journalist, Arthur F. Bentley, wrote a book entitled *The Process of Government,*[15] and in so doing gave the first full-length, detailed explanation of American politics in terms of what we will call the "pluralistic group model." Bentley's view of politics as nothing more than the actions of interest groups was not exactly a novel idea. James Madison had had similar ideas long before. But Madison did not give them the kind of elaboration that Bentley did. In Bentley's hands, the vague notions of group politics took on technical form. Later, his theories were to exercise profound influence over political scientists, to such a point, in fact, that today the pluralistic group model is *the* dominant model and approach to American politics. The most recent and probably best statement of the model can be found in David Truman's *The Governmental Process,*[16] on which most of our summary of the model will be based. The ideas, however, can be found in the writings of all group theorists.[17]

The pluralistic group model has striking differences from the previous model we considered. In the first place, few if any of the elements of the popular rule model are accepted as facts, and those which are used are radically altered. Whereas the popular rule image was based on autonomous individuals engaged in rational pursuit of the public interest, the pluralist image of politics sees interest groups as the major actors, concerned primarily with their own self-interest. Likewise, the pluralist model accepts man as less than rational and sees him participating less fully than the level desired by the advocates of popular rule. It sees decisions made not by majorities of free individuals, but by coalitions of groups that may not be majorities and do not represent all citizens. Oligarchies may and often do rule within each group. Decision-making is accomplished not by rational face-to-face debate, but in the exercise of power in bargaining—sometimes implicit—of oligarchs or group leaders. As few of these people hold public office, they therefore are not publicly responsible for their decisions. The politicians who deal with them are legally responsible, but, more often than not, they must respond to the demands of groups rather than vice versa.

The group model envisages a society made up of countless groups of individuals, each being constituted, in part, by members of still other groups. Moreover, each has a particular perspective on life and an interest that it pursues in a variety of ways, one of which is that of political action. While not all groups become politicized—that is, pursue their interests through action designed to influence governmental decisions—many do, and probably all will do so at some periods in their collective existence. And as each group attempts to attain its goals, it is likely to encounter resistance from others with contrary interests. Consequently, all groups concerned with a particular decision-making arena often struggle to influence government decision-makers and their decisions. Because interest groups are in conflict and because Americans are supposed to believe in democratic action, the government (decision-makers), given authority by the people, is actually in a position to determine who gets what, when, and how. In other words, the normative structure of the government and polity does count. What we have, then, is a vast arena of conflicting groups and officials, all engaged in interaction to shape public policies.

According to this model, almost everyone or group has some power to attain his expectations and demands. Should he, he at least can prevent or modify the demands of others, thereby forcing a compromise or bargain. In short, political power counts: it is not simply a derivative of economic and military resources. Nor is political action simply a matter of manipulation and command; more often it is a confused kind of bargaining taking place among countless shifting or unstable coalitions. No one person or small group of persons, such as the power elite—the next model to be discussed—gets all it wants. Generally, it is rather a case of everyone getting something, but no one getting all he would prefer. Group theorists thus do not claim that the distribution of values and costs is equal, but they do maintain that it is widespread. In our terms, both expectations and demands are made and realized by many in varying proportions. To be sure, resources are widely owned, but they are also widely distributed by the polity. In like manner, support for the various components of the polity and society are also widespread and fairly intensively felt. In any case, while more manipulated support is acknowledged than in the popular rule model, far less is acknowledged than power elite theorists see and condemn. As suggested above, the structure of the government and polity have important roles to play in the distribution of values and costs. Unlike the power elite model, group theory does not view the polity as operating as effectively for the interests of the few, nor operating automatically and consistently in an irresponsible manner. They also tend to believe, although not to the same extent as does the power elite model, that the polity functions rather slowly and that this factor tends to favor the status quo. And, also a contrast, they see much conflict that is in fact meaningful in terms of shaping decisions. Individuals do participate in politics, although not to the extent claimed by civics books, and they are effective. They can aid in the selection of their leaders, as well as control their actions to a considerable degree. Sometimes this control is based on negative factors such as cross-pressures and inertia, but nevertheless, it is a type of control. In the words of the group theorists, there is little hint of either a "mass," or an "individualistic" society. To be sure, all group theorists do not view the group struggle with equanimity; many fear the consequences of too much struggle and differential distribution of the values and costs. But rarely do they view the situation with the alarm expressed by some critics. About all that they ever suggest is piecemeal reform of the polity.

The power elite theory, as we shall see, may grant that intergroup conflict does take place, but that since such action occurs only at the "middle level of power," it is therefore largely meaningless. Group theorists, on the other hand, do not appear to divide society into levels of power, but see rather an amorphous and pervasive struggle, out of which emerges a kind of "equilibrium." By this is meant that everyone has a minimal amount of satisfaction, and accepts the decision as at least temporarily binding or authoritative. The struggle does not cease; it simply moves into different channels. In the 1930's, for example, management groups fought unions to prevent their legal recognition. Once the government enacted an authoritative labor law (Wagner Act), however, the management reluctantly accepted unions and proceeded to bargain, while holding union influence to a minimum by a variety of other actions, and pressing for greater governmental control over them. In 1947, the Taft-Hartley Law established a new equilibrium or set of working relationships among the affected parties, which has continued as the basis of their interaction. Such is the image held by group theorists of the political system or process.

Group theory, in effect, suggests a society of competing individuals and groups, but competing within a framework of norms, or "rules of the game," as they have been termed by David Truman. And while this framework of rules has been subject to criticism and change, it has also been remarkably stable in America. For the most part, these rules are of the democratic sort and consistent with a democratic political culture or, again, as Truman calls it, the "democratic mold." Dissenting critics, however, see these rules as trivial, viewing the belief system that underlies them as a myth used to justify and explain rulers and ruling that do not correspond with reality. For the critics, it is power—as they define it—that is crucial in society, not the formal rules or structures of government or polities.

A Critique of the Pluralistic Group Model

Entering a criticism of the popular rule model was almost embarrassingly easy. We shall be spared that problem in criticizing the pluralist model, for the good reason that it is a far more sophisticated and realistic picture of the power structure and the political process. Yet, criticisms may and have been made, some of which will be repeated here, and others added.[18]

As we stated in Chapter 1, the political system performs at least four general functions in society; allocative, integrative, goal-attainment, and system maintenance. While the pluralist group model provides descriptions and explanations of all, its strongest theory centers on the allocative function. Truman's work and the many case studies he used have all provided us with a better understanding of how political allocation takes place. But even in this case, the group or pluralist theorists have tended to emphasize but one of the processes by which allocation is accomplished. They have rightly stressed the bargaining process, but have de-emphasized such other structures as hierarchy or bureaucracy and class. Consequently, the description is both incomplete and misleading.

Another shortcoming of the pluralist model, although not a logical one, results from the greater theoretical concern over the allocation of resources and values than of costs.[19] In fact, the latter is not usually distinguished as an object of struggle. Thus, most research has been done on problems or situations in which an interest group pursues a greater share of the values to be had. How such groups behave to maintain or defend positions or to reduce their share of the costs of government has been much less adequately explained. For the group theorists, offensive action has proven to be of greater interest or fascination.

A third shortcoming, and one over which there has been some debate, has to do with the role assigned to the government in allocation struggles. Some critics have contended that the pluralist model underestimates the amount of influence that government officials—both elected and civil servants—exercise in the resolution of conflict.[20] The model seems to attribute most of the initiative to the groups and very little to the officials. But while the criticism is probably more true of Bentley's work than of Truman's, even the latter's image of the political system is one that makes the government something worked upon.[21] Perhaps the major instance in which the government and its leaders may assume the initiative more frequently and successfully is in the area of foreign policy. But as relatively few studies have been made about interest groups and foreign and military policy, few generalizations have been produced.[22] Generally, civic and foreign policy associations have a limited impact on decision-making, although the latter may be improving their status in this regard as foreign policy becomes more crucial. Where trade or economic policies are at issue, it may be that interest groups are powerful, but many policies are not immediately economic in their consequences. In any case, the pluralist model has had little to say about foreign and military policy making.[23] It has been rather, domestic policies that have provided the cases which perhaps may be due to the greater role of domestic issues during most of our history. As a result, the possible influence of the tighter system of bureaucratic norms working on officialdom (rational-efficiency or public interest models) has not been given much attention.

The explanation of the allocative process is deficient in still another way: group theory suggests that the outcomes of the allocation struggle are unequal, but it does not provide an operational means of measuring these outcomes. Presumably, one could look at the governmental actions during some specified time period, determine who got how much of what during that time, and then attribute this to interest groups. Then, presumably, one could devise an index in which each of the interest groups of the nation was ranked according to what it received. The pluralist model clearly suggests that this is what must be done. Yet, no effort has actually been made to rank interest groups in terms of their share of the societal values being distributed. Nor have we been told what sort of indicators to choose, except the vague one of policy. About the closest we have come to such a research project is by the reverse process contained in Truman's book. Here he has discussed a variety of factors that could be used in explaining outcomes. These factors, however, actually constitute a theory of "access" to decision-makers; they have not been tested with regard to outcomes. The factors include: those related to the group's strategic position (social status and goals) in society; those related to the internal characteristics of the group (cohesion); and, finally, factors peculiar to the structure of the polity.[24] Until group theorists actually do test the outcomes for the entire system rather than merely describing what happens in particular policy areas, we will have very little notion of the *distribution* of values and costs. No doubt, one could comb the literature of case studies in policy-making and come up with a number of hypotheses about allocative outcomes. That, however, has yet to be done.

There are, of course, other criticisms dealing with the outcomes of the allocation process. Those with a Marxist orientation, for example, or elite theorists believe that the pluralist model overestimates the equality of distribution of values and that it does not accurately describe or explain who makes the public decisions and the manner in which they are made. But as we would anticipate the next model by detailing these criticisms, they will be postponed for awhile in order to take up the question of the pluralist explanation of integration.

The popular rule model explained integration by assuming that various conditions exist which make it a simple problem. That is, the issues at stake are limited; the actors rational; the rules followed; and debate is resolved by appeal to facts. Although the pluralist group model is hardly as naive, its conception of integration, too, is not completely satisfactory. In the first place, less attention is paid to integrative structures and processes. In Professor Truman's book, for example, only one chapter is devoted to integration, while eight deal with the "tactics of influence" or "who gets what, when, how," with greatest emphasis on "how." Relatively little space is devoted to political socialization and control, the major means whereby integration is achieved in all societies.

The major mechanism suggested, by which integration is attained— and it is a questionable one—is through the working of what Truman calls "overlapping memberships." Simply put, Truman means that most citizens belong to two or more groups and that these multiple memberships are often conflicting. Because they are conflicting, it is likely that the cohesion of the affected groups will be diminished and the demands of each accordingly decreased, so that the limits of the struggle are constricted and compromise is made easier to achieve. The theory is an ingenious one and undoubtedly of some value in explaining integration. The question, however, is whether the assumptions underlying the theory are themselves realistic. For one thing, innumerable studies have shown that fewer Americans have *multiple* or *overlapping* memberships than is suggested by the theory. Furthermore, it is doubtful whether all these groups are in conflict. Indeed, it is possible that many of them are complementary, serving to increase the intensity with which a demand is made on society. In such a case, conflict might be increased rather than decreased. None of these doubts, of course, are easily documented, except the first one. But neither are the data that Truman advances very extensive or reliable. Other integrating forces he mentions are the "rules of the game" and values, but we are not told why they are accepted, nor how they came about. In short, we are really left in doubt altogether as to the processes of integrative and disintegrative tendencies in the polity. There is little doubt, however, that Truman believes that we are fairly well integrated.

The pluralist model is not successful in explaining integration because the concept is not operationally defined. Professor Truman, for example, speaks of a "viable" political system, but gives no precision to the meaning of the term. Nor do we know at which indicators to look, nor how to measure them, nor what to measure in regard to the level of conflict or its intensity. All we do know is that conflict is ubiquitous and perhaps least prevalent at the level of societal and political values. Otherwise, the analysis is devoted largely to allocative processes of bargaining.[25]

The last criticism of the model is one which others [26] have made, but which this writer believes is not always relevant, namely, the apparent lack of interest in developing a dynamic theory of the political process, that is, one which explains long-run changes. In short, while the pluralist model does propose to explain short-run movements and contains plenty of action, it does not explain in detail historic changes of the American polity, and certainly does not offer many predictions about the future. Elements of a theory are to be found rather in such matters as the increasing social and economic complexity of our life and the consequences for proliferation of interest groups and demands. But these elements, say the critics, are not the central core of a theory or model. While these criticisms are sound, they are somewhat misplaced in that no theory can explain everything and that to explain one facet of polities may mean sacrifices of another. Furthermore, there is no reason why we cannot gain understanding simply from a short-run model. Certainly economics has made a good deal of progress through the use of static models.

THE POWER ELITE MODEL

There have always been critics of the "American Creed," and most of them have had doubts not so much about our ideals as about our failure to achieve them. Not infrequently these critics have held to an ideal of America quite similar to that of the popular rule model discussed above, a world in which democracy would really be achieved and made meaningful to all citizens. Among these critics is the late sociologist, C. Wright Mills, whose critique of American life has appeared in a number of books, one of which, *The Power Elite*,[27] is most relevant to us. Taking his title as the label for our model, we will base many of our views on his book even though the ideas are not strictly Mills' alone.[28] Other political scientists and sociologists have entertained similar notions in the past and do so today. Nevertheless, to make the exposition simpler, we will rely mostly on Mills' volume. Later, we will introduce evidence from various empirical studies on community power structures to see where each of these models is or is not supported.

In its most concise form, the Mills' theory asserts that the major decisions affecting Americans and others, namely, those which have to do with the possibilities of war and peace, are made, not by the people through the formal structures of government as asserted in the popular rule and pluralistic models, but through the deliberate actions of a very small number of persons and groups whom he terms the "power elite." According to the theory, this small number of persons who really govern America consists of three groups: corporation executives, military men, and high-ranking politicians. Occupying key decision-making points in society, these three groups of men are subject to little if any control by others, and particularly by the ordinary citizen. Their decisions flow from a common perspective on life and common interests. Having control over economic wealth and military and political power, they are in a position to monopolize important control over major societal goals. More often than not, they act in "immoral" ways, or are "irresponsible" in the exercise of their power. In some instances they have not even acquired their power legitimately, and in any case, have had advantages over others, usually in the form of inheritance or economic gain.

Below these members of the power elite are a second layer of persons and groups consisting of Congress, state political machines, and regional interest groups who hold some power, to be sure, but hardly any with respect to the making of the big decisions in society. These men constitute what Mills terms the "middle levels of power," the levels with which social scientists and historians have traditionally concerned themselves in explaining American politics. Members of the middle level of power, as well as the professors who study them, are all members of the national middle class in terms of prestige and wealth. Locally, they may be regarded as the upper class. But while, typically, these politicians are negotiators, compromisers, and brokers of power, the significance of their actions and functions is not supposed to be what it once was in a society that was more responsive to middle-class demands. Modern technology and economy, as well as the present world situation, have changed all this. No longer is there a balance of power among the many groups of a pluralist community.

At the bottom of the pyramid of power, and making up the bulk of the population, are the masses, or, more accurately, the "powerless masses" of a "mass society." Here the average Americans pursue meaningless lives, manipulated by the power elite through the use of the mass media of communication. Almost by definition, such people are apathetic and cynical toward politics, and concerned only with mass culture and its fictions. There is no public discussion of the issues, nor any democratic resolution of them. Moreover, members of the mass cannot effectively bring their views—even if they have any—to bear upon the leaders.

Communications are owned by the few, and are not accessible to the many. Consequently, the mass can only respond to that which is initiated by others, all of which adds to the increasing gap that exists between the masses and the elite. Even the associations themselves, which once intermediated between these two groups, are vast organizations controlled to an increasing extent by elites or oligarchies. In short, there is no real, meaningful sense of participation in community or associational life. More and more, mass man is *told* who he is, what he wants to be, how to get or realize aspirations, and, perhaps most importantly, how to escape from the meaninglessness of life.

In terms of our conceptual scheme, Mills tells us that the demands and expectations that are fed into the polity are those of the power elite, just as are those which are acted upon and realized. Similarly, the resources required by the polity are commanded by the power elite, who, at the same time, manipulates the support that is to be given the system. Power, in short, is neatly circumscribed. Mass man makes no decisions and receives little; whatever he does receive is but a sop from the elite.

Again, according to the theory, the formal structure of the polity and of the government, in particular, is of little significance in the political process. Rather, power is in the hands of the elite, even though the middle levels actually do hold many of the offices. The latter's behavior is not important, however, except as a deception as to what really goes on in the society. If we want to know whose goals and values are being realized, we must look not at the structure of the government, but at the *nonlegal sources* of power—namely, economic and military resources and who commands them. One's political power is seen to depend upon other factors than the political, although a few men such as the President do wield great political strength. But even in that case we must look to see who backs him, who selected him, and who got him elected. If we look at the nature of political action, we can see that bargaining is not the crucial type; rather, it is *manipulation* and *command* that characterize the polity and its processes. And unlike the group theorists and others, Mills saw the polity as neither ineffective nor inefficient. Instead, the system works well for the benefit of those he called the power elite. Like these same theorists, however, Mills did see it as irresponsible, but to a far greater degree. According to Mills, the political culture that sets our ideas and norms is a kind of "superstructure" manipulated as a myth in the control of the masses.

All in all, then, Mills has leveled a provocative charge, not only against the power elite, but against the American society as well. It is neither what most of us want nor what we are likely to believe is the situation. For this reason, we will want to analyze the Mills' model with care to determine just how perceptive and accurate a picture it may be of the United States.

A Critique of the Power Elite Model

Research and theory are based upon assumptions and definitions, decisions which are largely arbitrary on the part of the researcher or theorist. Thus, if we want to check the reliability and validity of statements about reality, we must look at the assumptions and definitions used to direct the inquiry. In Mills' case, the crucial assumptions and definitions include: power; elite; and decisions.

The concept of "power" is obviously basic to the Mills' analysis, yet, curiously enough, he does not devote much time to making the term very precise. Daniel Bell, in a perceptive review [29] of the book, states that what Mills has actually done is to set no real limits to the term, defining it on but two occasions:

> By the powerful we mean, of course, those who are able to realize their will, even if others resist it.[30]
> All politics is a struggle for power: the ultimate kind of power is violence.[31]

The first observation that might be made about this conception of power and politics is its focus on the distributive aspect. That is, politics is seen only as a means for persons or groups to attain their own goals as against others. To be sure, power may and ought to be viewed in terms of this function, but we must also view it as a resource for collective purposes or societal goal-attainment as well. Mills' conception of power does not enable us to do this. And, as Parsons has noted, Mills' conception is based on the assumption that power is a kind of "limited quantity." Thus, for one person or group to augment its power means or necessitates a reduction on the part of another person's or group's power.[32] Consequently, in Mills' argument, the more power the elite acquires, the less either or both the middle level and the masses can command. Certainly power does involve interaction, but whether it is inherently limited is doubtful. How one would establish this alleged fact is never made clear by Mills.

A second point needs to be made concerning Mills' association of power and violence. Violence is only the limiting case and not the dominant one in the United States. To be sure, Mills does not claim that violence is the usual practice, but he does strongly suggest that violence is the ultimate kind of power and that we behave accordingly; in other words, our motivations to obey are dictated by this awareness of violence. Sociologists and psychologists, however, have indicated that obedience may be secured by many other means than that of violence. In Mills' theory, the role of values and norms in shaping action is minimized.

As in the case of power, Mills is not altogether clear in his usage of the concept "elite." One thing, however, is certain: "elite" does not neces- sarily mean moral or intellectual superiority. Indeed, if anything, Mills means that those he considers as members of the elite are morally irrespon- sible and, in many cases, ignorant. Generally, he uses the term "elite" to refer to those who occupy certain positions in society. These positions are strategic in the institutional structure of society in the sense that their occupants can make the major decisions affecting all others in America and elsewhere. Mills claims no interest in how decisions are made, nor in the personalities or self-awareness of the elite. Yet, as Daniel Bell observes, it is not enough to know the positions occupied by elites; one must also know what they are doing in terms of concrete behavior or decision-making.[33] Mills, however, tells us little about the decision-making process.

The third concept in the Mills' lexicon is that of "decision." We noted above that he specifically limits himself to what he calls the big decisions in society, those which have "terrible consequences for the underlying populations of the world." [34] His means for determining which decisions have these consequences are not spelled out because they are supposed to be obvious. Yet, the workings of society are also based on millions of lesser decisions, all of which in total make an enormous difference to the individuals who make and are affected by them. Mills, however, regards such everyday decisions of citizen and public official alike as insignificant at all levels of power but the middle one. The big decisions he actually discusses are but five in number, and all concern violence and war or the possibility of war. Richard Rovere, one critic of Mills, has analyzed each of these five decisions, and concluded that the power elite, as Mills defines the term, did not play a significant role, whereas the elected official—the President—dominated the decision.[35] The five decisions in- cluded (1) steps leading to intervention in World War II; (2) decision to drop the atomic bomb in World War II; (3) declaration of war in Korea; (4) the indecisions over Quemoy and Matsu in 1955; and (5) the decision regarding possible intervention in Dien Bien Phu when that city was about to fall in the French Indo-China War. These five decisions are all important, but hardly the only ones worthy of investigation. More important, the question still remains as to how it can be proved that they were ultimately determined by the "power elite" as defined.[36]

On the basis of these definitions and assumptions, Mills proceeded to construct the model we summarized above, making empirical statements about the power structure of the United States. Thus, in addition to the criticisms we have already voiced, it is possible to add others concerning the empirical aspects of the work. It is questionable, for example, whether the power elite is really as cohesive as Mills maintains it to be whenever decisions are to be made. For if the power elite is unitary, it must be unified not only among the three groups constituting the elite, but, by definition, within each of the groups, themselves. Yet Mills offers no convincing evidence on this score.[37] In fact, research along the lines of group theory has indicated that the business groups are united on but one policy matter—that of taxation, while the disputes that constantly divide the military are almost daily headlines. And, certainly the higher ranking politicians are seldom in agreement as was the case in some of the very decisions that Mills cites. On top of these intragroup divisions are those among the groups, *qua* groups. President Truman, for example, fired our highest ranking general during the Korean War on the advice of fellow generals, while civilian advisers cautioned against the action. Likewise, President Eisenhower opposed the advice of his military leaders regarding the Dien Bien Phu action. And some generals advised President Truman not to use the atomic bomb in World War II. If anything, the situation in the nation's capital is one of divided counsel and often inaction or delay rather than that of coordinated elite action regarding the big decisions. Indeed, if Mills' model mirrored reality, presidents would not suffer as they do over the agonies of decision. Cohesion in any group is a difficult state to attain. Given the amorphous situation of leadership in the United States and the existence of conflicts of interest as well as perspectives among these leaders, it is thus doubtful that an elite can rule in the way Mills maintains.

A second point concerns the position Mills ascribes to the masses, that of impotence in politics. An equally renowned commentator—Walter Lippmann—maintains that the masses do have power, and, in fact, from Lippman's viewpoint, too much power. His evidence is at least as reliable as Mills'. Nevertheless, Mills fails to weigh properly the influence that public opinion, through the various mechanisms of elections, and other practices between elections, operates on those who do make the final decisions. No doubt public opinion is manipulated in many instances and ways, but the manipulators themselves are frequently influenced by the public. Most importantly, Mills overestimates the amount of control that the manipulators are presumed to have over the variables involved in such operations. Even the best of our knowledge about the factors involved in public opinion—its formation and dissemination—is highly fragmentary. Mills, in effect, utilizes good social theory but draws extreme conclusions, and in most instances, unduly pessimistic ones.

While the Mills' analysis is primarily concerned with locating the decision-makers on great issues involving war and peace, it is clearly a theory of allocation, the chief object of which being power to make such decisions. On a lower level, Mills explains allocation in terms of a bargaining theory, but does not think it significant. It is rather who gets the power to make the big decisions that counts, and he who has this power also acquires other forms of value.

Nor is Mills' theory of allocation simply an explanatory one; a strong moral quality pervades the enterprise. He does not like what he sees in the United States. In this he differs from the pluralist theorists who generally approve of the ways in which allocation takes place even if they do occasionally prefer some readjustments in the direction of greater equality.

Like the popular rule and pluralistic group models, the power elite model also has a theory of integration in the political system. But unlike the other models, integration is achieved in a radically different way. In the popular rule model, we saw that integration came about as a result of rational agreement among individuals over problems that permitted rational solution. Integration was reasonably easy to attain because conflict was not as serious as we sometimes assume it to be. The pluralist group model, on the other hand, saw more and more intense conflict. But the conflict was channeled into legitimate forms ("rules of the game"), and reduced through the operations of multiple or overlapping memberships and the existence of potential groups. To a considerable extent, group conflict was seen as being transferred to the level of intrapersonal conflict where, presumably, it would be handled *outside* the political system. Some reliance was placed on the socialization process to inculcate the rules of the game into citizens, but this aspect of the theory was not spelled out in detail.

The power elite model explains the handling of conflict in another way: that of power and manipulation on the part of the elite and the media of mass communication over the mass society. Whatever sources of conflict may develop among the masses is suppressed not so much by violence, but by deception and "bread and circuses" to calm them down.

Meaningful political action is unknown; consumption of television, movies, crime stories, and Hollywood gossip are the substitutes. Enormous patterns of social control are the means of keeping the population ignorant, inert, and indifferent to political debate and struggle. Father figures, fads, and celebrities are the daily manna of the mass society. The mass media tell men what they want, how to get it, provide escapism if they do not succeed, and supply "identity." Clearly, citizens do not participate in either of the ways described by the popular rule or the pluralist group models. Their efforts are integrated by manipulation and power.

SOME CONCLUSIONS

The models just considered offer three different images of the power structure of the United States, each having a glimmer of the truth, but none portraying the nation accurately in all its complexity. Indeed, it is doubtful whether we can ever draw a picture complete in all its necessary details. Nevertheless, it is possible to go beyond the criticisms we have voiced of the individual models, and make some more definitive assessments of the American power structure. These assessments will take the form of a number of generalizations accompanied by bits of evidence and references to further data. All these generalizations are highly tentative; some are consistent with one or more of the models, but others are not. In total, they are expected to give us a somewhat better understanding of power in the United States so that we may comprehend the allocative and integrative processes that will be taken up in later sections of the book.

We will begin with a definition, since all the models did not use the same definition of power. *Power will be used to mean the capacity to state and realize the societal goals.* This definition seems to be consistent with similar ones in that it emphasizes capacities to realize ends or goals. In saying "societal goals" we do not mean to preclude private ones; in attaining a societal goal it is assumed that the actor will thereby realize his own goals, whatever they may be. What we are interested in, then, is: first, determining how much capacity each citizen has to state and attain the societal goals; secondly, what his power is based on; thirdly, the scope of the power or the number of decisions shaped, type of decision, and numbers of people affected; fourthly, how power is acquired; and fifthly, the stability of the power structure. The generalizations that follow will stem from and relate to these questions.

One extremely important point and criticism of all the above described models must be made, however, before listing our own propositions about the power structure. The point is this: none of the models convincingly test their propositions about power against the *outcomes* of the political processes. That is, they do not tell us whether or not a person or group has power by relating his presumed power against the actual decisions made in a given system during a given period of time. For the most part, the power elite models analyze the resources of power and assume that the possession of resources means they are fully, effectively, and efficiently used by the power-holders. Only Floyd Hunter has made any effort to test against decisions or outcomes of a political struggle.[38] To be sure, Professor Truman has told us that certain factors such as status, money, organization, or leadership skill determine the power or influence of groups. But he does not then compare one group against another nor test such comparisons against decisional outcomes. As a result, we get good descriptions of group action, but little or no predictive capacity from the Truman model. A description and explanation of the potential power that groups or persons may command is not a substitute for a test about actual power in particular situations. If we wish to test who has power, we must test against the allocation of values and costs in the polity. Those who get most of the values and pay the least costs, for example, have obviously benefited by power. Moreover, different groups may receive differing amounts of different values, and different groups may pay differing amounts of the costs levied by the system. We cannot, therefore, describe power systems as ends in themselves; we must instead relate potential power to actual outcomes of the allocative processes. This we will attempt in Part Six. For the present, we will treat power as a dependent variable.

PROPOSITION 1. *The resources on which power is based are multiple.*

No consideration of power in this country, or most others, can be based on the a priori notion that power stems from one source or resource. Power may be based on innumerable resources or be anchored in many parts of the total social structure. Consequently, those who assume that power is ultimately generated only by the economy or one's position in it seem wrong, according to this writer. This is not to say that at a given time, in a given place, among a given set of persons, that one type of power resource may not be the most crucial. But it is to say that in a society, the size and complexity of the American, it is highly unlikely that command over one type of resource is all that is necessary to the exercising of power. Even Mills agrees with this statement, for he has argued that power stems from three sources (business, military, and political) and that at different times in American history the balance among these three groups has varied. Where we differ from Mills is in the assertion that the resources of power are not restricted to the three he mentions. Others include such elements as personal skills of leadership, prestige, information, public office at all levels, numbers of voters, and public opinion. In terms of institutions or subsystems in society, power may stem from religion and the churches, education and the schools, and from the economy—both institutional and associational—including trade unions. The power of each of these resources or that which can be exercised by each is never a constant, as is assumed by Mills. Under differing conditions, each will wield or permit a greater scope for realizing goals.

PROPOSITION 2. *The aforementioned resources of power are unevenly distributed in the United States.*

Hardly anyone would contradict this generalization, for it appears as the most apparent one concerning power in any society. Mills and the group theorists have all supported the same idea as, indeed, they should. We need but look about us to notice that some people barely make a living, while others command great economic enterprises; that some men have great prestige, while others have little; that some men possess much education and information, and others hardly any; that some men hold public offices, while others never even vote; that some men can lead and others only follow. Under these conditions it does not seem realistic to assume that all men are politically equal. Indeed, the facts about the uneven distribution of the resources of power would seem to be incontrovertible.

PROPOSITION 3. *Command over the resources of power is likely to be, but is not necessarily, cumulative.*

For some time sociologists have noted that, in most societies, if a person has command over one resource, he is likely to enjoy command over others. We agree with this general observation. In the United States, for example, should a person have command or control over wealth, he is also likely to receive greater deference, acquire greater education, and exercise more influence in community decision-making. But these do not always follow to the point where but one person is powerful or that all who are will have common interests and goals. Nevertheless, the person who can acquire more of one resource will find others coming his way without as much effort. But power is never perfectly correlated with any of the above-mentioned factors or resources. According to a prominent student of social stratification, Bernard Barber:

> . . . One kind of influence does not guarantee equal possession of another kind. While one kind of influence can sometimes be translated into another kind, there is no universal or simple key to such translations. . . .[39]

PROPOSITION 4. *Potential power is unevenly but widely distributed in America*

Social theorists who concentrate on or are impressed with the facts about the unevenness of distribution of power frequently forget to consider the possibility that, even though this be the case, power still may be widely distributed. An analogy from the business world may help: in corporate enterprise it is well known that ownership of stocks is currently widespread, but in a highly unequal sense, with many millions individually owning one or a few stocks, while a few own much larger blocs of shares. Yet, control over corporation decisions stems not from ownership of enormous amounts of stock, but from the very fact of widely distributed ownership. Thus, a person who owns or controls but 2 or 3 per cent can out-do the many who own only a few shares. In the American polity, likewise, we find wide distribution of power, in the sense that each or many citizens have some power and a few have much larger shares. But the latter actually have only a small proportion of the total amount of power. The right to vote in itself, while hardly the only type of significant resource, is widely held, and, under many conditions, can overcome the other types of resources that are less equally distributed.

Indeed, one of the problems of political action in the United States stems from the fact that power cannot be readily mobilized by the polity, a fact emanating from the extreme decentralization of power, not only among office holders, but among the general population as well.

PROPOSITION 5. *Power and the resources of power are not used at full capacity.*

There is an assumption in much of political philosophy and science that all men seek power and that they employ it to the maximum on all occasions. Nothing could be further from the truth. Men are not restlessly seeking power in the polity, nor do those who have power, which, to some extent, includes all, exercise it to the fullest. Some citizens do not even perceive that they possess power, and others shy away from it, for the costs of acquiring and using it are deemed excessive. Indeed, one of the tasks of most leaders of private organizations and other groups is to unite their groups in order to mobilize power, but they seldom succeed in enlisting the full or even a partial amount of the power potential. Members have competing interests and values, with the consequence that building power is but one interest and possible value, and for many Americans, hardly the dominant one. In other cases, a power-holder may prefer not to exercise all his potential power for fear of inciting others into a struggle. Accordingly, he does not use all his power. Or, he may simply be inefficient.

PROPOSITION 6. *Those who may possess larger shares of the resources of power do not necessarily share the same values, norms, interests, and perceptions.*

In his model of the power elite, Mills attempted to prove that the membership of that elite shared the same perception, that is, they looked at the world through the same lenses and valued the same things. This he attempted to prove by inference from their common social positions and education. No other type of evidence was used at length or in detail. Yet, as a matter of fact, we know that all the men who make up what Mills termed the elite do frequently clash on their major values and norms.[40] The politicians do not value the same things as the businessmen or the military, nor do the latter two groups share the same affinities. And, as might be expected from their different roles, they frequently view the world from quite different perspectives; the politician understands and sees the social universe in terms of political power; the businessman, most often in terms of production and profit; and the military man, in terms of military strength. Each of these values and perspectives may often conflict in terms of goals of the polity and the means by which they are attained. To be sure they may also be complementary, but this has yet to be proved.

Even within the so-called elite themselves, there are frequent differences of interest, value, and behavior. Schools of thought exist within the military, for example, just as among politicians.[41] Because differences may and do exist, cohesion among such persons or groups as the businessmen, or the military, is not likely to be perfect. Struggles may and do take place among the more powerful, as Plato and Aristotle argued centuries ago. And the fact that they do often weakens their power position, while increasing that of the mass of citizens or other groups.

PROPOSITION 7. *There is no single power structure, but many such structures, in the United States.*

If the previous propositions concerning power are at all valid, we may thus conclude that a single, monolithic power structure is all but impossible in the United States. To exercise power is to control variables and conditions; but if these variables and conditions are as numerous, complex, and stable as we have frequently maintained, it then becomes almost impossible for one or even a few men or groups to control and thereby rule. Of course, decentralization of the polity may contribute to the rule of a few in that those who are ruled cannot be effectively united to prevent the highly rational, purposive group. This, however, remains to be proven. Indeed, there is another possibility—the direct opposite, in fact—that rulers cannot overcome the individual positions of strength that the countless ruled occupy. We may be ruled, in short, but we are ruled more by forces beyond the control of rulers and ruled alike than by the conscious efforts of the elite.

Whoever maintains that we are in fact dominated by a single power structure made up of a few persons or groups must prove his case by identifying the rulers, showing precisely how we are ruled, in what areas, and why it cannot be explained otherwise. For the reasons already stated, Mills has not offered such a convincing, logical, or empirically based explanation.

PROPOSITION 8. *Just as there are distinct power structures, so there are multiple types of structure, or configurations of power.*

Research on community power structures has indicated, if nothing else, that no one model can be demonstrated to serve for all communities. For example, in one community, such as that of Regional City, it may well be that a pyramidal structure exists and is constituted of the persons and groups described by Floyd Hunter.[42] In another city, say, "Cibola," analyzed by Robert O. Schulze,[43] or Bennington studied by Harry Scoble,[44] other types of community power structures may be found. Some of these take on a highly cohesive and tight organization; still others disperse power very widely and no one seems able to control the actions or decisions of very many other persons. There is no likelihood, however, that the variety of forms that power may assume is infinite; such a notion defies all that we know about human behavior. All the attempts of the classical political philosophers and contemporary social scientists suggest that the number of types of structures is very limited.[45]

PROPOSITION 9. *Power structures are seldom completely stable.*

No power structure can remain unchanged for long periods of time, the reasons for which are several: first, new persons must replenish those who leave for whatever reasons; and secondly, the changing structure of societies, resources, and political problems alters the relative importance and power of those who make up the structure.

Even C. Wright Mills claimed that the power structure of the United States has changed in that the positions of the three power elites has varied vis-à-vis one another. While for him there has been no change in the basic structure, there has been a shifting about of the three elites. We can summarize Mills' statement somewhat as follows: [46]

From the Revolution to John Adams' Administration
 1. Political
 2. Social and economic
 3. Military

Early Nineteenth Century: Jefferson to Lincoln
 1. Economic in ascendancy
 2. Political
 3. Military

Late Nineteenth Century to F. D. Roosevelt
 1. Economic dominates
 2. Political
 3. Military

F. D. Roosevelt and the New Deal
 1. Economic
 2. Political begins to challenge the economic
 3. Military

Post-World War II
 1. Economic
 2. Military
 3. Political

While Mills might argue about the order in which his elites have been placed here, he did maintain that it was not a simple matter of assessing their power, even though they shift about somewhat. According to Mills, the professional politicians have lost the most and the military have gained the most power; business, apparently, has always been at or near the top. Whether Mills' analysis is correct or not, the fact that he was willing to admit of changes among the elites, if not among the structure itself, is at least some confirmation of our proposition that power structures are not stable.

More in keeping with our own analysis is the fact that the resources on which power is based have changed as have the skills of those who use them in politics. In the earlier years of the nation, land counted for much more than it does today, and labor counted for less in an agricultural society. One might also add that education today counts for more than it once did. Indeed, today, technical information on society and science are highly valued commodities, with the result that scientists and educators are more powerful than ever before. Changing technology itself has called forth new skills as power resources. Also, various minority groups, including the Jews and Negroes, have come to occupy crucial electoral positions so that their power potentials have risen accordingly. Of course, changes in relative positions of the power-holders must also be related to specific situations. The position of the Negro, for example, may not be as powerful in the nation as in New York City; but his position is changing in both contexts, and that is what we wish to argue about power structures through time: namely, that they change in terms of both structure and persons or groups occupying them. Probably, there is greater change in persons and groups than in structure, but even that generalization is subject to qualification, as we have suggested in previous discussions.

Part Three

The American
Political Culture

WHAT we are now about to discuss could be handled in many ways. We could deal, for example, with the belief system and symbolic elements of our polity when interpreting the structure of the system, and with the various inputs of demands, expectations, resources, and support. In fact, we did that somewhat when discussing the power structure, and we will do more of the same in Parts Four and Five. Yet, the importance and the complexity of a political culture is such as to necessitate a separate and more detailed analysis. Setting aside an entire section of the book, then, must not be interpreted to mean that political culture is something distinct and unrelated to the polity and to our frame of reference. We are isolating this aspect for analytical reasons.

Gabriel Almond was apparently the first political scientist to coin the term "political culture," although he was hardly the first to detect and study the elements: beliefs and symbols. These aspects of politics have and continue to be the focuses of much of political science. And while it is dangerous to reify "culture," there is a sense in which one can speak of culture apart from the behavior of the members of society. That sense pertains to the fact that culture is not simply carried in the minds of people, but is also found in the form of objects such as libraries, books, museums, paintings, government buildings, music, and so forth. Similarly, in our interpretation, we will rely on a combination of approaches. We will study the objects of political culture as well as the behavior of Americans. Public opinion polls will be used for the information they may contain about beliefs and attitudes. Whatever the source of data, we are interested above all in interpreting the beliefs of Americans about politics and the symbolic apparatus that they have evolved to convey their values, norms, and beliefs. Each of these components has its effects or consequences for the inputs that enter the polity and, therefore, of necessity, for the outputs as well.

5

Liberalism

The American Belief System

In the present chapter, we are concerned with an analysis of the dominant American belief system toward political action. In somewhat simpler language, the concern is with the ways in which the American people view politics, and its place in their lives. We want to know how they see politics, both in terms of what *is* and what *ought* to be. Furthermore, we shall attempt to determine what the typical American views as his own proper role in the politics of the nation.

The analysis of these orientations can be considerably simplified by focusing upon a limited number of cognitive and evaluative beliefs about politics. We are not interested in reviewing the entire constellation of facts, values, and norms, but only those directly relevant to the course of politics. These elements of the political culture condition actual behavior, and are, of course, forms of behavior themselves. In fact, when a citizen expresses a value, he is behaving in an extremely important way, as, for example, when he studies a campaign and then votes on the basis of the evaluating he has done. He evaluates both before and when he casts his vote.

The typical American views politics in a somewhat different way than have most people during the course of history.[1] In the first instance, he views politics as a *democrat* and, secondly, as an *American* democrat. How this view expresses itself in political behavior is the substance of this book. It cannot be readily summarized. The concept of culture implies that there is a typical constellation of evaluative and cognitive orientations that form the basis for the behavior of most Americans. This constellation of views may be labeled in a variety of ways; the actual terms are of no great importance. Thus, some writers speak of the "American Mind";

others, of "attitudes"; and, still others, of "definitions of the situation." We will use the latter designation and the term, "belief system."

Another term, "ideology," employed by some social scientists, will be used here to signify a system of highly explicit beliefs about a program of action. An ideology constitutes a subclass of beliefs. As such, it too is a way of "defining the situation," of giving it meaning, of understanding or interpreting it. An ideology constitutes a way of looking at the world about one. Yet while no one lives without a system of beliefs—for it is a necessity of action and survival—not all elaborate ideologies.

Throughout history, the beliefs of most men have been of the implicit variety. Relatively few, including Americans, have found the time or the necessity of rigorously defining their own beliefs into elaborate systems of thought or ideologies. Indeed, only a few men need do that in any social system. For most Americans, then, beliefs consist of a collection of ideas as to what politics and government *are* and what they *ought* to be. These collections are seldom neat, logical, lucid statements; on the contrary, they are generally fuzzy, unclear, and frequently illogical. But whatever their character, they do serve the purpose of structuring the world for those who hold them. Whether the American ought to continue to see the world in the terms that he has is of no great concern to us in this book; our task is to describe and explain.

If beliefs are as described above, how are we ever to locate and discover their contents? The question is not difficult to answer, for the sources of a belief system are many. They include the explicit statements of leaders of the nation, newspaper commentary, the Constitution, the texts of political science and civics, the art of the nation, and, of course, the everyday expressions of the mass of citizenry. The ways in which Americans have traditionally defined the political situation has long been a dominant topic of scholarship. Thus, we have many authorities to turn to in our analysis, including many distinguished foreigners as well as Americans.[2] Determining the dominant views of Americans, then, should not be an overly difficult task.

The task will also be easier because we are concerned with the *major themes* in the American conception of politics. We will be less interested in the *distribution* of these themes among the population; nor will we attempt to specify the percentages of people who adhere to this or that belief.[3] We assume that not everyone will hold the individual beliefs that we describe nor hold them in exactly the manner they are herein analyzed. We will maintain, however, that the beliefs we indicate are widespread and, indeed, that they have no major competitor. That is, one and only one belief system holds sway on the American scene.[4] Variations on the themes do exist, but they are insignificant unless viewed against the background of dominant beliefs. If it be true that but one system dominates, we must then be prepared to accord it an important place in shaping American political behavior. For it is these beliefs that provide the basis of the formal role structure of the polity that structure policy alternatives and the expectations of citizen and leader alike.

THE LIBERAL IDEA AND IDEALS

The basic ideas of the American political "mind" received their most explicit statement in the Declaration of Independence. However, an English philosopher—John Locke—had expounded the same general ideas nearly a century earlier. His views were familiar and indeed commonplace among the men who led the revolt. The indebtedness of American leaders to this philosopher, plus the fact that it is convenient to draw upon his work, suggests the desirability of summarizing Locke's political philosophy as a prelude to an examination of the ideas of ordinary American citizens.

Locke is probably best known for his practical empirical outlook on society and the world.[5] Like many Americans, he believed that the world could be grasped only through the use of the five senses. In short, the universe could not be understood simply by intuition or reason. While Locke contradicted himself on this crucial matter when it came to explaining politics and his values, his empirical viewpoint is a fact and one that most Americans have always found congenial.

But while Locke was an empiricist, he also defended his views of men, society, and politics by invoking reason and intuition. He believed that men were born *rational, free, good,* and *equal.* None of these properties of human nature can be demonstrated empirically or by the means of science, but Locke believed in them, nevertheless. These views of man as rational, free, good, and equal are of profound importance, not only as providing the basis of Locke's political philosophy, but of providing that of the Americans as well.[6]

From these premises Locke deduced a system of government that he felt was an appropriate one in terms of being consistent with these beliefs, and one that would realize the ends or values implied in the premises. He believed that government was instituted or created by men to further their own ends. Government, in effect, was not a natural thing, but an artificial creation to be used only as long as it furthered the ends envisaged by Locke, namely "life, liberty, and estate." Government, he said, was created on the basis of a contract among the people and their rulers. Furthermore, this contract stipulated that government was to be essentially democratic or representative and therefore of limited powers. Since men, in Locke's view, were born with certain "inalienable rights," life, liberty, and property, a government must exist primarily to protect and further these rights. Should it fail to do so, it could be held accountable and even overthrown.

It was this set of beliefs that Locke expounded at the time when this nation was in its early years. And it was this ideology that was transported to America via colonists and books, where it found a favorable environment and reception. As a result it became the orientation of Americans, and formed not only the basis of their claim for freedom from England, but subsequently the basis of the Constitution itself. To this day, indeed, we are largely Lockeans; there are few Platonists, Hegelians, Marxists, followers of Rousseau, or any of the other European philosophers in America. Our own contribution to philosophy, pragmatism, is a descendant and variation of the basic tenets of Locke's liberalism. In the sense of adherence to the central doctrines of Locke, we are all "little liberals."

SOME MAJOR THEMES

Having outlined the philosophical basis of the American liberal belief system, as found in John Locke, we will now attempt to make these rather abstract ideas and ideals somewhat more concrete and immediate. This we will do by pointing out some of the more important ideas and ideals of the average American, which, as the reader will note, are part and parcel of the Lockean philosophy. Even if they were not stated originally by Locke, they are deducible from his premises and propositions. Further, in describing the American view of politics, we will do so only with respect to those ideas which are relevant to politics. Consequently, we will be mainly concerned with the role and status of politics in American life; conceptions of power and authority; citizenship; and the form of the government. Needless to say, various subsidiary themes will be introduced as we proceed.

Role and Status of Politics

Politics is not a way of life for very many Americans. In fact, with the exception of a few periods in history, the average American appears to prefer not being involved in active politics. This is so for a number of reasons, including conceptions of political action. For politics has long been thought of as a rather low form of behavior in which corruption, ignorance, and passion hold sway.[7] Obviously, this is not the type of activity in which one would want to engage, nor have one's children pursue, at least as a career. The preferred activity has been business and, more recently, the professions.

On a more fundamental level, the American has tended to believe that politics should be minimized in society and that private action should be the chief allocator and integrator. As Locke advised, government should be restricted to the provision of minimal rules of the game by which the allocation of values and costs and the integration of society can take place. Men are sufficiently good-natured not to require much central supervision. Their own self-interests will lead them to the best life. In Locke's estimation, the functions of the polity as outlined in a previous chapter were better served by depending upon other systems, particularly upon individual effort.

Political Power as Evil

Whether political action is thought of as, or in terms of, power, there can be little doubt that power is a central feature of political action. What the American people have traditionally thought of power thus becomes an important part of the analysis, for it is they who are the leading actors in the system.

If we define political power as we did in Chapter 1, as the capacity to shape societal goals and attain personal goals, it would seem reasonable to conclude that Americans have not been public admirers of power. In fact, they have been largely suspicious of it and, in particular, political power. Lord Acton's famous phrase that "power tends to corrupt and absolute power corrupts absolutely," while that of an Englishman, has nevertheless found greater acceptance in the United States than in Great Britain itself. That power will be abused is indeed a tacit understanding of most Americans. For these reasons, among others, the highly articulate founders of this country devised a governmental structure that would thwart any power holder or aspirant. So great was the fear of the abuse of power that it was felt that it could best be controlled by designing a system in which power was radically decentralized. In this way everyone would have some power but no one a monopoly. Thus, the federal division and the separation of powers on a functional basis were devised. In addition to these basic structural features, the Founding Fathers also relied upon the creation of many offices (elective), short terms, and competition between offices as well as among candidates and incumbents. Adding to these protections against the abuse of political power, the Constitution itself, particularly in the first Ten Amendments, makes it clear that power rests ultimately with the states and the people.

Since the early days of the republic many more protections have been built into the political system. Among them are such mechanical contrivances as recall, initiative, referendum, primary elections, direct election of United States Senators, regulation of campaign expenditures, prohibition of federal employees participating in elections, loyalty oaths, and many other laws affecting the behavior of politicians and administrators.

These attempts to control power by the use of formal laws have clearly indicated not only a recognition of the significance of power but also a fear of it. Interestingly enough, however, Americans have not depended very heavily upon internal personality controls and the socialization process to handle power; instead, they have relied mostly upon external or social controls. The British, for example, demonstrate a willingness—unknown to Americans—to depend upon the consciences of their office-holders not to misuse their powers. In this country the dependence is on external control with constant reminders to the power-holders that they are being controlled.

Yet while power has been widely dispersed during normal periods, the American people have also demonstrated a willingness to have power concentrated during times of great crisis as in a major war or depression. Under these conditions, executive branches of the government have been able to mobilize vast resources and support without much criticism. For the American tends to regard power in a practical or pragmatic way, as a tool to be used only for special purposes that are clearly defined. It is also assumed that power will be granted only under condition and that when the crisis is over, it will revert to its proper place among the people. Politicians, therefore, whenever faced with a crisis tend to justify their acquisition and use of power in these pragmatic terms. Power is not generally thought of in a mystical sense. This we find true not only in the language used to discuss power, but also in its symbols (Chapter 6). American officials, for example, seldom wear uniforms, and even when they do the uniform is hardly a striking or colorful one designed to elicit subordination.

A much less explicit aspect or assumption about power than its evil is the notion that power is a *thing* and *limited in quantity*.[8] In short, power is regarded as a "thing" possessed by some persons and groups and not by others. If the latter are to improve their position or acquire more of this thing, they must do so at the expense of others, since the quantity at any given moment is limited. It is because of this assumption as to the nature of power that Americans, including political scientists, are so concerned over its distribution and other values allocated by the polity. Indeed, most of political science is chiefly concerned with the patterns of distribution and the means by which the distribution takes place. The ordinary

American, likewise, tends to conceive of power in terms of "who gets what, when, and how." Because of this conception, and the belief that power is evil, Americans are not likely to think of power as being useful for the accomplishment of societal goals. Income may well be conceived of in functional terms, but not power. Thus, the concern with its distribution, control, and presumed evil consequences is a logical one. Should politicians request more power, they must present strong pragmatic reasons or justifications for doing so. Accordingly, power is not easily generated in the American political system.

But although the American does tend to think of power as a thing and as evil, he also tends to be somewhat ambivalent about his own personal power, whether as an individual or as a member of the political system. Thus, one frequently hears American politicians publicly deny their possession of power, or minimize their own puissance to control others. Conversely, they also have a pronounced tendency to overestimate the power of their opposition. The conservatives believe that the liberals have taken over the country, while the latter believe the opposite. Each will cite numerous illustrations to document their cases. Under another set of conditions—more private ones—many Americans, interestingly, will boast about their power or access to persons of influence. These are the individuals whom David Riesman has termed the "inside dopesters," those who claim inside information and want others to know of their relationship to the powerful, although they, themselves, may actually be impotent.[9] The ambivalence toward power, then, manifests itself in the belief that it is an evil and that one ought never to publicly exalt in his power. Hand in hand with this, however, is the secret pride that many take in being power-holders or of having access to them.

Rational-Legal Authority

Ambivalent attitudes toward power have produced a well-defined conception of the conditions under which political power may be wielded in legitimate or rightful ways. Authority will be defined here as legitimate power, legitimate, that is, in the view of those persons subject to the exercise of power. Authority, as we pointed out in Chapter 1, is an extremely important element in all political systems; it is no less crucial to the understanding of American politics.

Americans, as de Tocqueville observed, are a highly pragmatic people who will not allow ideas to stand in their way of accomplishing something that they believe needs to be accomplished.[10] This is the case with political action. Thus, despite their fears of political power, Americans are also willing to grant considerable power to the government and individual office-holders, provided that it is used, as stated above, for well-defined acceptable goals, under clearly specified conditions. In short, power is granted as a resource to be used for practical ends. But the power also must be carefully circumscribed and defined as in the allocation of power in the Constitution. Similarly, the public actions of elective public officials must be in accordance to the authority granted them in some legal document, both legally arrived at and accepted as authoritative.

The basis of legitimate power is therefore *legal,* the authority of the official resting not on his personality, charisma, nor tradition, but on the legal grant to his *office*. In a sense, it is not the official who commands, but the office. Moreover, the official must be prepared to demonstrate that his actions are within the legal scope of his office. He may even have to go before a court to prove his right to act in a specific case. At that time, his defense must be in legal terms, citing the proper documents such as a constitution or a statute granting him the authority to act. And, of course, the statute must have been arrived at according to legally prescribed means.

In the title to this section of the chapter, we used the word "rational" along with "legal" in describing authority in America. The term "rational" in this instance refers to certain properties of the rules or laws that define the office and powers (authority) of the office-holder. These rules or laws are *generalized* in the sense that they apply to all persons equally and impersonally, that is, for all who may occupy the office and those who may be subject to the commands emanating from the office. In this general sense, plus the fact that the laws or rules are logically consistent, do we understand the term "rational." Under rational-legal authority, the personalities of people are irrelevant. So long as the persons meet the objective criteria specified by the laws or rules, they are subject to them. Thus, a citizen cannot refuse to obey the commands of a policeman because he does not approve of his looks, personality, or religious affiliation. He may refuse to obey only should the officer exceed his authority. On the other hand, a policeman or an elective official legitimately selected, of course, cannot use his power outside the range of his official duties. He is like all other citizens, subject to the same laws as they.

Rational-legal authority is, therefore, a means—a major means in the United States—of controlling power in the polity. In short, power, to be regarded as legitimate, must meet the criteria of rational-legal standards. Yet, the fact that authority circumscribes the abuse of power does not mean that abuses are thereby automatically eliminated; they are not. In part, the disparity stems from a certain ambiguity in the authoritative documents so that the best-intentioned official may exceed his authority. Power is also abused through design. Self-interest or strong personality attributes may cause an official or officer to take advantage of his position. Generally, however, power has been effectively contained.

Rational-legal authority is hardly the only one operative in society or the polity. Indeed, the decisions and other actions of politicians may gain much support for reasons other than their basis in legal rights. Such a capacity may be based upon charismatic grounds, or upon a politician's own personal appeal to the electorate and other politicians. As such a person is often believed to have special capacities as a leader, and he is able for that reason to acquire their support. But while charisma does exist, it is not, as we have stated, a legal basis upon which to command performances nor is it as prevalent as in many other polities.[11]

Citizenship as a Duty

Many observers of Americans have noted their patriotism and the frequently loud forms it assumes. But it is also readily apparent that citizenship, or the relationship of the member to his country, involves much more than mere blatant patriotism. The American loves his country, for example, but tends to think of his rights before his obligations. And when he does consider obligations, he frequently thinks of them as odious and demanding. Even voting itself is sometimes considered a duty; indeed, election-eve pleas are generally couched in such terms—the duties of a good citizen. Service in the armed forces is something to be avoided or resisted. Instead of pleas to be of service to one's country and to be proud of the uniform and service, the American recruit is told that he will receive the best of food, clothing, and other services including education to prepare one to make money upon discharge. Similarly, service on juries is a duty, one for which the citizen must be monetarily compensated. The holding of public office is likewise regarded as a duty. Indeed, even the highest office in the land, the Presidency, is generally filled by men who claim that they are there only out of duty's sake. Sacrifice, in short, is the keynote of citizenship.

In the United States, citizenship apparently is something to be taken for granted. As a result, the people are constantly exhorted to be good citizens, to vote, and to pay their taxes. Many citizenship programs for all age groups exist primarily for the purposes of inculcating good citizenship: recognizing and doing one's duty. The League of Women Voters, the Citizenship Clearing House, and the many citizenship programs of organizations dedicated to other goals—all promote the duties of the citizen. The American Legion, while concerned with veterans' interests, also devotes much time, energy, and resources to various citizenship promotions.

Citizenship, then, is something distinct from social life generally, and therefore the object of special attention and organizations. The American's sense of belonging to his country cannot be thought of in the same sense, for example, as that of an Englishman.[12] To the latter, being an Englishman is so natural a thing that he hardly finds it necessary to discuss. As a consequence, the English do not worry as much about the loyalties of their fellow men as do Americans; these are assumed.[13] There are very good reasons for this state of affairs in both nations. The United States is a comparatively new country, made up of large numbers of immigrants who have had some loyalty to the "old country." England, on the other hand, is old and has not had to integrate millions of immigrants. Furthermore, the emphasis upon the individual of liberalism is such as to postulate a distinction between the individual and society so that loyalty is not automatic; it has to be secured by having society serve the individual. In times of stress, the obligations are reversed, and this often poses great problems of insecurity concerning the "real" loyalties of others. Consequently, intolerance and extreme demonstrations of loyalty are much more common in the United States than in Great Britain; they will continue to be so until Americans develop a more natural or implicit commitment to their country, and, in so doing, be less demanding and suspicious of others.

The conception of citizenship that a people has is, of course, a crucial variable in determining the levels and objects of support in the political system. Loyalty is not an undifferentiated product; it is allocated among objects. Which "objects" receive the most is problematical. In the United States we give more of our loyalties to the societal values and form of government than to the laws, policies, and personnel who may happen to be running the government at any given time. This must be the case in all stable systems, for the framework or structure of society and the belief systems are more crucial than are the momentary leaders and policies. To change the latter does not involve or necessitate a change in the former; but to change the system, *ipso facto,* is to destroy it.

Ambivalent Attitudes toward Compromise

Americans are well known among the people of the world for their informality, and willingness to adjust to others. Some commentators, in fact, have argued that we now have a cult of conformity and tolerance; that, in the language of David Riesman, we have become a nation of "other-directed" character types. No doubt there is a considerable amount of truth in the observations. Yet, it also seems that Americans in their public life, as contrasted to the private, stress themes of principle, which to all appearances seem the opposite of compromise and adjustment. This is especially notable in the judgments of politicians where compromise is regarded as bad and principle as good. For a politician to be known as a compromiser is to be condemned. Yet, in fact, we also seem to prefer the official who is not obdurant or obstinate, just as we prefer the agreeable person in private relationships. The typical American, then, has the same ambivalent attitude toward compromise as he has toward power. What Americans seem to like in their politicians is the appearance of steadfast dedication to basic principles and a pragmatic attitude toward compromise on subsidiary issues. The goals and values, as well as basic institutions of American life, must always be defended; but, decisions on policies and laws regarding lesser means may be compromised in the interests of getting the job done and reducing unnecessary conflict. That this is the case can be illustrated by the heroes Americans have chosen in their political history. Presidents like Washington are known and admired for their principles; presidents like Franklin D. Roosevelt for their ability to negotiate political compromises. "The Lion and the Fox" the latter has been called, and an apt description it is.[14] "Old Hickory," "Honest Abe" are but a few of the nicknames attached to politicians suggesting alternatives in the ambivalence of principle and compromise. The better-known public images, both verbal and pictorial, however, tend to stress the unbending character of the statesmen. On the other hand, politicians may gain a reputation for bullheadedness and obstreperous behavior that is not widely admired except for those who benefit from it; such is the image of Senator Wayne Morse of Oregon among many voters. Senator Robert Taft was another such figure, although his staunchness was also widely regarded as a virtue.

Whatever the views of any particular politician, the American is inconsistent in his views regarding compromise. He honors principles yet realizes the necessity of adjustment. And the fact that he is ambivalent makes the role of the politician even more difficult, for he is the one who must arrange the compromises while, at the same time, appear not to be surrendering important principles. Conversely, the voter in his private domain can avoid making the decisions politicians are required to make in public. Thus, he can go on being ambivalent with neither responsibility nor cost.

Responsibility and the Public Interest

Two of the more ambiguous terms in political science are those that head this section. Yet, they are no less significant for that reason either in political science or in actual politics. Responsible action on the part of public officials in the public interest is indeed a cardinal value of the American democracy. In fact, it would not be wrong to maintain that responsibility and the public interest have been institutionalized to a considerable degree, that is, have been formally made a value to be pursued by members of the system. This applies to interest groups and citizens as well as to government officials.

In the case of the officials, responsibility is secured in a number of ways, many of which are formally provided for in the definitions of their roles as officials. In outlining duties, the Constitution and laws attempt to ensure responsible action. In providing for oaths of office to be taken publicly and under great symbolic conditions, the polity also attempts to ensure responsible conduct. Likewise, the efforts of schools and other means of socialization to educate the citizenry into active participation in politics is an endeavor to attain responsible actions among those who control and demand values. In the case of the public officials, responsibility is to the electorate; this is assumed to be in the public interest.

The public interest has been defined in many ways, and will always be debated. But whatever the content, the public interest *as a symbol* is a most significant element in the American polity. It is that one object toward which all will profess agreement, a value that all prefer seeing attained, and by which all policies must eventually be justified. Self-interest is expected to be a goal or motivation neither of citizens, nor of the officials. For while it is an acceptable, if not *the* sanctioned, motive in the economy, such is not the case in the political system. Here the only publicly acceptable motives are public service, responsibility, and the public interest. No candidate for public office can thus afford to base his campaign on pleas to satisfy his own interests, material or otherwise. When an official takes the oath of office he pledges himself to defend the Constitution and work in the public interest. This becomes his public trust, his privilege, and his duty.

Politics as a Game

"The great game of politics" has long been a favorite phrase of Americans. And like all such phrases and aphorisms, it contains or reflects some important facts about the society in which it originates and is used. Americans, as we have pointed out, tend to think of politics in highly moralistic terms, but that moralism, more often than not, is reserved for special occasions. Frequently, in fact, politics is discussed in the terminology of games with the same sort of spirit that prevails at games. Thus, the American speaks of "throwing one's hat in the ring," or of "running" for office.

To conceive of politics as a game suggests that, while one hopes his team will win, the results are not so important that a loss can become tragic. Indeed, politics can be regarded as a game precisely because the outcomes in the United States are so comparatively unimportant under normal conditions. Furthermore, a return match is always provided for so that the score can be evened up. As Gabriel Almond has said, "A game is a good game when the outcome is in doubt and when the stakes are not too high. When the stakes are too high, the tone changes from excitement to anxiety." [15] There is still another prerequisite of the game conception of politics: that the rules be well established. No game can proceed, of course, unless rules have been decided upon, and are widely known and accepted. In the United States, the rules meet these conditions. A third condition or aspect is that the game have spectators as well as participants. In the United States, politics is to a great degree a spectator sport. Indeed, many people have no more sense of participation than that of witnessing the spectacle and enjoying it as a vicarious experience.[16] To be a spectator of a sporting event means that the event must not only have some interest, but, as Almond has suggested, some indeterminacy about the outcome. One is therefore attracted to witnessing the game and perhaps even to rooting intensely for one side. Yet, one always remains on the sidelines, never actually entering into the arena itself. Americans, to an unusual degree, do participate in this spectator fashion in the nation's politics. The conditions we have enumerated, concerning outcomes, indeterminacy, and rules, all permit, if not actually encourage, such a conception and behavior.

To say that politics is frequently viewed as a game must not be construed to mean that the game is not intense nor that some persons and groups are not vitally concerned with the outcome. In politics as in a real game there is to be found a genuine excitement and bitter partisans. Such partisans, however, make up a relatively small percentage of the total population.

Perhaps one of the best illustrations of the game atmosphere of politics lies in the campaigning and conventions of the parties. American campaigns and conventions are usually loud, colorful, and fun. Excitement rather than anxiety prevails. And the voters watch it all in an amused manner on their television sets. Even for the professional party members themselves, politics has a strong game appeal. No better description of this can be found than in James A. Farley's account of the 1932 National Democratic Convention held in Chicago, Illinois:

> There was a period of tense excitement and eager participation for those who were on the scene during the long week before the convention actually got under way at the Chicago Stadium. There was a thrill in the atmosphere, the feeling that a good fight was about to take place. The old party war horses love that sort of thing: it sets the blood coursing in their veins. They delight in wandering through the hotel corridors, looking wise, and whisper-

ing secretly about trades and agreements. They exchange views and swap gossip. They compare notes on what the various headquarters are giving out and take a squint at the candidates if they can. Many of the old-timers renew friendships that date back for as long as forty years. And, of course, each fellow has a weather eye cocked for the band-wagon rush. . . .[17]

The fact that politics may be thought of as a game, however, does not preclude its being thought of in other terms as well. In the United States, another major orientation is moralistic.

Political Moralism

The moralistic fervor of many Americans has long been a source of both amusement and confusion to perceptive foreigners. Admittedly, Americans do find it hard to think of politics without using moral terms and symbols.[18] Even when they are cynical about politics, as many are, they tend to derive their cynicism from moral premises that have not been met or honored. We have a strong tendency, in short, to judge politicians in moralistic tones. We also have a strong tendency to believe that human behavior can be shaped or altered by passing moralistic legislation, such as the Prohibition Amendment to the Constitution, and to perceive foreign affairs and people in the moral framework. Much of this moralism stems from the religious origins of the nation, most particularly from Puritan and later fundamentalist influence. For while we may believe that politics and religion should not be mixed, we are in fact among the world's greatest moralists regarding politics. The word of God is constantly used in political oratory. The Bible vies with Bartlett's Handbook of Quotations as a source of wisdom and expression among the public figures of America. Further, the kind of behavior that causes little or no comment among the people of other nations can be a source of great moral disapprobation among Americans. Our leaders are expected to be religious men, to live exemplary private lives, to honor Mother, condemn drinking, and do all the things good American boys are supposed to do.

Frequently, moralism has led to the most dogmatic and intolerant kinds of behavior. Vigilante movements, censorship groups, and all sorts of religious prejudice have stemmed from moralism.[19] Indeed, we sometimes seem to alternate between moral crusades against and complete withdrawal from the evil world of politics. Generally this has been the case with respect to foreign affairs where we have wanted either to save the world for democracy, or to retreat into isolation.[20] We have, to be sure, done both. Withdrawal and crusading, for the individual American, have taken the form of general indifference to politics for long periods of time. Then, when something goes wrong or appears immoral, we suddenly embark upon a political crusade to clean things up. Just as suddenly, after things presumably have been rectified, the good citizen returns to private life and makes money. According to this conception of politics, good intentions are all that are necessary. The man who has such intentions can do no wrong, or so many Americans believe. As a result, we have a fondness for men who appear to possess this virtue. Intentions, not political skill, is the admired quality under a moralistic code of judgment.[21] Thus, the skilled politicians always play down their skills and advertise the former attribute. In such fashion do they pay mouth honor to the moralistic orientation to politics.

Problem Solving and Optimism

Social life for the American is a man-created phenomenon. As such it can be shaped by the deliberate intentions and actions of men working in concert. No social problem is regarded as a product of nature and beyond the total control of men. If anything goes wrong in society we are to correct it, and the American tends to believe that the problem can be solved by the use of good will and hard work. Furthermore, he tends to believe that short-run improvisation is superior to long-run, complicated governmental planning, although the emphasis has been and is changing as the problems change. On the whole, however, the American tends to be rather optimistic about the handling of social problems. A good illustration of these several assumptions is to be found in the Volstead Act or the Eighteenth Amendment, which would presumably eliminate the problems of drinking. The innumerable schemes for the handling of other social problems such as juvenile delinquency and crime also show the American attitudes toward social difficulties and problem solving. These matters are problems and not man's fate; as such they can be resolved once and for all by the application of intelligence, good will, and hard work.[22]

When such problems do persist, the American will tend to attribute failure to neglect in using intelligence or hard work and sometimes to a lack of good will. Partisan differences about what ought to be done are regarded as somewhat evil. Everyone should regard the problem in the same way and therefore solve it in the same way.

UNIQUE CONDITIONS OF LIBERALISM

No doubt the reader will have begun to wonder how and why liberalism came to be established in America, and how it has managed to remain the major if not the sole set of beliefs defining the universe of politics for Americans. Although the answer is not an easy one to provide, we can perhaps indicate what a few of the historically unique conditions were and are for the maintenance of this single creed.

In the first instance, as has been argued by a number of commentators including Karl Marx, Alexis de Tocqueville, and, more recently, Louis Hartz and Daniel Boorstin, the United States began its national history without having to overthrow a feudal social structure. In the literary phrase of Tocqueville, America was "born free." The liberal ideology did not have to usurp another for there was simply none that contradicted it; everyone was a liberal. The dominant religious outlook was that of "liberal" Protestantism; and the age of Puritan theocracy had passed by and large, into the era of religious toleration. The social conditions of the time were the embodiment of liberal ideas and aspirations; men were already free. American society was, unlike the European, a land of free men who owned their own land, and voted in elections. Feudal estates, lords, fees to pay, or indentured slavery were nonexistent. Americans were free to develop from a clean slate. Liberalism had neither obstacle nor enemy.

Ideas, of course, are not the only forces that shape men's behavior. The physical conditions are also of very great importance and, in some theories, of the greatest significance. Whatever their general import, certain physical conditions found in America were of considerable importance in assisting liberalism to remain dominant.[23] For while a belief may lag behind changes in other elements of a society, it cannot be out of step for very long; either the belief itself will be changed or the physical conditions brought to consistency. In any case, liberalism was most appropriate to Americans, for they lived in a bountiful country in which it was possible and perhaps desirable to exploit the natural resources with private initiative and profit. Not only did the great supplies of resources permit individual exploitation, but property, which was so valued by Locke, could also be attained easily and defended as having been earned in the manner in which Locke defended the institution. The Lockean means for allocating values and costs seemed eminently suited to these conditions of plenty. We can appreciate the uniqueness and popularity of the liberal approach when we compare the conditions of the so-called underdeveloped lands of today.[24] Few people in these areas and even few Americans seriously believe that these lands can be developed according to the liberal approach. They are lands with a colonial background, often faced with dense populations and limited resources. To let men loose under the liberal rules of the game, if that were even conceivable, would end in tragedy and not development, as it did in America. Thus, the motivations postulated by Locke are not the motives we see today in these lands, nor even, to the same degree, in America itself.

Another unique condition, one that few other lands have possessed, is that of having been able to develop unmolested by the remainder of the world. Americans could concentrate upon internal development and protections of freedom without having to worry about invasions or war with other countries. As a result, the role of government could approximate the Lockean ideal of a minimal regulation. We did not have to raise great armies and finances to fortify the boundaries. Nor did we need to restrict personal freedom in the interests of national security, for there was really no security problem, as was faced by every nation in Europe. Unrivaled opportunities existed, therefore, for individual profits and liberty. The government thus has played a small role in the lives of the people throughout most of our history. Symbols of the political system were not often seen on the frontier and those that were were of the local governments, hardly very impressive. There was no powerful communist movement or state constantly threatening the liberal way of life. Internal subversion was hardly thought of; we had eccentrics, to be sure, but no revolutionists nor lords. Everyone seemed to be an entrepreneur, or had the conditions to be one simply by moving on West. Indeed, a man could hardly fail to succeed during most of the history of the country. The liberal ideology provided the motives; the conditions of the land provided the needed confirmation of the essential rightness of the ideas. In short, ideology and physical conditions worked together harmoniously to make America an enormous success.

6

The American Polity,
Public Office, and Symbolism

Social scientists and literary men have long recognized the significance of symbols, ceremonies, and ritual in social life. Periodically, political scientists have also attributed importance to these matters in political systems and behavior.[1] But, more generally, political scientists have tended to underestimate the power of symbols and to misunderstand their functions, engaging rather in polemic attacks against their use. Thus, symbols and ceremonies have often been regarded as irrational, the opiate of the people, and tools of the elites.

The symbolic component of political systems are at once more significant than political scientists have believed and significant in different ways. In this chapter we will explore the types and functions of symbolism in American politics. The discussion is hardly exhaustive; it is not meant to be.

A THEORETICAL NOTE

Symbolism may be regarded as the attribution of meaning by a person or group to an object.[2] Generally, the object is made to stand for something other than itself; it may be anything, including actions, concrete things, or an abstract sign as in mathematics. Symbolic objects derive their meanings from the actions and beliefs of persons, not from the objects themselves. Consequently, an object that possesses great or profound meaning for one person may be nothing more than a conventional item or practical instrument for another. Moreover, because symbols are attributed meaning, they act not only as resources, but as controls over the behavior of men, that is, those who attribute meaning to them.

123

The types of symbolism in which we are interested—political—derive their greatest significance from their relationship to the integration of society. Thus, some political symbols serve directly as integrating factors, while others appear to perform their functions by dividing the polity at one level of action, but by uniting it or some other system at another. Ceremonies and ritual of national holidays, for example, perform an immediate integrative function. The symbolism of partisanship, on the other hand, serves to divide the citizenry into opposing camps concerning the selection of leaders, but also to provide the latter with support for the implementation of their tasks.[3]

Political symbolism constitutes a discrete system, but it is not an isolated set of objects or meanings. Indeed, the symbolism of American politics is intimately related to other cultural objects of the society, and tends to be logically consistent with them and their meanings. We will attempt to illustrate this relationship throughout these pages.

SYMBOLISM AND THE AMERICAN POLITY

While American political life is rich in symbolic objects and meaning, it is rich in a different sense than are the symbolic systems of European polities, including the democracies. American symbolism, generally, reflects the unified, equalitarian, pragmatic, materialistic, religious, and idealistic value and normative beliefs associated with American social life. Likewise, its politics reflects these same meanings or orientations. That this is so is hardly unexpected in view of the special conditions of America's emergence into the world of nation-states. We are the product of deliberation, a revolution, isolation, a frontier, and, more important, a liberal ideology. As a consequence, our political symbolism tends to be simple, direct, and without complicated intellectual justification. Pomp and ceremony, while prominent in certain parts of our political life, are thus minimized as compared to European states with their monarchical backgrounds. It is significant, for example, that American elective officials do not generally wear special uniforms, but act in simple, civilian, business suits. Nor are class differentiations, particularly upper-class origins and affiliations, generally and deliberately reflected by American politicians, although the higher-ranking ones often do come from positions higher in the social structure than do their constituents. The point is that our officials reflect in their private as well as public life the same general value and normative orientations as do their constituents.

An interesting set of symbols of political relevance can also be found in the buildings and other physical objects of the government. In the first place, the power and authority of the polity is symbolized in almost every community and in the nation by governmental buildings and art objects. In most communities the largest and frequently the most ornate, if not artistically impressive, buildings are those of the government. The courthouse, city hall, and governor's mansion, not to speak of the number of structures in the nation's capitol city, are always prominent. And generally, these buildings have a special type of appearance, derived either from ancient Greek or baroque architecture. Yet, in many cases, if not all, both forms of architecture are quite incongruous with the American environment, although in the case of the Greek, not necessarily with the political ideals of the nation. What seems important is the attempt at attaining a symbol of grandeur to stand for the authority of government.

On a less imposing level are the countless art objects found in and around these buildings. Paintings, statues, and other mementos of the nation's past are found everywhere. The flag, of course, among the most obvious of these symbols, is placed on all public buildings. Likewise, many private enterprises, too, seem to feel some necessity for flying the flag above their properties.

But although there is a tradition of Greek architecture in the polity, there is also a tradition reflecting a less favorable view of politics and power. That tradition is represented by the run-down governmental buildings of many small towns and cities throughout the country. Post offices and courthouses are located in country stores, and countless state offices in business structures. Shabby and unkempt reminders of political authority are not uncommon; nor, in fact, are the Greek temple imitations always in good condition. This combination of Greek temples and shabby buildings symbolizes important political values, namely, our ambivalence toward power. We want political power to be honored, yet we also want to minimize the costs, both financial and psychological. The depreciation of government could not be better demonstrated than by the lack of attention we give many local governmental buildings. Conversely, the honor with which we treat certain aspects of government could not be better shown than by the wealth we have contributed to build Washington, D.C.[4]

Physical objects, however, are hardly the only elements of political symbolism. In the United States, as in all countries, we find a vast number of civic holidays, commemorations, festivals, parades, and all the events that accompany these patriotic occasions. And while in America most of these special days are signs for fun and frolic, all have highly serious aspects, as in the case of Memorial Day or, as it is now known, Veterans' Day. In all these events crucial moments of the nation's history, such as its birth, its war victories, and internal strife, are recognized and given meaning in the form of rituals. In turn, these rituals, stressing commonness, equality, and dedication to the past, present, and future, serve to integrate the members of the society. For a moment, at least, each individual becomes an American and not just another person. His life has been given meaning through the meanings which the events had and have in the history of the nation. Loyalty is reaffirmed by a tribute to those who have given the supreme sacrifice. Sacredness is the keynote. Yet, for most people, these same holidays are also days of sport and rest. Here is the affluent society that permits its members to view the world easily and confidently. Here is a society that permits its people even to ignore these essentially sacred rituals. Frivolity, solemnity, and patriotism, all are summed up in one day, in one set of events, just as the American tends to think of politics as both a game and the most serious of moral matters.

In all these symbols of the society and polity there is the sign of membership in a common community, of service to that community, of the power, the majesty, and the grandeur of the political system and its evolution. In all of these symbols are the practical actions of governing given artistic form. As Charles Merriam put it, in each of these symbols is "stressed the element of adoration in the psychology of power." [5] But it is more than that: symbols also give meaning to the citizen, and are not merely means of controlling his behavior.

But while buildings, emblems, music, art, heroes, and holidays are important elements of the symbolic complex, perhaps the most significant consists of the actions of the members of the polity, including both the officials and the citizens. The approach of the American to the exercise of power is one dominated by egalitarian norms in which the citizen does not demean himself before the public official. Nor does the latter conduct himself in a high-handed way. Political interaction is expected, and it is likely to be easy, free, and open, marked by gregariousness and a certain "game" aspect or atmosphere. Politicians, for example, are generally known by their first name or a nickname, although they are not so addressed in person except on the local levels where citizen and official may be friends. The language of politics itself also reflects these same norms; political discourse is colorful, and, while often partisan, it is seldom dogmatic in the sense of ideologies. The official language of government, on the other hand, is, as in the case of the judiciary and administrative agencies, highly formalized, legal, and dull. The structure and content of American political discourse also reflect the character of the process itself. Thus, political fights are generally fought in terms of a fairly common set of symbols, with the fight relating more often to means than to ends.

Soaring philosophical discourse is conspicuous by its absence. Although, to be sure, there is a set of symbols that refer to the generally agreed upon principles among Americans, and each side attempts to identify its programs with these principles as the only morally consistent and efficient way of doing things. The consensus of Americans, in short, unites all its symbolic system, Democrats and Republicans, alike, responding to the same symbols in essentially the same ways. *There are few sharply differentiated symbolic systems in American politics.* Even the few that do exist, as between the two major parties, are well within the more inclusive set uniting the people.

TYPES OF OFFICE AND SYMBOLISM

While the polity employs a wealth of symbols and symbolic activity, not all the offices constituting the government employ or function with the same set, nor do they have equal need for the symbolic presentation of their authority. And, certainly, all officials and politicians are not subject to the same searching inquiry concerning the meanings of their actions.

Of the three levels of government in the United States, the usage of symbols is clearly associated with the extent of power at each level. Thus, the national government and its actions are clothed in more formalized symbols and ceremony than are those on the local and state levels. From another point of view, symbolism seems to be directly related to the distance between the citizen and the office and official. That is, the greater the political as well as geographical distance, the greater the need and the greater the possibility of using symbols to suggest and justify authority. On the local level, the long-standing friendships and acquaintances with the members of the community really prevent a formalization of relations. It is much easier to call John F. Kennedy, "Mr. President," than it is to call one's lifetime friend in a small town, "Mr. Mayor." Indeed, it is more vital to the functioning of government that this be the case.

Then, too, the higher the level of government, the greater the power officials have to affect others. Apparently, the greater the power, the greater the need, as Merriam put it, for "garlands to cover the sadder aspects of the incidence of authority." [6] For this reason, a vast array of symbols tends to supplement the rational-legal system of authority by making it appear more beautiful and less dependent upon reason and logic.

Differentiation of symbolism also takes place along the functional division of offices as well as the geographical. For while certain symbols form the background for the entire polity, as pointed out above, others are

specialized to fit the needs of specific offices. The clearest case is that of
the judiciary, where may be found the most specialized and formalized set
of symbols and actions in the government. In the first instance, the court
is frequently an impressive appearing building with the historic symbols of
justice near its entry. The judges, wearing robes, are seated above and
in command of the proceedings. About them are flags, the gavel, law books,
and uniformed police officers. And the proceedings, themselves, are highly
formalized, with little left to chance. Above all, an impression is created
of objectivity, of fairness, of thoroughness, and of *finding* the law rather
than making it by arbitrary actions. The judge is treated with great formal
deference by all who participate in or witness the activities.

Legislatures also have their symbols and symbolic meanings, but they
are of a different nature than the judiciary. To be sure, legislatures too have
well-defined rules of procedure, but they may be and are treated instrumen-
tally for reasons of self-interest more openly than are those of the courts.
Indeed, the entire pattern of behavior on the floor of a legislature is quite
at variance with that of the judiciary. No one dominates the scene as a
judge; no one wears a uniform. The whole scene is one likely to create an
impression of great disorder. Few members, let alone spectators, know
with certainty what is taking place. And although hardly eliminated, formality is far less employed. Confusion and informality predominate as
members talk to one another, debate, walk about, and even sleep. The
scene may veer from one of great boredom to one of intense struggle and
bargaining. Courts, of course, are also the scene of a struggle, but of an
entirely different type. Here the tendency is to formalize the issue and
focus upon the position of a single actor, as in criminal cases, where someone is accused of violating a law and thereby opposing the state. The
legislature, on the other hand, represents not a struggle of one against the
state, but of diverse individuals and groups in society fighting to determine
the national policies. In a sense, the fight is more abstract than the court
battle, but no less intense. And all this takes place within a highly ornate
atmosphere, for the halls of legislatures are generally filled with objects
of historical meaning to the members and the citizen. Courts, on the other
hand, seem rather puritanical in their art work, which is perhaps in
accordance with the emphasis on dispassion and reason.

Executive offices and officials and action have still another set of symbols and meanings. In the case of the chief executive, the focus is not so
much upon the office, as in the case of the courts and legislatures, but
upon the individual who holds the office. Even while, in the end, his power
does rest on rational-legal grounds, the charismatic element is considerably
greater than that found in legislatures or the courts. Charisma has little

place in the courts for obvious reasons. Because legislatures are collectivities, it is almost impossible to create the conditions of charisma, for the fact of charisma is based not upon a group but upon an individual. The symbolism of a chief executive, such as the President, works to establish him as a leader as well as an official. Wherever he goes he becomes the focus of attention. His importance is symbolized by the provision of a mansion as his home and office. That we have had a tradition of equality and fear of executive power is partially suggested by the fact that some states have not even provided governors with executive mansions, although offices are provided in the capitol buildings. The chief executive, unlike other officials, receives far more deference and concern. He has police escorts, a flag, seal of office, higher salary, more aides, and help— all of which is appropriate, considering his duties and powers.

Administrative offices of the bureaucracy have still another symbolic setting. For the most part, administrators must work in offices that suggest efficiency, saving, work, and the humdrum of daily routine. Individual offices thus are not generally as attractive as those of either chief executives or legislators. Within the administrative hierarchy, symbols will differ, to be sure, depending upon position. But for the most part the impression is one of uniformity, categories, and orderliness as contrasted to the legislature. Likewise, there is not the solemnity of the court, nor the excitement of the executive office. Personality and individuality, as countless observers have noted, tend to be minimized. File cabinets, desks, and machines dominate the scene. Rational-legal authority rather than charisma and tradition is represented by these attributes and symbols.

These few observations on types of symbols attached or associated with different offices suggest an explanation for the distinctions. An important if not crucial aspect of all ruling is authority, or the basis on which power and commands are justified. The symbolic element of public office is intimately related to the type and extent of authority that predominates in that office. In the United States, all offices are based fundamentally upon rational-legal authority, but they do not rest solely upon that basis, nor is their operative ratio of types of authority the same. Administrative offices, based upon functional-specificity, affective-neutrality, universalism, and achievement norms, reflect these norms in the setting of their operation. Rationality and impersonality are hallmarks of the symbolic system. Consequently, the citizen who approaches an administrative building knows immediately that he is entering a different institution from that of a court, for example.

Executive offices, on the other hand, depend to a far greater extent on charisma than do the administrative, all of which is conveyed in the symbolic sets. Here the role of personality, of uniqueness, of identification, of warmth, of drama, is accentuated, unlike the administrative offices. Again, in Talcott Parsons' terms, affectivity, particularism, ascription, and diffuseness are emphasized, but not to the point where the rational-legal basis of the incumbent's authority is ignored or destroyed. Yet, while the latter is used by the executive to sustain actions, the charisma is also used to gain support for his policies and general handling of the office.

Judicial offices represent a quite different case and one that is not easily handled. For although dependence upon rational-legal authority is very great, it appears to be supported also by an appeal to emotions unlike the administrative offices. The appeal to emotions, however, is not charisma, but something closer to traditional authority. Certainly, the sometimes hallowed appearance of courts would lend support to this claim. Moreover, the ritualized proceedings, while based on rational-legal grounds, also present the feeling of tradition, especially to the layman. Dignity indeed has a premium in such surroundings. And while the courts do have a certain impersonality, it is more a product of tradition than of rational considerations of administrators.

This must be so, for the courts have the power to affect citizens as does no other governmental office. Life itself is often at stake. Such crucial decisions naturally demand the need for ritual and justification. Offices in which the range of discretion is narrower and of less significance have less need for ritualized proceedings, less need for complete acceptance of decisions; in other words, less need for authority. Citizens can be compelled to perform various actions with neither the official nor the citizen worrying unduly about justice. Consequently, elaborate "miranda" are less vital to effective implementation of decisions. The need for certainty is less compelling. And, as there is less need for "miranda," so there is less need for the elaborate justifications one finds in the decisions of courts.

SYMBOLISM OF PARTISANSHIP

Thus far the emphasis has been upon symbolization in the polity and in objects, and with specific types of offices. Yet offices are hardly the only roles in a democracy; another is that of the partisan. But if the place of symbolism in government has been slighted by scholars, the role of symbols in partisanship has been almost totally ignored. Yet, the partisan in his efforts to attain his goals engages in symbolic activities of a very important nature. The electoral process, for example—a focal point of partisanship— is a highly symbolic set of events, yet it is a facet of politics that no one has really explored for its symbolism.[7]

Let us begin by considering political parties, each of which has its own array of symbols, ranging from the verbal to the more purely artistic. In most cases these symbols are used quite consciously as devices to mobilize support. Moreover, the functions and environmental conditions of party action help to shape the kinds of symbols used. And, as might be expected, such symbols are combative in nature. A party is, after all, an organization interested in waging conflict, in defeating an opponent. This must be done, however, within a set of norms defining the limits of combat. The language of the partisan illustrates both of these requirements. Thus, there is usually a generous supply of combat words to please the traditional party worker, but also the more generalized symbols of being an American rather than a Democrat or Republican. While the symbols of extreme partisanship are used mostly at the conclaves of the party, the generalized American type come into use as the reference group (constituencies) of the party, particularly at election time, become more inclusive and heterogeneous.

A good illustration of the role of symbolism in parties may be seen in the functions played by conventions for the membership. The purpose of the convention is primarily one of selecting candidates and writing a platform. But these are hardly the only functions. Support must be generated, and this is accomplished by appeals to emotion as well as reason. E. Pendleton Herring recognized this when he wrote:

> The value of the convention lies in its permitting the rank and file of the party to participate physically and emotionally in a common enterprise. Here are the men who must carry the brunt of the campaign. Here they have a chance to meet, to shout together, to act together, to feel together. The excitement and turmoil of the convention fulfill a useful purpose. The relationship of the follower and leader is seldom an intellectual bond. A common bond of sympathy, a common symbol, is easily grasped and equally binding.[8]

Perhaps, we should add, more binding. In any case, Herring understood the role of emotion and symbolism in party politics.

As we noted earlier, the symbolism of partisanship has to be in accord with certain facts of American political life. As the major fact is that of a two-party system, each party thus finds it necessary to make an appeal to voters who are less than enthusiastic supporters. Consequently, if victory is to be attained in many constituencies, the vast number of independents or passive Republicans and Democrats who can switch allegiance must be appealed to by both parties. A symbolism reflecting this fact is apparent at each election. The candidates speak a common language and use many of the same themes, symbols, and national heroes. Both invoke the memory of Lincoln. Both use the same flag on their platforms; both revere the Constitution; both favor democracy, full employment, peace, and justice.

Once an election is over and the winner declared, tempers subside and the activity of governing begins. Before this can happen, however, certain highly symbolic events must take place over time, involving a great number of persons and groups. A candidate for office who was and is a *partisan* must now be clothed with the authority to rule others, including those who were and remain against him, a process both intricate and fascinating.

POLITICAL RITES OF PASSAGE [9]

Transitions from one role to another involve changes in a person's relationships with others. These changes include the creation of new relationships, the dropping of some with certain persons, and the addition of still others. By the very nature of the case, a crisis is created both for the person changing roles and the relevant others. Some sort of means is therefore required to assist this transformation if it is to be facilitated and accepted. In the case of the most serious role changes, such as those involving birth, death, marriage, and illness, the means include formalized events or rituals. In less crucial events, informal means are utilized. But in either case, certain "rites of passage"—to use the term of Arnold van Gennep—are developed from one role to the other.[10]

While the theory of "rites of passage" has not been applied often to political action, it would seem to be most useful in explaining certain phenomena. The theory is here applied to two political role changes: first, the transformation of a partisan into an authoritative public official; and secondly, the changes resulting from the death of public officials.

We noted in introducing this section that a partisan has to be given authority to rule and that this requires a change of role for the partisan and concomitant changes in the attitudes of the voters and others in the polity. Van Gennep contended that there are three stages in the rites of passage: first, separation; secondly, transition; and thirdly, incorporation. Without attempting a rigid application of these three stages, we will describe and account for the passage of a person from a purely partisan role to one of official authority.

In the first place, once an election is over and a victor declared, the rites are under way, but in a more or less informal manner. The candidate who loses usually concedes his defeat before the official count is over.

The rites have it that he should do this gracefully and at his own discretion. The victor does not initiate the event and, above all, he does not gloat publicly over his victory. Rather, he asks the loser for his support, although not always. The defeated, who usually refrains from blaming anyone for the defeat, then pledges his support to the country and the victor. The winning candidate thanks the loser, and may even suggest that his service to the nation is not over. The victor pledges his time, energies, and resources to the public interest. Always this is done with the greatest humility and with profound gratification for the trust shown in the man. He asks for continued support and invokes the aid of God. All this usually takes place within a matter of hours after an election, and even while informal, it does aid in the transformation of a partisan into a public official. Both the victor and defeated realize the change, and begin immediately to become accustomed to it.

The separation from fellow partisans begins when the newly-elected person must interact more frequently with the opposition and sometimes less frequently with his own party organization. The transition stage arrives when the politician has taken his oath of office, and is officially recognized as entitled to the powers of office. Let us consider this second stage at greater length.

In the higher-ranking offices the incumbent may be required to live a totally different style of life. Everything becomes public and subject to the norms of the public. Indeed, the incumbent's powers, responsibilities, and rewards are much greater than they were in private life. Because he is now accorded greater powers and responsibility, and because he so recently participated in a partisan election, it becomes imperative that some form of ritual be performed symbolizing to the populace that he is now entitled to the powers and emoluments of office. Likewise, it is desirable to inform the newly-elected official—in dramatic terms—that he is no longer just a partisan, but an official of all the people and held responsible for the public interest.[11] This ritual is the Inaugural Ceremony.

An inaugural is an investiture of power, duty, and privilege. It is a public event, reaching its most dramatic point when the official swears upon a Bible and repeats an oath of office. In the case of a President, for example, the oath is prescribed by the Constitution. Note what is sworn to:

> I do solemnly swear (or affirm) that I will faithfully execute the office of the President of the United States, and will, to the best of my ability, preserve, protect, and defend the Constitution of the United States (Article II, Sec. 1).

The oath is repeated by the President-elect, after the Chief Justice who reads it; it should be emphasized that the latter is generally thought of as essentially nonpartisan, of great dignity and responsibility.

After taking the oath, the President delivers a speech, the Inaugural Address, which reassures all that he is aware of what he has done and that he is prepared to represent all, equally. Research on inaugural speeches has shown that they are highly formalized and similar in content and symbols, regardless of the date, the man, or his party affiliation.[12] In all we find the symbols of unity being stressed, of dedication and tributes paid the people, the system of government, and "The American Way."

It is interesting to note that the entire ceremony is conducted in the presence of the outgoing President. In fact, he not only accompanies the newly-elected Chief Executive from the White House to the Capitol for the Inauguration, but also occupies a prominent seat on the platform. Symbolically, then, the nation and the out-going President are members of the same system, and are not going to conduct themselves in such a way as to flout the election results. Personal animosity may exist between the two opponents, but nothing in the ceremony is expected to show these differences. Another integrative aspect of the rites should be noted: men of God play their customary roles in giving the invocation and benediction. Thus, while state and church are separated in the United States, religion is accorded an important symbolic place in political events.

Presidents are not the only officials to experience the drama of "rites of passage." We have the words of one former Congressman, Jerry Voorhis, on the personal effects of such rites:

> I shall never forget Tuesday, January 5, 1937. It was the opening day of the Seventy-fifth Congress. Some of the events of the day are now blurred in memory but I can still feel my arm rising above my head and recall the members of the House repeating together these words: "I do solemnly swear that I will support and defend the Constitution of the United States against all enemies, foreign and domestic, that I will bear true faith and allegiance to the same, that I take this obligation freely and without mental reservation or purpose of evasion and that I will well and faithfully discharge the duties of the office on which I am about to enter. So help me God." [13]

Lest we think that the rites of passage are significant only at the assumption of public office, we can again gain insight from Voorhis. Leaving office, especially as a result of electoral defeat, and particularly in the case of the higher-ranking positions, poses problems for all concerned, especially for the defeated. The powers and perquisites of office must be surrendered to the victor. There are no "rites of passage" for the defeated, alone. His position, in the case of offices such as governor and the Presidency, is subordinated to that of the victor. But his presence at the inaugural ceremony is, of course, designed to indicate to the incumbent and the public that he has given up his office gracefully and peacefully. He neither rises and condemns his erstwhile opponent, nor does he reflect upon the capacities of the voters and their decision. Rather, after the election, the out-going official rationalizes his defeat. Voorhis, for example, after his defeat by Richard Nixon in 1946, had this to say:

> . . . I have given the best years of my life to serving this District in Congress. By the will of the people that work is ended. I have no regrets about the record I have written.
> I know the principles I have stood for and the measures I have fought for are right. I know, too, that, in broad outline at least, they are vital to the future safety and welfare of our country. I know the day will come when a lot more people will recognize this than was the case on November fifth.[14]

In his autobiography, Voorhis continued to rationalize by saying, "It was some satisfaction to have had the right people against me." [15] But he wrote Nixon that, "I will be glad to be of any help that you believe I can render." [16]

Unfortunately, for the defeated who are to resume private life, the nation does not express its gratitude in formalized ceremonies. Most of the burden falls on the defeated to adjust as best he can. All attention is accorded the newly-elected. And, complicating the problem for the defeated is the feeling, as Senator Charles McNary put it, explaining why defeated Congressmen seldom go home, that "as he [the Congressman] walks down the street . . . he thinks each person he passes is one of the votes that beat him." [17] Interestingly, in the case of Massachusetts' governors, a return to private life is rather strikingly symbolized by the fact that the retiring or defeated governor traditionally walks out into the crowd of people on Boston Commons after the swearing-in of the new man.

But while the focus of attention does usually rest upon the incoming official, there is one set of circumstances in which the focus is upon the man whose place he is taking; namely, when a particularly beloved official dies in office. The importance of the event increases, of course, when the office is an important one, or when death occurs during periods of crisis. We are not here concerned with psychological functions except insofar as they affect the role or sociological dimensions. It is significant, however, that the funeral services provide a means by which death can be handled for those who go on living. When a powerful and beloved President such as Franklin Delano Roosevelt dies during a war, the normal relationships of countless individuals are, as Sebastian de Grazia has shown, profoundly disturbed.[18] Descriptions of the death and rites of passage for Lincoln, at least as offered by Carl Sandburg,[19] convey some of the enormity of the loss suffered by the people. Indeed, the special type of services accorded to high-ranking public officials is ample testimony to the significance that society attaches to their service for the nation. This importance is further confirmed by the use of monuments and the marking of graves of distinguished citizens. In some instances, they become national shrines with the function of perpetuating great ideals of service, patriotism, and devotion.

RITES OF CITIZENSHIP

The significance of initiation rites in primitive societies has long been understood and described by ethnographers and anthropologists. To a lesser extent we also know something about such rites in private associations of Western nations. But a strange omission in the study of American society, and even of western European countries, is that concerning initiation into citizenship. If we accept the great importance attached to national and state loyalties—as we must in the twentieth century—the failure to study processes of citizenship is indeed paradoxical. Paradoxes, however, do have explanations.

Citizenship in the United States is prized, no doubt, not only by those who have it, but by many who hope and aspire for such status. Yet, it is interesting to note that with the single exception of the naturalized citizen, the United States does *not* ordinarily conduct ritualized initiation ceremonies for those who assume the duties of adult citizenship. Countless millions of Americans who become voters at the age of twenty-one years do so without any sort of formalized experience to inform them of their new status as adult citizens. Few Americans, in fact, even think about citizenship on that birthday; perhaps the closest they may come to such thoughts has to do with their being legally able to buy and drink intoxicating liquors. For most Americans, then, membership in the polity is something to be taken for granted. The only occasion on which it might not be so taken would be during wars and formal civic holidays when speeches on Americanism are typically delivered by public officials.

While the native-born citizen has no commemorative occasion to mark formally his induction into the American polity, those who voluntarily assume citizenship as immigrants do experience formalized rites even if they are not the most colorful and impressive. Indeed, naturalized citizens go through a fairly lengthy process, formally learning the new role in which they are taught something about the history of the country, their rights and duties as citizens, and the structure of the government. In addition, they take part in rites, which may be more or less formalized and intricate. The accompanying program [20] is an infrequent example of a general commemoration of citizenship. It is of interest because of the explicit use of many types of symbols that we have been discussing.

PROGRAM IN A HIGH SCHOOL AUDITORIUM

FOURTH ANNUAL I AM AN AMERICAN DAY IN HONOR OF OUR SONS AND DAUGHTERS WHO, HAVING ATTAINED THE AGE OF 21, AND ALL NEW CITIZENS WHO, HAVING BEEN NATURALIZED THIS YEAR, ARE NOW, ON THIS SOLEMN OCCASION, BEING INDUCTED INTO THE ELECTORATE OF THE STATE.

(Sponsored by Forty-Nine Organizations)

Presiding Officer .... Clerk of Courts
Music .... High School Orchestra
Advance of the Colors .... Four Veterans' Organizations
Invocation .... A Priest
Pledge of Allegiance .... Audience
The Star-Spangled Banner .... Audience
Marching On .... High School Choral Club
The Challenge of Citizenship .... A Judge
Acceptance of the Challenge:
    For the 21-Year-Olds
    For the Naturalized Citizens
Prayer of Citizenship .... A Rabbi
Violin Solo
Ode to America .... High School Choral Club
Presentation of Citizenship Awards .... The Mayor
God Bless America .... Audience
Retirement of the Colors
Benediction .... A Minister

Here is a formal attempt to enhance assumption of the adult citizen role. Thus, in the program or rite used as an illustration, the citizen is informed of the "challenge of citizenship" and noteworthily, by a judge, a symbol of the highly legal aspect of American citizenship. Presumably, the judge speaks of the responsibilities of the newly naturalized. Further, action of induction is recognized by the entire community through the sponsorship of "forty-nine organizations," private rather than governmental. The community also participates in and demonstrates its solidarity by the inclusion of religious figures and activities. A priest delivers the invocation, a rabbi offers a prayer of citizenship, and a minister gives the benediction. In addition, education is represented or symbolized by the use of the school auditorium, and by the participation of the high school orchestra and choral club. The government is symbolized by the presence of the Clerk of Courts who presides, the mayor, and the judge. Note that it is the mayor who presents the citizenship awards. Of great significance, too, are the representatives of four veterans groups, symbolizing dedication and sacrifice during times of national peril.

Nor are the participants themselves the only important element in the rites: various national symbols are also prominent, including the flag and music. The flag is in the charge of the veterans' organizations, while the music is participated in by the entire audience as well as the new citizens and officials. The songs—"The Star-Spangled Banner," "Ode to America," and "God Bless America"—are national and integrative. The words need no elaboration from us.

A focal point of the ceremony is, of course, the Pledge of Allegiance to the nation where everyone in the audience publicly dedicates himself and pledges his loyalty.

But although the rites of citizenship in this country are no doubt meaningful to those who immediately participate, few people, generally, do participate. "Swearing-in" ceremonies are usually attended only by the handful of newly created citizens, their closest family, and a few public officials. Generally, too, citizenship ceremonies are conducted in rather unimpressive municipal buildings such as courts or city halls. There is little if any pageantry or color. And, the ceremonies are concluded in a very short period of time. On occasion, various civic groups, patriotic societies, and the Immigration and Naturalization Service do attempt to create greater interest in such rites and to make them more impressive, but seldom are they successful. One result of such pressures was a Joint Resolution of Congress and a proclamation by President Roosevelt, in 1940, of "I am an American Citizen Day" for the recognition, observance, and commemoration of American citizenship. The day was to be the third Sunday of May in each year. The Proclamation encouraged civil and educational authorities of states, counties, cities, and towns to make plans for its implementation. Relatively few cities and towns, however, have seen fit to follow the President's lead or suggestion.

The symbolism of citizenship is consistent with the symbolism of much of American political life. It is simple, unostentatious, and in accord with the belief that membership in political systems is mostly a legal status. Furthermore, citizenship is regarded as something that can be learned by memorizing legal facts about our government and history and by passing an examination. It does not appear to be something extraordinary, requiring highly ritualized expression. Only occasionally are such rites used and seldom for the native-born who come of age. In short, we tend to take citizenship for granted.

Part Four

Political Processes

INTEGRATION AND
TENSION-MANAGEMENT

MUCH of political science deals with politics as though it were little more than conflict. Indeed, politics is often regarded simply as a struggle over scarce values, or, in the terms of one of America's great political scientists, Harold Lasswell, "politics; who gets what, when, how." The sources of division or disagreement, the waging of conflict, and the outcomes of this struggle are the focal points of such study. Little is said with regard to consensus, or the basis of agreements, or to the means by which a society such as the American handles tension and conflict so that the system maintains relative peace and stability. Little is said pertaining to the integrative elements and processes of American political life. To concentrate upon the allocation of values and the struggles of politics, however, is to have a one-sided picture of our politics.

In this Part Four entitled, "Political Processes: Integration and Tension-Management," we will be primarily concerned with looking at the structures and processes that serve to integrate and maintain our political system and society, thereby providing a basis within which conflict can be waged. We are additionally concerned with these matters because we wish to understand the allocative processes in which conflict predominates. Thus, while Part Four now stands alone, it will later serve as a foundation for getting at the allocation problems to be analyzed in Part Six.

If we assume that integration and tension-management are problems to be faced by all social systems, it is incumbent that we describe and explain how such problems are met. Many political scientists tend to assume a high level of integration and stability in our political system with the result that they concentrate their attentions on the allocative processes. No society, however, may be assumed to be perfectly integrated or cohesive. Disintegrative elements and activities are always at work. The extent to which a society is cohesive is dependent consequently on the balance or ratio of the integrative and disintegrative forces.

As sociologists have been most diligent in studying the means utilized and developed by social systems for the maintenance of order, we shall draw heavily upon their work in explaining our own situation. Generally, it is held that the major, although not the sole, means of order is accomplished through various processes of *social control* and *socialization*. The latter process is simply one of educating—in the broadest sense—the members of a society in the values, norms, information, and skills considered desirable and useful in that society. The emphasis is on the training or preparing of individuals and their personalities to be effective and contributing members of the society. Social control, on the other hand, is a process aimed not so much at the forming of personalities, but at controlling overt behavior along acceptable lines. External controls consisting of rewards and particularly penalties are thus developed to discipline people. Indeed, there is a sort of inverse relationship between the use of these two processes in the sense that the more a society uses one, the less reliance need be placed upon the other. If a society is effective in socializing its members, there is less need to depend upon external social controls. But in no society has there been an absence of control. Put another way, as no society ever fully succeeds in socializing its citizens, resort to controls is imperative. Those who will not or cannot accept the dominant and approved ways of doing things must be disciplined, first to prevent deviance, and secondly to punish those who deviate.

We will not study all forms of control, but only those that are either purely political or have political relevance. Likewise, we will not investigate socialization in its entirety, but only those aspects that have most immediately to do with political activity. The analysis will begin then with political socialization—the more basic of the means for the maintenance of values and norms as well as for controlling the amount of intrapersonal tensions that enter the polity. Then, we will turn our attention to the external controls employed by the political system to integrate members of society. The former process operates primarily on the personality level where political values, norms, and motivations are internalized from the political culture. Control and integration, on the other hand, have largely to do with the external restraints and commands used by the polity to coordinate the members of society. Socialization, in short, attempts to train people to want to do what the system requires, while control forces people to do what the system requires. The last chapter of Part Four, Chapter 9, will consider a number of supplementary processes used by the American polity to implement socialization and control. Some of these processes include smaller numbers of people than the major ones. Government officials, for example, engage in a variety of cooperative endeavors to overcome the decentralized power of our formal government. The fact that these ways are labeled "supplementary" must not be construed, however, to mean that they are of less importance.

7

The Socialization of Citizens

Children are not born democratic nor American; they must be taught the tenets of both throughout their lives. Indeed, if Hobbes and Freud were correct, children are born with egotistical and aggressive drives that require either reduction or redirection and adaptation if society and government are to be realized. And as the demands of democracy are high, the moulding of these assumed hostile natures into effective citizens cannot be an easy one. As Reinhold Niebuhr put the matter, "Man's capacity for justice makes democracy possible; but man's inclination to injustice makes democracy necessary." [1] Thus, the task of making or converting man's "capacity for justice" into concrete motivations and behavior sustaining democratic rule is a major task of the socialization process.

The concept "socialization," an old one in sociology,[2] is of very recent vintage in political science.[3] The notions conveyed by the term, however, are as ancient as Greek philosophy. Indeed, both Plato and Aristotle were greatly concerned over the training or educating of youth so as to preserve the social and political systems of which they sought and defended. The phenomenon of political socialization, then, is an ancient one, but one that has not been adequately studied in contemporary social science.

Socialization, in short, has to do with the civilizing of the members of society. From the political scientist's point of view, the important aspect concerns the creation of citizens by instilling them with the desired ideals and practices of citizenship. Most often, the socialization process is thought of with relation to the young, for it is they who have so much to learn. Yet all members of society are in the process of learning all their lives. One way of getting at the socialization of citizens is to ask a series of logically related questions, which might read as follows:

What is taught?
To whom?
By whom?
How?
Under what conditions?
With what consequences?

When we have acquired answers to this set of queries, we will have characterized the socialization process.

Before we begin our analysis of political socialization in the United States, it might be wise to identify its functions or contributions to the maintenance of our society and polity. And while it is difficult to specify in exact terms just how significant socialization is, it is relatively easy to state that socialization must not be underestimated as an integrative and tension-management process.[4] In terms of our analytical scheme, political socialization has much to do with shaping the *inputs* of demands, expectations, resources, and support that enter the polity. In like fashion, socialization has a vital impact on the *processes* by which these inputs are converted into *outputs* of power and decisions.

In teaching the young for citizenship we are, in effect, providing them with political motivation, notions of participation, and conceptions of their own role and others' in the political process. In short, we are preparing Americans for democratic citizenship as that ideal is understood in our culture.

Our analysis begins with some observations on the content of political socialization, or, in terms of the above question, "what is taught?"

WHAT IS TAUGHT?

The simple answer to the question posed in the title of this section is *citizenship*. But, correct as that may be, it is really not very informative. What we need is an elaboration of what goes into citizenship in the United States as contrasted to other societies.

Citizenship is first of all *membership,* meaning a set of actions and a state of mind. In the United States, we teach our people this state of mind, plus a set of appropriate behaviors or actions. They learn how to perform the various roles that constitute the polity and what to expect from others in different roles. On breaking down this state of mind and set of activities into its component parts, we note that the following types of things are taught as citizenship: political motivation; political values; political norms or roles; and political information. Let us discuss these elements of socialization in the order just stated.

Political Motivation

No social system can function successfully unless its members are motivated to perform the various roles that constitute the system. It is possible, of course, as we shall see in the following chapter, for a society and polity to coerce its members into action or obedience. But in the long run this is generally thought to be an ineffective and inefficient means of running the society. And in the case of democracies, coercion is expected to be, and is, minimized, for it is rightly considered to be morally inconsistent with the ethical foundation of the system. Democracies, therefore, devote considerable effort to inculcating the proper motivations into citizens so that they will voluntarily perform their functions and roles. Motivation, thus, is really a kind of "motive" force spurring citizens to action. We are not born with political motivation, but acquire it perhaps at great expense to both the individual and society.

It should be noted that we are interested in what motives are *taught* and not, for the moment, what motives actually govern Americans. Between the two, there may be some startling discrepancies. At this time, however, we are concerned with what is the approved pattern of motivation.

Perhaps the most persistently taught motive is that of active, dutiful participation in the polity. Americans of all ages are exhorted to take politics seriously, consistently, and "to do something about it." Thus, while the citizen is not generally taught to admire and aspire to holding public office, he is taught to make his influence felt in the forms of informing himself about the government, the issues, the candidates, and, above all, to *vote* regularly.

There is also a tendency to stress *nonpartisan* or public-interested participation rather than party membership and action. The sustaining motive behind all these forms or modes of participation is that of serving the public interest *as a duty,* rather than the self-interest of the citizen. No citizen is expected—in public, at least—to be motivated by self-concerns. More importantly, those who hold public office, or are candidates for such, must at all times contend that their motives are not selfish. The admission that one enjoys politics, likes its attention and prestige, or savors the exercise of power is strictly inadmissible and unacceptable. Self-interest has little legitimacy in American politics. Whereas in fact, self-interest aids the system to function, no one is supposed to recognize this except candidates who may accuse their opponent of being so motivated. That politicians do make such charges and that they are meaningful strongly suggests the negative role (disapproved norm) of self-interest in American politics.

The object of political self-interest is power—or the capacity to shape system goals and the means for their attainment. Power, therefore, is both an end and a means for implementing interests. As we noted in Chapter 5, however, Americans tend to hold liberal ideas as to power and its exercise. With respect to motivation, then, it becomes clear that power, its acquisition, and exercise are not highly regarded within the American polity. Citizens are not supposed to value power, and, if they do, it must be concealed. Nor is dominance, in the political sense, encouraged by institutions such as the schools and churches. In some ways economic socialization does honor such competition and dominance, but the polity itself does not. To strive for public office and power is, indeed, a somewhat suspect activity. Americans seem to be more conscious of the deprivations that political power may cause than of the advantages, seeing little good for society in the exercise of power. Curiously enough, certain other forms of power, such as physical strength, aggression in sports, and business power, are often highly admired and encouraged among the young as worthy of emulation.

Americans, it may also be added, seldom impress other people as being retiring, shy, pacifist, or self-effacing. In our international relationships we not infrequently wish to "show other nations that we mean business." Likewise, our domestic politics are marked by considerable verbal violence in contrast to the sophisticated, often erudite, and witty language of English and French politics. Thus, while aggressiveness is encouraged, at least verbally, it is not so much "power oriented" as it is justified on behalf of one's "rights." [5]

Consequently, only manifest or conscious motives for action are appreciated, and they must be of the approved type just described. We thus find it difficult to admit that our political heroes, at least, have been motivated by anything but noble motives or reasons. Unconscious striving for self-esteem, prestige, power, or income simply cannot be conceded. We find it difficult to conceive of Lincoln as neurotic, that he suffered from melancholy and had unusual dreams of personal grandeur. Sublimation of disappointment or compensation for some physical handicap may be admissible, as in the case of Franklin D. Roosevelt. But beyond that, we treat our Presidents in terms of their conscious goals and philosophies. Moreover, we hope to inculcate the motives of the young with the same admirable goals and philosophies.

It should be noted, once more, that these inculcated character traits can be directly related to the normative structure of the polity. Roles, in short, can be viewed both as to social function and as to personal motivation.

Political Values

No society is without a set of ideals or "things" valued. Certain objects, states of being, and actions are considered as more worthy to acquire, contemplate, and do than are other objects, states of being, and actions. In the United States, for example, high values are placed upon success, achievement, activity, work, efficiency, practicality, progress, material comfort, science, and, the individual.[6] Other societies, however, including both the advanced and pre-industrial, frequently place high value upon the very opposites of the American values. Efficiency, for example, is most highly esteemed in industrialized societies, while it is hardly ever heard of in the primitive and preindustrial communities. In India, mysticism is probably still more highly valued among many people than is science. There is, then, a relativity among societal values.

If we inquire into the values held by a society, we will discover that some of these values relate to the area of life we have designated as political. Political values are those having to do with the goals that the society collectively seeks and the means whereby they are sought. Accordingly, political values will be stated in terms of power and authority relationships among citizens and officials or governments, and in terms of goals that the society, as a society, would like to see achieved.

Before we begin our analysis of the specific political values of Americans, it should be noted that when we speak of American political values we mean those values that are most widely held (numbers of citizens), most intensely held, and those that have had the longest duration. To be sure, we have no very precise measures of these indicators, but qualitative analysis and the testimony of many observers of American life, both foreign and native, should prove ample.

It should also be stated at the outset that we look for evidences of values in the formal documents of American history, in the speeches of prominent or prestigious leaders, in the mass media of communication, in the daily behavior of citizens, and in the ideals preached in the classrooms. It must also be understood that we are looking for values or ideals, not at the actual behavior, between which there may indeed be a disparity. The man who preaches equality, for example, may not practice it in daily affairs. But to return: what are the dominant political values of the American people? [7]

Little acquaintance with Americans is required to detect a preference for, or high value being placed upon, *formal individual freedom*—perhaps the most frequently mentioned word in political discourse. The frequent occurrence of the word itself, however, does not inform us as to its meaning for Americans. Generally, they cannot give an explicit definition of what they mean. But it is possible by observing daily situations to infer what it is that freedom connotes to Americans.

To the average American, freedom generally means "freedom from formal restraints" rather than freedom to do certain things. Much of our history has been a series of attempts by various individuals and groups to remove certain barriers hindering their success or whatever else they may seek. Indeed, we sought freedom *from* Great Britain at the very outset. Just so, we devised a government subject to the restraints of a Bill of Rights that protects the individual *from* the government. Seldom do we speak of freedom *for* something.

Just as important in this conception of freedom is the desire of Americans to be rid of arbitrary restraint imposed by visible, concrete structures or identifiable persons. Americans complain less about the "free forces of the marketplace" in determining their places in life than about a specific monopoly. Nor do we as frequently complain of informal pressures. It is for this reason that we express more fear of the government than of nature, the presumably free forces of the economic system, or the informal, often unconscious, pressures of community life. For whereas a government is made up of visible persons issuing arbitrary edicts, nature operates through abstract forces, and the free enterprise system is thought to function through the freely determined decisions of individuals. In short, the American conception of freedom is not mystical, but very concrete and behavioral. If someone orders you to do something, it is a restriction on your freedom. It is for this reason that organizations such as the governmental and the military, who issue orders continuously, are viewed with suspicion and hostility. Many farmers, for example, consider nature and the marketplace to be less restricting than the government agricultural programs. In terms of objective consequences this may not be the case, but the American farmer often seems to think it is.

The converse of the freedom theme is that any restraint on freedom be justifiable. That is, the person or official doing the restraining must justify his actions in terms acceptable to the citizen's concept of freedom. The exercise of power, therefore, must be made authoritative. And, as we have seen, this means rational-legal authority. The official has a right to exercise power because he has been legally elected to an office and constitutionally provided with powers to act in restraining ways if need be.

We may not like the particular law being administered, the person administering it, nor its consequences, but we learn to accept his right to order others. Restraints upon freedom are acceptable, but they must be justified.

Although freedom, generally, is highly valued, it is political freedom that is the most vociferously defended and advocated. By political freedom is meant the formal or legal rights to select our officials and criticise and remove them if need be. The relationship of governor and governed, in other words, is the focal point of tension. We might even say that these freedoms are and have been considered so crucial that we have institutionalized them in the Constitution and laws of the nation. They have been formalized in the expectation that formalization will ensure recognition and protection.

Yet freedom, itself, is hardly the only value sought by Americans. Another and, according to at least one prominent foreign observer, the most manifest value is that of *equality*.[8] For our limited purposes, the question of priority is unimportant; what is crucial is that equality is demanded and expected. Put in the most simple terms, the demand for equality has historically meant the right to be treated as an equal, particularly in political affairs. And to some degree this demand has been realized; all qualified voters, for example, are given one vote each, regardless of their other characteristics and capacities. As voters, even though quite unmatched in all other regards, they are regarded as equals. Consequently, every minority group has sought equality, in the legal and political sense as well as in other social senses. And, frequently, the former has been a means to the latter.

Equality, then, has meant equal consideration in making demands upon the polity and equal sharing of the responsibilities in the forms of providing resources and support. To be sure, strict mathematic equality has not been achieved, and has been therefore a prime source of political conflict. Nor do all Americans prefer a state of equality, for the simple reason that they either feel themselves to be superior or to possess material means that they do not want to share. Generally, in the allocation of values and costs, it is the lower-status citizens who wish to have a greater share of the values, while the higher-status groups want greater equality in the distribution of costs. But while everyone is for some form of redistribution of values and costs so as to realize his self-interest, few people are for a radical or absolute equality. We most honor its demand in those spheres where we are obviously being treated as less than equal; we attempt to deemphasize its value in those areas where we have more than an equal share.

A persistent theme in the literature of political science and political discourse, generally, has been that of *responsibility*. In the case of Americans, the quest has been for political responsibility, that is, for governmental actions that are defensible in terms of our other political values. This has meant that we demand, or perhaps expect, that governmental decisions or policies be made with an objective of furthering our values of liberty and equality. Public officials and other politicians are expected to defend their courses of action in terms of their contribution to the furtherance of these values. This is regarded as responsible behavior.

But there is one other element in the ideal of responsible political behavior: that concerns the consistency of the actions with the norms of our society and political system. In this case, the chief norm or set of norms is that of the Constitution and the laws of long-standing regarding the powers and duties of public officials. Every action is expected to be defensible in light of the basic norms of the Constitution, which, then, is the major normative reference point. Indeed, much energy and intellectual skill have gone into interpreting the document and applying it to the daily actions of citizens and officials. The Supreme Court, of course, has become a specialized agency in this task.

Yet, while Americans demand responsibility in the above sense of the word, they have not seemed to demand responsible action on the part of our political parties. It is commonplace for students of politics to remark on the almost total lack of responsibility of the parties to implement their promises of campaign time. Few Americans, however, would like to see the party system altered. But whether changes are wanted or not, the value of responsibility is high as it applies to public officials.

Another value conspicuous for the frequency of reference and demand is that of *efficiency* in government. Few if any citizens demand inefficiency. Certainly, the preference for efficiency is understandable given the materialistic, empirical, practical approach of Americans to life and their addiction to economic values. It is because efficiency is regarded as a necessity in economic activities and the source of profit that we often feel that it ought also to be a political value and norm. Generally, however, Americans tend to think of the government as being inefficient. And, as a result, a long tradition of reform has been dedicated to the attainment of capable operations. The early Progressive Movement, for example, sought as goals efficiency and low costs. Within the administrative management movement, one also finds a dedication to efficiency as an end in some cases, but always as a norm to be applied.[9] Proposals are constantly offered from editors' desks, legislators' proposals, and executive requests for increased competence of operation—a demand that is both a continuous and strongly advocated value among many Americans.

Efficiency, however, is not always consistent with the other political values. But consistency, of course, seldom disturbs many of us where values are concerned. Thus, we seem to want liberty, equality, responsibility, and efficiency at one and the same time even though logical analysis and experience indicate that all may not be possible or that one might entail measures that diminish the probability of attaining or maintaining the others. Efficiency, for example, may reduce the amount of freedom each of us has or, conversely, the extension of liberty may reduce efficiency. But whatever the relationships involved on the logical level, we do—as a people—value all these objectives.

Partisan Values

The rather abstract, although meaningful, values we have been discussing are those taught by all the agents of political socialization and which command widespread and deep respect among the American people. Yet, they are hardly the only values taught; we are also instructed in the values of political preferences or partisanship, in the sense of political parties. *We learn, in other words, to be Republicans or Democrats.* And each of the agencies of socialization has something to do with these identifications, and their reinforcement. To be sure, some of the agencies are more involved in this than others, but all participate in some manner in different ways and in different directions, with somewhat different results. In short, no agent of socialization can be neutral in the matter of party affiliation, although some try and others pretend to do so. The schools and the churches are usually among the latter category. On this, we shall have more to say.

One learns not only to be a Republican or a Democrat, but also to prefer certain approaches to the operation of government, to prefer conservative or liberal public policies. A citizen's views of government's responsibilities, its role in public welfare, the level of its expenditures and taxes, and its regulation of business, agriculture, and labor—all are matters of preference that must be learned. They are not biologically inherited And while they may be influenced profoundly by self-interest, self-interest is not something that registers itself automatically upon the mind. It has to be perceived, even if falsely.[10] We learn our party preferences and policies, in short, through experience and the conscious teaching and appealing of others. To this end, every agent of socialization participates and, in some cases, competes, as is the case with the parties and interest groups. Obviously, the agent who gets to the child first—the family and the father, in particular [11]—has the greatest advantage. Because of the family, as most voting studies confirm,[12] most of us become "little Republicans" or "little Democrats" at a very tender age. We have no awareness of why or how, of course, except that Dad always says nice things about one of the parties and not the other, or at least not as often. Consequently, every primary school teacher can predict party preferences of the parents of her students with considerable accuracy by the simple test of identifying the preferences of the children. Unlike their parents, the latter normally suffer no inhibitions about the public expression of preferences.

Political Norms

Earlier chapters have indicated the crucial importance of rules or norms of behavior in every society including the American. What we want to do, now, is to delineate some of the more politically relevant and significant political norms of Americans. Before doing so, however, it will be necessary to enter a note about two highly important distinctions regarding the norms we analyze; the distinctions pertain to the sources of the norms and to their functional primacy. With respect to the sources of the norms, we must distinguish between those norms which are learned and have first application in the primary groups and private associations, and those which specify behavior in the nation-state. The norms of behavior that apply to the family, the neighborhood gang, the peer-group at school, the trade union, the corporation, and other associations may not be the same as the norms that apply in an adult's role as a citizen. Whether they do or not is, of course, an empirical matter; for the moment, we simply call attention to the distinction. Another distinction pertains to the functional consequences of these various sets of norms. For while all norms have consequences for both the allocative and integrative processes in a society, individual and certain other types of norms may have greater significance for one of these processes than the other. Thus, while the norms of "fair play" have their greatest consequences for the allocation of values, norms of loyalty are most relevant to the integrative problems of society or its solidarity.

Let us start at the beginning of the norm-learning process, in the primary groups and secondary associations. It is in the family and at school among the peer-groups that children learn their first norms of behavior, or what is considered proper and wrong.[13] They learn the rules by which values and costs are distributed, and the norms of loyalty to the group. In other words, the child at this time has his first experience as a "citizen" in a group, learning his roles, and learning about loyalty, conflict, leadership, power, and authority. He is participating, in fact, in a small-scale social system with a polity, an informal one to be sure, but a polity nevertheless. And, if Freud is correct as to the enormous importance of childhood to later adult behavior, we must attach considerable meaning to these early experiences as a "citizen" for later adult citizenship. But what, in the sense of political norms of behavior, is learned at this stage?

One of the first norms taught to every child, whether he learns them or not, specifies that he control his *demands* upon others, that is, that he not be selfish. The norm of self-discipline, of course, is a rather diffuse and generalized one, and not always easy to define. Indeed, most of the parent's problems stem from trying to get the child to be less self-oriented, urging him to think of others before making demands or holding expectations of them. The parent usually tries, then, to control the demands made by the child, just as does every other group with which the child becomes affiliated. The interests of the group, or the public interest, is thus experienced and learned.

Along with learning the need for self-discipline, the child is subjected to norms relating to the *allocation of resources* within the group. He learns that he is expected to contribute his time, energy, and whatever other resources children can produce to keep the group functioning. This may mean providing sports equipment, marbles, a play-space, and the like for the other children. In older groups it may mean holding office or doing any of the numerous tasks that all clubs require in order to survive. The type and quantities of resources are matters for each group or organization, but all require some kind, and each member must learn what they are as well as the expectations of others regarding resources.

The last set of norms learned concerns his *support* for the group: what to support, how, and how much. Generally, this set of norms defines patriotism or loyalty. Thus, the child learns in some families that loyalty to the family is the alpha and omega; that all internal squabbles end at the front-door; and that the family present a united front to the world. In the gang, the boy learns not to "rat" on his buddies and to defend them at all costs. Indeed, every primary group and most secondary associations have some definition of treason and minimal support, even though we seldom think of these more casual activities in such terms.

Now, the question is, what are some of these concrete norms? Among the more important ones, perhaps, is that of *"fair play,"* [14] a notion that has no single clear-cut meaning in every group. It does denote or suggest, however, that in one's relationships with others, particularly those in which allocation of values and struggle, or conflict, is entailed, that one compete according to the rules of the game or situation, without taking advantage of the other person. Even when one is losing, he is expected to honor the rules and fight fairly. School coaches, for example, seem to pride themselves on teaching their charges to conduct themselves as gentlemen on the field. Losing, they say, is better than cheating or harming the opponent. Yet it should also be observed that while we teach our young to do everything that is *fair* to win, we teach at the same time the need *to win*. Later in life, this means fighting elections hard and down to the wire; in war, it means fighting, not to settle for a negotiated settlement, but to win. Americans may not revere rules in the same way as do Britishers, but they too have definite notions on how to recognize and honor them.

Along with the norms of playing hard to win and playing fair is the norm of being a *good loser* should that be necessary.[15] Americans do not like complainers, or persons who offer excuses, particularly those who focus the blame for the loss on others. Yet, so great is our emphasis upon winning that the need for rationalization is correspondingly increased among those who must lose. And, in most of our games and economic opportunity there must be a loser, for the stakes are limited or are scarce. Not everyone can be a winner.

But at the same time that rationalizations must be available, they must also be of a certain type to be acceptable. In games, for example, the officials may be castigated, but one does not accuse the opposing players of cheating, nor does one accuse the spectators of poor behavior. "Luck" or "that's the way the ball bounces" are the most legitimate rationalizations. In adult politics, the losing candidate may accuse the opposition party of unfair campaigning, but never the winning candidate personally. Nor does he accuse the voters of stupidity. At worst, they may be thought of as dupes for having been manipulated by the opponent. Likewise in governmental actions, a disappointed citizen may accuse government officials of poor judgment, corruption, weakness, and partisanship, but seldom can he explain his failures by saying that the formal structure of the polity itself is at fault. Good administration would not have allowed or permitted the alleged injustice. In short, specific rules or structures may be criticized, but not the basic constitutional arrangements. That would verge on disloyalty. To say this does not mean that the various taboo types of rationalizations are never made; it means simply that they are not viewed with widespread favor, particularly by the middle classes. In European countries, failures to achieve great success are not blamed on the individual, but, if a rationalization is at all sought, upon the system. For this reason, socialism has had a much greater appeal to Europeans than to Americans with their individualistic orientation. For socialism attributes the problems of life not to the individual, but to the economic system. Reform of the former is viewed as settling nothing, and indeed is regarded as impossible without fundamental alterations of the latter system. In America, on the other hand, the belief is that the principles of right organization of society have already been discovered and are in operation. Thus, whatever misallocations of value may occur are the fault of the individual, and can be corrected only by his actions.

Loyalty and support are the focal points of still other norms (informal) among the primary groups. In fact, in the eyes of the membership, norms affecting group cohesiveness may well be the most important ones. The demand for conformity is in itself a type of norm. Many observers of youth peer-groups have noted the absoluteness of the demand for loyalty and the striking degree to which such groups achieve their goal. Indeed, unacceptability or rejection from a youth peer-group is usually regarded by the young as a traumatic experience. Criminal gangs and military units that are effective are also marked by powerful demands for solidarity or loyalty. "One for all and all for one," is not an atypical expectation in the primary groups. This may mean not "ratting" on fellow members, or such less dramatic acts as wearing the proper tie, clothes, using the meaningful words, or giving the secret handshake.

To most people the demand for loyalty is meaningful for the simple reason that the group provides meaning and purpose to the member or aspirant, in addition to the more concrete material rewards that may be attained by membership. Thus, while loyalty may be a cost, it is—in itself —also a rewarding experience for most men. We learn to appreciate those who, especially under crisis conditions, "stick with you" and ask nothing in return.

At the adult level, we see evidences of loyalty at work in political parties. It is most apparent among the professional politicians and party workers. As one perceptive politician, Edward Flynn, has observed: "Loyalty is a big word among politicians." [16] Rewarding friends and punishing enemies is but another manifestation of this. Loyalty is also found in the relatively stable party preferences of voters; few voters change parties in the course of a lifetime and most voters, 74 per cent, declare themselves members of one of the parties.[17]

While party loyalties among politicians are strong and the stability of party preference is marked, there can be little doubt that loyalty to the nation is the most pervasive and most demanded. And, significantly, it is not an adult monopoly, but one that is acquired early in life, both as a matter of informal example in the family and through deliberate teaching on the part of the formal agencies of political socialization: schools, primarily, and churches. Love of country and its political institutions is instilled as one of the first functions of the school system.

Political Information

Historically, one of America's most cherished ideals has been that of a highly informed nation and electorate. To this end, we have devoted a considerable amount, although not percentage, of our national resources. Over 40 million students are enrolled in our colleges and secondary schools. And, today, more than 97 per cent of the people can read and write.

To a large extent, the purpose of this educational faith has been to prepare citizens for a democratic way of life. In our conception of that way of life we have, traditionally, placed great faith in the efficacy of political information of the factual sort, that is, the learning of countless facts about our history and formal political institutions. There is great faith in the rational solution of social problems by people who must know what they are supposed to be doing. In America, this means reciting facts, not philosophy. Consequently, the required courses for our students are more often American history, American government, or a civics course, than they are courses in logic, ethics, or psychology. It is widely assumed that one can attain an understanding of our politics if he memorizes legal facts about the government. For generations, primary and secondary students, especially, have thus committed to memory such things as the number of states, the size of Congress, the Bill of Rights, the legal procedures of the legislatures, the sizes of city councils, the dates of Civil War battles, and the Gettysburg Address. Presumably, these facts equip one to be a useful and appreciative citizen.

According to the above conception, political information is the key to active mastery of the political world. Without it we cannot be good citizens. Nor must we terminate our studies at school graduation, for facts are constantly changing and the citizen must keep up with the news. Thus, we are exhorted to keep informed about both national and international events. To this end, literally dozens of organizations, programs, and events are sponsored daily. Thousands of radio and television stations, newspapers and magazines, books, and special publications are distributed or broadcast to keep a flow of news to citizens. In short, there is no paucity of a certain kind of political information.

STUDENTS OF CITIZENSHIP

We observed at the beginning of this chapter that everyone in society from the youngest to the oldest, from the poorest to the wealthiest, is being continuously socialized. Not all, however, are being equally socialized in politics. In general, it may be asserted that children, having the most to learn about everything, are engaged more continuously than their elders in learning how to be members of society. Yet the question is moot as to whether they acquire most of their *political* awareness, information, norms, and values during the younger years. No doubt they do learn a great deal. Nevertheless, much of what they learn in the family and schools is often in for some sharp changes as they mature into adult citizenship. Early beliefs about authority and power may well be influential throughout one's life, but practical experience as a citizen with the act of voting and dealing with political officials may also provide some new perspectives. In any case, a person learns about politics all his life, though certain early orientations may form the basis of all that is later selected from the environment.

Among those who learn most in adult life about politics are those who actually participate in politics, either as party workers or as politicians. Learning then frequently becomes an unlearning of much that was formerly uncritically accepted. Men who become politicians, for example, must discover how to campaign, run their offices, and deal with the public, press, and other politicians. For some men such learning is one of the more significant experiences in life. Moreover, for those who had highly unrealistic images of political life, a major reorientation in values and perspectives is a definite possibility.

THE AGENTS AND MEANS OF SOCIALIZATION

No one is ever solely self-taught; teachers are always present in the learning situation. This is no less true in the political system than elsewhere. Becoming a citizen, a partisan, a government official, or a member of an interest group, all requires instruction from others even though it be informal and hardly a conscious or deliberate activity on the part of teacher or student.

Schools and Formal Education

As might be expected in a complex society the size of the American, the agents of political socialization are many. For convenience we might approach the matter by first classifying the types of agents as either formal or informal and organizational or nonorganizational. Societies almost never allow the general socialization process to take place without having developed a set of formalized or highly institutionalized agencies of education. Thus, in all industrialized societies, a school system is a conspicuous element. And, from our point of view, the most important aspect and function of this school system is its role in making citizens out of the children entrusted to it. Indeed, the long history of public education in this country partially confirms the idea that schools are considered to or actually have a prime responsibility in citizenship training.[18] The elementary and secondary schools provide the most dramatic instance of political socialization, but hardly the only one. Universities and colleges also perform functions along these lines, and particularly state universities, which are required by state law to teach a certain minimum amount of political science or American history to the students. Another aspect of education in politics and the obligations of citizenship can be found in the requirement at many state universities that military training be a part of the male student's preparation for serving his country. Yet the colleges and universities of the country tend to treat the socialization process somewhat differently than do the primary and secondary institutions in that *knowledge* of politics is stressed rather than values and norms. But even this statement must be qualified, for the values and norms are more or less assumed to be democratic. Few if any professors of history, political science, or any of the social sciences, for example, ever deliberately educate students to believe that systems other than democracy are worthy. Fascism, communism, and varieties thereof are almost never taught as exemplary models for Americans. And while information about them may be conveyed, it is usually accompanied by condemnations. Indeed, the higher institutions of learning appear to operate on the belief that truth leads to greater faith in democracy. In any case, these formal institutions are important agents of political socialization in terms of developing citizenship. They are also important in another regard suggested above: that of equipping students with the knowledge and skills to become not merely citizens capable of performing the minimal duties of citizenship, but citizens capable of developing into future leaders for the polity. The fact that most of our leaders are college educated should come as no surprise.[19] Moreover, it may be assumed that many of their skills received their first sharpening during college years, either in the classroom or in campus politics. The law schools, too, seem to play a profound role in the preparation of political leaders.

Mention should also be made of the specialized role engaged in by our public military schools, West Point, Annapolis, and the Air Force Academy, in developing skills which, though devoted generally to violence, are nevertheless an integral part of the polity. The military is employed by the state, not by private agencies. Obviously, military education contains a good deal of political socialization. In the United States this usually means that the future generals and admirals are taught to view patriotism as the highest virtue and party affiliation as bad. They are also taught that the politicians and politics, itself, are evil and useless or, at best, necessary evils. What is important to remember is that these military institutions, regardless of the content of the values and norms, do socialize their students.

The way in which the educational system implants the proper ideas and ideals in the young is a highly complicated one. It consists of both formal and informal methods, and both conscious teaching and unconscious setting of experiences and examples. Among the formal means are, of course, the regular formalized course offerings in civics, history, economics, and literature. In addition, the school uses symbolic occasions including patriotic holidays and rites to inculcate respect and affection for the country. Plays, pageants, and recitations are all a part of the process. Little children learn to pledge allegiance, to sing "The Star-Spangled Banner" and "God Bless America," and to recite the opening lines of the Declaration of Independence, the Constitution, the Bill of Rights, and the Gettysburg Address. Later on, the teenagers are taught to participate in politics through student government in their classrooms and the school assembly. Here they learn that governing is supposed to consist of elections and rational discussions. All this is done, however, within the close supervision of the school authorities. The students themselves really handle very little authority. In addition, the schools participate in providing such political experience as mock conventions of the political parties, "model United Nations" at the college level, or Boys' State or Junior Statesmen in some states, in which the boys learn how to elect officials and then meet government officials for a day or two. The young in some cities are allowed "to take over the reins of city government" for a day. All these techniques are meant to give understanding and appreciation through actual experience. Whether they do or not, we do not know.

The schools are the focal point of still another kind of experience for many children, an experience in politics stemming from their activities in peer-groups during the off hours. Clubs of all sorts develop and are recognized by the school as legitimate organizations. It is in these clubs and informal groups of friends that the children learn American political values and norms. It is here that they learn authority, loyalty, and rebellion, plus something about the processes of accommodation, conflict resolution, and leadership. How these lessons may be transmitted to adult political behavior is, of course, difficult to ascertain. But it is highly unlikely that such crucial experiences early in life will be forgotten or will be without effect. For they are the conditioning and reinforcing factors in the acquisition of values, norms, and attitudes.

In the United States, the school is the official agent of political sociali-zation and, as such, occupies a strategic position in the communication and inculcation of political values and norms. It is of some significance, therefore, to determine *who* influences *what* is taught in the schools. In the United States, schools are locally controlled by elected officials called school boards, of which there are about 200,000 members in the public elementary and secondary schools.[20] These men and women have great power, for they decide who the executive officers of the schools will be, who the teachers are, the course curriculum, the textbooks used, and what the school system will be used for outside the official school hours. In addition, they decide on matters of great importance to the teacher's career, such as their participation in the community, salaries, requirements, and the general standards of education in the local area. Who these people are, therefore, is a significant fact.

Most studies of school board members indicate a heavy preponderance of business and professional men, although these groups constitute but 15 per cent of the population. Form and Miller,[21] in summarizing the results of a number of studies conducted in several cities and states, and a national sample, concluded that the percentage of business and professional men on school boards totaled as high as 76 per cent in the national sample, while the percentage of laborers was only 3 per cent. In no case did the per-centage of business and professional groups drop below 66 per cent, nor did the total of working men rise over 6 per cent. Unfortunately, as the study did not distinguish between business and professional men, we have no information as to their distribution.

Also, as the relationship between social background and political values is not an easy one to establish, what we have to say on such relationships must be highly tentative. Nevertheless, businessmen and professional men do tend to vote Republican and to be somewhat more conservative than do the lower income groups. And while they may not dictate precisely what each teacher is to teach, it is highly unlikely that a school board composed of such men would long tolerate teachers and texts that departed sharply from the values and norms held by the school board as dear and essential to the welfare of America. Indeed there have been many instances in American history of the recent past that would suggest that deviant phil-osophies die a quick and most mortal death.[22] But, even if the board members themselves do not bring direct pressure to bear upon teachers to conform to their own values, the teachers often anticipate such pressure, and subconsciously, and sometimes quite consciously, conform. At the very least, they often shape their courses and discussions so that hostility will not be engendered. Thus, statements on the United States and its politics are softened, and few criticisms are voiced of any severity. Thus, civic *problems* are not really taught, and conflict is played down. Thus, the role of radicals, unions, co-operatives, and socialism in our history is either ridiculed or passed over without comment. The student is generally taught only to revere, not to condemn, to be a "good" citizen, not a partisan making demands. The failure to do the latter tends to lend support to those who make up the bulk of the school boards. Not only does the Republican party tend to benefit from the treatment given politics in the school-room, but middle-class views of politics are also apt to prevail, all of which satisfies the school boards.

The Family

No one would seriously disagree with the proposition that the family is the major agent of socialization in all societies. But while we are all familiar from personal experience, if not from academic study, with the role of the family in creating civilized beings, many of us, including political scientists, have forgotten how vital is the family in creating citizens. Our knowledge of the processes involved is not extensive, but there is reliable data on certain aspects of the process and particularly on the content of what is taught by the parents to their children. We will consider this data shortly. For the moment, we are simply concerned with the family as an agent of political socialization.

The family is apt to be crucial in the entire socialization process for the simple reason that the child spends most of his more formative years within its orbit. It is here that the child has his first experiences with power and authority. And authority, as we have indicated, is fundamental in the polity whether it be in a family or a nation-state.

One of the better-known facts about the United States, for example, and one which distinguishes it from many other societies, is the looseness of the kinship system and the permissiveness with which children are raised by their parents.[23] The father is not usually a powerful authoritative figure either toward the wife or the children, as is the case in, say, Germany. In many situations, the whims and wishes of the child are indulged to the extent that the child learns little if any form of self-discipline. All this is done in the interests of democracy and personality development in which expressiveness and adjustment are regarded as prime virtues. At one time, "children were to be seen, not heard"—a maxim that has disintegrated today with a vengeance.

The child growing up in such an environment sees power diffused among at least three persons: mother, father, and himself, and, perhaps, other children. Because he sees the mother on a more or less equal plane with the father as an authority, and his own wishes taken into account, he is likely to learn not only that power need not be respected, but that indeed it may even be manipulated.[24] Thus, he soon learns to play the parents off against one another and thereby to gain his own ends. He will also note that he may be used by one parent against the other, and appreciate the bargaining strength he has acquired. All this means that the child views power not in mystical terms and unquestioned obedience, but as a pragmatic thing with which one can bargain. Thus, rationality of action and skepticism about power-holders are encouraged. It should also be noted that these two approaches to power are further stimulated by the practice of justifying the exercise of power by appeal to reason, either to the child or in front of him. When the child is expected to do some chore, for example, he is generally *asked,* not ordered, and provided with reasons for so doing. American children soon learn, therefore, to demand "why" when commands are given; likewise, parents soon learn to ask or request, not order.

The child learns not only how power and authority operate within the kinship group, but also acquires certain attitudes toward power-holders outside of the family unit. Thus, while parents and other elders may not be politically-oriented, this attitude in itself, plus the comments on such authorities as the father's boss, the police, the politicians, and the bureaucrats, are apt to become internalized by the child as his own set of attitudes. Especially important in this regard are the stereotypes of such persons and the manner in which they are discussed before the child. The words "copper," "flatfoot," "politician," "boss," "political deal," and many others are not apt to convey favorable impressions of public authorities. Likewise, the behavior of parents before authorities will impress the child in striking fashion. Should the father talk back to the policeman who has flagged him down for speeding or should he defer to the officer, the child may respond in similar ways himself as an adult. The respect shown by a parent for public property is also preparation for the adult civic life of the child. These, then, are illustrations of a basic orientation that children learn from the parents, an orientation concerning one's rights and responsibilities as a citizen. In short, whether a child grows up to emphasize rights and demands on the government or to fulfill his own obligations is surely strongly influenced, if not actually determined, by early family experiences.

In America, authority tends to be minimized, and made pragmatic. Thus, it should come as no surprise to discover that the child is taught to stress his own rights rather than his duties to the state. He is taught that government exists for the people, and is supposed to be run by them. He learns to question the actions of authorities who are regarded as "no better" than himself. And he learns to believe that politics is riddled with corruption. Following this same inexorable logic, however, he also learns that he must not despair, for he has "inalienable rights," and can pit one party against another, one official against another, one level of government against another, just as he did with his parents. But, for all the pragmatic and sometimes unpleasant beliefs he amasses, he also acquires a firm belief in the greatness of America and its way of life, its riches, and its form of government. He acquires a lively if sometimes blatant sense of patriotism, but one that allows him to be something of a businessman with respect to winning profits from the government and the polity.

These basic beliefs are not the only products of the family socialization efforts. The child also acquires attitudes about daily politics, its personalities, policies, and parties. Indeed, according to the voting studies, the family is probably the chief influence on the voter. As V. O. Key, Jr., has written:

> The processes by which party identification is established and maintained are not well understood, but it is clear enough that the family is influential in building a sense of party identification. Commonly, 75 per cent or more persons vote as their parents did and those whose parents were independents tend to be independents in high degree.[25]

Perhaps we can gain a more striking impression of the influence of the family on the voter if we quote from the responses of interviewees when asked about their party affiliations in a recent national poll.

> I'm a borned Republican, sister. We're Republicans from start to finish, clear back on the family tree. Hot Republicans all along. I'm not so much in favor of Eisenhower as the party he is on. I won't weaken my party by voting for a Democrat.[26]

The child's attitudes on the policies and politicians of the day are also likely to be accurate indicators of the parents' most recent pronouncements. And although the standards by which these matters are judged are not likely to be spelled out, they will become influential with the child, if only implicitly. How could it be otherwise with one who is still unable to reason on such indirect and compex matters?

Youth Organizations

Although American youth organize themselves in both formal and informal groups, they are also organized by their elders into groups having considerable relevance for political socialization.[27] Usually these organizations are set up for more general socialization, but all inculcate political values, norms, and information. For some, moreover, it is their *raison d'être*. Organizations such as the Boy Scouts of America, Girl Scouts of America, Future Farmers of America, and 4-H Clubs of America are all generalized socializing groups, but each devotes much time to matters of political relevance. Other groups, including the Young Democrats and Young Republicans, are purely political in orientation. Still others, including the American Legion Baseball Leagues, are meant to provide recreation, attempting in the process to instill values and norms such as "competitiveness" and "good sportsmanship" that may serve to condition later political values and norms.

Each of these organizations inculcates ideal notions of citizenship and indoctrinates American values. Dominant values include: thrift, respect for private property, self-control, self-reliance, duty, good deeds, clean living, courtesy, productivity, and reverence for religion. Basically, these are the traditional values of the American middle class, and as such serve to rationalize and defend the status quo. In addition, the youth organizations also support the existing order by isolating youth from political conflict. American youth seldom learn or engage in the extreme forms of political behavior typical to the young of other countries. Nor are the youth of this country an active force in politics; their attentions are devoted rather to preparing for an occupation, and having a good time in the meanwhile—orientations that are supported by youth organizations.

If we look at some of these group's activities we can gain a better understanding of their possible impact. We have already noted that all these groups emphasize productive values and self-control rather than expressiveness, particularly political expression of the conflict type. The 4-H Clubs, for example, teach how to do things around the farm and in the household. The same is true of the Future Farmers of America. The Scout Movement likewise teaches productive living, but perhaps is more oriented to the development of good citizens than are the farm organizations. Conservative values are instilled through the wearing of uniforms, the earning of "merits," the Oath, and above all, through the examples of their adult leaders who are generally from the middle class and value the American Way of Life. Active participation in the governing of the organization is also permitted on a limited basis by the leaders. In such participation the young members learn that they have a right to their opinions and to give them expression, but that they must also be well within the majority views. The importance of norms or rules of behavior and the conduct of meetings is also instilled. Ideas of social status are conveyed through the symbols of the ranks in scout troops and the system of rewards for achievement. In short, the members of all these organizations learn what is expected of them as ideal American citizens. By the bye, they may also learn many unintended facts, but the leaders do their best not to teach them contrary notions.

The role and function of private youth organizations become still clearer when we recognize the fact that they are largely under the control of the "better" people in the community. Although systematic data is not readily available, casual observation would seem to suggest that the schools are operated by the same groups of occupations, ethnic groups, religious affiliates, and civic-minded organizations among adults. In politics, these are the people most likely to vote Republican, to be conservative, Protestant, and to fall within the middle income range.

Political Parties

Most discussions of the functions of political parties suggest, if they do not prove, that parties serve to educate the citizenry.[28] How well they accomplish this function is debatable, but surely it is true that the parties do attempt to educate the citizens in their voter's role. Indeed, parties devote enormous amounts of time and energy, as well as other resources, in trying to communicate with the voters. And while their objective is obviously a self-oriented one—to win elections—they also convey information in the process about issues, candidates, and the parties. They also disseminate norms and values for the voter to use in his own process of evaluation. And they generally exhort the voter to vote regardless of the direction of his vote. Thus, by encouraging citizens to take advantage of one of their basic rights, voting, they thereby contribute to the polity.

Parties in the United States are agents of citizenship only in a partial sense in that they do not exist to socialize, nor do they "teach" continuously. Rather, their actions are likely to be periodic or cyclical, mounting in frequency and intensity as elections approach, then suddenly diminishing and leveling off during the long interim periods. In short, they do not directly impinge on many of the citizens for any sustained period of time. Then, too, the parties are less concerned with the provision of factual data about political processes than with providing evaluative clues or perspectives. They train in partisanship.

But the inculcation of partisan values and information is not the only contribution made to political socialization. The American parties also teach and preach the superiority of our way of life. Both parties are nationalistic and both honor the political system that created and maintains them. Thus, even while the parties may each have their partisan emblems and other symbols, they also have national heroes, display the national flag, sing the national anthem, pray for America and divine guidance, and claim to speak for the United States. Their candidates do not claim to be just Democrats or Republicans, but Americans first and party members second or third in the hierarchy of loyalties. In such ways do the parties socialize both for partisanship and integration.

The ways in which the parties accomplish these functions is, as was said above, somewhat unsystematic and erratic. Some are accomplished through the formal methods of campaigning and the distribution of literature. Much, however, is done informally and symbolically by the actions of office-holders. Moreover, each party is organized at all levels of government, but not evenly throughout the nation. Services are provided by party officials ranging from ticket-fixing to legitimate help during crises. Many social events are utilized by parties, especially around election time, to educate the voters and maintain supporters. Clubs of all sorts are used to spread the word. To reach the young, each party has a Young Democrat or Young Republican affiliate, as the case may be. Thus, conscious teaching and learning from experience in internal party activities serve to socialize those who have contact with the parties.

Interest Groups

Interest groups, like political parties, are also primarily concerned with "educating" the adults of the community.[29] And, like the parties, they are mostly interested in providing evaluative cues to their members and the publics outside their domain. As interest groups want to realize specific goals, usually to augment their own positions in society, they too teach value positions. What information is provided is dealt with as it relates to the goals or objectives of the group. Thus, they maintain bulletins or newspapers with political sections or columns to keep members informed on the group's political action. Likewise, they publish and distribute special studies having to do with political affairs, and often engage speakers from public office and universities to inform them on political issues. Indeed, campaigns may well be run to encourage their members to participate in politics. To this end, books and lectures are provided to show how such activities can be accomplished. Apparently, the encouragement of political action by members is becoming increasingly popular. These groups, of course, have always engaged in politics, but have deceived themselves that only their opponents do so. Some even run schools as do the trade unions with COPE, or Committee for Political Education.

Interest groups cannot help but be agents of political socialization.

They become so simply by being members of the political system. What distinguishes the modern interest group from the old is the self-conscious manner in which the former approach their activities. They have become highly specialized bureaucracies in socialization. In still other words, interest groups are rationalizing those aspects of political socialization in which they are interested. Note the programs they conduct to "educate" the citizenry or public opinion to aid their cause. To accomplish the task, highly skilled technicians in mass communications are often employed at high cost.

Some interest groups, especially those which tend toward being patriotic, attempt to broaden the scope of their education by educating for civic participation and loyalty. These groups, of which the American Legion or the Daughters of the American Revolution are good examples, attempt to instill citizenship ideals, not just economic interests. The Legion, for example, conducts contests for school children in which essays on American history or patriotism are awarded for excellence as determined by the Legion. Likewise, they bestow civic commendations and awards to adults, awards that generally go to persons strongly identified with being a patriot and a conservative.

The Mass Media

In one sense, the mass media are simply a technical means of socialization. To treat them only as such, however, would be highly superficial. Those working with the mass media are, in fact, agents of socialization who have particular ideas of what should be conveyed to their consumers. In order to appreciate those in the mass media as agents of political socialization, we must then have some knowledge of who they are, of what their interests consist, and how they operate. Fortunately, students of public opinion have been quite diligent in collecting such data, and it is to their work that we will turn for most of what we want to know.[30]

By mass media we mean to include television, radio, newspapers, magazines, and books. These are the media that reach or are intended to reach large audiences, although considerable differences do exist in the sizes of the various audiences of each. Television, for example, influences many more Americans than do books. But whatever the differences, the numbers involved in even the smallest sphere are sizable.

One of the more crucial facts about the mass media is that they are largely and increasingly controlled by small numbers of people. For to own and operate a concern engaged in mass communications is a major task requiring great investments and technical skills. As a result, fewer persons are in control of most of the communications that go on in the country. Indeed, in terms of the numbers of publishers, television and radio stations, and newspaper publishers, there is less and less competitive activity. Even while there has been an increase in the daily subscriptions of newspapers, for example, the number of daily papers has dropped approximately 20 per cent during the year 1930–1947.[31] In 1953, the percentage of daily circulation held by owners of papers in two or more cities was 45.3 per cent.[32] The cities having competitive papers in 1954 represented only 6 per cent of the total number of cities with daily newspapers.[33] These figures suggest an increasing concentration of ownership. And, they also suggest another hypothesis of considerable significance to the socialization process: namely, that mass audiences are receiving a more uniform set of political perceptions or images. Newspapers, of course, are hardly the only mass media providing such uniform images. All the media tend in that direction, just as all are becoming more centrally owned and controlled. But, unlike newspaper publishers, radio and television owners are restricted to some extent by government in the number of stations they may operate. On the other hand, there has been an increase in the number of jointly owned radio, television, and newspaper firms. As of 1957, 21.2 per cent of the radio and television stations were identified with newspaper ownership.[34] Likewise, in the area of book publishing, recent years have witnessed a number of mergers and thereby a reduction of the number of large publishing houses. To be sure, book publishers, unlike their newspaper counterparts, do put out a less uniform product, but its audience is, of course, far smaller and probably more sophisticated.

Regardless of who operates the mass media, it is imperative to study the content of their offerings to the public. We have already noted that there is a tendency to produce a uniform product. But we have not indicated what that content is nor the uniformities thereby contained. In the case of newspapers, especially, the contents reflect an overriding concern for violence, sex, sentimentality, and the ignoble aspects of life generally. The amount of space—over time—devoted to political issues and news is not unusually great.[35]

THE PROCESS OF SOCIALIZATION

One of the less known areas of political socialization has to do with the *processes* of teaching and learning. We can only convey impressionistic notions of the techniques or methods and informal processes.[36] If they should sound familiar to the reader, we shall have at least partial confirmation of their reliability.

How a person is taught and learns citizenship in a democracy is not likely to be a very clear picture, for many influences impinge upon the individual, and not all may be equal in their impact. Only one thing is certain: namely, that all of us are subject to both formalized teaching about politics and informal pressures to perceive and act in certain ways. No one group or institution employs a single procedure; all engage in many methods. Thus, the schools formally teach history and civics and engage in rituals of respect for the nation. The teachers themselves act informally as symbols of power and authority for the students and even their parents. And, in the schoolroom, the teachers—unknowingly in some instances—convey political preferences via verbal and nonverbal expressions. In other cases, they do so knowingly and openly. On the school grounds, the child is socialized by the peer-group with ideals of group behavior, and learns notions of authority, leadership, loyalty, bargaining, and conflict. All these "lessons in citizenship" are taught and learned informally without awareness of the process, as such, to its participants. Later in life, the adult citizen will have his political preferences constantly confirmed by the groups to which he belongs, even though he has no awareness of the acts of confirmation. And, he may confirm these same preferences by an unconscious selective choice of the mass media.

Although political socialization is considered of paramount importance in this society as in all societies, it is a highly confused and unsystematic process. Both formal and informal techniques are employed by all the agents and agencies, with greater reliance placed on one or the other. The schools, for example, tend to formalize their methods and become very self-conscious about education. The family, on the other hand, socializes by example and imitation, both primarily informal and even unconscious means.

THE RESULTS: SOME INTENDED
AND UNINTENDED CONSEQUENCES

The time has now arrived for an evaluation of the results of all the energies and resources we devote to the socialization of our people in politics. It must be remembered, however, that the fact that we commit all these resources to creating citizens is no automatic guarantee that they are effective or efficient. Undoubtedly, we do shape behavior as a result of socialization, but are the results the ones the agents of socialization hoped for? While our evidence on such questions leaves much to be desired, we raise the questions, nevertheless, and will attempt partial answers with full awareness that they may be magnificently wrong.

Some Intended Consequences

Most Americans are loyal patriots and support their country by fighting its wars, paying its taxes, obeying its laws, and participating in many ways in the functioning of its political system. Insofar as Americans do share common values and norms, and possess political information, we must credit the socialization process with success. That the ideals have not been met entirely is, of course, manifest; we will consider them in the next section, and provide evidence for this claim. But as no society has ever achieved complete success in this regard, our noting these discrepancies must not be construed to mean that no success has been attained. For it must also be remembered that the socialization process teaches other things besides ideal behavior. Recall, too, that the society has not one socialization process, but many, and some inculcate contradictory ideals, norms, and information.

On the whole, however, we must say that the kind of citizenship taught *is* actualized. Most Americans remain Americans and do not migrate. And, most Americans are more American when abroad than at home. More important, perhaps, most Americans cherish the liberal belief system described in Chapter 5.

Some Unintended Consequences

What teachers teach and hope for by the way of results never approximates the ideals. But worse, what is taught can sometimes end in situations totally unexpected or undesired. For instance, the father who teaches his son, by example, to revere authority may create the opposite result; namely, a son who rebels not only against the father but against all authorities.[37] Likewise, the minister who teaches his children to be Christians may produce in its stead atheists or agnostics, or a nation that teaches liberalism, as this one does, may end up, as Louis Hartz has argued, with some very dogmatic illiberals, or people who insist that everyone be a liberal.[38] Yet, whether we produce the opposites of what we intend, we do not produce at the level held as an ideal. Indeed, most of this section is concerned with the discrepancy between ideal and achievement rather than the kind of situations described above. But we will have a few things to say about the latter as well.

The discussion is based on results as related to political values, norms, and information. And while the indices and measurement of results or consequences are not the best, they are better than sheer speculation.

Distribution and Acceptance of Values

The teaching of political values does not mean that everyone in a society will accept them as his own personal values, nor that he will govern his behavior by or in accordance with them. In every society, there will be a pattern of distribution. That is, some members of the society will accept the values taught, while others will be indifferent, and some will reject them altogether. Our concern is with determining what that pattern is in the United States. In short, we want to know who accepts what values and how. Information on this problem is scattered and scanty, but we will make the attempt to answer the question, if for no other reason than to raise it.

Generally speaking, observers of America have tended to agree that Americans possess a remarkably homogeneous set of beliefs, attitudes, and values, and that this has been true almost since the inception of the nation. Of course, since these observers state their generalization at a rather high level, variations, which may appear crucial in daily life for most of us, have not struck them as important. Thus, Professor Hartz has maintained that all Americans believe in an empirical approach to life, and that they value life, liberty, and property.[39] At the level of abstraction used by Hartz, this is probably the case. But if these abstractions are reduced to empirical hypotheses to be tested, they become somewhat suspect, as do any generalizations about Americans. We can illustrate this contention by reference to an investigation conducted by Raymond Mack among college students at Northwestern University.[40]

Professor Mack was concerned with learning what students thought about the Bill of Rights, namely, in terms of their approval or disapproval. The study indicated that when students—the sample included 560—were asked whether they approved of the Bill of Rights as a whole and without identification of its elements, they approved it by an overwhelming majority. When asked about specific rights, however, not identified as parts of the Constitution, they showed considerable doubts and reservations. The Sixth Amendment, for example, which guarantees the right to confront an accuser, was disapproved of by 67.5 per cent of the students. Double jeopardy, in the Fifth Amendment, was accepted as desirable by 71.8 per cent of the respondents. The three amendments of the Bill of Rights that drew the most widespread agreement were those parts of VI which relate to habeas corpus (94.8 per cent); trial by jury (89.6 per cent); and, the First Amendment guaranteeing free speech and press (82.5 per cent).[41]

However, we must be careful in analyzing and accepting data of the above type, for the situations are posed in a highly unrealistic way. The Bill of Rights, for example, gains its support and viability not in formally structured experiments, but in the daily activities of the courts and political life. Of course, it is important to know that not all Americans believe equally and strongly in civil liberties. Professor Samuel A. Stouffer's study of American attitudes [42] toward communism and civil liberties demonstrated this point rather conclusively. It also showed that the protection of these political values is more dependent upon certain groups of citizens than others; the former including the higher income, better educated, urbanized people who also tend to be the leaders of the nation.

To be sure, no society, including the American, is without its authoritarians, and these personalities can be found in all ranks or classes.[43] But if they are to be found, it is rather the proportions that are crucial. In the United States, it seems safe to say that they are a very small minority. Indeed, our socialization efforts have probably created many more organizational types than authoritarians who must engage in political sadism, escapism, and cynicism. And even these few can be protected against by the existence of a Bill of Rights and the political system. But it may be that Edward Shils was right when he argued that every political system, including the democratic, requires a few authoritarian personalities to perform certain of the tasks of criticism and leadership that better adjusted people find it difficult to do.[44] In any case, we need not fear the existence of a few such people.

Prestige of Government

One might assume that the citizens of a democracy would hold their political system and its officials in high repute, for they are taught to believe that it is a "government of the people, by the people, and for the people." But assumptions on such matters are dangerous to make, as we are about to see.

Again, the evidence on such attitudes as faith in government and the prestige of politicians and administrators is scanty and doubtful. Nevertheless, if understanding is to be gained, we must consider what evidence there is. The data seem to indicate many contradictions or ambivalences among Americans. In 1944, for example, the National Opinion Research Center questioned a national sample of some 2,560 adult citizens to determine whether or not they would like to see their sons become politicians.[45] Sixty-nine per cent did *not* want their sons to enter politics. While there were variations among the different groups asked, in no case did less than 51 per cent oppose such careers. On the other hand, in another poll, conducted in 1946, in which respondents were asked to rate a long list of occupations in terms of their prestige, no less than nine of the top-rated thirteen positions were governmental or political.

These top-rated offices and their ranking were as follows: (1) U.S. Supreme Court Justice; (3) State Governor; (4) Cabinet Member in the Federal government; (5) diplomat in the U.S. Foreign Service; (6) mayor of a large city; (9) U.S. representative in Congress; (11) government scientist; (12) county judge; and, (13) head of a department in the state government.[46]

When citizens were asked whether they would prefer to work for the United States government or for a private firm, still another set of data emerged. This set of data, however, would seem to indicate that the prestige of government service or work is on the up-grade, and that it may even have surpassed that of private employment. We are fortunate in having some reliable trend data from three different studies on the matter: A *Fortune Magazine* poll in 1940; a U. S. National Survey (AIPO), 1947; and the Detroit Area Study of 1954.[47] The earliest poll by *Fortune* indicated that some 40 per cent of the respondents preferred working for the U. S. Government, while 50 per cent said they preferred a private firm. The remainder had no opinion. By 1947, 41 per cent favored governmental work, 40 per cent private employment, and 19 per cent had no opinion or preference. In the Detroit Area Study, 56 per cent preferred governmental work, 30 per cent private positions, and 14 per cent had no preference or opinion. The rise from 40 to 56 per cent seems significant with respect to the status of governmental positions. Indeed, the security that government employment offers would appear to be more attractive today than ever before.

Levels of Participation

Among the more evident of the unintended consequences is the solid fact of low levels of participation in political activities. Certainly those agents of socialization who have made a fetish of widespread and intense participation have cause to worry, for the American people are simply not participating to the extent hoped for by idealists. There are many forms of participation, and while not all are investigated, the indicators that are used have demonstrated much indifference. One of the better known studies has concluded that few Americans engage in any political activity, as defined by the investigators.[48] Using such measures as voting, political discussions, organizational memberships that involve political action, writing and speaking to public officials, working in elections, and contributing money to political campaigns, Julian Woodward and Elmo Roper measured activity with a scoring system such that the highest score was 12 points.

When this was done and the results tabulated, it became apparent that only 10.3 per cent of the adult population could be described as "very active." [49] Moreover, this score was computed on a rather minimum amount of activity. The very inactive totaled 38.3 per cent. Classical democratic theory would surely place greater demands on the citizen than did Woodward and Roper. Had the latter done so, the scores on participation would have been correspondingly lower.

We should note, however, that when political scientists and public opinion pollsters measure participation, they tend to measure only those active forms that have most to do with the allocation processes of the polity, namely, the contributing of time and money, or voting. Many other modes of participation, which have enormous significance for the integrative processes, are neither studied nor measured. Such activities as paying one's taxes, attending political rituals such as a Fourth of July parade and ceremony, obeying the laws all are ignored, but all contribute to the solidarity of the nation. Of course, those responsible for the socialization of citizens may be credited with encouraging these forms of participation. "Obey the laws" is a favorite theme among such groups as the churches, the schools, and the Boy Scouts of America.

Indeed, integration rather than disintegration is likely to be more strongly stressed in all social systems. What the agents of socialization want is participation, but not of the type which is disruptive; few socializers teach the "right of revolution." And especially among the young, duty, not rights, is bound to be stressed.

Level of Political Information

A third unintended consequence of the socialization process has to do with the extent of political information among the citizenry. The hope of the founders of this country, and of most agents of socialization to this day, is that we would have, and indeed require, an informed electorate. However, the facts of the matter indicate that these hopes have not been and are not likely to be soon realized. By the standards of the agents of socialization, themselves, the level of knowledge of Americans concerning government and politics is not very high. Yet, as such evidence is very meager and tentative, our conclusions must of necessity be tentative and partial.

One of the rare studies of citizen attitudes toward government, done by the Bureau of Government at the University of Michigan, questioned a sample of 764 families in the Detroit Metropolitan area as to their knowledge of certain specific government services and some more generalized areas.[50] Of those who had attended college only 53 per cent were able

to provide right answers to the generalized questions. The following quo-
tation from the study suggests some of the dimensions of knowledge
concerning generalized information:

> Thirteen per cent knew about what portion of the national budget was
> spent on national defense and foreign aid.[51]
> Twenty-eight per cent knew that the Board of Education was made up
> of elected officials.[52]
> Fifty-six per cent knew the amount at which income taxes started and
> income tax returns had to be filed.[53]

The investigators also attempted to determine the levels of "instrumental knowledge." Whereas "general knowledge" indicated "an awareness of the system and how it operates," "instrumental knowledge" was
considered as "crucial information about the immediate consequences of
administration as they impinge upon an individual; it is information, essential to an individual, about his rights and obligations with respect to a
specific agency." [54] It was expected that the levels of "instrumental knowledge" would be higher than those of "generalized knowledge," for the
former comes largely from personal contact, and is acquired as a matter
of self-interest. The results, however, were not significantly different from
those relating to generalized knowledge; both were very low. Questions
were asked, for example, concerning the operations and programs of three
governmental agencies that vitally affect countless citizens in a metropolitan area: Bureau of Old Age and Survivors Insurance, the Michigan
Employment Security Commission, and the Detroit Board of Education.
The results were as follows:

> Twenty-two per cent knew the length of coverage under unemployment
> insurance.[55]
> Twenty-six per cent knew of both major types of protection—old age
> and survivors insurance—under the social security system.[56]
> Fifty-six per cent were aware in the most general terms of an appeal
> procedure under the selective service system.[57]

Another area of political information on which, according to classical
democratic theory, we might expect extensive knowledge of politics is
that of familiarity with issues, what the government is doing about them,
and how the parties and candidates (during elections) view them. Fortunately, a considerable amount of research does exist on these items, most
of it a product of the voting studies. Familiarity with selected issues,
framed in very general terms, was studied by the Survey Research Center
of the University of Michigan during the 1956 Presidential campaign. This

is what they found.[58] First, familiarity with issues is increased when framed in general rather than specific terms. Secondly, familiarity with issues, and what is being done about them by the government, is also increased if the issue has a history and has not recently emerged onto the public scene. Thirdly, the issues of domestic affairs are more familiar than foreign issues.

When we turn to even more generalized information presumed to be important to the contributing citizen of a democracy, we find that the low levels of information are even more startling. Hyman and Sheatsley,[59] in evaluating the results of many public opinion polls over a twenty-year period of time (1930–1950), illustrated their contention that the levels of information are generally very low. They reported that, at the height of the 1948 Presidential campaign, 12 of every 100 adult Americans did not know that Dewey was the Republican candidate, and 9 did not know that President Truman was running for reelection. Other findings are just as startling. During that same election, between 60 and 70 per cent had no knowledge of the party platforms; the average citizen could identify but six of Truman's positions on the major issues. Three years after the United Nations was founded it was discovered that 25 per cent of the people had not even heard of the organization. The authors then informed us that tests of information invariably show at least 20 per cent of the public totally uninformed, and that usually the figure is closer to 40 per cent. One survey [60] mentioned by Hyman and Sheatsley showed that 31 per cent of all adult Americans said that they had never heard of the Bill of Rights; an additional 36 per cent said they had heard of it but could not identify it; and another 12 per cent gave incorrect versions.

FINAL REMARKS

We have now explored the socialization process, identifying its functions, its agencies, students, contents, processes, and some of the consequences. We have found that Americans are not all taught the same things by the same sorts of persons and processes, nor do they all behave in the same ways as citizens.

Consequently, socialization is one of the most complex of human affairs and one about which we know very little, especially concerning political aspects. Fortunately, recent developments in political science portend well for the future of research in this crucial area.[61]

8

The Means of Political Control

Understandably, students of democracy have been more concerned with the study of the means by which the people control their governors than with the ways in which governors control the people. We say understandably because democracies are distinctive in the fact that the ordinary citizen has some say about who his rulers will be and the policies they pursue. But even in democracies, governors must rule, must state goals, and must implement these goals. Put in more blunt terms, democratic rulers must also control citizens. Our immediate problem is to describe and explain some of the means by which control is exercised in the United States.

In the last chapter we said that every American underwent a socialization process that "made" him an American citizen. In so doing it provided him with a set of values, norms of political behavior, partisan preferences, skills, and political information to assist him in his role as a member of the polity. We also said that one of the functions of the socialization of citizens was to make them their own policemen, that is, to enable them to govern themselves without being told how to do so at every moment by a governmental official. We also noted, however, that socialization is not perfect; that some citizens do not—for a variety of reasons—become perfect little citizens who do no wrong.

Political control may be quickly and simply defined as the external means that political systems employ to control the behavior of its members. That is, it refers to the control of behavior by external checks rather than internalized processes dealt with under socialization. In terms of our conceptual framework, we are interested in the output of controls or "feedback" produced by the polity.[1] Perhaps we should refresh our image of the polity with the figure we first used in Chapter 1.

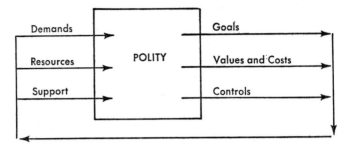

Figure 4-1. Input-Output Model of the Polity.

In Figure 4-1, we suggest that the polity is not simply the passive agent of the inputs stemming from society, but is itself—primarily through its agent, the government—an active force shaping or affecting the demands made upon it. Resources are made available for its use, and it is accorded support by the goals, means, and personnel of the government. Citizens, of course, may attempt to make illegitimate demands upon society such as robbery, vandalism, and corruption; or, they may fail or deliberately decide not to contribute their expected share of the needed resources and support. Controls, then, are necessary in the polity because socialization is often inadequate. Put in other terms, we maintain that utopias, or non-controlled societies, are both unknown and not likely to be soon realized. Whatever the future, political controls now are a very present reality.

Our inquiry into the means of political control will be guided, as it has been before, by asking a set of related questions. The questions are raised in the following order:

> Who controls?
> Whom?
> How?
> And, with what consequences?

THE AGENTS OF CONTROL

In a very real sense, every citizen is an agent of control over the behavior of others, but no polity could remotely begin to rely upon such a complex system of command. Instead, societies maintain *functionally-specialized* agencies of control endowed with authority of some kind. In democracies such as the United States, the agencies are highly *institutionalized* and given *legal-rational authority* to control the behavior of citizens. Even while informal controls may be exercised by ordinary citizens, they cannot, except under rare circumstances, exercise the power of the state. For the most part, then, the agents and agencies of control are institutionalized, highly *visible* to the population (some wear uniforms such as the police), functionally-specialized, possess *limited powers,* and must exercise their powers according to well-defined rules. Some of the agents are selected through the process of election, others are appointed, but most are chosen by civil service examination on the basis of merit. Many of the over 500,000 elected officials are agents of control at least a part of the time: 3,053 county sheriffs, 135,000 urban policemen, 20,000 federal police, and 10,000 state police, plus 80,000 rural and suburban policemen, engage in law enforcement.[2] On the national level, the President himself obviously plays such a role. It is one of his less prominent ones however, because he engages in such activity indirectly through the actions of countless lesser officials. Appointed agents of control include such officials as deputy police, U.S. district attorneys, members of regulatory agencies such as the Interstate Commerce Commission, Federal Trade Commission, Federal Power Commission, Civil Aeronautics Board, Maritime Board, Federal Reserve System, Securities and Exchange Commission, and many similar boards and commissions at the state and local levels. Civil servants include all those who work for these various elected and appointed officials: the state police forces, Treasury agents, FBI agents, and many others. In addition, several thousand courts and judges serve as agents of control.

Most of these agencies and agents have become, as stated above, highly specialized and even professionalized, as is the case with medical people engaged in public health problems, lawyers acting as government attorneys, and the police forces. We might also include the armed forces in our discussion for they too have regulatory functions in maintaining law and order. Their personnel, and especially the professional officer corps, are specialists in violence. While they are not generally used in daily domestic life, they are employed occasionally in extreme situations to quell strikes, demonstrations, and rebellions. Although less violent forms of control are employed by most agents, these forms too call for technical training and skills, some of which are acquired in formal schools such as the universities, others during "in-service" training or on the job.

Highly visible and specialized agents of control are not the only kinds in America. As stated above, most of us act as controllers over other people, but do so in very informal and even unconscious ways. Thus, the father who tells his son not to throw rubbish on the highway because it is not the right thing to do is implementing the police and the laws that prohibit such actions. But there are even more significant and interesting examples of informal control.

One extreme kind may be illustrated in the following. Throughout American history we have experienced and witnessed the control activities of many citizen's groups or vigilantes who have taken "law and order" into their own hands.[3] During the latter quarter of the nineteenth century, the very frequency of lawlessness and violence on the frontiers of the West caused many good citizens to form such groups in order to maintain peace. Very often, however, the means used were inconsistent with the laws and values of our society, but they controlled nevertheless. Throughout the history of our country we have also witnessed the rise and activities of groups concerned not so much with the maintenance of law but with the control of political beliefs and actions. There have been periodic "red scares" in which some Americans have seen fit to worry about the patriotism of others and to implement their fears with overt action. The "Know-Nothings," the Ku Klux Klan, America First Committee, the American Legion, various citizens' leagues, Daughters of the American Revolution, and many others have devoted either full or part time to other citizens' beliefs and political activity. Control was and is accomplished through a variety of techniques, including rumor, insinuation, lies, brutality, economic sanction, alienation, spying, accusation, and ridicule. On another level, big city machines have controlled voters and others by the use of force, promises, and penalties. Indeed, the political boss became known as expert in the use of such techniques as fraud and violence.

Vigilante groups and individuals operate more or less sporadically as crises occur in society. And while their attempts at control are perhaps not the most effective over the long run, since they depend to such an extent upon emotionalism and crisis, they are among the most dramatic. More important in everyday life are the efforts of other types of groups whose major concerns are nonpolitical, but who engage, nevertheless, in political action, and whose actions have political consequences regardless of intent. Such groups include the corporation, trade union, church, business firm, and others. Each of these groups exercises controls over its own members and nonmembers who have contact with the organization. At the turn of the twentieth century, for example, corporations and other businesses actually "owned" or controlled many members of the United States Congress. Many of these same businesses controlled local communities through their preponderant economic power. Today, according to the research of sociologists such as Floyd Hunter,[4] we know that economic enterprises exercise a preponderance of political control over the decisions of many large cities, as in the case of Atlanta, Georgia. Other studies have confirmed Hunter's findings.[5] Vidich and Bensman, in their interpretation of the power structure of a small upper New York village, have argued that controls rest in the hands of a small number of persons.[6] Earlier community studies, including that of the Lynds' on Muncie, Indiana, definitely show the power of business at the city level. In each of these cases, community decisions of significance are made by the economically powerful; as such, they act as controllers of political life.[7]

Yet, the actions of these groups and persons are done in such a way as not to suggest totalitarian control. The actions are those of democratic procedures. Thus, the economically powerful may control the public offices, have influence with those who do, or set the alternatives for the officials and people. Or, they may exercise a negative power through the veto of community projects they do not want to see pursued. But whatever the means they do exercise control over the behavior and destinies of other citizens.[8]

CITIZENS AS OBJECTS OF CONTROL

No one escapes regulation or control by the polity and government. Indeed, hardly a day passes that we are not in some way controlled by the agents we have just described. But most of the time we are quite unaware of the fact of control, although periodically we are physically confronted by the agents and other evidences of regulation. In the former case, we are usually regulated indirectly through controls on still other citizens. An example of such might be that of "fair trade" laws affecting the prices that druggists can charge the public. What we as consumers pay is determined by regulations on drug manufacturers and retailers. More interesting and vital to us, however, are not the indirect controls, but those which affect us directly in the person of an agent. A policeman issuing a ticket, the Internal Revenue Department demanding the payment of an income tax, a property tax assessor assessing our house, a license bureau requiring a driver's test, the Selective Service commanding our induction into the armed forces, and being refused a passport to travel aboard—all are but a miscellaneous and very partial listing of the types of situations in which we as citizens are directly regulated.

In controlling citizens the polity is concerned with two quite distinct matters: *beliefs* and *overt behavior*. In terms of the number of legal controls, actual behavior is of greater interest to the controllers. Administrators generally are unconcerned as to whether the citizen likes a particular law or regulation so long as he obeys or complies. This is usually the case with the lesser regulations such as traffic laws, business regulations, and the like. Of course, laws that have greater support among the controlled are easier to enforce. The controls that create the greatest furor—pro and con—are those that go beyond the regulation of overt behavior, particularly those involving little more than everyday behavior, and affecting a person's beliefs whether political or otherwise. Certainly American history has not been without a good many such incidents. Generally, however, the tradition has been to minimize such control on the part of the government. Still, many private persons and organizations, both directly and indirectly, have attempted to control thought. Usually, this has been done by attempts to limit the number of alternatives presented the people and by imposing heavy sanctions upon the person declaring a contrary belief. Fear and intimidation, for example, have been used to discourage others from stating their views and implementing them. Fair hearings have not been allowed unconventional social, religious, and political beliefs. Public opinion has been used to create a situation of unanimity and fear, until a citizen's fear has become his own personal policeman. In short, control is no less effective because invisible.

Of course, we do not all feel every regulation or control that exists. Indeed, most controls apply to but small segments of the population, and relatively few to all citizens. None the less, when a law or norm is violated in a democratic society the outcome can be most dramatic and most consequential. Consequently, the person to whom control is most important is the *deviant* from the law, the person who has failed, either through innocence or design, to comply.

DEVIANTS AND DEVIANCE

A deviant may be defined as one who does not comply with the laws and the informal norms, or accept the belief system of the political system. No evaluative connotation is attached to the terms "deviant" and "deviance"; they are meant simply as descriptive categories in analyzing the behavior of citizens.

A citizen, of course, is neither a deviant nor perfect citizen; rather, all of us at times are deviants and at other times—most of the time—observers of the laws, norms, and beliefs of our country. In explaining deviance, then, we need to indicate what we deviate from; the answer, as suggested above, is from the formal laws of the polity, the informal norms that inevitably develop within the political system, and the elements of the political culture. In the last category it is the belief system that is most relevant. Deviance from the formal laws is, of course, the easiest type to detect, while deviance from the informal norms and beliefs is the most difficult. Why this should be so, we shall presently explain.

First, however, it is necessary to say something about the extent of deviance in the polity. Although the problem is an empirical one, it does seem possible to anticipate the findings of research, as well as to take advantage of previous findings from other areas of deviance than the political. Social scientists have long noted that norms are generally observed in stabilized societies. This general observation can and has been reduced, however, to a mathematical curve that has a definite shape, similar to the letter "J." [9] What the curve "says" is that the frequency distribution of a pattern of behavior is such that many more members of the system perform the action than do not. In filing income tax returns, for example, most people do file, a few occasionally do not, and still fewer never do. The position and exact shape of the curve or distribution is obviously dependent upon the law being considered. Few of us would find ourselves occupying the same position on the curve for all laws and norms. But whatever the individual case, the people who occupy positions near the "sometimes" and "never" are the deviants. And it is instances of deviance that pose problems for control.

Sources of Deviance

Any theory having to do with the explanation of political deviance must pertain to the sources of such behavior. That is, it must provide explanations of why such behavior occurs.[10] While there are several explanations based upon biological, psychological, and social factors, we will not give equal emphasis to all. Instead, we will emphasize the social-psychological variables, placing more or less equal stress on each dimension.

If we approach the problem of deviance logically, it would seem that we ought to consider; first, the nature of the normative system defining legitimate and illegitimate behavior; secondly, factors relating to the deviant person or group; thirdly, factors relating to those who are responsible for the enforcement of norms; and fourthly, social conditions affecting citizens, agents of control, and the norms of society.

When we view the normative structure of American society and polity in particular, it is fairly apparent that the number of norms is incalculable. Indeed, these many norms vary in the degree of formality, precision of statement, severity of sanction, type of sanction, explicitness, rigidity, and consistency of enforcement. And the simple fact that countless norms of behavior, whether formal or informal, do exist is likely to generate situations in which the citizen and the public official will often be confronted with conflicting norms. One may require one kind of behavior, and another the opposite. Thus, in our complicated federal system, it is not uncommon that contradictory laws apply to the same situation. Eventually, such conflicts of laws between state and national government, or state versus state government, are resolved in a federal court or the Supreme Court. Until that moment, however, a citizen or official caught between these laws often finds it difficult to honor both.

Another kind of conflict of norms deals not with laws, but with relationships between informal norms and laws. Consider the instance of a politician who is required by law to state his campaign expenses, but who is also "required" by an informal norm among the politicians to be less than honest about the sources and amounts of his expenditures. Or, consider the situation of a public official—say, an Attorney General—who is required by law to enforce federal laws that might embarrass certain fellow party members and, indeed, the party itself and the President. What should he do? The law says one thing; the informal norms of party life say another. Or, consider the possible conflicts that may arise among informal norms. The public, for example, expects a President to select the best man for a certain post, the party expects him to select a deserving party member and worker. These illustrations are but a few of the many possible ones posing dilemmas for the citizen and the public official. If the person obeys one, he is likely to disobey the others. Of course, there are solutions to such dilemmas; these we will deal with later.

Another source of deviance in the political system stems from the ambiguity of some of the norms that govern us. Both the laws and the informal norms are subject to such ambiguity. The former may be obscure because the law is couched in generalized terms as is the case with our fundamental law—the Constitution. Indeed, citizens, officials, lawyers, and the courts, all have often been perplexed by the equivocal nature of Constitutional dictates. One of the fundamental provisions of the Constitution, for example, that of federalism, is nowhere systematically defined. Likewise, a famous and important item, the "necessary and proper" clause, dealing with the powers of the national government, is hardly self-explanatory. The manner in which government is to be continued in the event that a President becomes ill is not spelled out, nor are all the conceivable relationships among the three branches of government. In like manner, the Constitution is not very illuminating about the meaning of many of the first ten amendments or the Bill of Rights. Nor does it inform us as to the exact meaning of freedom of speech, press, or assembly. As a result, many cases of arrest and subsequent court action have resulted in an attempt to implement or determine the meaning of Constitutional principles. Indeed, citizens and officials have often deviated from the law simply because they did not know what the Constitution meant or could be construed to mean. Consequently, we find that equally honest and capable judges and lawyers have debated these meanings again and again as a result of the original ambiguities left by the Founding Fathers.

A third characteristic of the normative structure also requires examination: it pertains to the sanctions rather than to the norms themselves. Many of the norms—from the legal to the purely informal—are backed by sanctions that are not very stringent or demanding. And in some cases, the sanction may be equally as ambiguous as the norm. In other instances, norms are quite clear but the sanctions themselves are ambiguous. This is especially the case with the informal norms that operate among politicians. In the United States Senate, for example, one finds norms such as "one must select some fields in which to specialize," and "one must do his homework on his legislative tasks." But while these norms are fairly clear, the sanctions for failure to perform accordingly are neither very specific nor explicit.[11] On a much higher level, we may observe that although the Constitution states various rules about the powers of each branch of the government, little is said regarding any evasion or abuse of these powers. That sanctions may be unclear or weak may be regarded as a condition favorable to evasion and transgression.

Let us now consider the objects of control—citizens and officials—as possible sources of deviance. That is, let us look at these people with the intention of discovering, if we can, certain factors that might be conducive to deviance.

The most obvious factor is that the persons subject to norms are not adequately socialized in the norms and values of the society. Indeed, we noted at some length in the last chapter that many Americans do not turn out as the agents of socialization had hoped. In short, they are not ideal citizens from the point of view espoused by the socializers. Knowing little about the facts of political life, they participate very little as evidenced in high nonvoting figures. Nor do they know or behave according to all the American values and norms. Of course, the fault may not and probably does not reside in the ordinary citizen, but rather in the ideas, ideals, and methods of the agents of socialization. Whatever the reason, however, the immediate source of deviance is the deviant himself, the citizen. In some instances, no doubt, the citizen has failed to learn his roles because he could not or would not as the case may be. The political aspects of life may simply bore him or he may find them obnoxious. And so, he deviates.

A fact aiding and abetting evasion of norms is that such evasion can, in some cases, be readily justified or rationalized. Laws can be ignored or violated because the citizen feels that he is not a part of the system: "The big shots get away with it"; "I didn't do it for myself"; "They all do it";

"What difference does it make?"; "Why pick on me?" [12] Each of these rationalizations is convenient for the deviant and an acceptable one in our society. Indeed, since we ourselves are somewhat ambivalent about the "law," such rationalizations are important; because they are available, persons feel that they can violate norms.

One last factor deserves attention in that it is similar to the possibility of rationalization: this is the possibility that deviance may be legitimized by the subculture of a group, and that loyalty to that group is of primary importance to the member who deviates. Instances of this sort can be found in the unwillingness of Communists and even ex-Communists to testify against their fellow members. In the first place, membership in the Communist party is not in itself illegal. Furthermore, Communists believe that what they seek is not only consistent with American values, but may be identical; they can see no inconsistency therefore between their beliefs and actions and those of non-Communists, but even if they do see an inconsistency, they still may be moved by group loyalties not to jeopardize in any way the positions of their colleagues. In common parlance, they will not "squeal" on their friends, and this, of course, is a traditional informal norm among most Americans. Deviance, then, is sustained and justified by these considerations of belief that one is not really a deviant and, secondly, by a sense of loyalty to the subgroup.

In a society with as many laws and other political norms as this one, and with countless agents of control, it seems rather likely that some of the agents will not, for a number of reasons, enforce the norms. In other words, we have a certain degree of lax law enforcement. To enforce the laws demands energy and involves costs for both the individual agents of control and the society. Yet we as a nation do not always adequately finance enforcement; we cannot be perfectly efficient, therefore, in law enforcement. The Internal Revenue Bureau, for example, cannot possibly check on every single tax-paying citizen, given its resources. As a result the Bureau is forced to rely on spot checks and the honesty of the citizenry. Both are sufficient to deter more tax evasion, but neither is fully effective. For the Bureau to check everyone would entail spending more in enforcement than is derived from the receipts of such an operation. In effect, then, perfect law enforcement is too costly at the margin; bringing in an additional dollar would require the expenditure of much more than a dollar.[13]

The above remarks deal with situations in which rational calculation on the part of the control agency suggests that laws not be rigidly enforced. In many other types of situations, however, rationality is not the crucial factor explaining light enforcement. The control agent may be simply lax, lazy, or even unsympathetic to the laws being enforced. Police may sleep on the long lonely vigils of the night. Administrators may not approve of a law they are expected to enforce and thus resist implementing the policies. In fact, they may actively attempt to make them unworkable. In other cases, as with the Prohibition Amendment, the law enforcement officers, particularly at the local level, simply sympathized with the people who wanted to drink and so overlooked the violations as often as possible.

In addition to the above factors influencing the agents of control, there is the obvious fact that some agents are actively corrupt in their work, regarding their positions as opportunities for personal aggrandizement. Corruption, of course, has always been found in American politics, and apparently will continue for some time. Many commentators, especially during the period of 1860–1932, observed an incredible amount of corruption in the government. It was most noticeable, however, at the state and local levels. Even at the national level, Senators were bought off, Cabinet Members of Harding's Administration sold out for money, and administrators lined their own pockets. At the city level, crime and corruption so prevailed among citizens and officials that Lincoln Steffens could write a book entitled *The Shame of Our Cities.* And even today the regulatory agencies in Washington as well as at every level of government offer lucrative opportunities for the selfish and immoral to abuse their rights and powers. Not infrequently, businessmen and others who can profit from a failure to comply with laws will make various rewards available to those agents of control who are in a position to help. Thus, municipal regulatory agencies such as health and sanitation boards will overlook dirty restaurants; safety officers will fail to inspect factories and other hazardous places of work; or fire inspectors will be paid not to be too searching regarding tenement dwellings. Indeed, these are but a few illustrations for which one can find plenty of evidence in American life.

But while the agents of control may more often be corrupt in the sense of not performing their duties, they are sometimes overzealous in their work of law enforcement. Police, for example, are human beings with all the foibles of other men, and occasionally they allow their foibles freedom.[14] A case in point is that of the policeman who dislikes various minority groups with whom he may have contact. It is fairly well known, for instance, that the police of many large cities in the North as well as the South enforce the law more rigidly and consistently over Negroes than whites.[15] One and the same law is differentially employed to the disadvantage of the Negro. We also know that, during the earlier years of the union movement to organize workers, police often acted as strikebreakers and made life difficult in other ways for the unions. In some college towns the local police seem prejudiced against the students, while around military installations the police seem to be very sensitive to the offenses of soldiers. In all these cases, the police give the impression of overzealous law enforcement. In short, they seem to be more concerned with compulsive enforcement against particular groups than with being servants of the people.

Types of Deviance

Whenever one begins to type phenomena, he is confronted with the problem of deciding upon the basis of classification; deviance is no exception. The way in which the decision ought to be made rests, of course, upon the objectives of the investigator. And these objectives must be made clear, for there is no single way of classification.[16] The same phenomena, moreover, may be classified in different ways and should be if their meanings are to be completely understood. We will attempt various classifications of deviance, therefore, in accordance with our several objectives.

One way of classifying deviance is to do so according to the numbers of people involved. Another is to base the differences on the types or forms the deviance assumes, for example, violent or nonviolent. A third means of classification relates to the degree of illegitimacy involved, for some forms are considered more unacceptable than others, and some are even regarded as legitimate. Let us begin by cross-classifying the first and second approaches. Figure 4-2 illustrates some of the possibilities.

	Violent	Nonviolent
Individual	Assassination Vandalism Sabotage Treason Murder Assault	Corruption; perjury Espionage Tax Evasion Kick-backs Bribery Civil Disobedience
Group	Vandalism Rebellion Revolution Riots	Tampering with elections "Sit-ins" Communist agitation Sit-down strikes

Figure 4-2. Types of Deviant Behavior in the Polity.

Another means of clarifying deviance is to distinguish between the goals and means of political behavior. Thus, we can classify deviants on the basis of their acceptance or rejection of goals or means used in the polity. Here, we take our scheme from Robert Merton's well-known typology of individual adaptation to social structures.[17] The following table shows the various combinations, with the $(+)$ signs signifying "acceptance" and (−) signs denoting "rejection." The (±) sign means "rejection of prevailing values and substitution of new values."[18]

Table 4-1—A Typology of Modes of Political Deviance.

Modes of Deviance	Political Goals	Institutionalized Means
Innovation	+	−
Ritualism	−	+
Retreatism	−	−
Rebellion	±	±

A person or group may engage in any one of the forms of behavior found in Table 4-1 depending on personal decisions and political conditions beyond the control of the individual or group. It should also be noted that some of the modes of behavior are more acceptable than others. Thus, innovation and ritualism receive more approbation than does rebellion. Of course, none of these various forms are as acceptable as conformity, in which one accepts both the political goals and institutionalized means.

Innovation, to be sure, does have a good ring for most Americans as long as it is an abstract value. But when it means that one's own position, interests, values, and goals appear threatened thereby, support is not likely to be shown. Furthermore, few Americans appreciate the desirability of major changes in the political values and goals of our society. Indeed, few people in any society willingly take on new and different values and goals. Thus have Americans strongly rejected many socialist-type objectives. Nor is the innovator of such departures, a deviant in the polity, seldom appreciated in his own time. To be sure, innovators are welcomed by some people some of the time, and by many more especially under special conditions such as depressions. But at the level of goals themselves, innovation is not generally well received.

Ritualism is a somewhat different type of deviance. In this case, the norms of behavior are honored by performance, but the approved goals are not sought. In politics this may be taken to mean that the citizen has scaled down his expectations and demands, believing that the higher ones cannot be achieved. Such a citizen may continue to obey the laws, pay his taxes, and even vote, but he will do so with little hope that these actions will have much influence on the policies of the government. He plays it safe by not expressing opinions and by "minding his own business." Superficially, such a person may appear to be a conformist, and in a certain sense, he is. But he is also different in that he does not honor goals to the same extent. From the point of view of the polity, he is not a "problem" because he does not rebel. While there are no data on the number of these people, it would seem that they are more numerous than the innovators. Ritualism is a convenient means of adapting oneself to the polity.

Whereas the ritualist rejects the hopes for higher goals, the person who retreats rejects both goals and means not so much by a conscious and overt act, as by ignoring the political situation altogether. One is, as Merton has said, "in" the polity, but not "of" it.[19] Escaping from the problems and conflicts of the polity, the retreatist tends to feel alienated, and does not want to be bothered. Citizens are likely to feel this way when the demands of the polity are heavy and conflicting. And while no one really does escape, a person "in his own mind" may reduce his anxieties, tensions, and insecurities by devoting greater energies and time to other than political action and thought. How often does the citizen who feels burdened by politics complain of being sick and tired of it all? Defeatism, quietism, futility, and resignation are all characteristics of this type of behavior.[20] Feelings of effectiveness, if they exist at all, are extremely low. Obviously, there are varying degrees of alienation and retreat from public responsibilities. Extreme cases are probably not frequent. However, data from a number of studies seem to show that greater numbers of the alienated exist than our belief system would have us believe.[21] Additional data have suggested that the persons most subject to feelings of impotence are women and less educated, lower income, lower status, and rural people.[22]

Rebellion is the fourth form of deviance from the ideal norms. In this case the rejection of goals and means is accompanied by the substitution of other goals and means. Further, rebels are generally easy to identify because their behavior is in accordance with their beliefs and feelings. The rebel announces his position and fights against the status quo. His convictions are pronounced and his courage great. Usually his goals are the opposite of the prevalent ones as in the case of the Fascist. Usually, too, his means are opposed. This is so because he does not believe in the equity of the institutionalized means, and, as a result, may advocate violent overthrow of the government. Anarchists, Communists, "Know Nothings," the Ku Klux Klan, and American Nazis—all are examples of groups who may be considered to have been or who are rebels in the United States. Yet it is not likely that we will find many rebels at any given time because rebellion itself is an extreme action having little attraction for many citizens. In most instances, only extreme conditions affecting the individual and society will produce a rebel.

SOME MEANS OF CONTROL

The ways in which citizens are controlled are as many and varied as the ways in which they are socialized. Yet, there are differences in the types and extent of controls used in various political systems. Some, including the totalitarian, tend to depend upon violence or terror to a greater extent than do the democratic. Likewise, the latter tend to employ controls with greater consistency and regularity, and according to more universalistic standards than do the totalitarian societies. Finally, it is probably fair to say that democracies, including the United States, attempt to institutionalize controls and to minimize them, preferring greater individual freedom and the socialization process as the lesser of evils.

It is usually said that the basis of the state is legal coercion or, more accurately, that the state has the ultimate right or authority to employ coercion, including the most violent form—death—for offenders. This holds true for the United States as with every nation-state. Indeed, no subsystem or institution other than the polity can command such awesome authority and power. The power of the polity to administer the death sentence is hardly the only institutionalized authority, but it does illustrate the means of control in the ultimate sense of the word.

Formal Law

A law is a type of norm—a prescription—of what may be done, of what must be done, or of what is prohibited from being done. And attached to laws are various *sanctions,* such as jail sentences, fines, surrender of rights, paroles, and the like, for the purpose of discouraging deviance and for penalizing those who do deviate. Having authority because it has been enacted through institutionalized procedures, a law is regarded as consistent with the basic norms: in our case, the Constitution. By definition, then, laws as types of controls and norms are most explicit, institutionalized, and precise. This does not mean, however, that Americans are legally literate. Most of us, indeed, are not, and must depend upon specialists or lawyers for advice and defense. For our legal system, including the law itself, is highly complex, enormous in scope, and detailed in particulars. Moreover, it is not very organized or systematized because, like Anglo-Saxon law, it is produced on the basis of daily needs and precedents. We have not codified our laws as have the continental countries, influenced by Roman law traditions. Consequently, for the laws that control us as American citizens, we have no single source from which to consult.

Given the American's propensity to write laws and a pragmatic approach to life, they have, not unexpectedly, developed an amazingly varied repertoire of legal controls. Business, for example, today is controlled by common law, statutes and ordinances, administrative regulations, franchises, certificates, licenses, taxes, subsidies, contracts, and industry codes. The need for legal staffs in business organizations hardly requires comment. The same may be said with regard to governmental agencies and branches. In short, law is the major form or type of control whether judged in terms of the number of such controls, persons affected, administrative officials, or areas affected. A polity characterized by rational-legal authority could not be otherwise.

Violence

Although the American people and political scientists have had a tendency to avoid confronting the fact of violence in our society and political system, violence has long been a fact of American politics and society. There is, of course, legally recognized and sanctioned violence in the form of the death penalty that only the state can administer. But there is also the possibility and historical fact of much illegal and extralegal violence connected with both the integrative and allocative processes. Around election times in some areas of the nation, for example, one finds violence and intimidation a not infrequent visitor and decider of the election. More dramatic and unhappy than sporadic election violence is the persistent application of it to Negroes in the South and other areas of the country to prevent them from performing as citizens. Periodic violence so serves to warn the Negro that in proscribed areas of conduct he acts on the basis of anticipated harm. Likewise, the labor unions for many years had to experience clubs, stones, and policemen's arsenals of control. Violence, indeed, was a major fact in the early years of unionization. Other evidences of continuing violence are evident in police brutality against minorities and lower classes in most of the major cities. Then, too, there is a great deal of underworld brutality being exercised against their own kind and even over the more reputable citizenry.

The ugly presence of force is, of course, a part of every political system and society. Fortunately, however, it seems that no society or polity can be integrated solely and for long periods by brute power alone. Certainly the American political system is not very dependent on such. But it would be foolish to overlook the historical fact of power; the Civil War, for example, served as the ultimate means of reintegrating the American society and political system. Riots and minor rebellions have always been put down by the authoritative use of force and other weapons by police and soldiers. In 1958, for example, President Eisenhower found it necessary to quell rioting in Little Rock, Arkansas, by the use of military force. Likewise, President Roosevelt resorted to the Army to control veteran pension marchers in 1932. Earlier, Cleveland used the armed forces to handle the railroad strikers. And still earlier in the nation's history, the Whiskey Rebellion was squashed by force. Throughout the settling of the Western frontier, armed force was repeatedly employed to bring about law and order. The Army, for example, was continuously engaged in attempts to overcome Indians and bandits. In short, we Americans are accustomed to violent measures whether used by authorities of the government or by informal agents of control.

Propaganda

Violence is, of course, a very costly means of maintaining control over large numbers of citizens. In addition, it is morally inconsistent with the belief system of the American people and of all democrats. To employ violence, therefore, requires extraordinary conditions and justifications, many of which are not the daily fare of most stable societies. For this reason, control must be largely based upon more peaceful means such as law and custom. At times, however, even both of these means can be ignored or violated. The problem, then, is one of securing compliance or obedience without having to invoke costly penalties or sanctions. One of the ways in which conformity and support can be acquired is through the use of direct persuasion of the public.

Persuasion, or propaganda, may be simply defined as the manipulation of information and symbols designed to elicit certain political behavior. The information may be true or false or misleading, but in any case it is used to produce specific responses of support, compliance, or action. Nor is propaganda employed only by advertisers, politicians, and political parties. It is being increasingly used by the government itself.[23] Indeed, what are generally referred to by governmental administrators as informa- tion services and press officers are nothing more than propaganda and propaganda officials. And hardly a department in the federal and state governments is without a number of such people whose primary goal is to build support for their particular programs and services. From these officials come press releases, speeches, booklets and other forms of printed information, movie reels, and the like, all of which are used as techniques in opinion formation.

One of the primary sources of propaganda in government is of course the Presidency, for it is he who is now the focal point of effective action as well as the major symbol of the polity. When the President propa- gandizes, however, he does so in two roles, one as the leader of the

United States, and one as a partisan leader of a political party. His propaganda thus reflects both of these roles. In both he commands the attention of the nation and world, and has the resources of the government to propagate beliefs and desirable goals. Consequently, opponents find it difficult to mobilize as many resources for an opposed point of view. It is for this reason that the President, as well as most incumbents of public office, has an advantage in the partisan struggle.

The government in a democracy does not, however, have a complete monopoly of propaganda services and resources. In fact, the government is but one competitor in the entire system of control. Many other agents of control also exist, most of whom are private and partisan. They, too, manipulate information and symbols to build support for favored policies and actions. In the United States, these agents include the newspapers, radio, television, political parties, corporations, unions, churches, and all the other interest groups who participate in the allocative and integrative processes of the polity. Each is able to mount a certain offensive in support of their positions. In fact, for some students of government, the actions of these groups constitute the major focus of politics. Whether such an exclusive focus is justified or not, what is crucial is that all such organizations propagandize the American people, and many do so in opposition to the actions of the government. Thus, the monopoly and effectiveness of the government are weakened and democracy, thereby, may very well be protected.

Political Customs

Customs are ways of doing things that do not have the sanction of laws, nor are enacted in the same deliberate manner, but evolve through long passages of time. For the most part, customs are enforced not by external forces or agents, but by the socialized consciences or habits of the citizens. But there are always some citizens who do not accept all the political customs of the nation, and to them such customs act as controls just as do the laws. Whether accepted as legitimate or not, however, customs are present and must be accounted for in the political system.

Customs derive their force, or sanctions and legitimacy, from the people and their history as a nation. For this reason, they are not necessarily enforced by legal sanctions, but rather by public opinion. A citizen, for example, may defy opinion and not go to jail for so doing, yet his effectiveness in reaching his goals will not be enhanced, and, in all probability, will be reduced. But to return, what are some of the American political customs?

Perhaps the most important one is the two-party system; there is no constitutional provision saying we must have a party system, let alone two parties. The fact remains, however, that we do. And while the system may and does now have legal foundations and protections, it is still a custom that has been given legal recognition. For the citizen who would like a greater number of choices or alternatives at elections, the custom of having a Republican and Democratic party is a serious control over his wishes.

Another political custom of considerable significance to both the citizen and the politician has to do with the residency requirement of the latter in seeking office. In the United States, most candidates are expected, although not legally required, to be residents of the constituency from which they are running for public office. In England, such is not the case, and many members of Parliament represent districts where they have not resided.

Public Opinion

One of the most powerful controls over the behavior of Americans happens also to be one of the most difficult to describe and explain: public opinion. Many commentators including Tocqueville, Hartz, Shils, and Riesman have focused on the enormous influence that public opinion, or what citizens think others are thinking, has over their own behavior and beliefs. Tocqueville, for example, said:

> In the United States the majority undertakes to supply a multitude of ready-made opinions for the use of individuals, who are thus relieved from the necessity of forming opinions of their own. Everybody there adopts great numbers of theories, on philosophy, morals, and politics, without inquiry upon public trust; and if we look to it very narrowly, it will be perceived that religion herself holds her sway there, much less as a doctrine of revelation than as a commonly received opinion.[24]

Unlike some of the other controls we have mentioned, public opinion is a *diffused* control in that it is enforced by multitudes, not by a single or small group of specialized, legally authorized persons. Although, to be sure, opinion leaders are certainly an important element in the development and dissemination of views. Public opinion is also an *informal* means of control in that it is seldom given legal expression. Usually people simply say "they say" this, that, or otherwise. And, unlike law, public opinion does not have explicit sanctions. Opinion is, then, a control of the people or citizenry over that very same citizenry.

According to Tocqueville, public opinion is the major control, and one with frightening possibilities, chiefly because democracies such as the American exalt equality of men and therefore equality of beliefs.[25] One man's opinion is thought to be as good as the next, particularly where politics is concerned. And, since this is supposed to be true, it becomes necessary that the majority opinion be *the* opinion. Nonetheless, it is doubtful that America has suffered from public opinion to the extent of which de Tocqueville considered possible. Indeed, the very diffuseness of the process operates to make its sanctioning power less effective. Moreover, the varying conditions of American life have been such as to permit if not always encourage variety in opinion. Admittedly, at the level of basic social and political values, public opinion has been remarkably similar throughout the United States both historically and geographically. On the levels of public policy, however, much greater variations are to be found. Public opinion seems to be most powerful during periods of rapid change and crisis when fears are generated about the survival of personal values and the nation. Thus have Richard Hofstadter [26] and Talcott Parsons [27] explained the "pseudo-conservativism" of the 1950's. But regardless of the particular explanations given public opinion and the demand for conformity, no society has ever been ruled completely by the views of the masses. Rulers of course may be more or less influenced by what they believe opinion to be, but few decisions are ever dictated by public opinion. Nevertheless, opinion in democracies does form the background of official actions, and citizens do worry lest their neighbors think badly of them. In these senses public opinion is an important control in the American polity.

SOME LIMITATIONS ON CONTROL

Lest an impression be created that the polity and government can do whatever they will with respect to controlling citizens, a sharp and immediate denial must be entered; they cannot do so in a democracy. In the first place, explicit constitutional limitations are used to restrain formal governmental controls. These restraints are generally to be found in the Bill of Rights, but also in the so-called Civil War amendments— Thirteenth, Fourteenth, and Fifteenth—and in state constitutions. Each of these constitutes a guarantee of personal civil liberties from infringement by the various governments. To be sure, no such guarantee is self-enforcing; someone must be deprived of his freedoms before a case can arise, and then he must be willing and able to carry the case through the court system. As many persons and groups are in no such position, rights, therefore, are often violated through the exercise of governmental controls, particularly at the local level where police power is most dominant. Likewise, citizens are often not protected as well as they might be from controls exercised by other citizens or groups in the polity, who are not members of the government. Thus, a corporation or trade union may transgress a right, and little can or will be done about it. Nevertheless, these many rights are bulwarks against the growing controls of the government. Indeed, not only are Americans generally aware as a result of their socialization that they do have rights, but political leaders, too, are aware of this. We sometimes forget that our politicians and administrators are also citizens and that they have been socialized just as the average citizen to desire and respect personal rights. Nor must we forget the role of private associations in the protection of rights and resistance to governmental controls. They provide the individual not only with assurances of his beliefs, but also with resources that can be used in actual litigation should that be necessary. Thus, the businessman who resists governmental controls gains support from his membership in business associations, just as does the farmer from farm organizations. In addition, there are civil rights organizations dedicated to the preservation and extension of individual liberties: the Civil Liberties Union, for example, promoting liberty through propaganda and the provision of legal aid.

A point should be repeated that the government is hardly the only agent of control. In fact, as we pointed out on several previous occasions, the private agents—which may involve most people at sometime or other —may more often infringe upon rights than do the governmental authorities. In these cases, the government is looked to as the restraint or control. The injured parties may expect the government to enact legislation in order to protect their rights from other citizens. Thus, the federal government in 1957 enacted the Civil Rights Act. In addition, there is a President's Committee on Civil Rights. The Department of Justice itself has a Civil Rights Division for the exclusive purpose of protecting individual liberties. These are but a few of the governmental protections offered the citizen against groups or persons transgressing the civil rights of others.

There are other types of limitations on governmental control that are seldom mentioned, but are important, nevertheless. Here we refer to limitations, not in the sense of explicit, rational devices such as mentioned above, but limitations that stem rather from shortcomings or gaps in the regulatory process itself. One such limitation on governmental control is the very *costs* of regulation. As direct command and control are very costly, and since the government depends largely upon taxes for its revenue, there are distinct limitations on the resources put into control, and thus on the effectiveness of control itself. Secondly, control is also limited by the fact that it is generally *complex,* and must apply *to large numbers of people.* It is simply impossible for the government to observe and regulate much of the behavior that takes place within a society, even within the smallest ones. For this very reason, totalitarian societies have their own problems in exercising controls, in addition to the problems of cost. Finally, *the government must depend on agents of control* who may not be in sympathy with the controls they are asked to enforce. But while all these limitations are important, they are hardly the most significant. Liberties, in the final analysis, depend upon a population who takes its belief system and values seriously. To the extent that Americans do, they are protected. But it must always be remembered that legal institutions and inherent characteristics of control play important roles as well.

SOME CONCLUSIONS ON CONTROL

There can be little doubt that controls are or have been increasing at a rapid rate since the advent of our industrialization and urbanization. These twin developments have given birth to an increasing interdependence and frequency of contact among Americans. And as this interdependency has manifested itself more and more, citizens have demanded that the others with whom they have contact be controlled in some way so as not to injure themselves. The demand for the regulation of others, and the growing expectation the political system will help to guarantee security in a highly fluctuating society and economy, has meant an enormous increase in controls on the part of the polity. Thus, no segment of the economic system, for example, or other subsystems, is free of governmental intervention and control. In short, we have attempted to use the resources of society in a rational effort to control the circumstances under which we live. Businessmen want security as well as the laborer and the farmer.

But internal developments toward increased specialization and interdependence are hardly the only reasons why we now have more controls than ever before. One need only look at events in foreign affairs and international relations, and at the threats posed by the challenge of the Soviet Union, China, and other nondemocratic systems to the continued security of the United States to understand why the government has been driven to take measures to increase national strength. And this in turn has meant growing control as to the demands made by private individuals and groups over the resources of society and over the input of support into the polity. We have, in short, become extremely security-conscious. Indeed, it is a rare important governmental decision that is not conditioned by foreign policy developments. Consequently, individual freedom is no longer what it once was; there simply is not enough room for its unrestrained exercise. More and more we are controlled by the agencies of government and by the means of compulsion, direction, and investigation, a fact that has led some commentators to fear that we may soon cease being a democracy and become a garrison state.[28] Other commentators fear that we are already too bureaucratized. Still others fear that we are controlled, not so much by the polity as we have defined it, but by a power elite of mostly private persons.[29] Whatever the actual situation, there is little doubt that the number of controls has significantly increased, that the number of citizens controlled has increased, and that the number of agencies of control has spiralled. No longer do we depend on automatic types of control that once presumably regulated the economy and public affairs, too. Increasingly, our controls are of the overt, direct, legally enforced type. The unseen hand of Adam Smith or the "popular democrat" is still with us, to be sure, but unfortunately, it is of much less importance.

9

Conflict

Real and Potential

Chapters 7 and 8 were intended to show how the American society and polity meet the two most general and universal problems of integration and conflict management through socialization and political control. We have suggested all along that, while one of the functions of the polity is to integrate the larger society, it is also necessary for the polity, itself, to be integrated as a system if the larger function is to be served. But complete integration of the membership in a social system is not a prerequisite of action. Such a state, in fact, cannot even be attained.[1] Indeed, some would maintain, including the writer, that such a state is neither attainable nor desirable. In a democracy, conflict of certain types and within certain levels is both preferable and necessary.

But conflict must be conducted in such a manner that it is productive in the sense of enabling us to realize individual and societal goals and values. The problem, then, is one of figuring out how the American system *handles* conflict or potential conflict so that its worst consequences are reduced and its benefits increased. While political socialization and control of course are basic to the problem, they are not the only structures and processes by which potential conflict—or tension—is handled. In the present chapter our major concern will be with some of the other structures and processes that supplement or implement the basic ones, in both reducing the level of tension and handling it in more peaceful ways.

We will begin our analysis with a distinction between two general types of processes; the socio-psychological and the political. The argument, in brief, will be that we depend upon the former to lessen the development of conflict as well as to divert that which exists or is generated to other channels than the polity. In this regard, we will consider both personality and social mechanisms. The political processes on the other hand are found in the polity and are primarily oriented to the handling of conflict once it has developed. One cannot be dogmatic on this score, however, for the polity also attempts, under some conditions, to reduce conflict.

The reader should also be aware that each of these mechanisms or processes may be classified or looked at from other points of view. For example, we might classify them according to whether they are deliberate, consciously operated, or unconscious means. From time to time, then, we will indicate in a few words whether a particular process functions at the conscious or unconscious levels in social behavior, as well as point out the characteristics mentioned above. It should also be said in a direct and somewhat uncompromising way that the various structures and processes we discuss are neither purely integrative or disintegrative, but rather a combination of both. However, we do maintain that there tends to be some functional differentiation with respect to these processes, and that at least these dual aspects can be distinguished. Thus, when we argue that elections, for example, serve integrative purposes, we do not mean that conflict is not also encouraged. Rather, each is encouraged at different levels and at different times in the political process. These distinctions must be kept in mind throughout the analysis.

SOCIO-PSYCHOLOGICAL STRUCTURES AND PROCESSES

In this section we will discuss a variety of factors that serve either to reduce or channel potential and overt conflict and tension away from the political system. By way of introduction, they may be summarized as follows:

1. Resources and the belief system.
2. Diverse goals.
3. Social opportunity and mobility.
4. Control of demands and "affect."
5. Displacement of hostilities.

Resources and the Belief System

The abundance of natural resources in America has been stated, *ad nauseum,* by social scientists, historians, and other commentators. What has not been so frequently observed are the consequences of such affluence for beliefs, attitudes, and political behavior. One historian, however—David M. Potter—influenced by behavioral social science, has drawn some very explicit generalizations about the relationships of abundance and American character.[2] In addition to a brilliant argument that abundance is a precondition of democracy, Potter also claims that abundance has shaped our views of political action. We can do no better than quote him on the matter.

> Not only has the presence of more than enough seats, more than enough rewards for those who strive, made the maintenance of a democratic system possible in America; it has also given a characteristic tone to American equalitarianism as distinguished from the equalitarianism of the Old World. Essentially, the difference is that Europe has always conceived of redistribution of wealth as necessitating the expropriation of some and the corresponding aggrandizements of others; but America has conceived of it primarily in terms of giving to some without taking from others. Hence, Europe cannot think of altering the relationship between the various levels of society without assuming a class struggle; but America has altered and can alter these relationships without necessarily treating one class as the victim or even, in an ultimate sense, the antagonist of another. The European mind often assumes implicitly that the volume of wealth is fixed; that most of the potential wealth has already been converted ino actual wealth; that this actual wealth is already in the hands of owners; and, therefore, that the only way for one person or group to secure more is to wrest it from some other person or group, leaving that person or group with less. The British Labour Party, for instance, has, I believe, placed greater emphasis upon the heavy taxation of the wealthy and less upon the increase of productive capacity than an American labor party might have done. The American mind, by contrast, often assumes implicitly that the volume of wealth is dynamic; that much potential wealth still remains to be converted; and, that diverse groups—for instance, capital and labor—can take more wealth out of the environment by working together than they can take out of one another by class warfare.[3]

Ever-growing demands for more, in this perspective, do not mean demands relative to someone else, but simply more for everyone. The character of American politics is, therefore, as Potter has stated, different from European politics, for we contend with the environment more than with one another. Consequently the polity, in a very real sense, has had less stress placed upon it. The existence of large quantities of resources and the belief in the possibilities of abundance have not created any great demand for utopian political changes. The tensions that exist otherwise in countries with smaller supplies, and with beliefs in politics as a kind of "zero-sum game," have thereby been reduced.

Not unconnected with these considerations is the additional fact that the goals which Americans seek, regardless of the means, are diverse and not all in conflict. Let us see how this variable is tied to integration.

Diversity of Goals

All men do not covet identical goals. Even given a limited supply of resources, not all men will engage in the same struggle over the same resources for the same goal. What one finds rather is that some of the people some of the time will be engaged in a struggle over the same goals. Instead of one enormous struggle in which all participate against all, we see a mere handful of citizens fighting, and the bulk of the populace either uninterested or not participating.[4] Compared to the situation of many nations, there are countless small-scale conflicts short in duration. Indeed, the number of citizens who directly participate at any given time in allocative battles is actually miniscule. Emile Durkheim expressed it well when he wrote:

> In the same city, different occupations can co-exist, without being obliged mutually to destroy one another, for they pursue different objects [goals]. The soldier seeks military glory, the priest moral authority, the statesman power, the businessman riches, the scholar scientific renown. Each of them can attain his end without preventing the others from attaining theirs. . . .[5]

In short, the heterogeneity of our population tends to encourage a variety of goals or "objects," as Durkheim called them. This tendency works toward minimizing the number of competitors in any given struggle for a scarce resource. Competition will, of course, persist among those who do participate and covet the same object, but the important point is that the total number of competitors is reduced. Thereby the shares of each may be increased. Since we are not all pursuing the same goal, we can afford not to participate in many of the allocative problems of society; we need not get agitated over every struggle, for the stakes are not at issue for us. Much of American indifference to politics is explained by this simple but seldom recognized fact.

Social Opportunity and Mobility

One of the great promises of America for the European immigrant as well as the native American is the opportunity or possibility of advancing either himself or his sons up the social scale of income and prestige.[6] That this has historically been the case to perhaps an unequalled degree has meant that the attentions and energies of citizens could be directed to the pursuit of social gains on an individual basis. And while there are classes, they are relatively open to upward movement and interchange of members. In societies in which class is stronger and the avenues of entry are closed, men become and remain members of a single class. Their aspirations, if any, are of a class nature. That is, the individual cannot hope to climb by himself as in America, but he may benefit by class action. This usually means a combination of economic and political action through class movements. Politics, then, is the major means of improvement of social position. In the United States by contrast, the ambitious young man devotes his energies not to politics or strikes, but to *individual* efforts at climbing by himself the social-economic scale. He does this not by challenging the status quo, as does the young political malcontent of many other lands, but by demonstrating his acceptance of it, and his ability to work within the accepted system. If he aspires to business success, he is likely to espouse business values and sound Republicanism —hardly a challenge to the status quo.

Control of Demands and "Affect"

Because politics, like religion, involves man in some of his most crucial beliefs, it is small wonder that his political feelings or sentiments are likely to be intense and seek expression. Not only are such sentiments likely to be highly emotive or affectively charged, but, when given an outlet, they may also stimulate considerable conflict and hostility. In a democracy it is inevitable that the political atmosphere will be charged with much emotion for the obvious reason that democracy is intended to allow as much free play of ideas and sentiment as is felt possible. Yet, entirely free expression of emotion or affect may also be disruptive in terms of goal-attainment, system maintenance, and integration. No polity, of course, allows complete freedom, or much less encourages an undisciplined expression of sentiments.

In all political systems, one finds a variety of mechanisms for the control of sentiment or affective behavior. As might be supposed, these means consist of both the formal and informal, external and internal, the conscious and unconscious, and active and passive types. The United States is no exception. In fact, we will argue that it uses all these mechanisms in great number, and is generally effective, although not so effective as, say, Great Britain and some of the Scandinavian countries. On the other hand, the United States is more completely controlled in this regard than Italy or France, when one looks at the frequency of overt conflict. Whatever the extent of control, let us analyze how affective expression is limited.

In the polity as a whole, affect is limited in the first instance by the existence of explicit rules, such as slander and libel laws, prohibiting extreme verbal aggression. Also, speech *leading* directly to violence has been punishable, though, in view of the First Amendment, the lines drawn are less clear. Indeed, the Supreme Court, in many of its rulings on freedom of speech, has devoted a great deal of attention to making such considerations explicit. Does the speech concerned tend "to incite violence" or unlawful acts; are "fighting words" used; is there a "clear and present danger" that the words used will bring about "substantive evils" that governments have a right to prevent? In such cases the Court has examined the affective content of such speech, and made judgments as to its potential for creating illegal conflict.[7]

Affective expression is also limited by the existence of many informal norms or standards of courtesy and taste in political discourse and conduct. Political oratory, for example, is no doubt highly exaggerated and emotional, but it is seldom marked by the use of profanity, obscenity, or hysterical speech in public. Laws also regulate this type of expression on the public media of communication. But above all, there is the general understanding that politics is to be conducted in certain more or less dignified ways. The higher the office that is being sought or the more important the issue in the nation, the greater the chances that political language will be couched in morally acceptable terms. No one, for example, would tolerate an outburst of profanity among Presidential candidates. Indeed, candidates for almost any office are expected to honor common standards of decency in their behavior, to act reasonable, and to control their tendencies, if any, to vent personal emotion. Further, acceptable emotion in political oratory is highly ritualized. Alarm is raised, for example, over abstract, nonpersonal problems about which there is much agreement: communism, corruption, or loss of national prestige. And while these matters can be the source of public disorder, they rarely contribute to violence.

There is one area of political life in which affective expression is highly charged, but also highly circumscribed, namely, intraparty activities. Party conventions, for example, are marked by invective, complaint, charge, countercharge, and declarations of undying loyalty. But although the tension and emotion of most party conclaves run high, they are still circumscribed in a variety of ways, namely, by basic agreements with the opposition party, ritualized emotion that few people take seriously, and a "fun" atmosphere. In short, the norms of party struggle are such that violence is minimized, and the verbal battle is treated as something of a sham.

Control of affect is even more noticeable in the formal governmental structure. Take administrative organizations as an illustration. In bureaucracy we see the norms of universalism, functional-specificity, and effective neutrality at work, both with respect to internal behavior as well as to external relations. The administrator is expected to run his organization according to the dictates of reason or rationality rather than emotion, and he is usually successful. In fact, many critics argue, too successful, regarding bureaucracy as cold, efficient, and impersonal. But the administrator, expected to govern his decisions by resort to facts and rational justification, would get nowhere with the legislature or the client if he frankly admitted basing decisions on feelings. We even protect or provide conditions to facilitate this type of action by the use of civil service rules and by prohibiting administrators from using their posts for political purposes. Administrators, then, are discouraged from emotionalism, or even support-arousing political activity.

We have accomplished much the same, if not more, with respect to controlling affective display in the court system. The processes of the judiciary have been reduced, in effect, to a highly ritualized kind of rationality in which rules, or procedure, and the need for evidence and reasoned arguments are exalted to the highest degree. We further protect the judiciary by isolating the judges from the need or desire to participate in the more emotionally charged political process.[8] This has been done by both formal and informal rules; for example, by appointing judges for life, that is, for good behavior. This preservation of distance from affective dispute is most marked in the case of the Supreme Court, clothed in such formality and ritual ceremony. No politician or interest group would dare attempt in any direct way to interfere with its isolation. Witness the failure of Roosevelt to "pack" the court in 1938, when he launched a direct attack upon its neutrality.

The legislative situation is also a case in point. That legislatures wage more overt and continual conflict than any other branch of government does not preclude them from attempting to reduce the extent of affectivity.[9] Not only are rules of procedure very much in evidence, but both formal rules and powerful informal norms exist to govern the amount of emotion expressed in legislative debate. In fact, one might argue that much of legislative debate is very boring precisely because affectivity is not encouraged or always permitted.

Neither profanity nor questioning of a colleague's motives is permitted by formal rule. Gentlemanly conduct is expected at all times and is seldom violated. Cases when it has been are remembered precisely because they are so exceptional. It should also be noted that American legislatures do not debate as much as is generally thought to be the case. Rather, many speeches are delivered, but these are for the constituents back home, and of little concern to the members. Indeed, the entire membership is usually not even present on the floor. The stirring debates of history, either in Congress or the state legislatures, are few and far between. Furthermore, much of the content of legislative concerns is dry, factual, detailed, and unemotional. As a casual glance at the *Congressional Record* would indicate, the speeches of legislators are filled with statistics and facts.

Until now, we have described the social aspect of the control of "affect" by illustrations. We have yet to touch upon the psychological aspect, or the processes that occur within the individuals making up the polity. To do so requires a few words on "repression." The phenomenon of repression is one of the basic processes in the personality, and, as such, has come in for a great deal of emphasis by psychologists.[10] Interestingly, we may note that it has an analogue in the political system, as a system. But first, a definition: an act of repression is an active effort to suppress information or feelings (conscious and unconscious) that are somehow regarded as undesirable to recognize. Thus, many Americans attempt to repress their hostility toward other persons with whom they may be daily required to live or work. We have some interesting examples of this sort of thing among citizens as individuals and in our government.

Citizens frequently repress partisan feelings when in the company of others whom they know are either identified with the opposite party or of whom they are unsure. Sometimes this activity has been interpreted to mean that Americans are indifferent to politics. Actually, it may often mean that politics is a matter of such intense conviction that citizens would rather repress their sentiments than engage in divisive action with their neighbors. The voting studies, for example, have demonstrated that communication among voters at campaign time is most likely to be structured in such a way that Democrats discuss politics with Democrats, while Republicans talk politics only with fellow Republicans.[11] Thus, the parties are integrated while the nation itself is polarized. During the periods between elections, however, we find this repression serving to integrate people who would otherwise be enemies if they discussed political values and beliefs. Arguments about baseball and fishing or cars can be readily conducted without bad feelings, but not so politics. Under these conditions, the rational thing to do in the interests of the maintenance of friendship is to repress the political. Such is the case with many citizens.

Another way in which repression functions as an integrative device stems from the fact that citizens do not normally run to the government or make political ultimatums out of all their demands, expectations, and frustrations. In fact, it is highly doubtful whether a very large percentage of the total demands an individual might have are ever given political expression. To measure this assertion poses tremendous problems, but casual observation would seem to suggest that most citizens look for nonpolitical structures and means of realizing their demands more often than not. Since one's irritations at many of the government's regulations are either repressed or vented in private, the politicians and the polity simply do not hear many of them, nor are they forced to act on all of them. Likewise, many felt injustices are never raised to the level of public complaint nor brought to the courts for adjudication. Repression of these demands and expectations is not only regarded as less costly, but in some cases as proper, in order that one not be regarded as a poor loser. Thus, Vice President Nixon, on losing so close an election for the Presidency as he did in 1960, did not complain publicly. He accepted the loss gracefully, and did not ask for recounts of the ballots in many exceedingly close electoral districts, although many of his party managers did press for more. Political leaders constantly repress demands in the interests of societal integration, especially where it is part of their role-expectation. A famous instance of this occurred during the 1944 Presidential election when Thomas E. Dewey agreed to a request on the part of President Roosevelt not to use certain materials in his campaign against the latter in the interests of the nation at war.[12] Many lesser instances could be cited, but these are sufficient to suggest the role of repression among leaders and citizens.

We will now shift to the system level, and analyze the governmental activities as they serve this function. Office-holders in government constantly repress information. Or, to put it another way, they refuse to divulge information that either might be embarrassing for their group in the government or useful to an enemy or that might otherwise put them at a disadvantage. In particular circumstances, Presidents can legally repress or suppress information, that is, not disclose it to Congress or the press. Such nondisclosure, upon protest, is usually *explicitly* justified as being "in the public interest." The implicit aim—to restrict the area of controversy—is often quite obvious. Presidents as individuals and partisans may also attempt and succeed at repression of political conflict. Indeed some Presidents and other politicians, having strong dislikes for conflict, have often attempted to avoid or suppress it in ways which protect themselves as individuals and divert the citizenry from believing that conflict is widespread or serious in the society. In such cases, emphasis is accorded to the agreements rather than to the discord that may exist. Symbolic rather than instrumental action is preferred.

Parties, themselves, may also find repression to be the best way of handling conflict. This is normally considered the best course of action when the conflict reaches high levels of intensity. For example, E. E. Schattschneider, tells us that:

> Sectional conflict before the Civil War was so explosive and dangerous that both major parties treated it warily and avoided offending the sectional interests so successfully that they concealed the depth and passion of the conflict in the country. As a consequence the contest over slavery was carried on *outside* the parties. . . .[13]

Although some politicians do benefit from the exploitation of dissension, many more treat such conflict with caution, for the outcomes are seldom certain. Under such assumptions, the rational action would seem to be one of allowing the conflict to be waged by others, if, indeed, it is to be waged at all.

But while the control of affect is manifest, we are still left without an explanation of why Americans have tended to place limits on the emotive side of political life. The answer, or so it seems to this writer, apparently stems from the belief system. We have seen how certain themes of work, practicality, rationality, science, technology, and simplicity dominate the American beliefs concerning life and its values. We have noted also that our beliefs show a strong liberal foundation and that Protestantism holds sway over the religious scene in America. Keeping all this in mind, our argument, then, can be summarized by saying that the American belief system is a composite of beliefs arising out of science, liberalism, and Protestantism and the central characteristic of each of these various orientations toward life and politics is one that stresses norms of *rationality* rather than emotion or affectivity. In fact, each thought pattern attempts to control the display of emotionalism, substituting in its place *facts* and *logic*. No thought system, of course, can completely eliminate affect. But some do deemphasize it and attempt to control its expression. Thus, Protestantism has reduced the amount of pageantry in religion and churches; liberalism honors laws and not men in government; and science obviously tries, and largely succeeds, in reducing or eliminating the affective component of thinking. Each of these belief systems, in turn, then reinforces the other in the reduction of affectivity in American politics.

These are elements of our belief system that become an internalized restraint on our political conduct through the socialization process. In addition, they become the basis and rationalization of the system of external controls adopted to limit affectivity in the various branches of the government. All these controls seem quite natural to us for the simple reason that we have been educated to believe in them as axioms of conduct.

Of course, affectivity is not thereby eliminated from the polity, nor is it likely to be. The reasons for this are apparent: emotion is required to provide motivation for participation; an advocate of a completely emotionless system would soon lack followers. Also, affectivity is ever-present because conflicting interests and values are ever-present. In short, the polity—without reifying it—has a considerable amount of affectivity or emotion below the surface, constantly seeking outlets. No one can have all his demands satisfied; *ergo,* a high level of tension. Then, too, we require affectivity to provide patriotism, an emotion that is hardly based upon interests or reason. Indeed, emotional identification is its major basis. In effect, we attempt to direct affectivity into the areas of agreement, such as patriotism, and away from the more contentious issues and areas.

Displacement of Hostilities

Harold Lasswell once said that, "One of the principal functions of symbols of remote objects, like nations and classes, is to serve as targets for the relief of many of the tensions which might discharge disastrously in face-to-face relations." [14] Hostilities among members of a society can be reduced, in other words, by transferring or displacing them on people outside the society. At the same time, it becomes possible not only to reduce internal tensions, but to create greater solidarity among those who would otherwise be in conflict. Many social scientists would agree with the observation of Georg Simmel that:

> The group in a state of peace can permit antagonistic members within it to live with one another in an undecided situation because each of them can go his own way and can avoid collisions. A state of conflict, however, pulls members so tightly together and subjects them to such uniform impulse that they either must get along completely with, or completely repel, one another. This is the reason why war with the outside is sometimes the last chance for a state ridden with inner antagonisms to overcome these antagonisms, or else break up definitely. . . .[15]

The way in which displacement occurs is relatively simple to understand. As Americans share more values, norms, and perceptions among themselves than they do with other societies, each of us is capable of forgetting or minimizing our differences when faced with a *common* enemy or threat to our sense of security. Since the dawn of civilization, political leaders seemed to have known this elementary political fact, and have not been in the least reluctant to use it. American politicians are no exception. European countries, and the U.S.S.R. in particular, have and are serving the American people as objects for the displacement of hostility that might otherwise have been vented on our own people, institutions, and behavior.

THE POLITICAL SYSTEM AND CONFLICT

The discussion has proceeded in terms of a number of socio-psychological mechanisms, and their application in America, which have relevance to the handling of conflict. The argument has been that each of these mechanisms serves to generate conflict under certain conditions and to reduce or redirect it from the polity under still other conditions. For the most part, they have served to minimize conflict in American history either by reducing or by so structuring it that it can be more easily handled if and when politicized.

Little has been said, however, about the political system, itself, and the effects it may have upon the handling of conflict and the integration of the society. Thus, we will now view the polity as it shapes and handles the inevitable problems of differences. The argument will be largely consistent with the preceding: namely, that the American polity, while generating conflicts itself and making integration difficult, does, nevertheless, deal with conflict in such a way that integration is possible on a higher level than might otherwise be the case. We will deal with the situation in terms of both the political culture and the structure of the polity and government.

Institutionalization of Conflict

The waging of competition for public offices, whether electoral or civil service, has come to assume legitimate forms since the founding of the Republic. The desire has not been one of denying competition nor of reducing it, but of giving it a legitimacy in terms of the value and normative systems. Accordingly, Americans have regulated political competition both by legal and informal norms, and have justified the competition as being good or beneficial. The crucial point for us, at this time, consists of the fact that we have regulated or institutionalized the process itself. Various norms or requirements, for example, are specified in law as to the time of elections, who may vote, who may run for office, how he must qualify, how many votes he must gain to win, how he may campaign, how the votes are counted, and how the winner is to be declared and installed in office. Each of these phases of electoral competition is regulated in detail.

Still, we sometimes forget the significance of institutionalization. But, imagine if you will, what the struggle for public office might be without a highly stable set of norms. Under such conditions, it is entirely possible that there would be no regular or periodic elections, that competition might assume violent forms, that losers would not concede offices. Norms, of course, may be and are violated, but still they serve the function of control with remarkable effectiveness in all stable political systems. Competition, therefore, assumes a definite pattern, and is predictable in the sense that we as citizens know how it will be conducted, just as football fans know the game of football. Consequently, we spend our election days much as we do any other day of the year; we need have no fears about the events, for they are, in fact, regulated by a complex, but highly effective, set of norms.

American Political Culture and the "Public Interest"

One of the more used and abused concepts in the history of political science is that of the "public interest." [16] We need not enter that fray to make use of the term, nor will we. Yet, whatever the meaning of the public interest in any given political struggle or issue, it is clear that the *belief* on the part of many citizens in the existence of such an interest tends to counter the quest for a self-interest or to appease the charge of self-interest. We see evidence of this in the fact that every interest group and politician attempts to garb his own special interest in terms of the public good, whatever that may be. The doctrine of a public interest therefore encourages individuals and groups to either modify their demands in anticipation of arousing an angry public, or it forces them to justify their interests and demands in accordance with higher values, such as presumably make up the public's interest. Indeed, the very effort of rationalization causes an interest in viewing things from another point of view. Furthermore, it also offers a convenient means for representatives of Congress, say, to question the demands of partial interests. In short, one's own demands must be reconciled with those of others. And the fact that the government's officials may invoke such standards does aid, it would seem, in controlling demands and political conflict.

Clearly, certain kinds of demands are not even given a hearing because the public interest appears manifest. The manufacture and sale of poisonous drugs and dangerous weapons, for example, cannot be advanced as a legitimate goal by interest groups because it cannot easily be rationalized, unless controls are accepted. From the point of view being argued here, the belief in a public interest is a means of regulating conflict. It may not be the most effective, but it is nevertheless one of the means.

Political Symbolism and Symbolic Acts

In Chapter 6 we detailed the role of symbolism in the polity, saying that its greatest significance had to do with the integration of the polity. Here we wish to recall and emphasize that point; namely, that political symbols and symbolic actions on the part of our leaders are extraordinarily important as integrative devices. An appreciation of this contention can be gained by observation of the daily activities of Presidents, governors, and other executives in the political system.

Presidents devote a large proportion of each day to seeing a great variety of delegations and individuals not connected with an official position in the government—sessions that are usually photographed and printed in the newspapers for all who would to see. The significance of these countless meetings is to demonstrate to the people concerned and to the public the President's interest in everyone from the crippled children used in antipolio campaigns, to the leaders of industry, arts, education, labor, and the churches. Each segment of society is granted recognition in a symbolic act, and while they may not get more from the allocative processes, the *recognition* itself is important. The world of the arts, education, and other groups, for instance, not so fully recognized by an Eisenhower Administration, now seem gratified by the recognition of the Kennedy Administration. Interestingly, President Kennedy has also made strenuous symbolic gestures toward the business groups who had some reservations about his sympathy. Likewise, President Eisenhower made gestures of a symbolic nature toward labor.

Other types of symbolic integrative actions include all the historic and memorial events that serve as our rituals of civic solidarity. Normally, public officials are the major figures in these events, and on each occasion the unity of the nation is stressed.

Decentralization of the Polity

One of the more elementary facts about the structure of the American political system is its *decentralization of decision-making or power*. The significance of this fact, however, has not always been appreciated in terms of its implications for conflict. *A decentralized political system tends to decentralize the conflict that takes place within its bounds.* The reason for this is quite simple. In the United States, the offices or decision-making points are the focal points of the conflicts; and with many of them independent or semi-independent of one another, the conflicts between them also become independent or semi-independent. Conflict may be waged between each, in short, with little reference to the others. This frequently happens, and is abetted by the additional fact that elections are staggered so that the issues of one level of government cannot be injected easily into another. Local elections tend to be local elections and not state or national, although, as V. O. Key, Jr., has shown, there are mutual influences.[17]

Nevertheless, potential general conflict is isolated into lesser but more numerous conflicts. Fewer persons are involved, and the objects of the conflict are lesser in scope than they might be were the governmental structure centralized. Another important consequence flows from the decentralization of political power, namely, that the defeated in an election at one level or set of offices need not fear for their exclusion from power; they may win in some other office or set. Certainly, the costs of defeat are hardly as great as the game played under "zero-sum" rules where the winner takes all and there are no return matches. In addition to the geographic decentralization of power, it is also "decentralized in time." That is, frequent elections give the defeated a chance to recoup their losses fairly soon. Once again, the costs of defeat are reduced and the rewards of victory curtailed, so that the participants have neither as much to lose or to win, and therefore may play a low-pressure game with lower stakes.

Elections

Political scientists have traditionally treated elections as devices whose sole purpose is that of selecting leaders in the political system and whose major consequence seems to be that of inciting conflict. Admittedly, elections do provide a means for the selection of leaders and, to a lesser extent, the choice of public policies. But the fact that elections create and sustain conflict is still less consequential than is ordinarily assumed. For while elections heighten conflict, they also resolve it. Elections thus also act as mean for the mobilization of support for the various elements of the polity.[18] Let us see how this is done, first, in theoretical terms, and then with empirical data.

The heated arguments of some partisans during election campaigns are somewhat misleading if they are not analyzed in detail. To be sure, opponents do appear to attack one another vehemently throughout the elections; but in the process they also *reaffirm* their *mutual* faith in the laws of the nation, in the political system, and in societal, as well as political, values. Figure 4-3 illustrates the point.

Elections are means, then, of choosing leaders and of indicating the broad directions of public policies, as shown by the bottom two lines in Figure 4-3. It is at these levels that we will find the most disagreement

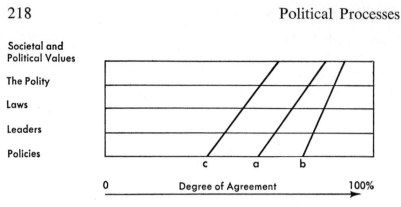

Figure 4-3.   Levels and Objects of Conflict and Support.

in American politics. But under some conditions, elections also serve to resolve conflict at these same levels and to build support for both the leaders and the broad basis of policy. Just as important, elections serve as public, institutionalized means of reasserting our common faith in our laws, the polity, and values as indicated by the upper lines of the diagram. The curves in Figure 4-3 are hypothetical and are meant to suggest the general situation of conflict on election day (*a*), and shortly thereafter (*b*). We note that (*b*) is somewhat to the right, indicating greater solidarity or agreement after the election. Citizens who may have opposed the winner or his policies are seen as less antagonistic, and, indeed, even willing to give the winner a chance to see what he can do. This is the period of the traditional "honeymoon" enjoyed by politicians during the first few months of their incumbency.

What evidence do we have in support of the theory of elections as integrative mechanisms in the polity? Admittedly, the evidence is limited, but it is convincing, nevertheless. For example, Paul Lazarsfeld and his colleagues [19] discovered in their study of the 1940 Presidential election that voters were quite lenient toward the opposition even in the case of so controversial a figure as Roosevelt. At the most intense stage of the campaign, the writers noted, "only 25 per cent of the respondents were in what might be called wholehearted agreement with their own parties. . . ." [20] They also observed:

> Another indication of this lenient attitude toward the campaign is provided by the changes in opinion of some Republicans toward Roosevelt just after the election. Even a week or so after Election Day, when the smoke of the campaign battle had hardly had time to clear away, 22 per cent of the Republican voters had already bettered their opinion of Roosevelt, now that he had again been elected president. Most of the Republicans, of course, still maintained the opinion they had held before Election Day.[21]

There is additional support for the theory that voters adjust their attitudes toward the winner where pollsters have discovered that more voters claimed to have cast their votes for the winner than he, in fact, received on election day. The most recent Presidential election offers further confirmation of the theory. Consider the findings of Dr. George Gallup who has kept a continuing check on the popularity of Presidents since Franklin D. Roosevelt. One of his attempts to test public opinion showed that, although President Kennedy won by less than 1 per cent of the votes cast, only two months later (January, 1961), he had the approval of the voters by a ratio of 9 to 1. President Eisenhower, in January of 1953, had an even greater amount of support than on election day. Only 4 per cent of the respondents disapproved of the way in which he was doing his job.[22]

A well-known reporter, James Reston of *The New York Times,* noted the above phenomena concerning Kennedy when he wrote in his column:

> As a result, an interesting thing has happened. The mail reaching the capital now is full of letters from Republicans testifying that they feel much better about Kennedy's victory today than they did two months ago, and the President-elect is thus approaching Inauguration Day with a larger margin of support than when he was elected.[23]

One last bit of evidence can be interpreted to show the integrative functions of elections. Namely, that with but few exceptions—the Civil War election of 1860, and those of 1896 and 1928—elections have tended to draw the parties closer together than they would have been otherwise had there been no elections or had there been longer periods between elections. In the same vein, it should be noted that candidates at the national level, if not always those at lower levels, tend to modify their positions during such times, and sound very much alike. To be sure, the election itself is not the cause of the drawing together, but it is the mechanism that releases integrative actions. The politicians are forced at election time, as at no other, to appeal to the large moderate sector of the population in order to gain majorities.[24]

Like all generalizations, however, it is necessary to state the conditions under which the various consequences develop or result. Certainly not all elections result in greater cohesion. Indeed, some may, as did the 1860 election, produce or exacerbate conflict (curve *c*). But generally in the United States, an election may serve integrative functions, if for no other reason than that we already have a considerable degree of agreement at the higher levels of values and acceptance of the structure of the polity (curve *a*). Were this not the case, an election would raise questions and issues of disagreement and make them more difficult to handle. Given our situation, however, many elections in the United States do serve as rituals of integration, demonstrating that we can afford to disagree over minor matters because we are more united on the higher ones. Elections also serve to indicate that the outcomes are often so insignificant that nonvoting may be a rational form of behavior. Under a truly divided society an election would attract many more voters for the simple reason that there was something to resolve.

Significance of Political Outcomes

What we are about to discuss is intimately related to a number of the other factors already denoted, and may even be somewhat repetitious. A new slant, however, may sometimes clarify. Also, there are some new elements in the explanation.

Many observers have berated the American people because they do not seem to participate in politics in any great numbers nor to care very much about the opportunities to participate. Others have been so unkind as to say that our party system does not afford very many clear-cut alternatives either in the way of candidates for office or public policies. We choose, if we choose at all, between Tweedledee and Tweedledum. Without realizing it, the critics have pointed their fingers at some very important factors involved in tension-management and ultimately in both the integrative and allocative processes and their outcomes. Let us now see how these criticisms can be used to explain the situation in the United States.

While elections may or may not be thought very important by many political scientists, it is becoming more and more evident that many citizens do not seem to regard them as being crucial. In other words, the outcome—who wins—does not seem relevant to their daily lives, nor do their major values appear to be at stake. Fortunately, there is some evidence on that score from the polls of the Survey Research Center at the University of Michigan. In their study of a national sample of the voters in the 1952 Presidential election campaign, the voters were asked, "Do you think it would make a good deal of difference to the country whether the Democrats or Republicans win the election . . . or that it won't make much difference which side wins?" [25] In the resulting answers, about *one-fifth* thought it would make *much* difference, and *nearly* a *third* said it would make *no* difference. *Two out of five* thought it would make *some* difference. Table 4-2 [26] from the study gives a more accurate breakdown on the figures.

Table 4-2—Perception of Importance of Election to the Country.

"Do you think it would make a good deal of difference to the country whether the Democrats or Republicans win the election . . . or that it won't make much difference which side wins?"	Percentage of Total Sample
A good deal of difference	21
Some difference, minor differences	40
It depends	1
No difference	32
Don't know or not ascertained	6
Total	100
Number of cases	1,614

In other words, our assertion may be stated as meaning that the 1952 Presidential election was not regarded as so crucial in terms of the voters, preferences that they could view possible outcomes with alarm or consider leaving the country. And while the 1952 election is but one election among thousands, it hardly seems wise to suggest that most local or state elections are more crucial. Indeed, at the national level, many elections might well be thought of as less important than that of 1952. Professor Key seems to believe that we have had only a very few of what he calls "critical" elections (those of 1860, 1896, and 1928).[27] These were the elections that altered the power structure of the country and the distribution of values and costs. But the question still remains whether even these elections were *perceived* by many citizens as having crucial stakes.

While it is somewhat more speculative, we may also suggest that not only do Americans tend to view the outcomes of elections with a considerable amount of indifference, but they also tend to view the outcomes of political struggles between elections as being somewhat suspect, not so suspect, however, that they are greatly dissatisfied with the results. Although the evidence on the proposition is lean, many of the matters we have thus far used do tend to lead our logic in that direction. Put in the form of a graph, a curve might be drawn to illustrate the thesis.

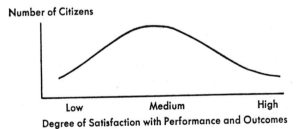

Figure 4-4. **Satisfaction with Political Performance and Outcomes.**

Figure 4-4 indicates that a few citizens are not very satisfied with the outcomes of the allocation process, a few are highly satisfied, and that most citizens fall somewhere in between, or are moderately satisfied. The curve, of course, is a hypothetical one and not an empirically based schedule. But regardless of its precise shape and position, it does seem to be reasonably consistent with most of what we know about the situation.[28] Surely it is more consistent than would be an inverted, or U-shaped, curve or one that ran either downward and to the right or upward and to the right. The latter would suggest utopia, the former, revolution.

Voluntary Coordination among Government Officials

In speaking of voluntary coordination among governmental officials, we are concerned with the means by which a highly differentiated and decentralized political system and formal structure of the government are integrated so that effective action can be taken with respect to selecting and implementing system goals. The cooperation of which we speak exists for both phases, but is particularly relevant to the implementation of policy. We need not further emphasize the matter of the decentralization of our system. What is imperative to realize is that effective action in the American polity may be extraordinarily difficult, posing many problems for official leadership. Thus, contradictions arise from different units of the system pursuing the same goals differently, or not at all, or pursuing divergent goals.

Role Factors Encouraging Cooperation

These several means of cooperation and coordination of action do not come into being out of goodness alone. But certain aspects of official roles do encourage cooperative efforts that contribute to the realization of general governmental goals. In the first place, officials, and particularly administrators, since there are so many of them, find it advantageous to cooperate if by doing so they are able to attain *mutual* goals. Thus, police departments, sheriffs, state police, and federal agents attempt to cooperate as much as possible in order to handle crime. To this end, they aid in training one another, maintain mutual information services, and so on. Likewise, county clerks find it expedient to be on good terms with county treasurers, and each finds it useful to maintain communication with others of the same office. Shared or mutual goals, then, are a condition of coordination and cooperation.

Another condition that makes coordination and cooperation possible is the fact that public officials are all Americans, speaking the same language, and above all sharing a common perception of the social universe. Like the rest of us, they too are "little liberals," a product of our system. In addition to the same general cultural orientations, they are all governmental officials, and as such develop certain professional approaches, ethics, and behavioral patterns. These are, of course, fostered and encouraged by professional associations and journals. According to one count, there are some 184 local government associations alone.[29] Almost every office has an association and regular meetings for the discussion of common matters and problems. Such activities obviously increase the potential for cooperation.

A final factor also needs some mention: namely, that of the common experiences which many officials have had in other branches of government or levels in the federal system. Quite often, indeed, their attitudes and role definitions are shaped by these earlier experiences, and form the reference point for subsequent behavior. Many of our Presidents were state governors; many Congressmen were state legislators; and, many local officials served in a variety of other local offices. Tables 4-3, 4-4, and 4-5 can give some notion of the importance of the claim.

Table 4-3—First Public Office Achieved by 180 U.S. Senators.

Type of Office	Number	Percentage
U.S. Senator	17	9
State Governor	4	2
U.S. Representative	7	4
State Legislator	38	21
State-wide Elective Official	8	4
Local Elective Official	25	14
Law Enforcement	50	28
Administrative Official	26	14
Congressional Staff	5	3
	180	100

Of course, Table 4-3 [30] does not suggest the variety of offices that U.S. Senators have held; it merely indicates which office was first held. Thus, a Senator may have been a state legislator, a governor, and a Congressman before becoming a Senator. We get a little better picture of the experience of Senators, at least, from Table 4-4 [31] regarding their total political experience (in years) prior to the Senate.

Another indicator of the amount of comparable experience found among politicians is that of Presidents. As this is the highest office in the

Table 4-4—Levels of Political Activity before Reaching Senate.

Number of Years in Public Office before Senate	Percentage of Adult Life in Office				Totals
	0-19	20-39	40-59	60+	
0	10	0	0	0	10
1-4	10	1	0	0	11
5-9	7	15	3	0	25
10-14	0	7	12	2	21
15-19	0	2	9	7	18
20-24	0	0	2	9	11
25 or more	0	0	1	4	5
	27	25	27	22	100
					(179)

land and normally comes at the culmination of a career, we might expect
that considerable political experience has been accumulated; and it generally has. Table 4-5 [32] lists the types of positions that have been held
by Presidents, and the number of Presidents having those experiences.

Table 4-5—Political Experience of Presidents.

Type of Office and Experience	Number
Ministers to Foreign Countries	7
Governors of States	13
Vice Presidents	10
Members of President's Cabinet	9
U.S. Representatives	14
U.S. Senators	13
Members of Both Houses of Congress	8

Again, some Presidents have served in more than one office. We may
note a few more facts about the comparative experiences of politicians
before moving on. Roughly 32 to 35 per cent of the Congressmen at each
session have served as state legislators.[33] About two-thirds of our Presidents have served as legislators, and the same is true of the Vice
Presidents.[34] Approximately one-half of all Supreme Court Justices also
have served in their state legislatures.[35] From 1789 to 1938 some 125
members of the President's Cabinet had started their careers in state
legislatures; and a good many state officials had moved on to the
Congress.[36] Thirty-two justices have been members of Congress, and
eight have been state governors.[37] From this recital of facts in words and
tables, we can readily see the amount of mobility within the government
and therefore the amount of comparative experience that officials have in
office. This experience, enabling them to understand and appreciate the
problems and situation of other officials, thereby makes the conduct of
public affairs easier.

Examples of Voluntary Coordination

Since the constitutions do not spell out what officials are to do each day with respect to one another, the development of voluntary means of cooperation has been long and uneven. Means have developed, nevertheless, and they are numerous. As each can be specifically labeled and thereby made understandable, they need not be discussed in detail. The following types are indicative of their variety and also of the ingenuity which politicians and administrators have shown in overcoming the dispersion of authority created by the American Constitution:

1. Interstate compacts and commissions—using formal or legal means.

2. Orderly transitions from one Administration to another.

3. Workshops or training institutes among officials from different political units.

4. Professional associations and journals providing professional norms and information in common.

5. Comity between houses of the legislatures and of Congress.

6. Liaison officers among branches of government.

7. Mutual honoring of requests for information and assistance.

8. Joint committees in legislatures—again a more formal means of cooperation.

9. "Errand-boy" functions by legislators for citizens—working out citizens' problems with administrators.

10. Party activities—creating a common tie for different office-holders.

Part Five

Political Processes

ADAPTATION AND

GOAL–ATTAINMENT

THE primary function of the polity with respect to society is that of mobilizing resources for the achievement of societally sanctioned goals. Along with the attainment of goals is that of assisting society to adapt to its environmental conditions. While the latter is chiefly the problem of the economy, the polity is not without its own problem of adaptation. We will consider both processes, but emphasis will be placed upon the goal-attainment function.

The first item on our agenda concerns the problem of goal-attainment in the United States: the goals sought, the conditions shaping the process, and, finally, some comments on certain structural characteristics of goal-attainment. Chapter 10 is devoted to these facets of the problem. Chapter 11 continues the discussion by focusing on the process, itself, that is, on the ways in which goals are achieved. Three phases of goal-attainment will be distinguished and elaborated: selection, legitimation, and the implementation of goals. Of course, some members of the polity are more concerned or involved in one phase than another. Likewise, different types of action are used. It is matters such as these that will be discussed in Chapter 11.

10

Goal-Attainment

Agents, Instruments, and Processes

In the twentieth century, increasing attention has been accorded the attainment of societal goals. The rise of totalitarianism, the demands of the newly-developing states, the increasing emphasis on collective efforts in western democracies—all are striking illustrations of the desire to achieve new social goals, as well as many older ones, by collective effort rather than by private individual activity. Americans have not avoided these tendencies. In fact, slowly, but inevitably, the polity has become the major means of achieving social goals. Whereas the individual, the family, and local governments were once considered the best means of achieving goals or meeting the problems and dilemmas of life, many more people now consider the federal government, and the polity more generally, as providing the only solution. Employment, social security, juvenile delinquency, police protection, housing, and health are but a few of the areas in which societal concern and resources are used to allay the resources of individuals.

What we are concerned with, then, are the means that the United States employs to achieve social goals. In terms of our conceptual scheme, we are interested in learning *how the polity converts its inputs of resources and support into an output of achieved goals.* More specifically, which members of society are chiefly responsible, how do they perform their tasks, and under what conditions? Different societies, of course, will rely upon different types of roles and use different instruments and processes. We ought not overemphasize distinctions and will not. But the United States does have its own "style" of mobilization, and achieves societal goals by distinct patterns and processes.

SOCIETAL GOALS

What societies may desire to attain collectively is probably infinite in variety. In any case, what Americans have been interested in seeking has included an increasing number, and perhaps even rate, of new social goals. The demand to use system processes rather than private ones has resulted from dislocations in the society and lives of the individual citizens, particularly economic dislocations. But it also stems from other sources such as the external threat to the nation from communism and the Soviet Union. As these various environmental dislocations and threats have occurred, many people, particularly the opinion-leaders, have become sensitive to them and have articulated beliefs that something must be done to counter them. Moreover, since many of the domestic crises have appeared to result from the operations of private goal-attainment processes, blame has been placed upon them, with the demand and hope that public means of goal-attainment will prove to be the better. Consequently, many more people, today, demand greater services, benefits, and protections from the polity than ever before. Collective resources and organization are looked to for providing national defense, housing, full employment, social security, and many other goals.

But although the dependence on collective means has been rapidly increasing, we must recall that private, voluntary means are still the chief methods by which Americans attain goals. Indeed, every proposal that sounds as though it might increase the government's role is subject to criticism on that point. Accordingly, the rationalizations and legitimizing of any collective goal-attainment endeavor must be careful not to challenge many of the tenets of the liberal belief system. The liberal rhetoric is, in fact, frequently employed to justify such changes.

Many societal goals are widely accepted as such, and are expected to be achieved by political or collective endeavor. Such goals include national defense, provision of domestic order, education, some transportation, the postal system, regulation of monopolies, and various protections for the consumer. These goals and public efforts to attain them are widely accepted because they readily appear as having a common interest and because most people are likely to believe that none could be easily achieved by private enterprise. The United States, of course, does pursue goals that are less than widely approved; some goals, in fact, may well be intensely disliked by various elements in the polity. Among these are those goals that impinge upon the particularistic interests of occupational groups including labor, business, and agriculture. Consequently, benefits for such groups are often resisted by other groups, while various controls are opposed by the groups being controlled. How support is related to the achievement of goals is considered in the following section of the chapter, so we need not develop it for the moment. What is more crucial at this juncture is the hierarchy of goals in American politics.

Given the possibilities and high probability of multiple goals, and the impossibility of all being achieved simultaneously and equally, the question is which goals are given priority. Since goal-attainment is closely connected with the processes of allocation, we will delay the analysis of how goals are selected until Part Six. For the present, we will restrict ourselves to outlining the hierarchy of goals. Historically, the ranking of societal goals changes as new needs and desires arise; our account of present day goals must therefore be recognized as time bound. And while there are some problems involved in determining the rank-order of goals, one of the better indices is that of the national budget, that is, the willingness of the members of the polity to devote their economic resources to various alternative uses. We have in the budgets a handy quantitative measure of these decisions.

But while handy, governmental budgets are also tricky indicators and measures of societal goals because their categories are generally broad and sometimes noncomparable. As a result one must be very careful in their interpretation.[1] Then, too, a budget may represent the balance of power in society rather than the pattern of goals. This is so because some minorities are in crucial or strategic positions that allow them to shape goal decisions against the wishes of majorities or collections of minorities. Nevertheless, a budget is still an indicator, and a useful one for our purposes.

If we examine the pattern of *all* governmental expenditures in 1959, for example, we note that the proportions devoted to the major activities of the various governments were ranked as follows: (1) national defense and international relations with 39 per cent of the budgets; (2) education, 14.6 per cent; (3) police protection, about 8 per cent; (4) highways, 7.8 per cent; (5) natural resources, 7.4 per cent; (6) interest on the general debt, 5.6 per cent; (7) health and hospitals, 4.2 per cent; (8) public welfare, 3.3 per cent; and (9) the remaining 10.1 per cent going to such items as air transportation, social insurance administration, housing, and the like.[2] There is nothing startling about these figures or the hierarchy of goals they represent. As we stated above, they suggest that the greater the common interest perceived, and the more likely the goal can only be achieved by the polity, the greater the likelihood that government will be used and public funds spent on its attainment. Thus, national defense is perceived as essential and possible only through national agencies. Health and hospitals, on the other hand, are still regarded as being primarily the responsibility of private individuals and groups. Consequently, only 4.2 per cent of the budget was given to the achievement of health.

Two characteristics of the goal pattern deserve special mention: one, their secular character; and secondly, their immediate, practical concerns. Regarding the first point, we should note that American governments do not spend money on the construction of religious facilities, nor do they contribute to daily operations of religious organizations. In this respect, the separation of church and state is quite complete and sharp. The second point is of unique importance, too; namely, that no American government is likely to devote vast resources, in the fashion of many ancient societies, to the erection of political-religious monuments such as the pyramids of Egypt. Resources are expected to be devoted to promoting useful facilities for improving and furthering secular activities like commerce and industry. Here, much of the debate in legislatures is revealing, because legislators seem preoccupied with the justifications for each item in the budget and particularly whether each is justifiable in *practical* terms.

Along with the concern for practical, secular goals has been an accompanying rejection of messianic goals. In spite of a certain minor theme in American history about "Manifest Destiny," the resources of American society have not been devoted to transforming the world in the manner in which Nazism and Communism have attempted. Indeed, the unrestricted commitment of societal resources to such "supra" goals is almost unthinkable to most Americans. Liberal political values and geographical isolation have conditioned Americans to preferring the improvement of their own standard of living to the conquest and reformation of the world. The returns or outcomes of such endeavors as the latter appear neither very immediate nor favorable. In short, the use of resources for collective goals must always be justified in terms of the dominant values, and proceed according to the norms of political acquisition and commitment—values and norms that are generally antithetical to messianic fervor.

THE PROBLEM OF MOBILIZATION

Goal-attainment is chiefly a problem of combining resources and building support for goals among those who must contribute their resources, support, skills, information, or simply compliance. How successfully a nation achieves its goals depends on a number of factors, including the type of goals, the availability of resources, their quality, and the amount of support, leadership, and the nature of the system that is to mobilize and convert these variables into goal-achievement. Our problem, of course, is to assess these variables in the case of the United States. But while some aspects of the problem are easily dealt with, such as measuring the resources, others are highly qualitative assessments. The reader, therefore, should recognize that our interpretations are nothing more than that: interpretations of conditions that affect goal-attainment.

Abundant Resources

Most discussions of this type begin with some attempt to assess the resources available to the society and polity for goal-attainment. We will honor this custom herewith. In Chapter 2, we pointed out the wealth of the nation as compared with that of other societies. And, indeed, the United States is an extraordinarily wealthy society by almost any index: national income, productivity, capital wealth, or natural resources. We need not detail these matters, but a brief review might serve to indicate the dimensions of the matter. With respect to the human population, the United States has one of the largest (fourth) in the world. Furthermore, it is a relatively young population, highly educated, skilled, mobile, and industrious, with a high literacy rate (97.5 per cent). Whether measured in terms of total output, or average per capita output, the economy is probably the most productive the world has ever known. With this human and technological basis for goal-attainment, the polity stands in good stead.

Human resources, however, require natural resources to implement goals and here, again, the United States is well off. With some 6 per cent of the world's population, and 7 per cent of the land area, Americans produce around 20 per cent of the free world's wheat, 50 per cent of its corn, 33 per cent of its meat, and 50 per cent of its cotton.[3] In addition, Americans, in 1955, produced about one-third of the free world's coal, one-half of its oil, one-quarter of its cement, one-third of its iron, one-half of its steel, and one-half of its electrical power. In short, the United States produced about 40 per cent of the world's industrial goods.[4] While these illustrative figures certainly do not afford a basis for systematic comparison, they do strongly suggest that the United States has a decided advantage over other nations with respect to resources potentially available for goal-attainment. One result of this is that Americans are seldom scarcity conscious, nor pessimistic, about their nation's potential power. Given its resources, in short, the United States can generate enormous power to achieve its goals.

In considering resources in society, it should also be pointed out that all of these resources are not automatically and immediately available for collective goal-attainment. This is particularly the case in the United States where, historically, these resources have been largely considered as being the private property of individuals and groups. To be sure, the government has been accorded great powers such as that of eminent domain, and during war-time, almost dictatorial powers to command resources, facilities, and support. *Legal* limitations, however, are almost always attached to these powers. No American government can, under normal circumstances, command resources with the assurance of a totalitarian regime. Nevertheless, as we stated in Chapter 8, the power of the government is increasing with each new kind of crisis.

Abundance of resources in and of itself has little meaning, of course, until judged against the demands made for their use, or for the goals that society desires to see achieved. When viewed in supply and demand terms, the favorable picture we have drawn becomes somewhat less impressive because the demands on these bountiful resources are still greater than are the resources. One of the commonplaces of political science and much popular writing on the subject is to the effect that governments at all levels are confronting shortages of financial resources to meet the growing demands of an expanding population with greater needs. Frederic Dewhurst, in his monumental assessment of America's needs and resources, indicated considerable disparities between them in almost every area of American life.[5] Similarly, the well-known Rockefeller Reports of the late 1950's pointed up the same problems. In a more polemical piece, John Kenneth Galbraith criticized the American failure to use or redistribute its resources so that this affluence could satisfy the "public needs," including better education, recreation, housing, transportation, and other facilities.[6] All of these proposals have called for more resources dedicated to societal rather than private needs of specific individuals. The assumption is that the total stock of resources is ample, but that it is improperly allocated. Given the public demands, however, the supply of resources is, in fact, limited.

Problems of Support

Continued, if not always enthusiastic, support by the citizenry for governmental programs is usually assumed in America as in other democracies. Perhaps because support has been assumed and generally accorded our polity, we have seldom inquired into its dynamics and failures. But support, in fact, is contingent depending upon a number of factors about which we think we know something, and undoubtedly upon many more about which we know very little or can even identify. As we suggested in an earlier chapter, the level of support for the societal and political values, for the structure of the polity and its symbols, appears to be rather high, while support for particular officials, laws, and policies apparently is less widely distributed and less intense. These varying levels and intensities of support pose crucial problems for the polity, particularly for those in official posts who must gauge it and make the best of whatever the situation allows. For while support is closely related to the maintenance and integration of the polity, it is also a crucial variable in the matter of goal-attainment. Admittedly, goals can be attained without widespread support or strong intensities, but without either or both, the task of goal achievement becomes that much more difficult.

Most goals pursued by the United States, as indicated by its legislation, probably do not require widespread, highly intense, active forms of support from the citizenry. In other words, most of the goal-seeking is routinized and conducted not by citizens but by bureaucrats. The former simply give passive support, with the largest percentage of people entirely unaware of the goals or of the means they might use to prevent their attainment. Occasionally, however, certain goals do become well-known, and citizens form attitudes about them and frequently act accordingly. The prohibition of liquor by Constitutional Amendment, for example, legitimized by that sacred symbol itself, failed to win much popular support or official enthusiasm for enforcement. The results are well-known: prohibition did not succeed, because officials were not often zealous in their duties and the citizenry saw to it that bootleggers supplied their demands. In this case, many people were affected in an important and adverse way. But few laws or goals are such that widespread active resistance is encountered. Today, of course, we have such an instance in the South where whites actively and intensely oppose the efforts of the federal government to attain equal rights for the Negroes. Generally, however, few citizens are directly and knowingly affected by any single goal-attainment effort.

Thus, while we may assume that active opposition is not commonplace, and that goal-attainment may proceed in reasonably peaceful fashion, it must also proceed without much fervor or enthusiasm. The ordinary citizen, indeed, is likely to find himself in a peculiar relationship with his government, one that is most likely to be distant, formalized, impersonal, and discontinuous. Face-to-face, intimate, warm, and informal relationships of governors and governed are hardly apt to be the case in a nation of over 180 million persons. Few citizens perceive their relationships to the polity and the government as similar to their familial or social group memberships. The persons who direct the goal-attainment activities are distant figures, holding public offices, and paid to do their jobs. Thus, most meetings with government officials tend to be somewhat formalized

and segmental. The government is often thought to be "they"and not "we,"
or "my government." To be sure, personal identification is frequently encountered with respect to specific individuals holding elective public office,
such as the Presidency. But most offices—being functionally specific
universalistic, and based on legal authority—do not offer favorable conditions for such identification. Instead, the citizen fulfills a formalized role
himself, engaged in such formalized, impersonal actions as paying his
taxes, performing military service, acquiring licenses, filling out various
forms, and voting. Because of these sharply attenuated relationships, mobilizing support may be rather difficult in many situations requiring goal-
attainment.

For the citizen who would like to find ways of identifying with his
political system, the opportunities are limited. It is extremely difficult for
the citizen to know how to participate and involve himself in the goals of
the United States. Expressive support, in short, has few outlets. Politicians,
teachers, and other leaders, for example, often exhort the citizen to participate and "do something" about some public matter. Yet, seldom do
these same leaders accurately specify the means for desired courses of
action, other than to mention some other formalized ritual such as "writing
your Congressman." When Gallup recently polled the nation as to whether
they stood ready to answer President Kennedy's inaugural call to "ask what
you can do for your country," some sixty-six million Americans offered
to do something.[7] President Kennedy, however, did not stipulate what it
was that they might do. Thus, when Gallup asked the respondents what
they thought they might do, they found difficulty in answering. The usual
responses were made: some would write their Congressmen, others would
be more scrupulous in filing income tax returns, and still others would try
to be better citizens by obeying the laws, keeping informed, or being
honest. Another study, using a sample of 260 adult New Yorkers who
had witnessed the Kefauver hearings in 1951, which exposed over television big city crime and its political connections, gives eloquent testimony
to the problem of citizen action and support in a huge, complex city such
as New York.[8] G. D. Wiebe interviewed these persons to discover their
behavioral intentions and responses to the hearings. What he found, in
brief, was that while most of the respondents were quite willing to act
against crime, few were willing to do much that was instrumental in at-
tacking the problem. For the most part they simply talked to friends who
agreed, or indulged in undirected behavior in which power fantasies held
sway. They tended to feel impotent about affecting any changes in the
situation that Senator Kefauver had brought to light. These same feelings
of impotence have been noted and confirmed in other studies by Robert

Agger and his associates,[9] Angus Campbell,[10] Murray Levin,[11] Morris Janowitz and Dwaine Marvick,[12] and strongly argued by such commentators as David Riesman and Nathan Glazer,[13] Morris Rosenberg,[14] C. Wright Mills,[15] and others. All agree that, to the extent that citizens are asked to give active support for some particular goal-attainment effort, many are not going to know how, or be able, and as a result will indicate frustration, cynicism, and impotence.

Of course, we must not create the impression that all citizens are raring to go and are frustrated by factors beyond their control. Such is not the impression intended. If our interpretation of the belief system in Chapter 5 is correct, we may confidently expect that, historically, Americans have not been primarily concerned with viewing their political system as a great societal goal-attainment agency. It would appear that the polity has become significant in this respect only with reluctance on the part of many Americans. In the past, with the polity given only minimal tasks, the problem of support was also minimized. Likewise, in an earlier day, with the population smaller, with a less complex social structure and fewer problems, the relationship of the citizen and government could be closer. Today, even local governments are highly complex and impersonal.

Structural Limitations of the Polity

One of the reasons why mobilizing high levels of support is difficult stems from certain properties of the polity. Yet even where support is not a problem, the structure of the polity is still a difficult condition that confronts or shapes the goal-attainment process. Goal-attainment must take place within the structures constituting the polity. Thus, even high levels of support and resources do not mean that they will be used effectively or efficiently by the system. Under some conditions, such structural features as its size, complexity, dispersal of power, formalized roles, and procedures may act as a formidable obstacle to goal-achievement. Likewise, the fact that the system operates in this manner also contributes to a great frustration potential in the mobilization of support. The very slowness of response on the part of the system to most stimuli is likely to cause frustration among many segments of the polity.

Indeed, many of the cherished legal requirements that are intended to protect the individual citizen, such as the "rule of law," and "due process," tend to slow the tempo of goal-attainment. A commonplace example is that of eminent domain; the government is given the power to command land, for example, to build highways. But the process through which the government must go to get the right-of-ways is complicated and time-consuming, for the citizen whose property is being taken must be consulted, and he also has the right of appeal on prices. In addition to these basic elements, bureaucratic reporting requirements are such that much "red tape" results to complicate and extend the period of goal-attainment. A great variety of clearance and coordinating procedures and devices that aid the integration of the decentralized polity also work to complicate goal-attainment.

Consequently, the leader who wishes to attain goals other than those of the status quo is not likely to find the system an ally nor a comfortable one in which to work. Support is eroded by the inevitable passage of time and the dilatory actions of the defensive groups. Indeed, the only times the structural elements of the system have been overcome are under extreme crisis as was the case during World War II. Even then, the system had practically to be abandoned for what Clinton Rossiter has called a "constitutional dictatorship." [16] At that, it took three years for the society to fully mobilize its resources. And this was accomplished with many favorable conditions such as unused productive capacity, isolation from direct contact with the enemy, and a high level of support for the war effort. To be sure, the polity did perform effectively in the sense that it did mobilize the necessary resources and won the war; but it did so under what may be unusual conditions in the future, and it did so inefficiently. The Founding Fathers designed a system, not to respond immediately to demands for social goals, but one designed to prevent or slow down the process of societal goal-attainment in the interests of protecting individual citizens from governmental controls.

MOBILIZATION AGENTS: POLITICIANS AND BUREAUCRATS

We turn, now, from the conditions under which the mobilization of resources and support takes place to the agents of mobilization. Up to now the discussion has surely suggested that all the people do not participate equally nor in similar ways with respect to the mobilization process. In the previous section, we strongly implied that most citizens do not participate in direct, active, meaningful ways in goal-attainment. We said, in fact, that most citizens participate in more indirect, impersonal, formalized, segmental, and discontinuous ways. Nor does everyone participate in all goal-attainment efforts. For while the government pursues many goals, and while we all participate in them in the generalized sense of providing tax money for their finance, there are many specific goals that involve only a small percentage of the people.

Given our *gesellschaft*-type system, we tend to parcel out goal-attainment activities to specific persons whom we may call *leaders* and *bureau-crats*—the "officials" in our system. These relatively few persons perform the major tasks involved, setting goals and mobilizing support and re-sources, and converting them into actualized goals. Let us begin, then, by considering the leaders.

Leaders in Mobilization: The Politicians

In many societies the determination of societal goals is the work of a relatively small number of persons. In the United States, however, the selection of collective goals is the task of many men, some of whom hold public offices, while others act in their private roles as officials of organized groups and as opinion leaders. Precisely how many leaders one might find is difficult to ascertain because the criteria of leadership vary. Alexis de Tocqueville, for example, thought that nearly every American was a leader in the sense of participating extensively in public life. But he did not carefully specify the criteria of participation and leadership. Since de Tocqueville's time, others have attempted to define these terms and test them. Woodward and Roper, for example, attempting to measure par-ticipation among adult Americans, and by using a very generous scoring method (see page 357), concluded that even so only 10.3 per cent of the population participated very actively.[17] Today, with a population of about 108 million adults, the number of very active persons by this scale would be slightly more than ten million. Whereas Woodward and Roper suggested that one of ten persons is very active, Alfred de Grazia has maintained that only one of every 62 are what he calls "politists." [18] Re-gardless of the differences in estimates, it is clear that, in absolute figures, a very large number of persons are active in politics and, to some extent, may be thought of as opinion leaders in the selection of goals and the mobilization of support for their acceptance as formal goals of the society. Of these active people, however, perhaps not more than a few thousand are highly placed and influential.

More directly concerned with goal-attainment than the several million political activists are those who hold public office and who have been accorded formal responsibility for goal-attainment activities. A 1957 estimate of the number of elective officials has them numbering about 523,000, of whom 514,000 are local officials and the remainder, national and state officers.[19]

These various officials and political activists have as their chief func-tion the specification of goals for society. To be sure, many of the local officials particularly are more often involved in administering than in goal determination, but all participate in it somewhat. In any case, these highly active persons do articulate and propagandize for societal goals. In performing this function, they attempt to translate private demands and expectations into public policies. And as a result of their function and positions, they tend to develop certain perspectives or orientations toward the polity and goal-attainment.

The politician, as a mobilizer of opinion and support, performs a distinctive role in the polity. He tends, therefore, to structure his orientation according to *affective* standards, that is, to stress the emotive rather than the factual aspects in most situations. The feelings of his constituents are more crucial than are scientific facts of whatever may disturb them. Consequently, the politician is likely to show more concern for welfare than for truth. *Goals* rather than means are emphasized for the latter are more often the concern of the administrator. The politician wants to elicit approval—or at least a predisposition—on the part of the citizens to support the goals he wants enacted into public policy. Sensitive to the interests of his constituents, he thereby shows his *particularistic* orientation. Pork barrel for the constituency and patronage for his party organization are the traditional, particularistic concerns of the politician. Likewise, he is more interested in his constituents' *ascriptive* qualities than in their achievements. "Balancing the ticket" with members of different groups or interests is one such expression of the concern. Unlike the administrator or professional, generally, the politician treats his relationships with others in a *diffused* manner. That is, he does not restrict his involvement to carefully circumscribed areas like a doctor dealing with an illness, or a lawyer dealing with financial matters of a client. He interests himself in almost everything of vital concern to people. Accordingly, he considers it part of his job to intercede for constituents in all variety of problems, to attend funerals, loan money, and provide welfare and jobs. But, like the administrator, the politician also has a *collectivity* orientation in that he too stresses common interests and loyalties. Patriotic oratory and public ceremonials are commonplace grist for his mill.

That the politician performs this process of mobilizing support, and does so within the above orientations, means that he will more than likely encounter conflicts with others in the goal-attainment effort who perform somewhat different roles. Thus, in dealing with goals, the politician being affective and particularistic, often runs counter to both the citizens and administrators. With respect to the former, the citizen is apt to see the politician as vacillating, compromising, and untechnical in matters of interest to that citizen. The administrator, on the other hand, is apt to see him as nonrational, interfering with universalistic norms, inefficient, and generally inexpert. Because the segmental and differentiated polity creates these varying perspectives, overcoming them is a difficult and tenuous job. Moreover, the fact that different actions within the goal-attainment function are performed by somewhat distinct groups means that the process is slower. To bureaucrats and others, consequently, the task of eliciting support by the politician often seems to be a highly nonrational, complex, and uncontrolled activity. But, more on this matter in the following chapter.

Bureaucrats: The Workhorses in Mobilization

Given a population of over 180 million, enormous land area, literally thousands of societal goals, a highly differentiated polity, and many leaders, it is not strange that the implementation of societal goals is accomplished by a relatively small number of highly organized persons with considerable powers. The United States, like all large-scale states, depends upon a bureaucracy for this accomplishment rather than upon the voluntarily coordinated efforts of individuals and small groups. Moreover, achieving social goals requires the technical mobilization of vast resources as well as support. While the latter activity is provided primarily by the citizens, the former is supplied by the bureaucracy.

Although the American bureaucracy shares a number of characteristics noted by Max Weber as inherent in such organizations, the American, unlike Weber's model, has a number of more unique variations. These we will consider below. For the moment, we will deal with the more generalized properties. Both, of course, have important consequences for the polity and particularly for the mobilization of resources. The first observation that needs to be made about the bureaucracy as the instrument of mobilization is that it is large, in terms of numbers of agencies and personnel, and has been steadily growing throughout the history of the nation. In 1800, for example, the government employed around 5,000 persons; today, the federal government employs nearly 2.5 million, the state governments 1.5 million, and local governments about 4.7 million persons.[20] With a total potential work force of some 65 million, it is apparent that approximately one of every eight people, over the age of fourteen, is employed by the government. Not all of these people are "bureaucrats" in the strict sense of the word, but they are employed by the bureaucracy. Should one compare the numbers of elective officials with the number of bureaucrats, it will be clear that the latter are far more numerous. For while there are only 523,000 elective officials, the bureaucrats total, as noted above, 8.7 million persons.

The bureaucrat, as we have stated on a number of occasions, has a highly specialized role to play in the achievement of national goals. Unlike the citizen, he is a professional who performs a more or less technical service, on a full-time basis, for a set salary, and within a highly organized and hierarchical system. Unlike the politician who acquires his role by winning elections, the bureaucrat is recruited through competitive examinations that emphasize *universalistic* norms such as the acquisition and use of information and logical thinking. Unlike the politician, too, the bureaucrat tends to emphasize *means* rather than ends. Moreover, he seems more concerned, than does the politician, with pursuing his tasks in an *affectively-neutral* way. His involvement with other people is like that of the professions, *functionally-specific* rather than diffuse as is the case with the politician. In the bureaucratic setting, rationality and efficiency are more likely to be prime values and norms than in the halls, say, of Congress. Unlike politicians, the bureaucrat is also aware of his increasing professional standing, forming countless organizations based on narrow professional concerns. Then, too, at least some elements of the bureaucracy have very intense feelings of the *esprit de corps* variety, of which the FBI, the Forestry Service, and the Foreign Service are outstanding examples. Neither the citizenry nor the politicians have developed such identities.

The American bureaucracy, though functionally differentiated, is still compatible with its cultural environment. Unlike its European counterpart, American bureaucracies are not bound by the same degree of tightness and tradition. The social distance between the citizen and bureaucrat is much closer and governed by greater informality and less deference on the part of the citizen. The American bureaucrat has not, traditionally, had the same social status as the European bureaucrat, although his status has been increasing. Rather he has had to perform his functions within an atmosphere of hostility, lack of respect, and stereotyping on the part of both citizen and politician. And while the scope of bureaucratic power has greatly increased, this power has been granted reluctantly and with many controls attached. As a result, the bureaucracy in America is more likely to be ineffective and inefficient than all-powerful, as was the case in Prussia.

PROCESSES OF GOAL–ATTAINMENT:
SOME STRUCTURAL CHARACTERISTICS

Having identified some of the more important conditions under which the American polity seeks goals, and the agents who assume the major roles in goal-attainment, we will now discuss the structures by which the system operates. We will do this by noting some of the more crucial properties, somewhat in the fashion of Chapters 3 and 4. We cannot provide, nor does it seem necessary, a colorful detailed description of specific cases. A number of such studies will be referred to, however, in the course of our own interpretation to which the interested reader, wishing to gain a more empirical understanding, may consult.

In passing, it should be said that many of the properties noted here as characteristic of the goal-attainment function are identical to the entire system and to certain other processes we have and will discuss in subsequent chapters. This is to be expected for the various processes all take place within the same political system. Consistency of normative structure is, therefore, quite understandable, as are the actual processes themselves. Yet while many properties are held in common, we should not overemphasize this fact. For given the different functions each process and set of structures perform, certain peculiarities are also observable. We will attempt to do justice to each.

Rationality of Action

Since Freud, at least, it has been popular to emphasize the irrationality of individuals, not to speak of society itself. Indeed, profound limitations on rationality do exist in both the individual and social group. Yet we must not forget, as Herbert Simon has cautioned, that men do perform many actions in highly rational ways. When we speak of the rational character of American goal-attainment, we mean nothing more than the effort to be intelligent, that is, to use information and analytical skill in order to devise appropriate means for the realization of ends. The American polity employs far more of these efforts and norms than do all traditional societies. That the American system fails to achieve perfect rationality is hardly surprising; what is surprising is that so much effort is given it and that the outcomes are as rational as they are.

Americans, with their cultural background of science, Protestantism, and liberalism, are understandably concerned with the achievement of purposive behavior at the collective as well as individual levels. Note, for example, the fantastic amounts of effort, words, and study that go into our political debates over which goals to achieve and the selection of means for their attainment. The pages of the *Congressional Directory* are but one indicator of these efforts; the special study commissions and groups instituted by both the government and private groups are others; and the amount of resources that educational institutions devote to consideration of national values, goals, and policies is still another. All these people, time, effort, and other resources are applied to the goal-attainment process. They are attempts to increase social control over the established goals and their achievement. And whereas Americans are highly conscious in their choice of goals and means, most other societies have been largely ignorant or less conscious of *what* they have aspired to achieve as a group.

In fact, among many peoples of history, societal goals have not been considered even as a possibility. One simply lived within the dictates of nature and whatever rulers one had. Americans, on the other hand, have, through their "instrumental activism," rejected this belief, substituting in its stead the conviction that life is lived to achieve goals and that one has the power and capacity to devise goals and means. As a result, great emphasis has been placed upon individual aspiration and achievement, with increasing reliance upon collective means to achieve collectively-shared goals.

Institutionalization of Goal-Attainment

As we have repeated on several occasions, most of American political life is institutionalized through legal rules. The same holds true for the processes by which goals are determined and resources mobilized. The intricate ways in which goals are selected are determined by the Constitution in broad outline and, more specifically, by our patterns of politics. The same is true of the means of implementation. Both are illustrated by the complex route that legislation must take in becoming law and by the incredibly complex regulations that must be followed by the bureaucracy once goals have been selected.

The institutionalization of goal-attainment confers legitimacy upon the goals selected by partisan leaders, just as it confers legitimacy upon the sanctions used by bureaucrats to implement these goals. Indeed, the significance of this legitimacy is hard to overestimate because societal resources are being committed to uses which at least some Americans may not support and, in fact, may bitterly oppose. It is precisely because the degree of institutionalization is so high that the effectiveness of the polity in achieving goals has been considerably increased. Americans, consequently, do not often attempt to deny their services, facilities, and resources to the government. Nor do they often openly rebel against participating in goal-attainment. Admittedly, grumbling is prevalent and listened to by politicians and bureaucrats, but it is not regarded as tantamount to a refusal to serve.

Functional Differentiation of Goal-Attainment

Again, let us re-emphasize a point: goal-attainment, like all other processes, tends to be distinct in the sense that the process is different, that it is performed by different persons, and that this is done according to different norms. Of course, no set of political structures and processes is ever completely differentiated. But there is a powerful tendency in that direction in the United States, and, when compared with traditional societies, the extent of that differentiation is remarkable. Leadership and bureaucracy and the norms that guide their respective behavior are all visibly distinct. Likewise, the role of the citizen in goal-attainment is explicit. His model norms in this capacity are to obey the laws, to pay his taxes, to render service if called, and to recognize the "public interest" when his own goals lose out.

Because the bureaucracy is so important in this context, it might be useful to note the extent of differentiation in it alone. The *United States Government Organization Manual,* in the 1961-62 edition, runs to almost 800 pages of listed bureaucrats, departments, bureaus, divisions, sections, boards, commissions, and the like, which make up the federal bureaucracy. Much the same extensive differentiation exists within the state governments and many local governments; and although the scale for each is smaller, it is of course multiplied manifold.

One consequence of this extreme fragmentation and differentiation requires mention: namely, that the problems of coordination and efficiency become primary and perennial ones. Both are greatly reduced by structural differentiation, regardless of what values may be acquired in the process. Not only is the attainment of goals made more time-consuming and costly, but the impact that any one person may have on the process is also greatly reduced.

Compulsory Element in Goal-Attainment

Practically all political theorists are agreed that compulsion or, as Weber put it, "imperative coordination," is a prime characteristic of political systems, regardless of the type of system. But while compulsion is found in all the processes we have specified as basic to the polity, it would seem that goal-attainment and integration entail more compulsory actions than do allocation, system-maintenance, or adaptation. Notwithstanding the ratios, enforced cooperation is clearly a significant aspect of the mobilization of resources. Once goals have been set, resources are required; to get them, one can seldom rely on voluntary acts of the citizenry. Thus, the American polity, like all others, requires that citizens pay taxes, observe various laws, be drafted into military service, serve on juries, testify in court, and refrain from disruptive actions such as rioting or rebelling. For those who wish to do otherwise, choice is restricted once a goal has been adopted as a public policy.

Stability of Process and Policies

As we have heretofore noted the general stability of the American polity; so we may observe it in regard to goal-attainment. That the process is institutionalized does tend to make it stable and predictable. Consequently, the ways in which goals are selected and implemented do not change from day to day, but remain fairly similar over the years.

Not only does the process indicate stability, but the outcomes or policies themselves are also quite constant. Indeed, some commentators, especially those who feel adversely affected by these policies, are prone to believe that it is almost impossible to change a policy once it has been instituted. Certainly there have been dramatic shifts in societal goals during the history of the nation, but seldom have they been erratic, as has sometimes been the case with dictatorships. American foreign policies, for example, have remained fairly stable in terms of their goals, although the means have changed frequently. Nor have radical shifts in domestic goals and means been characteristic of the United States. Unless driven by circumstances, changes in fundamental direction take a long, long time.

That the goal-attainment process should be this way is not surprising: a number of elements in the polity serve to produce that consequence. Among them is the widespread agreement on societal values that we have repeatedly suggested. And, as social scientists know so well, individual perceptions, values, and norms also have built-in means of continuity. More directly related to the issue at hand is the fact that the two-party system works in such a way that moderation and similarity of policies are encouraged in the search for support. We may also note that alterations in party control of government are not frequent. Indeed, in most communities, states, and the federal government, there tends to be a long-term cycle, with the same party often in power for decades.

Even while the turnover rate among the various actors who perform in the mobilization process does vary considerably, it is still doubtful that instability is rife. To be sure, the turnover of politicians in some offices, such as state legislatures, is high; but among other local, state, and national offices, the rates are considerably reduced. The civil service, for example, has a high turnover among the lower ranking personnel, but much less so at the more crucial, middle ranks, other than the appointed officials. Personnel, then, are not constantly shifting so that each administration has a completely new set of workers. The extent of stability in each of these categories is, of course, still something of an unknown, because there are no systematic comparisons. But on the basis of theory and bits of evidence, we might conclude that the extent of structural stability in goal-attainment is such that the process is probably the most stabilized, while policies and personnel follow, in that order.

Development of the Goal-Attainment Function

In the previous section we observed that the process of goal-attainment and the policies that it produces are characterized by a high degree of stability. We wish now to note that the secular trend by which goal-attainment has become important has certain properties. These include, first, an ever-rising amount of resources being given it; and, secondly, an uneven short-term movement. What is referred to are the amounts of resources, energies, and attention paid to the achievement of societal goals. Since 1900—by whatever index one may choose—the amounts of money, the number of employees, the number and scope of goals, and the quantity of capital assets of the government have all risen greatly. But while there have been very few down-turns, and only slight ones at that, the course of development of goal-attainment has not been even. This has been especially marked during years of crisis, wars, and depressions. During such times, attention to goal-attainment increases rapidly, demands multiply, and the system responds with overwhelming effort and energy. Witness the sudden and feverish bureaucratization during World Wars I and II, and the Great Depression. Indeed, the number of government employees almost quadrupled during World War II, while during the Great Depression, the increase was something like 33 per cent. Expenditures have also increased by enormous amounts, but drop sharply immediately after wars, only to begin climbing later.

11

The Mobilization of Resources

The processes by which entire societies mobilize their resources are as fascinating as the conditions under which they operate. This is certainly the case in the United States. Given the conditions described in the last chapter, it becomes something of a puzzle to figure out how the Americans can organize effectively to do very much. That mobilization is largely successful in the sense of the nation surviving and meeting most of its problems hardly seems debatable. The next problem, then, is how this is accomplished.

PHASES OF GOAL–ATTAINMENT

The complexity of goal-attainment is such that a vast amount of simplification and classification is vital if anything is to be accomplished in describing it. To interpret the action of groups and societies in achieving goals, various writers and researchers have used a variety of schemes including "decision-making," "group theory," "problem-solving" in small groups, and others. Many of these analyses are similar, though they employ different concepts and categories. But, all appear to deal, at least implicitly, with a number of "stages" or "phases" in the process.[1] It would seem useful then to consider societal goal-attainment in the same manner, that is, as consisting of different phases during which different activities take place and, to some extent, are performed by persons fulfilling different roles in the polity. This approach, cross-cutting the conventional descriptions of what goes on, gives in so doing a somewhat more functional interpretation than would otherwise be possible.

We will begin by considering the first phase of goal-attainment to be the devising and selection of goals to be attained by collective means. The input of "demands" and "expectations" is the most directly relevant source of these goals, while the polity, itself, is the major mechanism for their selection. In a large-scale political system, one may expect that many potential goals are put forth; the problem then is one of selection from among all the proposals. Actually, as we shall develop below, the number of potential goals is not large, nor are they unpredictable. Certain factors serve to limit them, and particularly those which come to be accepted as authoritative goals of society.

The second phase, although hardly a distinct one in the sense of occurring during a separate time sequence, is that of legitimizing the goals selected. Here the "support" input is of greatest significance. And many political activities and institutions serve to perform this function. In the fulfillment of the legitimacy aspect, we will look at the role of legislatures, the legislative process, the role of the Supreme Court, and the President. Much of what we had to say in Chapters 5 and 6 on political culture is once again helpful for seeing the importance of legitimation and the ways in which it takes place.

Once goals have been selected and legitimized they must be given effect or be implemented if they are, in fact, to be attained. At this point or phase of goal-attainment, the problem is one of administration and control. But the fact that bureaucracies have been set up and controls devised does not mean, *pari passu,* that goal selection and legitimation are completed; they are not. Goals continue to be devised, modified, accepted, and legitimized as the circumstances of mobilization change. Nevertheless, for analytical reasons we can make sense of these complex processes only by subdividing and simplifying them. The classification used, here, is only one; how useful it is will remain for the reader to decide.

SELECTION OF GOALS AND MEANS

Without doubt, the most complex phase of goal-attainment is the first, the selection of goals. And because the first phase is so crucial, political scientists and others have devoted a vast amount of energy to clarifying the situation. Yet, considerable ambiguity still surrounds the process.

We will not provide extensive detail on the legislative process, but rather point up a few general but pertinent characteristics of the selection of goals. These generalizations relate to who selects goals, how, and by what processes support for them is acquired.

A major figure in goal selection, today, is the chief executive, whether at the federal or the state levels, and, apparently, in many local governments as well. This is not to say that many other persons, both in and out of official posts, do not also participate; they do. They tend to participate, however, by winning the attention and support of, or resisting, the chief executive. It is he who defines the issues, although he may not initiate them. And it is he who specifies the program of action to be debated in the polity. The President, for example, puts forth his program in his Budget Message, State of the Union address, and other messages to Congress; the bills he submits, and the support he tries to evoke in the system, provide the focal point of the entire network of political communications. Congress cannot or has not provided this same leadership for most programs for a long time. Nor can the Supreme Court, except under rare circumstances, provide daily leadership. Certainly private individuals and groups, except under unusual conditions, are not in authoritative positions to exercise leadership. Responsibility, in short, rests with the President.

To some extent, although one must interpret the results with many qualifications, the data on the origins of bills in legislatures and Congress suggest that the chief executive is the primary source. Lawrence Chamberlain's classic study of the problem indicated that from 1880 to 1945, on some ninety major bills, the President initiated many more of them during the entire period than did the Congress. The latter, however, did reach high points prior to 1900 and around 1925 when it surpassed the President.[2] A study of the New York state government also strongly suggests that in one year (1941) administrators, through the Governor, initiated some 46 per cent of the measures, or more than any other source.[3] Interestingly, too, the Administration-sponsored bills had a higher rate of acceptance; in the case of New York, the 46 per cent of such bills introduced provided 56 per cent of the laws passed.

The President on the national level and the state governors at their level also provide the focal point of political communication and debate. It is their programs of goals and means that are debated by others. Indeed, what takes place in Congress is largely determined by what the President has raised as issues, what he has set forth as proposals. Congress acts, therefore, not as the chief mobilizing agent, but as an institutionalized arena for the discussion, amendment, rejection, and legitimation of societal policies. That Congress takes these activities seriously is attested to in a variety of their actions including the increasing use of investigating committees, longer sessions, an ever-growing volume of work, and their performance in the rejection of substantial numbers of the President's proposals. With regard to the latter index, it is evident that during the past eight years—even with popular Presidents—the rejection rate has been very high. The highest percentage of acceptance was in 1954 when President

Eisenhower managed to have 64.7 per cent of his proposals enacted into law. During his remaining years, however, he never attained more than 47 per cent of his program; and during his last year in office, he received only 30.6 per cent of his program. President Kennedy during his first year attained but 48.4 per cent success. Over 50 per cent of the President's proposals have, then, been rejected by the Congress during the past seven years.[4] This record testifies to the important role Congress has in the selection of goals, but it also suggests that the role is very much one of selecting from given alternatives proposed by the President, of approving or disapproving. For even though the Congress does reject a large proportion of the President's proposals, more of the measures that become law are sponsored by the Administration than by any other single source. Indeed, administration support is almost a necessary condition of legislative success.

The actual selection of goals and means for their attainment is one of the more mystifying processes in the polity. Identification of the more relevant actors, such as the President and administrators, by no means tells us how they and others interact to create and select goals and means. From the voluminous literature on the general area of governmental decision-making, it is apparent, however, that the number of persons directly involved in making these decisions is small in number and a small part of the total adult population. Proposals tend to be initiated by several groups in the polity, including the President, members of Congress, bureaucrats, and interest groups. According to one authority, Richard Neustadt, decisions on these matters during recent years have been made to a very great extent by the bureaucrats and the immediate members of the President's advisers, with particular influence being exercised by the Bureau of the Budget.[5] It should be observed, here, that while interest groups do play an important role in suggesting goals and implementation procedures, it is the politicians and bureaucrats or the persons with authority who play the major role in shaping the President's program and, therefore, the agenda of goals and means.

Once goals and means have been established through a complex process of bargaining and competition within the Administration, the same thing goes on throughout the government and polity, with bargaining and competition the major processes for the building of support on the part of these various proposals. Fairly conscious and rational efforts are made by the proponents as well as opponents to develop the necessary coalition of support to have these proposals adopted as official policies. The repertoire of political action for the mobilization of support among politicians, interest groups, and the general public is amazing in its imagination and complexity, its expenditure of resources, and demands on time.[6] In the initial stages of goal selection, the President will hold staff reviews and briefings, call for reports, have cabinet presentations, and negotiate with party members from Congress. After a program has been produced, the President will formally unveil his selections by a series of formal presentations. These include the State of the Union Address, the Budget Message, a series of special messages to Congress on particular issues, measures introduced as "Administration bills," and, perhaps, a series of speeches to the general public. Press conferences may also be used to elicit support. For publicity reasons, private conferences with legislative leaders, important persons, and newspapermen may also be employed. Highly complicated strategic and tactical maneuvers will be devised by the Administration and its Congressional supporters to push the program through with a minimum of cost.

In playing his role of leadership for the establishment of goals, the President operates, however, within a system of many constraints. Consequently, Presidents who expect to present highly organized, articulate programs of action to the Congress and the people, and have them accepted without revision, are apt to be in for a painful lesson. Conversely, the President who provides limited, piecemeal programs, not very different from those which have gone before, is more likely to succeed and maintain his position of power. Programs of action require support from many sources to be enacted; thus, only those programs that have something to offer many of these groups, without, at the same time, offending other members of the potential coalition, are assured of much success. Accordingly, the President and his leaders must arrange negotiations and bargains with all the affected in hopes of being able to arrange exchanges of advantage. No neat program can long stand the modifications that each group will want made. Nor will everyone be able to attain all he prefers. The problem of the President is to so lead that what each group gets is sufficient to enable them to support the program without alienating other groups. Some Presidents apparently, are better at this than others. Henry Pringle writes of Theodore Roosevelt that he "would progress to a certain point in his program to ward off socialism and unrest, and then make energetic efforts to appease the right wing." [7] President Truman has been similarly described by Samuel Lubell: "This faculty for turning two bold steps into a halfway measure—no mean trick—is Truman's political hallmark. . . . When he takes vigorous action in one direction it is axiomatic that he will contrive to move in the conflicting direction." [8] To those who hold to programmatic goals, much of this sort of action and bargaining is deeply disturbing. Yet, this higgling and backstepping are the necessary means or process by which societal goals come to be established.

In addition to the constraints mentioned above requiring some form of competition and bargaining over goal-attainment, there are a number of others, many of which we have dealt with in other contexts and to which we will return in considering allocation. The complexities of the polity require bargainings, just as does the two-party system within which the President operates. Likewise, the presence of innumerable interest groups with their Constitutional rights to be heard and be influential requires coalition building and bargaining. Besides helping to shape the process by which goals are established, these various factors also act as constraints on the freedom of the President and other leaders to achieve the goals they deem vital to the nation. Hardly an action of the leadership is not conditioned by their presence. Hardly a societal goal is not strongly affected.

The selection of goals does not, of course, proceed in purely haphazard manner; nor are the actual goals chosen based on a purely desultory basis. Our discussion in the previous chapter suggested that certain parameters prevent this from occurring: a widespread acceptance of a single belief system (liberalism); and a highly institutionalized goal-attainment process, which structures both the process, the outcomes, and limited resources. Previous chapters have also indicated that the unequal distribution of power tend to shape the consideration of issues and the alternatives available for choice. Nevertheless, if we are to make sense of the actual goals selected, we need to pursue this matter of goal selection somewhat further. A number of "givens" structure the outcomes, and they need to be further spelled out than was possible in Chapter 10.

Earlier we noted that in America legally specified societal goals and means tend to be secular and short-run in character. We may now add that the alternatives are further restricted by the strong rejection of doctrinaire programs of action. The sorts of proposals that a socialist or intellectual reformer might wish to advance are not accorded an equal opportunity to be considered in meaningful debate and choice. Nor has the nationalization of basic industries been offered the citizenry as an alternative in the sense in which lesser alternatives are given at election times. On the other hand, fascist-type programs dependent upon extensive programs of control are also excluded from serious consideration.

Another alternative excluded from serious debate regarding societal goal-attainment efforts is that of fundamental reform of the system itself, that is, of the polity. Few would accept as a worthwhile issue, and probably fewer still as an acceptable alternative, the abolition of federalism, the separation of powers, bicameralism, and reforms of the other fundamental structural elements of the political system. Through slow and almost imperceptible or piecemeal change, reforms of these elements are made, but not by conscious once-and-for-all decisions altering the entire structure.

The goals that are selected for attainment are rather likely to be those falling within the traditionally accepted framework of legitimate goals. This means that the usual ones of law and order, defense, some welfare, and certain facilities for transportation and communication will be the major areas of goal-attainment. Totally new goals such as those of socialism and fascism are unacceptable. Yet, within the traditional framework, goals may be shaped and old ones increased in scope. Of course, resistance is always a factor in the adoption of new goals or even in the broadening of the scope of an accepted one. In the American polity, those who have fought the adoption of a new goal or its increased scope usually manage to delay and minimize these goals and the resources devoted to their achievement. Rarely, however, have they been absolutely able to prevent very many proposals—other than those completely outside of the boundaries of the belief system—from being eventually selected. Many of the socialist goals of the early part of this century have now been adopted in gradual, piecemeal fashion. Today's liberals, reformers, and socialists no doubt are discouraged at the progress made, but so are the conservatives and reactionaries. Competitive and bargaining solutions often leave the competitors and bargainers both unhappy, for each has had to accept something that is less than desirable.

One of the more interesting aspects of goal selection concerns the frequency of changes and the nature of changes of those goals and the way in which they are attained. The constant adoption and substitution of new goals is not a feature of American politics in the sense that each year sees new ones added or old ones discarded. Great new goals are infrequent, and tend to cluster only during periods of great disturbance for many people. This is particularly the case with goals of a domestic type such as providing full employment and social welfare. Ordinarily, it would seem that goal-attainment is "incremental" or "additive," that is, that Americans do not change goals so much as they debate over whether to add more resources for their successful achievement.[9] Thus, since unemployment insurance was adopted to further social welfare goals, the debate has been whether to broaden coverage and whether to provide greater benefits (more money for longer periods of unemployment), not whether to abolish the program altogether as improper. Once goals are given official status or achieve legitimacy they are seldom replaced or abolished.[10]

Even party changes do not produce sudden and dramatic shifts in goals or means. If anything, changes tend to occur more frequently with respect to the means of implementation rather than with goals themselves. The Eisenhower Administration, for example, did not suddenly and completely overthrow Democratic goals nor means. Indeed, not a single major reform of the Democratic Administrations was totally repealed. While many lesser practices of Administration were changed, life went on mostly as it had under Truman. Likewise, the election of Kennedy, in 1960, did not see a wholesale rejection of Eisenhower goals and programs.

THE LEGITIMATION OF MOBILIZATION

If our interpretation of the American polity has been substantially correct, it would follow that one of the crucial phases in goal-attainment is that of legitimizing the process itself, particularly the outcomes or the specific goals selected and the means for their implementation. What is involved in societal goal-attainment is nothing less than the appropriation of resources. Especially involved are the human services and cooperation from private individuals and the commitment of these resources to goals of which at least some members of society did not and do not approve. Obviously, the legitimation of these actions is of extraordinary importance in a democracy. How, then, does the polity justify its actions? What sorts of actions does the polity or its representatives perform?

The legitimation of goals and the mobilization of resources are of considerable importance not only because the United States is a democracy which requires that the people—in some sense—approve of the decisions that are made in their name, but also because of the peculiar kinds of processes by which decisions are made. The highly complex, and not always visible, process of bargaining, with its "deals" and compromises, in a nation that has ambivalent attitudes and beliefs about these practices is not likely to stimulate unquestioning admiration nor confer authority on the outcomes with ease. In fact, a good deal of cynicism may and usually does result. The transformation of partisan demands and expectations into authoritative societal goals is, therefore, something of a problem. The need for legitimation is vital.

Rites of Passage: From Partisan Demand to Authoritative Goal

National goals do not spring into being without opposition, nor do they attain legitimacy automatically and immediately upon conception. Rather, each proposal that is intended to become a national goal must go through a long, tortuous, and complex process or "rites of passage" before it becomes law. That few proposals manage to be so recognized is indicated by the fact that only about one out of twenty of the measures introduced into Congress each session ever becomes enacted into law, and only a few of these can be said to be major legislation. Not more than a half dozen such bills, in fact, are really considered significant.

What happens in the intricate enactment of a law, and an especially important program of action, is that the process has the effect of conferring legitimacy on the measure and, thereby, of building support for it among both the leadership of the country and the populace. The most basic factor at work, of course, is the formal process itself, namely, that the proposal must and does go through the prescribed channels of Congressional debate and hearings, and wins the signature of the President. The very length of time it takes draws attention to the proposal. And since hearings and debate go on, much in the light of full publicity, nothing can be "put over" on those who oppose the goals. Indeed, most all who wish to be heard may in some manner be given voice on the issue.

The struggle that goes on within the government and polity, and most importantly within the legislature, is usually interpreted as conflict that divides men. And, so it does. But this same conflict, filled as it is with private interests, strategies and tactics, and bargaining, is also the means whereby support is garnered for the proposal as a societal goal. It also prepares the people, and particularly the opposition, to accept it as authoritative once enacted. This contrasts rather sharply with the practice in totalitarian states where new goals are simply announced to the public without a great deal of preparation other than manipulation of opinion. The adjustment that Americans must make to a new societal goal or program is much less abrupt and arbitrary, and allows some sense of participation in shaping the outcome, even when one loses. Much of this sense of participation may be and is indirect and symbolic, but even those forms are important. If nothing else, the ordinary citizen may participate vicariously through his representatives and interest spokesmen; and, of course, he does have a representative. There is, indeed, something circular —"equilibrating"—in the process whereby those with highest expectations, the participants and the attentive, also, by involvement in the process, contribute to legitimation.

At this point, we might note some interesting symbolic elements in the "rites of passage." As the major formal rules have it, legislation must come from Congress or state legislatures, as the case may be. It should be noted, then, that all bills in Congress, for example, begin with the words "Be it enacted by the Senate and House of Representatives of the United States of America assembled, . . ." Already the symbols of agreement are used by the partisan. The same words appear on the final printing of bills passed, that is, of public laws. After the legislation has passed and been certified as accepted, it goes, of course, to the President for his signature or veto. Most laws are signed by the President, in spite of the attention given the number that have been vetoed. The highest number of bills vetoed by a President actually amounted to only about 12 per cent; Cleveland was the President. Only seven Presidents have vetoed over 2 per cent of the bills sent them. The result, then, is a considerable amount of agreement between Congress and the President, thus insuring widespread support for the law. When Presidents sign important measures, especially those they have initiated or supported, they frequently do so in a blaze of publicity of symbolism. Thus, all the more intimately involved and associated sponsors of the law are seen as witnesses to the ceremony. Several Presidents have also seen fit to deliver a short speech on the measure, stating its significance and benefits. Occasionally, too, the President will sign the law using several pens, which are then distributed among those present as mementos of the historic occasion. If possible the President will include bipartisan support, as in fact he tries to do throughout the struggle for the law. Statements on the part of normally opposing party members is one means of building support and legitimacy for the proposal. Thus, the support of Senator Vandenberg of President Truman's foreign policies has generally been interpreted to mean that the distinguished Republican Senator immeasurably aided American foreign policy to change from that of isolation to active participation. Presidents also appoint bipartisan commissions to build support for goals just as they also appoint opposition members to their administrations. And, above all, Presidents are apt to remind the citizenry, and particularly opponents, that they speak for the "public interest" since they are the only official who is elected by all the people.

While the Congress and President do play major roles in the legitimation phase of mobilization, they are not alone; the court system, too, plays a role, especially at the higher levels. Indeed, the Supreme Court, with its power of judicial review, has therefore the power to declare certain goal-attainment efforts unconstitutional. But while the Court has exercised this right in some eighty-one cases (not all affecting goal-attainment), it is imperative to remember that this is a very minute proportion of all the cases the Court hears. Where the Court does not declare a law involving goal-achievement unconstitutional, it is conferring legitimacy on it as a proper activity of the government and polity. When the Court does rule it unconstitutional, the effect on legitimacy is immediate and obvious. Should the Court be closely divided, this too casts a reflection on the legitimacy of the measure, but not a decisive one when the law is approved as Constitutional. Nevertheless, the acceptability of the measure is questioned and support lessened in such instances. That is why the Court prefers unanimous or nearly unanimous decisions to bare majorities.

As the final legitimizer in the process of goal-attainment, the Supreme Court, indeed, plays a crucial role. This role is heightened by the fact that the Court is popularly thought to be the protector and interpreter of the Constitution, which, since it lays down the ground rules, is the basic symbol affecting the legitimacy of all political processes. To contravene the basic rules is, perhaps, the most illegitimate action that can be taken in the polity. Thus, in political debate over new program proposals, opponents will often resort to the argument of unconstitutionality. If they are persuasive in their arguments, they can often avoid pleas as to desirability. Consequently, we can well appreciate the importance of the Court in goal-attainment as well as in other political processes. Charles L. Black, Jr., has written that the "legitimating work" of the Court through judicial review is of supreme importance in the instances of new goals and means on the part of the government.[11] He has written vividly of the role that the Court has played throughout American history of legitimizing change, particularly of the New Deal, which, in its sweeping changes of goal-attainment, made it difficult for many citizens to accept. Even while the Court fought these changes for a time, it finally reversed its stand and "imparted legitimacy to the New Deal." [12] According to Black, there was no other alternative.

GOAL IMPLEMENTATION:
BURDENS AND PROCESSES

The administrative process is universally so familiar to most political scientists that they often overlook the distinctiveness of the ways in which the American polity achieves its goals. This uniqueness can best be sharpened by contrasting the situation with that of a totalitarian state such as the Soviet Union, and the newly-developing states. To be sure, many of the formal elements of goal-attainment found in the United States, the U.S.S.R., and the newer states are similar. Yet, not only are the values of the variables different, but, in the case of the Soviet system, some crucially different ones are also added. We might note first, that the formal polity of the United States does not involve itself, directly, in goal-attainment activities to the same extent as does the Soviet Union. The proportion of expenditures, for example, which go into public activities are much smaller in this country. Likewise, the numbers and percentages of citizens who are employed by the government are far fewer in the United States than in the Soviet Union. And, as we have pointed out above, the goals through which Americans seek their polity are far more restricted than in totalitarian societies. On the other hand, the United States government is more involved in societal goal-attainment programs than are most underdeveloped societies.

Further, the American polity does not impose the same great demands as does the Soviet Union upon its population. While the latter seeks, for example, to achieve through societal action an extraordinarily rapid rate of industrialization, the United States has been content to allow private development of the economy over a much longer span of time. The constant and repetitious exhortations of the government in totalitarian societies to their people to produce are rarely given voice in the United States. Here, we have relied rather upon the sanctions of private gain and a work ethic ("Protestant") to encourage productivity. The all-powerful, enforced, collective patriotic drive of the totalitarian regime, with its common zeal to achieve societal goals, is virtually absent in America except during a popular war. The burdens that have been imposed on the Russian people—extreme deprivation in order to develop capital goods, the food scarcities, forced population movements, and disruptions of family life incurred during successive economic development plans—all are absent or minimized in the United States. In fact, here, there have been no equivalents of the Five-Year Plans. The closest Americans have come to such endeavors is a declaration of generalized goals by the President in his annual messages to the Congress and the people. Governmental controls, while numerous and disturbing to many people—especially businessmen—are hardly to be compared to the all-pervasive controls of the Soviet Union. Nor does the American bureaucracy have the capacity to control vast numbers of citizens as does the Soviet regime. Limited goals imply limited means of implementation. The demand and support inputs to the polity are more or less givens for American administrators and politicians; for Soviet leaders they are much less constricting.

But while the point about goal-attainment can be easily made when comparing the United States to the Soviet Union, it is less easily made with respect to other democracies. However, the burdens placed upon the American do seem less demanding than in several other democracies. Thus, the United States government appropriates a smaller percentage of the national income through taxation than do Great Britain, France, West Germany, and Italy. While the comparability of figures is always a bit doubtful, and the amounts somewhat outdated (1952), the following estimates of tax receipts in these countries are about as authoritative as are available. In 1952 the United States government garnered about 24.7 per cent of the Gross National Product, while Western Germany took 33.0 per cent, Great Britain about 32.7 per cent, and France 31.2 per cent.[13] In proportion to Net National Income, the percentages run something as follows: Western Germany is highest with 42.2 per cent going into taxation, France next with 41.3 per cent, Britain with 39.2 per cent, Italy 32.5 per cent, and the United States only 29.6 per cent.[14]

From these figures on taxation, we can readily see that the American people, with higher personal incomes, pay a smaller percentage of their salaries and other earnings into the government than do four other democracies, abroad. We might also note that, in addition to paying out less of their earnings, the Americans have not previously had to serve or perform peacetime military service as European countries have historically required of their citizens. These few examples suggest that the American's share in the costs of goal-attainment is probably less than those of citizens in some other countries. As comparative data is extremely difficult to find on matters of this type, however, our observations must be regarded with considerable skepticism.

If data are difficult to find on objective costs, they are still more difficult to come by on the more subjective aspects of goal-attainment costs. Yet, we might hazard the guess that Americans, while very patriotic, seldom seem to take great personal pride in the accomplishments of their polity. A new city hall, for example, may be constructed but few citizens will give any overt indication of having personal satisfactions from the accomplishment. Civic pride does not seem to be highly developed. Rather, many governmental projects are viewed as burdens that might better have not been built. Little sense of personal involvement and identification appear among many citizens. On the other hand, the increasing competition being provided by the Soviet Union may well stimulate a greater sense of personal involvement in the achievements of the nation as a nation. Likewise, the fact that more national goal-attainment efforts are emanating from the government than from private organizations may direct the attentions of citizens to the collective enterprise, allowing them to identify with it.

Whatever the burdens that goal-attainment places on the American people, it is clear that the implementation phase must be conducted with limited resources on the part of the government. In Chapter 10 we argued that the physical resources potentially available to the government are plentiful and of high quality. Yet, it is also correct and necessary to say that the government is deficient in the amount of power it has to mobilize these resources. Seldom have the American people seen fit to grant the government sufficient power except during major crises such as wars. In short, authorization must be sought in all instances of goal-attainment. The totalitarian states do not face the same limitations. On the other hand, the United States government does have far more power than do the newly developing states and societies, which lack not only the economic resources but the political skills and organization to implement their very high aspirations. Comparatively speaking, the United States is far advanced in terms of goal-attainment. Indeed, the provision of law and order, social security and welfare, transportation and communications, and national defense are commonplace activities. As contrasted to the underdeveloped societies, goals can be easily implemented. But unlike the totalitarian societies, the American does not rely exclusively upon public or political goal-attainment.

In terms of the implementation of societal goals, we can say with considerable confidence that the American polity relies to a large extent on *private* means to achieve its goals. Unlike the situation in many other nations where socialism, communism, or a state-directed economy have taken the place of private development, the American economy in providing facilities and resources for society is primarily privately owned and managed. More immediately political is the situation so frequently encountered in countless American cities and towns where private associations perform many of the activities that could be expected of government. Practically every city and town has dozens of private organizations such as the Red Cross, Chambers of Commerce, Junior Chambers of Commerce, Kiwanis Clubs, Rotary Clubs, unions, Lions Clubs, veterans' organizations, and many others, all of which are either engaged in full-time community action, or have various special projects that may be closely related to social goal-attainment. Reliance on such associations stands in sharp contrast to many other countries, including industrialized, democratic ones like France and Italy. Few countries, indeed, have as many private associations and few depend on them as do Americans. Totalitarian states discourage them, and underdeveloped societies have not yet created the skills nor realized the social conditions for private associations.

Edward Banfield has observed that only in Western Europe, the United States, and Japan have people learned how to discipline themselves to working in concert for a common objective over the long run.[15] More particularly, he described the differences between a Southern Italian village and an American town in terms of the far greater number of private organizations and goal-directed activities of the latter. If goals are to be achieved in Italy, they are achieved by the central government; in the United States, they are attained through both the efforts of governments and private organizations, with much greater dependence on the latter than is the case in most other societies. The existence of some 200,000 voluntary organizations with a membership of close to eighty million men and women outnumbers all other countries. To be sure, they are not all continuously engaged in public goal-attainment, but a considerable amount of activity is so directed.

In spite of the identification of the polity with power and control, we must not underestimate the role of private cooperation in the achievement of public goals in America. Policing, prosecution, orders, licenses, and the like, are hardly the only means used by the United States government. Considerable reliance is placed on voluntary compliance with the necessities of collective goal-attainment. For this reason, consent and collaboration on the part of the concerned parties to the problem are often sought. Under the short-lived NRA, for example, private industrial groups were used to formulate rules and enforce them. In agriculture, the farmer's associations are consulted on the determination of policy and its implementation. Referenda are held to determine whether restrictions will be adhered to by the farmers affected. In antitrust cases, consent decrees are often used to settle the issues. During World War II, the government practically turned the regulation of transportation over to the American Association of Railroads. These illustrations of voluntary action, of government counsel, mediation, and fact-finding in collaboration with private groups suggest the variety and dependence of the polity upon voluntary participation and compliance. Indeed, the extent to which this is so distinguishes this country culturally from other democratic systems.

Governments, of course, do not stand idly by, awaiting the citizen to develop his own motivation and willingness to commit his resources to the public. Some commentators, in fact, have worried because the government takes too active a part in mobilizing support for its programs. The bureaucracy, in particular, given its responsibility for mobilization, has developed and uses a number of techniques to encourage voluntary support. Advisory committees made up of citizens or interested spokesmen are used in a variety of administrative situations. This is especially so in situations involving business where such committees aid in winning approval of goals, thereby making their attainment less burdensome and more effective. A similar practice of governments, particularly at the federal level, is the appointment of "blue ribbon" commissions, such as the two Hoover Commissions to promote support for governmental reorganization and efficiency. Still another technique of increasing inducements to participate and comply is the practice of what Philip Selznick termed "cooptation," that is, the incorporation of outside elements whose cooperation is vital into the organizational leadership.[16] Such was the practice in the TVA, according to Selznick.

A similar purpose is served—stimulating private efforts—by the use of honorific rewards, although not to the extent employed by European polities. The armed services, for example, reward valor with medals, and even with financial benefits. But unlike the British, the Americans do not confer titles; the Constitution, in fact, explicitly prohibits them (Sec. 9, Article 1). These many techniques of creating and using inducements to participate in and support collective goals are primarily *positive* sanctions, that is, rewards. Certainly negative sanctions are also used extensively, but the elaborate and varied schemes of rewarding and placating the potentially resistant citizen are the product of American democratic culture. Interestingly enough, where specific resources are to be mobilized as, for example, taxes and military manpower, negative rather than positive sanctions are the order of the day. Of course, these immediate sanctions to secure compliance also rest upon a widespread acceptance of the system, its values and norms. Generally, too, no such program can go into action until it has won a substantial amount of support and legitimacy. A conspicuous exception was the prohibition of liquor manufacture and sales (Eighteenth Amendment), which, of course, could have been termed a failure even before repeal because it lacked support. The basic inducement to support the mobilization process is acceptance of the goals and the process by which they are adopted. Legitimacy of the action, then, provides the foundation. More concrete forms of inducements, however, both negative and positive sanctions, are needed and used to convert a generalized support of the polity and its goals into effective programs of action.

A fourth characteristic of the implementation process follows from the previous ones and the structure of the polity: namely, *decentralization*. Although the federal system alone provides the basis for such decentralization, it is also in accord with the belief system emphasizing local control, as well as the demand for division of labor. Some notion of the decentralized character of the process can be obtained from the figures on the number of government employees at each level of the government. In 1960, the federal government had somewhat more than two million employees; the state governments 1.5 million; and local governments 4.7 million.[17] Furthermore, few of those who work for the federal government work in the national capital. In fact, only 235,000 persons work in Washington, D.C. And, of course, many state employees reside and labor throughout the state rather than in the state capital itself. In addition to the decentralization of personnel, many goal-attainment activities are farmed-out by the federal government to the states and local governments. This is the case with civil defense, National Guard operations, TVA, and, of course, federal grants-in-aid to assist in the performance of a wide variety of goals in which the federal and state governments have a concern. Decentralization of operations is indeed almost a shibboleth in American political debate. He who would centralize always has the burden of proof upon his shoulders. It is fortunate that our cultural values here coincide with technological necessity.

The fifth characteristic of the implementation process is so obvious that it is seldom emphasized: namely, the *empirical* character of the mobilization process. In Chapter 10 we observed that goal-seeking was highly rational; here, we wish to develop the point further and comparatively. Americans do not practice much of what could be described as magical behavior in administration and mobilization. Many societies throughout history have, however, practiced such magical rites in their goal-attainment efforts. Bronislaw Malinowski has described, in great detail, how the Trobrianders of the Pacific engaged in magic in order to facilitate their economic quest for food.[18] Others have also shown how magic was used before and during wars among primitive societies. Almost all peoples go through some sort of ritualized performances before entering war, but some depend more upon magic than others, and for different reasons. The United States, as suggested above, uses religion, in a highly generalized way, to give legitimacy to the American goals and "American Way." But magic is neither invoked nor relied upon to control the environment and attain social goals. Active mastery of the environment through the use of scientific techniques is rather the accepted way of dealing with social problems. There is no specialized role for the administration of magic included in the political processes.

The empirical quality of goal-attainment can be attested to in a variety of situations and practices. Indeed, an entire study, that of political science, has arisen to higher status in America than elsewhere as a useful tool for the educational preparation of politicians and administrators. An even more specialized study, that of administration, is dedicated largely to the improvement of goal-attainment processes. Moreover, a significant number of professional associations, research organizations, and technical journals are concerned with the advancement of the study and practice of political goal-attainment. Likewise, constant efforts are made by a variety of public commissions and private individuals to improve the effectiveness and efficiency of goal-attainment. That the product of all this analysis is not always useful may well be true. But it is neither the work of magic, nor are the practitioners medicine men.

A FINAL NOTE

Just as Part Five began with the observation that goal-attainment is receiving increased attention in most societies, so it is in the United States. The future, as a consequence, is apt to see the goal-achievement function and processes emphasized far more than it has been in the past. For the nation is no longer isolated, nor simple in structure, nor confronted with but elementary and relatively few social problems. The United States, today, huge, powerful, highly interdependent within itself and with the rest of the world, is indeed, the leader of the Western nations. As such, societal goal-attainment has become an imperative. The problems posed both within our society and by the challenges from without will thus entail the increased use of collective resources and organization. As we pointed out in Chapter 8 on political controls, the number and scope of these controls will continue to increase in spite of our preferences.

No longer can social welfare be completely or efficiently attained by private effort alone. National defense cannot be provided by General Motors nor by any combination of private concerns. The exploration and conquest of outer space cannot be financed and organized extensively by private enterprise. These illustrations indicate the dimensions and gravity of the problems confronting the United States. To meet these problems, and achieve the goals that future generations may wish to achieve, more taxation, more controls, more leadership, and more cooperation and support will be demanded from the citizenry. America, for a long time, was severely tried by problems of integration and allocation of values. Today it is being tried by goal-attainment and adaptation to its environment of the world. Future books on American politics will be apt to emphasize these problems, functions, and processes to a much greater extent than we have in this volume and to a far greater degree than have previous studies.

Part Six

Political Processes

THE ALLOCATION
OF VALUES AND COSTS

PART Five dealt with the ways in which the American polity mobilizes societal resources to attain societal goals. We summarized these processes under the rubric of "goal-attainment." Among the various facets of goal-attainment considered were the nature of American collective goals, the kinds of conditions under which mobilization takes place, and the consequences thereof. Leadership and bureaucracy were said to be primarily concerned with performing these tasks. Goal-attainment, in short, was viewed as essentially a leadership and organizational problem.

Our perspectives of the polity will now change from that of the system attaining goals to that of the individual members struggling to realize their own private desires. We are now interested in the ways in which members go about shaping societal goals, through their own activities in the political process. Thus, we will take a look at their expectations and demands, how such matters become politicized, and the processes of adjustment among citizens in pursuit of conflicting ends. The first two chapters, 12 and 13, will elaborate this well-recognized area of political science.

The remaining chapters will be concerned with the outcomes of these struggles or processes. In other words, we will attempt to determine *who gets what and how much from the allocative process*. To this end, we will present data on the allocation of authority—for example, who wins office—economic benefits, economic costs (taxes), and psychological expenditures.

12

Expectations and Demands

Our interpretation of the goal-attainment processes leads us into a whole swarm of interesting questions about the distribution of the costs and personal values entailed by the collective goals. In Lasswell's terms, the problem is "who gets what, when, and how." If we are to find answers to these questions, it is necessary to begin somewhere; that somewhere, in this case, will be with the expectations and demands of the citizenry themselves. What we are about to discuss is not unrelated to societal goal-attainment for a relatively simple reason: namely, that in shaping collective goals, citizens also take account of their own personal aims. Or, conversely, in taking account of their own goals, citizens shape the goals of America. Likewise, they are confronted with the problem of their own share of the costs. Thus, while some persons and groups are more interested in the values to be derived from the system, others appear more excited by the projected costs of existing and proposed programs. For some time now, we have called the former "liberals" and the latter "conservatives," although history has from time to time played some tricks with these definitions. Men like Hamilton, for example, were conservative but also in favor of a strong central government and greater taxation: today's conservatives appear to be against both a powerful central government and heavy taxation. In any case, we are primarily concerned with today's situation and the more abstract problems of how expectations and demands arise and become parts of the political process.

TYPES OF POLITICAL EXPECTATIONS

What citizens get from their political system depends, of course, on what they *demand* of it and the *availability of resources* for goal-attainment. Thus, if we are to understand the American polity, we need first to know something about the kinds of expectations and demands that Americans have typically made. To the reader who has read Chapter 5 on the belief system, many of these demands should already be familiar. Liberal beliefs form the basis of our conceptions of legitimate expectations and demands, and will be viewed as such in the present analysis.

A distinction must be recalled, however, before we proceed: for some important reasons, the terms "expectations" and "demands" require differentiation. Let us start with political expectations. Political expectations, as we have defined them, are a set of beliefs that people have concerning the behavior of government and citizens. We expect, for instance, that government officials will behave in certain ways and not others. We expect that interest groups will act in certain ways and not others. These sets of expectations are both empirical and normative. That is, they are in the form of prescriptions as well as factual statements. Indeed, many of the basic expectations that Americans hold about the performances of politicians and themselves, as citizens, are rather *amorphous, indefinite, inarticulate, implicit, and even contradictory.* But they are no less significant for that reason. There is, for example, a generalized expectation that governmental officials will or ought to be honest and live decent family lives. These expectations are not always spelled out, except when violations occur and people become articulate and precise in their reactions. For the most part, these expectations are a kind of background of normative judgments that are "there," but not consciously acted upon each day. And while they are generally widely-shared attitudes, they are not shared by all with the same intensity.

Before enumerating some of these expectations, it must be said that they are apt to change with time and new conditions. Today, for example, Americans generally assume or expect that the government will take a more positive approach to economic problems and distress than did Americans of the nineteenth century. Indeed, in terms of both scope and quality, we expect more of the government today than ever before. But what are some of the most pervasive expectations? The following list is merely suggestive and not exhaustive.

1. That government will be honest.
2. That government will be efficient.

3. That officials will be accessible and courteous.
4. That the public interest will be the guide to policy.
5. That violence will not be employed.
6. That decisions will be rationalized as legal and reasonable.
7. That citizens will be treated equally by government.
8. That government will be limited in its powers.
9. That government will be as public as possible.
10. That government has a positive responsibility to serve the people.

While the listing has been derived from more or less casual observation, it is not without some supporting data. The data, however, are indirectly related and may not be representative for the nation, since they stem from the study of one community. Janowitz, Wright, and Delaney, in their survey of the Detroit area, tried to get at some of the perspectives that Detroiters have of government and, particularly, administration.[1] To this end, opinions were asked about the public schools, local officials and bureaus, state officials and bureaus, local police, and state police. The results are as follows: only 9 per cent of the sample rejected or were hostile to the performances of all five sets of administrative authorities.[2] Outspokenly critical remarks ranged from 16 per cent on schools to but 2 per cent who evaluated the state police in a highly unfavorable way.[3] These same people, on the other hand, had a somewhat different response to the necessity for "red tape" in government. To the question: "As we all know, all government bureaus have some red tape. On the whole, how much do you feel is really necessary?," 47 per cent thought that less than one-half or none was necessary.[4] Likewise, a total of 41 per cent felt that taxes were too high.[5] Interestingly, some 45 per cent felt that they were about right.

These few bits of information shed a little light on expectations such as the ones we have suggested. But we also need surveys that will get directly at the problem of expectations (both empirical and normative). Until such time as they are conducted, we must rely on casual observation and scattered bits of data.

The above list of expectations is a fairly generalized one about which we may assume rather broad agreement. However, there are other types of expectations or latent demands over which there is less agreement. These deal with such matters as the scope of governmental activity and the worth of governmental programs and costs. As such, they are much more likely to erupt into demands than are the generalized expectations enumerated above. Happily, recent research has provided some light on such potential or latent demands, most of which has come from the students of community politics. We will report but a small part of their findings.

Janowitz, Wright, and Delaney, in the study mentioned above, state that some 46 per cent of the sample felt that the national government was doing "about right"; another 40 per cent said that it was not doing enough; while only 7 per cent felt that it was doing too much.[6] Still another 7 per cent said that they did not have an opinion or that their opinion was not ascertained.[7] The distribution of opinions varied of course with age, social class, and race; with the younger, the lower class, and the Negro race tending to believe in a broader scope of governmental action.[8] As these results apply only to Detroit, doubts about representativeness for the nation are admittedly in order. Scott Greer, in reporting on the metropolitan St. Louis Study, tells us that, while 80 per cent of the sample had some suggestions for changes, there was little consensus as to the changes desired.[9] But, "there was no significant criticism of most major services of government." [10] While schools were the subject of continual public agitation, less than 5 per cent of the subjects identified it as a "problem area," [11] showing the difference between actual demands in politics and public opinion. The former may be noisy, but they are not numerous. According to Robert Lane, "American politics tends to express the needs and wishes of the more contented and satisfied citizens at every level in society, rather than the discontent and alienation of the dissatisfied." [12]

POLITICAL DEMANDS

Portions of the background of generalized expectations we described in the previous section sometimes become translated into overt behavior in the form of political demands. At such times, demands on the polity are *active* and not passive like the expectations from whence they derive. It should come as no surprise, then, to find that it is the demand input that is responsible for most of political action, particularly for that aspect which is concerned with conflict.

Indeed, the demands that men make upon one another and the groups to which they belong are varied and frequently in conflict. The object of a demand is, of course, related to the goals and processes of the polity, for it is through political action that the person or group making the demand expects to have his goals realized. We need to know, therefore, the sources of demands, types of demands, conditions under which they become politicized, and, finally, the determinants of the success or failure of a demand to be realized.

When we speak of the sources of demands, we refer to the social-psychological conditions that have produced them. We are saying in a sense that the demand would not exist if these conditions did not also exist. It is important to know then from whence demands arise. In the first place, they are the products of individuals acting within a framework of groups and their cultures. Consequently, we need to understand both the individual and the group environment if we are to understand the demand and its forms. Moreover, a demand may serve either conscious or subconscious desires within the individual. In the first instance, it contains an explicit goal a person wishes to attain. Thus, a citizen may desire that the city government repair a sidewalk in front of his property, or provide more efficient and less costly fire protection. These are illustrations of conscious, deliberate goals toward which a person might want to have his political system work. In the same vein, an interest group may work in favor of some specific piece of legislation being considered by a state legislature. The goal in these cases is clear-cut and rationally derived. Much of American political behavior, particularly that which is involved in the struggle of interest groups over the allocation of values and costs, is of this sort.

Not all political demands, however, are derived from such conscious sources. Many may also serve psychological functions for the individual.[13] A person may, for example, want to run for public office, offering as his manifest reason for doing so, his desire to perform a civic service or responsibility. But it may well be that he is also involved in finding an outlet for his need to exercise power or be accorded deference. We must not automatically accuse such a person of hypocrisy; indeed, he may not be in the least bit aware of subconscious motives. He may actually believe that what he is doing is for the sole reasons he offers in public.

Still other demands may be made on the polity by persons displacing their private frustrations and hostilities.[14] For although many of our political institutions operate to minimize the amount and success of the displacement of hostility, they do not automatically prevent it from arising and breaking out temporarily. We would therefore be foolish to believe that all American political action is founded on, or has its sources in, purely explicit goals. Much of the demagoguery we have known is based precisely upon sources such as aggression. And certainly, many of our attitudes in international relations have their basis in the displacement of hostility by Americans onto foreign countries.[15] At least some of the treatment that Negroes have received at the hands of Southern whites stems from socio-psychological sources that have no direct bearing on politics, but which are politicized into power relations.[16] And who can assert that some of the hostility demonstrated by extreme partisans in political campaigns comes solely from a rational assessment of the situation? In like manner, the demand that we need a man with charisma to save us in times of crisis is not a purely rational one, yet many Americans will make just such a demand, given certain situations. These examples serve to indicate that political demands may often have their roots in subconscious and unconscious wants. This is particularly obvious where the hostilities are intense, or where the demands are expressed in extremist fashion. Not even our fairly stable and widely accepted political institutions can prevent these from being the basis of political action.

What a citizen demands in the way of public policy can seldom, if ever, be said to arise solely from the individual's intellectual effort. The demands that men make have been socially conditioned. Note that we say conditioned and not determined. What a person may deem as a suitable policy usually arises because he has become sensitized to various needs and desires cultivated by the conditions of the time and place. The demands for strong governmental control over the economy during the 1930's, for example, could not have been so widespread or vigorous had not a severe depression set in to create a need for some form of action. Likewise, current demands concerning national defense are far more widespread and intense than in former eras, the situation in world politics being such that defense is now a real problem that it has not been for much of American history. To be sure, not everyone recognizes a problem at the same time; thus, a few men may see one long before others. Often, those who are personally confronted with difficulties are not the first to diagnose the situation. Other men then become the leaders, and, as such, shape the awareness and action of the affected with respect to that problem.

As might be expected, the volume of demands in the United States for governmental action is enormous, regardless of the indicators used for measurement. We need not overwhelm the reader with statistics to make the point. Taking Congress alone as a place in which demands are registered, we may note that approximately 20,000 bills are introduced during a single Congress (two years).[17] With so many demands, the Congress finds it necessary to meet for about eight months each year to consider their disposition. In the process, Congressmen have come to fill over 33,000 pages of the *Congressional Record* during each two years.[18] In addition to Congress, of course, are the state legislatures with their growing work-loads. Demands are made, too, at many other access points than legislatures. These include both formal and informal ones such as courts, chief executives, administrative agencies, and the like. The volume of demands is very great indeed.

And while the volume of demands has increased steadily and rapidly with the years, their diversity has also increased. Governmental budgets in the nineteenth century were not only smaller than present ones, but less complicated. In other words, they were made in response to fewer and less diversified demands. Some eras, of course, are more concerned with some problems and demands than other periods, just as some areas of the nation are more involved in some problems than others. In the nineteenth century, for example, a great many demands revolved about such issues as slavery, the incorporation of new land and states into the union, the National Bank controversy of Jackson's time, silver in the latter part of the century, and reconstruction of the nation after the Civil War. In the twentieth century, new problems and variations on old ones have come to the front. Thus, the United States has had to deal with conflicting demands regarding the regulation of property, the recognition of labor unions, the quest for social welfare in a complex, industrialized economy, domestic security against internal subversion, protection from external enemies, and, now, the growing demands centered about population explosions, urbanization, and education.

Founded on these competing demands are, of course, political alignments. Because the demands change as problems change, so the alignments are subject to various alterations. Since dealing with these several relationships would take us away from our immediate concern, we will leave them to the many good history books.

AVAILABILITY OF RESOURCES: SCARCITY AND DEMANDS

To ask the sources of political demands is to ask why demands themselves arise in society. And while the answers to the question are many and varied, all rest ultimately upon a single assumption; namely, that the object of the demand is *scarce* relative to demands for it. Allocation could not possibly be a social problem if there were no scarcities, for the simple reason that everyone would receive all he wanted. It becomes a problem in politics only when the members of society demand more of the object than there is available to satisfy their felt needs. Note that we say "felt needs," implying that objectively there may be no shortage of an object. But if men feel that there is such a shortage, they are likely to act as though there were and actually create one. In large measure, indeed, many of the struggles of politics boil down to struggles over scarce values and resources.

But what are we to understand by the notion of "scarcity?" [19] Are not many of the things government does quite unconcerned with measurable goods and services? The answer to the latter question is a firm yes, and these aspects will be discussed later. Yet, regarding many of the objects of demand, it is still meaningful to speak of scarcity. The primary object, *power*, is a case in point: many of the *resources* that produce power are, in fact, measurable and scarce. Not only are the formal public offices that constitute the government limited in number, but only a relatively few men may hold them at any given time. The office of the President allows but one man to administer it, and that man is the one who wins a simple plurality of the votes cast in a presidential election. The loser, even if he should lose by a single vote, has no legal power whatsoever. Likewise, there are but fifty governorships in the nation and only fifty men may hold them. The same thing goes for all other offices in the government. Obviously, the demand for these various offices is greater than the supply. Not surprisingly, many of them are the objects of extreme competition during primaries and general elections.

If power may be thought of as limited in a certain sense, what of the other objects of political action? Obviously, *income,* or goods and services with monetary value, are also objects that are measurable and limited at any given time. Indeed, citizens struggle over the distribution of governmental expenditures every day of the year. Some want one program, some another. Or, in the case of agreement on the general program or policies, arguments often ensue over the distribution itself of the monies and goods involved. In this regard, note the case of federal aid programs. Some groups and individuals want aid to be distributed on the basis of need, some on the basis of population, some on the basis of equal contributions, and still others, on some combination of factors. Another illustration of considerable contemporary interest is that of the distribution of educational funds in the states. And, of course, the greatest struggle takes place over the general allocation of all governmental revenues: shall we spend it on welfare, defense, regulation, or what? These struggles arise because the funds being allocated are limited, because everyone in the society cannot expect to get all he might prefer acquiring. Income and monetary values are, therefore, primary objects of political demands, and are limited. When one person or group acquires a greater share, others must surrender an equal amount.

Power and income, then, appear to be limited in quantities. And even while some other objects of demand appear to be less so, they too, since power is frequently a means to their attainment, are also limited. Thus, one may think of deference, knowledge, and skills as being restricted in the sense that the means of acquiring them through political action are circumscribed. Admittedly, it is doubtful that each of these objects or values are in themselves limited, to the extent that for one person to gain is for another to lose. But as the means of attaining them, such as power and income, are constrained, so too, in effect, are these abstract values.

The general problem of scarcity manifests itself in at least two distinct ways: the first is a situation in which the goals are given or agreed upon. In this case, the problems are those of distributing the shares to be realized in attaining the goal, or the costs thereby entailed. The second case occurs when the resources are given and the goals undetermined. Both types of situations constantly occur in this country and others and, indeed, seldom present themselves independently of one another. The citizen and politician are faced with both allocative problems in bewildering confusion and numbers. To deal with but one is impossible, for the settlement or handling of it usually has implications for all problems confronting the polity. Each day, some of us are required to make decisions about what to seek as public policy and how to get it; each day, some people must make decisions about how much others are going to receive and how much each is to pay. Thus, conflicts of goals and means are ever with us as citizens as well as economic beings.

In focusing on the fact of scarcity, we do not wish to imply that all the conflicts stem solely from shortages of resources. Rather, the notion of scarcity must be understood in terms of *demands* and *supplies*. Given the levels of resources existing in the country, we could conceivably reduce the amount of conflict among Americans over their distribution *if* everyone, or many, reduced their demands. Few of us, however, are so willing; we are a demanding people, especially in regard to material goods. In fact, we are taught early to believe that increasing our private standard of living is one of life's highest goals and values. And in our efforts to improve our standards of living, both psychic and material, we resort to the polity in increasing numbers.[20] As a result, the allocative processes have had an increasing burden placed upon them. In the process, the system functions of integration and tension-management have been severely tried. We may as well repeat here that our treatment of these various processes as distinct factors has been done only for analytical purposes. In reality, they become largely interrelated.

Given the generalized problem of scarcity, what sorts of *conditions* are conducive to scarcity and thus to new demands on the polity? The answer is to be found in the dislocations that arise in a rapidly changing society.[21] These dislocations may be found in any part of the society, including the economic system, the stratification system, the family, church, and educational institutions. Societies, of course, particularly one the size and complexity of the American, are not likely to be completely integrated, stabilized, or ever in a state of equilibrium. Nor are the various sub-systems, including the polity, apt to be in complete harmony. Because they are not, tensions arise that must be handled if the society is not to disintegrate. As a result, much of the action in society constitutes an effort on the part of members to handle and resolve dislocations, contra-dictions, and conflict. Let us now consider some of the more probable sources of dislocation in the American society.

We will begin with the economic system. As a highly interdependent industrialized society, whatever changes take place within that system are likely to be felt throughout the remainder of the society. Because the American economy is primarily privately-owned and operated, it is often subjected to a great deal of strain, for private individuals and firms make the key decisions, and these are expected to be integrated without the use of a central planning board. In other words, millions of decisions concerning buying and selling are made each day by millions of people. And most of these decisions are made without consultation with the other persons; indeed, they cannot be so made. Yet it is expected and predicted in economic theory that all these separate actions will be coordinated by the market mechanisms. Given the situation, it is, of course, hardly surprising that the system is not perfectly coordinated. Decisions are made that do not constitute rational adjustments to other decisions by other people. As a result, the system is subject to much movement and variations. Nor do production and employment neces-sarily proceed along a nice even line. Rather, each is subject to great changes or depressions and inflationary periods. Since men are adversely affected by these movements in the economy, it is not entirely unexpected that they will attempt to control the situation, or at least to find means of adjusting to it. Among the means of control are, of course, resort to political action. The dissatisfied members of society turn to the polity, in other words, as the most inclusive power system in society, in order to express their grievances and seek amelioration or justice.[22] Even men who ordinarily dislike governmental controls will often ask for govern-mental assistance. Thus, businessmen seek to curb unions and to receive tariff protections, subsidies, price laws of various sorts, and other govern-mental help. Laborers and unions look for protection from the power of corporations and their managements. Farmers seek protection from the dislocations of the marketplace, the means of distribution, and nature.

In such a highly complex society, there are bound to be many situa-tions that are beyond the control of individuals and groups. It is these sorts of situations that most men attempt to control by resorting to political action. Since the economy is a major fact in the lives of most people, it is to be expected that they will be sensitive to its functioning. Thus, we find the economic system the subject of so much political attention. We need not be Marxists to appreciate the tremendous significance of economic behavior for the polity. Even so, the economy is not the only source of change and dislocation in society.

Other sectors in which change and disruption may take place include the realm of ideas and knowledge. From time to time, new ideas or new applications of ideals develop, winning the allegiances of men, that have little to do with economic considerations. The demand for female suffrage, for example, was such an instance. The demand for the prohibition of liquor during the twenties was another. But the most crucial ideas have been those relating to science and technology. We frequently forget that technological developments are founded on changes in ideas about nature.[23] The development of nuclear physics in the twentieth century, for example, is causing manifold changes in the social relationships and behavior we describe as American. Indeed, many of these innovations are in the process of changing our lives this very minute; and, many of the changes are quite unknown to us and will be understood only by future historians. One technological change that has already vitally affected politics has been the revolution in forms of transportation and communication. Democracy under conditions imposed by horse travel was a very different democracy from that in which the country can be traversed in less than five hours. The fact of geographical mobility has also made politics different by creating new problems and a search for new answers. Ultimately, this mobility is based upon technological innovations. The polity has inherited the consequences in the form of the traffic problem, regulation of traffic, provision for roads, and support for older forms of transport now obsolescent, such as the railroads. Not only do we face new and greater problems in the regulation of air travel, but soon, we will have to deal with space travel as well. As this revolution in transportation has taken place, we have had new domestic and foreign problems created. Almost always, these problems have become political at some stage or other, for no other solution has seemed adequate, at least to the interests of those directly involved.

POLITICIZING OF DEMANDS

Thus far, we have located the sources of demands by pointing out scarcity and various types of dislocations in social life that cause men to turn to politics in order to overcome the difficulties. Social dislocations need not become politicized, however, to be resolved. Yet some do, and still many more, it appears, are becoming the responsibility of the polity and government. How are we to explain the manner in which a problem or a group becomes politicized?

Turning to political action appears to be done for a number of reasons. *First, in the United States, there is the opportunity to do so.* We believe in the right of citizens to make demands known and to do so through political action. On the other hand, the traditional belief has been that other forms of action are preferable to the political, and should be exhausted before making one's demands a political issue. Thus a group will turn to the political system as the most inclusive and powerful in society, when it becomes impossible to gain satisfaction for its demands by private actions. And, with more of the rules of society being made by the polity, it thereby becomes a highly rational course of action to attempt to shape those rules in ways deemed more favorable to one's own position. Or, in less dramatic cases, it becomes rational to attempt to influence the ways in which existing rules are administered, for administration can completely reverse the intention of the rule-makers.

A second reason, or condition affecting the manner in which a group becomes politicized is a prerequisite of political action itself; namely, *the expectation that something can be accomplished to relieve the frustration or dislocation.* That the American polity affords many points of access does, in fact, encourage political action. Nevertheless, this is no guarantee that action will be forthcoming or that it will be successful. In fact, the multiplicity of access sometimes has the consequence of frustrating action. On balance, however, it would seem that the American polity does encourage action among the citizenry and that citizens generally do believe that politics is or can be efficacious.

A third condition completes the discussion of the politicization of *demands: the presence of leadership to give voice to the demands and to mobilize the necessary resources for their implementation.* Demands have often been present and probably always will be. Yet, some are never acted upon, or at least not successfully, because effective leaders have not been available. The improvement of the Negro position, for example, has come about in part because he now has effective leadership and organization capable of performing the functions of leaders. The same was true of the working class after the 1930's, when skilled leaders and organizational resources appeared on the scene and collaborated with politicians. In a sharply differentiated polity, coordination of action is imperative and leaders are expected to do the job. Thus, if citizens are to control their situations, leadership—although traditionally decried in democracies—is vital.

Further resources than leadership are also required if demands are to be heard and acted upon. A person or group without the ingredients of influence simply cannot succeed in making himself heard. Without such other resources as *money, social status, and a strategic position in society,* in short there can be little hope of success in attaining one's goals or in acquiring one's expected share of values. We shall have a good deal more to say on this matter in the following chapter.

We may summarize the conditions necessary for the effective politicization of demands in the following way:

1. A frustrated expectation or demand.
2. Opportunities to make demands known.
3. The expectation that something can be done.
4. Leadership and organizational resources.
5. Other resources: money, social status, and strategic position in society.

MEANS OF EXPRESSING DEMANDS

Once a demand becomes politicized, what happens? To explain in brief, the politicizing of a demand means that it becomes *publicly expressed or made known* to other citizens and to the officials who make up the government. But, how is this accomplished? What means are employed to give public expression to demands?

The American democracy, like all democracies, affords a variety of channels by which the citizen can express himself. These means vary from that of an individual addressing informal requests to a politician, to highly institutionalized procedures of a formal nature. The latter type are of the greatest significance, and will be treated first.

Institutionalized Means of Expression

Two kinds of institutions are used in expressing demands: one revolves about elections and the selection of leaders or officials; the other relates to various procedures used to influence officials between elections. Let us view elections as institutionalized means of making demands known. An election, obviously, is a device for making known demands concerning who shall have public authority and office. Moreover, they are fairly clear means of expressing these demands or desires, for they do select officials.

But the facts of electoral behavior would suggest rather strongly that they register only the opinions of those who participate which, as we have seen, are few in relation to the entire adult population. And, as we will see in Chapter 14, many consequences flow from the types of elections we have in this country. We need not anticipate our findings at this point, but state only that consequences are important, and will be dealt with later.

While an election may provide a choice of candidates and officials, one thing it does not provide is an accurate expression of the policy preferences of the citizenry.[24] Indeed, given the vagueness of our party positions, and the workings of the electoral system, it hardly seems possible to interpret election results—in many cases—as accurate indicators of views on policies. Seldom are clear-cut mandates found in elections. Politicians and their followers may believe the converse to be true when they win, but examination of the election would seldom support these expectations. Typically, the issues are so muted in American campaigns that a voter cannot easily tell which candidate will best serve his own demands. At best, he can make a judgment of the sort that says "Candidate A appears to be more sympathetic to my generalized values and norms than B." But he cannot be certain that A will act very differently than B when confronted with specific problems and situations. Finally, elections as indicators of preferences among policies are not very reliable for the same reason that they are not good indicators of "majority preferences" over candidates. That is, they do not attract large percentages of voters. Even if elections did offer alternatives among policies, they would probably still register majorities of those who participate rather than the nonparticipant.

Elections should be seen as means of selecting officials and control over their behavior in the broad sense that officials are reminded that they are elected and beholden to the citizenry.[25] They are, in effect, important symbolic controls. They are not, however, very effective controls over policy.

A second set of means for expressing demands is found in the multiple ways in which our polity provides for representation of demands between elections. Some political scientists call them "access points"; we see them as institutionalized means for expressing demands and expectations. Most of these ways are found in conjunction with the three branches of government at each level: local, state, and national.

The most visible and best known points of access are those found in or around legislatures. Formally, the legislatures provide for citizens and their representatives to appear before legislative committees in order to present their views on legislation affecting either themselves or the society.

Witnesses constantly appear before the committees of Congress giving formal statements and informal answers about their views. Moreover, legislators also make themselves available to citizens for private conversations about issues, problems, and their positions. Other sources of information to the legislator are the mails and public opinion polls. Investigations are still another means of the legislature to solicit demands and information about society. A legislature, then, is accessible to the public, although not equally so for every citizen.

For a few people, demands may also be expressed to the President and other chief executives through personal contact, and for many more, indirectly through their assistants. The President is, as might be expected, much less accessible than the Congressman. But he is not completely isolated, for he is a politician, not a King. Even so, demands are made known to the President largely through the work of his assistants, various Departments, and other politicians. The Congress, in a very real sense, is a major institutionalized means for making local demands known to the President. Constant use is made of the legislative chamber and other means to criticize his stewardship.

Courts are also access points for the expression of expectations and demands, although they are not generally conceived in such terms. Consider the role of the Supreme Court, for example, in judicial review. Here, private persons make their demands known regarding certain legislation or laws by challenging the constitutionality of the law. Simply presenting a case to the courts is, especially in civil suits, a means of expressing expectations and demands that involve the government and society. Indeed, certain groups have even made political progress by using the court system as the place to express grievances. Thus, unions during the 1930's, and the Negroes during the past ten years, have given vent to their felt deprivations of economic and civil justice. In these instances, the courts have acted as leaders by improving the position of minority groups who otherwise would have had little chance to be heard or to have had favorable action given their goals. Consequently, the court system must be regarded as a part of the political system, one which participates in the goal-attainment activities of citizens and in the allocation of values and costs just as do the other branches of government. To be sure, the courts may be somewhat more sheltered in the matter, and possess a superior status, but they are participants nevertheless.

Thus far, we have indicated the access points through which the citizen and his organizations make their demands. We have, in a sense, treated the matter as though the politicians and other officials are simply recipients of demands. In many ways, of course, they are. Citizens do write letters, make personal calls on them, threaten them; and the leaders of opinion fill newspapers with editorials, make speeches, and wage campaigns to affect the official's views. But seldom do the politicians sit and await these demands. They are elected because they have some views themselves, which were expressed in the campaign and in previous years of office-holding, if that be the case. Congressmen, for example, devise legislation—not in the technical sense—but in the sense of deciding what sort of public goals ought to be realized and how. Indeed, politicians probably devote more thought to public affairs than does any other group in society. It is not, therefore, unusual that they should take a creative and initiating role in policy-making. It should be emphasized, however, that politicians are only one such group among many. Administrators, at all levels of government, are a prime source of political demands. Working with regulatory problems every day, and having daily contact with special clientele or groups in society, they are, therefore, in a highly favorable position to know what ought to be done. In fact, it would now seem that a bill in Congress has much less chance of being enacted if it is not a product of the Administration and of the governmental administrators who are responsible for the implementation of the legislation.[26] Citizens who want to have a pet idea made into public policy are thus better advised first to convince the administrators and the President than the Congressmen. Much the same may be said about the state governments; increasingly, governors and administrators are becoming the people to see. But in whatever branch, office-holders are the major articulates on policy matters, raising and shaping issues themselves, even if in conjunction with key external groups. It is they, after all, who have the most direct "access," namely, the means and perquisites of their own office.

Noninstitutionalized Means

While institutions are generally effective in governing the behavior of Americans and others, they are never completely so. Nonlegitimate means will also be found for expressing demands and behavior when the institutions appear to block intensely felt demands. Americans have not avoided this channel.

Demands have been made through the use of violence in the forms of civil rebellion, riots, unlawful assemblies, and even assassinations. Each of these forms of behavior is most likely to occur under extreme conditions in which the participants are led to believe that they cannot attain their goals via legitimate action. They are, in effect, a kind of last resort. But, admittedly, they have at times been successful in attaining goals or preventing others from attaining theirs. The southern whites, for example, have long employed violence to prevent Negroes from attaining full status as citizens. Today, the younger Negroes are turning to tactics that, while not involving violence themselves, do involve or create situations that may lead to violence on the part of whites.

The ingenious are not without noninstitutionalized, nonviolent means of making their demands known, and the more acceptable ways are probably used more frequently than the violent. Plain threats of violence, or even of perfectly legal but morally questionable action, can be ways of making one's political demands known. The lobbyist or the voter who threatens a public official with reprisal at the polls is an example of a legally acceptable threat. Then, too, demands may be reinforced with the offer of benefits or bribes. But while public officials may be subject to many threats, they are not exactly defenseless. The ambitious politician, in fact, may himself use his office to attain goals by nonlegitimate means. Mayor James Curley, of Boston, used to threaten the bankers with turning the city water mains open on their premises if loans were not forthcoming.[27] Putting it this way, the loans were generally advanced.

But while a variety of noninstitutionalized ways or means of expressing demands has been mentioned and illustrated, we must not conclude that such means dominate the system; they do not. Although it is not easy to estimate the frequency of this form of behavior, we may still conclude that no democratic polity could long endure if violence and other forms of noninstitutionalized demands were, in fact, dominant.

Some Limitations on the Expression of Demands

The mere fact that we can speak of "institutionalized" means of expressing demands strongly denotes limitations on the sorts of demands that may be expressed and the manner of expression itself. Democracies, if they are to survive, simply cannot tolerate all forms of political behavior.

But while most of the limitations are well-settled, some are subject at times to interpretation, and all to some form of change. Generally, demands are limited in formal ways as to the means of expression, means that are highly formalized or institutionalized and that are set forth in law and tradition. Indeed, the very structure of the government and the enumeration of powers is illustrative of this contention. But, as pointed out in Chapter 9, we do place limitations upon the types of demands as well as upon the forcefulness with which they are presented. We rule out riots and revolutions, for example, as much as possible, even though they may occur and certainly are a means of making demands. We tend, also by our norms, to rule out violence, whether verbal or physical, as an honorable means of politics. And we tend to require that demands be moderate and defended by reference to our value system and normative views. Only under unusual circumstances does the politician who rants and raves command the most honored position in the system. Moderation is the alpha and omega in the socialization process.

In the formal processes of government, the expression of demands is subject to even more extensive and detailed control. Witness the complex formal and informal rules of procedure in legislatures, courts, and official relationships with the citizenry. While all these rules constitute severe limitations on how things may be done, the belief system of the country tends to limit what sorts of demands themselves may be made. The formal structure also limits the types of demands in the sense that each official can only act on certain types and no others. In short, our politics may produce much noise, but it does restrict demands, nevertheless.

By way of a reminder, the objects of allocation in the polity can be almost any value, resource, and cost required to maintain the system. Such objects or values include among others power, income, prestige, security, welfare, and liberty. Of these values, the most crucial is, undoubtedly, that of power because it is the most generalized resource, one that can be used as a means to the attainment of still other values and resources.

13

Allocation

Competition and Bargaining

Having explored the realms of expectations and demands, we are now in a position to tackle the problem of how these many and frequently conflicting demands are handled by the organized political system. We are not so much interested in the situation of action as in the action itself. Presumably, all we have said up to this point will aid us in comprehending the structures within which the actors contend over who gets how much of what, and how. Likewise, we are concerned not with detailed day-by-day accounts of political struggles, but with describing the over-all characteristics of allocation patterns. As usual, we will sacrifice the color, detail, and passion of more topical approaches, but we hope to give a somewhat broader perspective to the ways in which Americans divide their political values and costs.

No political system, however simple or authoritarian, depends on a single means for allocating benefits and costs.[1] Allocative processes are more the products of history than of once-and-for-all-time decisions and plans. Yet, human endeavor to gain valued ends in a social setting appears to consist of but a few possible combinations of means, among which are command, competition, and bargaining. Each may assume somewhat different forms under differing conditions, but they do seem basic. Each society relies on some combination of these means or processes. What is crucial in distinguishing types of polities from this point of view is the peculiar combination. Thus, both the Soviet Union and the United States depend upon command, competition, and bargaining. But while the former uses more command situations, the latter uses more bargaining and competition. Furthermore, the character of competition itself is different:

the Soviet Union has not institutionalized competition for leadership roles: the United States, through elections, has.

It is our contention that competition and bargaining are the major means of allocating scarce values in the United States. Admittedly, we do not contend that political competition and bargaining are strictly analogous to the marketplace, nor do we contend that each is conducted under perfect conditions. Just as perfect competition is rare in the economy, so is it rare in politics. Something more akin to monopolistic competition is probably the chief form of political market, but purely competitive situations and monopoly are also to be found. But let us now return to a point made above: namely, the institutionalization of allocative processes.

THE INSTITUTIONALIZATION OF COMPETITION

Although competition is very nearly a universal phenomenon and recognizable to all, it is not necessarily an easy matter to define and describe. But, perhaps, we can identify what we mean by stating a few of its dominant properties.[2] We might say that, first, competition is a type of human behavior in which two or more persons strive for the same goal for which resources are limited or scarce. No party to the competition can acquire all that he would prefer; in some cases (zero-sum situations) what one party acquires, another must of necessity lose or fail to obtain. Whether zero-sum or nonzero-sum situations predominate in politics is an empirical question, but both, we may be assured, are present in all political systems. And we may also be assured that scarcity is still a condition and problem regardless of the extent of that scarcity.

Given the facts of mutual striving and scarcity, one can easily imagine, as did Hobbes, the ultimate case of a war of all against all. A look at reality, however, would suggest that, while Hobbesian limiting cases are possible and have occurred, it is also a fact that competition in social life has assumed more peaceful forms. But regardless of the historical origins of peaceful competition, it is clear that men have regulated competition. In other words, rules have been formulated to govern competition in many spheres including games, economic behavior, mating, and politics. Even war is regulated to some extent by the existence of rules or norms.

Democracy itself may very well be regarded as a set of norms to institutionalize competition in the political arena.[3] Democracy, in fact, is one of the most complex efforts by man to control the behavior of contenders. But for what do men compete in politics? As we stated in the previous chapter, the chief object of competition is power—its distribution and use—as a resource for the attainment of personal and societal goals. Along with power, of course, go other values: prestige, income, and safety. And as societies, including the American, become more politicized, so will the competition for these values become more politicized, as is already the case in the underdeveloped states and totalitarian societies.[4] Most immediately, however, Americans compete for public offices—elective, appointive, and civil service—and for public policies regarding the distribution of both values and costs.

The Norms of Competition

Though competition is widespread, its forms may be quite different for the simple reason that the norms or rules of the game vary considerably. There would be little point in elaborating all the kinds of norms one might find even in a single political system, but it is possible to delineate some of the outstanding characteristics of the competitive norms in the United States. Generally, it would appear that political competition is expected to be *universalistic*.[5] That is, the competition is presumed to be free and open to all qualified citizens. That it is not, of course, is manifest. Nevertheless, the belief does exist that the process should be open to all. To facilitate this end, Americans have provided rules that limit unfair competition, whether it results from intimidation, monopoly in communications, excessive spending in elections, or falsity in public statements (libel and slander). These various norms are all based on a belief system emphasizing equality: equality of opportunity or of representation, whether in a court, legislature, or in contacts with the bureaucrats. Both sides in court litigation are expected to be given a hearing. All sides are expected to have an opportunity in legislative debates to influence the outcomes. Appeal is provided for in every internal process of the American polity; lose now, but carry the case on to other decision-makers in some other form, if necessary.

Equally as important a characteristic of the normative structure is the emphasis on *achievement*.[6] Competition is expected to be waged on the basis of skills or achievement, not on the ascriptive qualities of the competitors. When a candidate for public office campaigns, he does so on the basis of his past achievements (private or public) and the promise of further ones. He does not make overt appeals to ascriptive characteristics or identifications. To be sure, ascription is hardly ruled out, and, in fact, has been quite prominent in some areas and periods during American history. Witness the balancing of tickets, or the appeals that one is of the same race, region, people, or class. Yet, even here the ascriptive quality is not to be raised overtly. Raising the issue of race, for example, in such elections would be frowned upon. Rather it serves to emphasize that *any* special group has a right to compete by universalistic norms. The clearest case of achievement norms can be found in the increasing reliance being placed on civil service examinations to fill the bureaucracy. Even local governments are beginning to place their employees under civil service. And, in the case of appointive officials, the rationale of any given appointment is usually cast in terms of achievement. The achievement norm is powerful in America because of its consistency with the liberal, individualistic belief system. We may expect that politics as well as economic behavior will be shaped by it.

One last characteristic of the competitive situation requires further treatment, namely, the possibility of *appeal,* or of continuing the competition once defeated. In the United States, the allocative processes are not like games with definite time periods after which one side is regarded as the victor and the other the loser. Rather, in American politics, the game goes on continuously. A contender may lose at one stage in the electoral process, the legislative debates, a court trial, or a departmental hearing, but be assured that he will have further opportunities for appeal of his case, or demands and policies. Such appeals may take years, as they frequently do in the judiciary, and decades, as in the political process more generally. To be sure, there are some political games that do end at specific times and for which there are no further appeals; court proceedings have their termination as do elections. Nevertheless, there are further elections, even through a "court of last resort" in the legal system.

The significance of this aspect of the normative situation in political competition cannot be overestimated. What is so important about the nature of American political competition is that the outcomes—because they are authoritative—win the acceptance of the people, including the loser. In almost all instances, continued support for the system, if not for the policies, laws, and personnel, is assured. Indeed, a polity that could not maintain the support of the losers in allocative outcomes would be highly unstable. In the United States it is common to say that "he had his day in court," "it was a good fight, hard fought," or some equivalent thereof. Acceptance of a loss is expected in our system. The legitimacy of the outcomes, and the processes by which they were determined, is extraordinarily crucial in all polities. Competition in American politics produces many more "good" losers than "bad" ones. To gripe or complain about an outcome is considered poor form.

Deviations from the Norms

Yet competition, in spite of its normative regulation, is likely to be somewhat unstable. The reason for this stems from its very nature, namely, the mutual striving for scarce resources and values. Moreover, the desire to acquire gain or position is especially strong in the United States; indeed, it is so strong that competitors are frequently enticed to overstep the boundaries of fair competition.[7] And, as we have seen in Chapter 8, deviance may result from the vague and sometimes contradictory norms that are supposed to govern competition. We need not go over these matters again except to remind ourselves that competition is subject to deviance and instability. Reams of exposé literature, both journalistic and scholarly, have been produced to indicate some of the dimensions of nonnormative competitiveness in America. Lincoln Steffens' *The Shame of the Cities* was hardly the first or the last of the accounts of corruption, violence, and intimidation in American politics. Since his time we have heard from many Congressional committees as to the extent and types of unfair competition in the political system. What is interesting in all these exposés is the fact that they are produced. In short, we have corruption, but it always makes people indignant. Politicians, fully aware of this, often use it for their own purposes, especially in campaigning for public office against "the bosses," "the interests," or against any who have come by their lot presumably by unfair means. Our moralism at once makes our deviations more apparent and less happy. Voting frauds, nepotism, incompetence, income tax evasion, inside information, bribery, and the like are part of every political system, to be sure. But their incidence in American politics has always drawn greater indignation and protest than is the case in many other societies, including democracies. Paradoxically, the standards of public office and individual political behavior are so high, and quite unrealistic, that cynicism and further cheating have probably been encouraged thereby.

BARGAINING: THE MAJOR FORM OF ACTION

Since bargaining in the marketplace is unquestionably familiar to many readers as a personal experience, it is therefore an easier process to describe than is bargaining in the polity. Then, too, as the media of exchange and the terms of economic bargaining are much more concrete and measurable, more precise statements can be made about the process and its outcomes. Yet, political bargaining is a fact of life, and, in America, the predominate fact in the politics of allocation.

By bargaining is meant a process of determining societal goals and means through the peaceful exchange of advantages between two or more persons or groups.[8] Person A desires something of which person B has control, while B prefers something of which A is in command. Since each controls what the other wants, it becomes possible for each to enter a bargaining relationship with the hope that advantages can be mutually exchanged. Each person or party to the process then enters a series of strategies and tactical moves that he anticipates will maximize his own advantages while at the same time making an exchange profitable for the other party. In recent years, these various moves have been described and explained by "game" theorists as well as by economists.[9] Our own limited needs hardly require game theory to explain political bargaining; the interested reader can check the bibliography for some of the more interesting and relevant treatments. Rather, the important matter now is to identify the bargainers, spelling out the necessary conditions in which bargaining takes place, whether in the marketplace or the political arena.

The Bargainers

In one sense, all American citizens are participants in the bargaining process. From the point of view of allocation, however, it is highly probable that only a small percentage of citizens *directly* engage in bargaining over societal goals and means. Certainly, studies of political participation would suggest rather clearly that the "actives" in politics are few and far between. But, who are the bargainers? Robert Dahl and Charles Lindblom [10] tell us that the following persons and groups seem to predominate:

1. Leaders of national, state, and local party organizations, including politicians in the executive branch and Congress.
2. Congressional committee chairmen.
3. Leaders of government bureaucracies, including bureau chiefs, department heads, the President, and other politicians.
4. Leaders of nongovernmental, nonparty organizations organized primarily for purposes other than bargaining with government leaders, including leaders in trade unions, business firms, religious organizations, professional associations, and the like.
5. Leaders of nonparty organizations primarily to bargain with government leaders, namely, special-purpose pressure groups, including organizations like the National Association of Real Estate Boards, veterans' organizations, and the Farm Bureau Federation.
6. Opinion leaders working in communications, particularly mass communications, including publicists, newspaper editors, reporters, columnists, and radio broadcasters.
7. Individuals of special prestige, status, or control, including men like Bernard Baruch, Herbert Hoover, and General MacArthur.

Yet while this listing may seem formidable in terms of numbers, it is actually but a small percentage of the total population. Floyd Hunter managed to list the names of but two hundred persons who might be termed key national "influentials" or, in our case, bargainers on the national scene.[11] Whatever the actual numbers, it is probable that the percentage will be very small indeed.

Of these individuals and groups, the key bargainer is the *politician*. He not only does most of the arranging of bargains, but also has *public responsibility* for doing so. Whereas private individuals and groups may do a great deal of the bargaining among themselves and with politicians, it is the latter who tend to lead and accept the public responsibility for the particular bargains achieved. Consequently, interest groups are seldom blamed for governmental policies that go wrong; rather, it is the politicians identified with them who are considered culpable, as was Hoover for the depression of the 1930's, and Truman for the Korean War. Private groups and individuals who may have shared in influencing the decisions leading to these events are seldom identified or blamed or congratulated, as the case may be. The politician, on the other hand, is involved, whether he be a bargainer himself or an intermediary between conflicting groups. It is he who is held responsible.

Conditions of Bargaining

In defining bargaining, we have already indicated or suggested some of the conditions by which it is permitted and encouraged. In addition to *permitting* and *encouraging* such activity, we should also add the *requiring* of some form of action, whether it be bargaining or some other process.

The first condition that makes bargaining a possibility and necessity is that the parties to the transaction have *differences* which require resolution.[12] Were there no differences over goals or means, there would be no point to entering negotiations. The fact that differences do exist, however, does not guarantee that bargaining will, in fact, take place. In other words, differences are a prerequisite, but not a sufficient cause.

In order for bargaining to take place, additional conditions must be present; among them is the *incentive* on the part of persons with differences to profit by exchanging values.[13] Having differences is one thing, but having differences plus the incentive to exchange is quite another. It is the latter qualification that is necessary before bargaining can commence. Each party must be in command of something that the other wishes to attain. A desire to gain is thus a requirement.

Another requirement has reference to the area of disagreement, or, conversely, agreement. Bargaining seems possible only if the area of disagreement is relatively narrow. Put another way, bargaining is possible only if there are rules by which each party governs its behavior and if the goals over which they bargain are goals rather than final values or principles. In short, there must be *agreement* within which or on which disagreements can be discussed and advantages exchanged.[14] An illustration from American history may illuminate the matter: the issues over which the Civil War was fought were treated in the nature of final values and principles for which men would rather die than bargain. Prior to the war's outbreak, there were attempts to bargain over these issues in the political system. The final rupture, of course, meant the breakdown of all such possibilities. Today, Southerners will again bargain on racial integration. Obviously, what is bargainable changes through time, and from people to people. Some peoples, for example, will bargain over their economic goods; others will not. One of the problems in political bargaining, not frequently confronted in the marketplace, is that issues arise in which basic values come to the front more quickly thus discouraging or even preventing bargaining. It is interesting to note that, although bargaining is the major kind of behavior in the American polity, we have always been somewhat suspicious of the process and the people who conduct the negotiations. Admittedly, the Puritan heritage of moralism is a powerful one.

We have now listed three general sets of conditions necessary for bargaining; but, what is the situation in the United States with respect to politics? In what manner are these conditions satisfied?

The condition of *differences* hardly requires elaboration. A nation with 180 million people of diverse situations, traditions, and interests, and a complex polity is likely to promote bargaining. With respect to these points, and particularly the latter, Dahl and Lindblom tell us that:

> In the United States the structure of government prescribed by the Constitution, court decisions, and traditions vastly increases the amount of bargaining that must take place before policies can be made. Federalism; the composition and procedures of the Senate; the bicameral legislature; the separation of President and Congress, and the checks and balances between them; differences in their constituencies; fixed and overlapping terms of Representatives, Senators, and the President; constitutional restraints on legislative authority; judicial review; the amending process; a decentralized party system; and the devolution of power to committee chairmen in Congress whose position is automatically derived from seniority —all these provide a variety of narrow defiles where a skillful and aggressive group may fatally mine the path of any group of threatening leaders. The necessity for constant bargaining is thus built into the very structure of American government.[15]

Furthermore, as we do have scarcities of the values that men want, competition is inevitable and bargaining a possibility. Differences do not have to be encouraged; they exist. And, in a country where Lockean individualism, capitalist values, and democratic rights predominate, who can deny the existence of incentives to bargain? Not only are Americans taught to desire and demand more, but their interest groups also make a profession of this very teaching. Our notion of progress reinforces the desire to bargain even if Puritan ideals condemn the means. And finally, Americans can bargain over their differences because they share many basic values and agree on basic norms of political behavior. As each of these conditions has been analyzed in greater detail in previous chapters, this brief summary should suffice.

Types of Bargaining

No human process is so simple that further differentiation of types is not possible or desirable. The same may be said for bargaining. A bargain is an agreement, and it is on this fact that we can distinguish types of agreement that will enable a more precise statement of what really goes on in the way of political, as compared to economic, bargaining. At least three types of agreement present themselves: *explicit* bargains, *implicit* bargains, and *conjectural* bargains.[16]

An *explicit bargain* is the one that most of us think of almost automatically when we consider bargaining. It is one in which the parties to the agreement are known to one another and into which they enter with as clear and unambiguous knowledge as is possible.[17] This is the sort of agreement one finds in contracts where each party has spelled out the conditions in writing. And while explicit bargains are much more frequent occurrences in the marketplace than in the polity, here, too, there may be such agreements. In one sense, the Constitution, itself, was a kind of explicit bargain—the result of many "agreements" at the time of its formation—although it has subsequently been elevated to symbolize the command of "higher law."

An *implicit bargain,* on the other hand, is one in which the conditions of agreement are not spelled out with the same clarity, nor are the conditions equally binding.[18] Usually, one party is expected to do something to which the other party is expected to reciprocate at some eventual time; but this is not always guaranteed. The nature of the reciprocation, in fact, is seldom made clear. A politician will vote for a measure to please another politician with the *hope* that eventually the latter will repay the assumed obligation. But while implicit bargaining occurs more frequently than explicit bargaining in American politics, it is difficult to provide empirical evidence of the former because the bargainers are seldom willing, given American attitudes on bargaining, to describe their experiences. Furthermore, implicit bargains, by definition, are not easily observed by the public or the social scientist. Casual observation and the commentaries of newspapermen and biographers of politicians, however, strongly suggest that implicit bargaining is much more prevalent than the explicit variety.

In terms of importance and frequency, the chief form of bargaining is the *conjectural bargain,* or the case in which neither party to the bargain is sure of the terms or conditions.[19] Such is the normal situation during campaigns and elections when the candidate puts forth a belief system, or some of the elements thereof, but not enough nor clearly enough for the voter to know precisely how the politician will act once in office. On the other hand, the politician, himself, knows very little about the voters' views nor whether they will support him either in the election or after, if he should win. Neither party, then, has a very clear notion of the other's conditions or terms. But they do know something, or have some indicators of conditions. Politicians do belong to parties and some voters do make their preferences known in unmistakable terms. Were this not the case, elections would be totally worthless. Nevertheless, ambiguity reigns free in American politics. Under such conditions, many politicians prefer being cautious, and thus one cannot be absolutely certain how a candidate, once elected, will respond to either old or new issues.

The same may be said about bargaining among the politicians themselves. At any given time during a legislative session, politicians are usually reluctant to predict the outcome of many of the struggles. Yet, if majorities are to be constructed, bargaining must continue. The same may be said with reference to bargaining among politicians and administrators. Elements of bargaining are present, but they are vague, and the task of the politician is to divine these lines and get things done that are compatible with his ideology and program. Small wonder that American politics seems so bewildering and senseless to many foreigners.

SOME CONSEQUENCES
OF POLITICAL BARGAINING AND COMPETITION

Laudable as it is to describe the processes of politics, it remains insufficient unless some concern is shown for the results or consequences of the processes. In fact, one might say that the consequences are our major criteria for judging the means by which they are attained. So it will be here. Of course, the many processes of our political system have multiple consequences. At this point we will resort to our conceptual scheme for guidance.

As our major concern in these chapters is the allocation of values and costs, so our concern will also be with the impact of the process of bargaining upon allocation. Outcomes, or who gets what as a result of competing and bargaining, is a crucial problem. Because actually determining how much of what values and costs go to each person, group, and section is so crucial and difficult, we will devote three chapters to the outcomes. But there are a number of general propositions that can be advanced concerning competition and bargaining outcomes and that and the polity deserve statement before the more detailed materials on outcomes are presented. The remainder of this chapter, then, will be devoted to an enumeration and discussion of these several generalizations. None of them are particularly novel. Indeed, we have not sought novelty, but rather a means of understanding, whether novel or not. Most of the generalizations will be familiar to the political scientist, and, while they are not exactly noncontroversial, they do tend to have rather wide acceptance among students of American politics.

PROPOSITION 1-1. *No unified, cohesive, acknowledged, and legitimate representative leaders of the "national majority" exist in the United States.*[20]

Most political analysis in the public press, as well as in political science, assumes that on any given issue Americans are divided into a majority and a minority. Seldom is this the case, however, if we include in the base of the calculations all qualified voters in the nation or even within the constituency analyzed. At best, in a Presidential election, only 60 per cent of the voters vote, and many fewer participate at the state and local elections. If we analyze the numbers of citizens participating in public decision-making between elections, we are likely to find still fewer making any efforts and still fewer with influence. What we are leading up to is the proposition that majorities—national majorities—do not exist, and that since they do not, it becomes impossible for leaders to claim such followings.[21] The institutional arrangements we have developed for making public opinion possible and felt have not been able to create majorities. Consequently, on any given issue that may arise, but a very small percentage of the public is aware, interested, and effective in its resolution.

Even on issues that do cause greater interest and participation than is normally the case, such groups cannot be considered as cohesive, for they will split on the very next issue that arises. Consequently, a political leader who wishes to lead majorities is in for some trying moments. Not even Presidents can speak for a majority. Majorities are fictions, albeit useful fictions in some contexts, but fictions nonetheless.

What exists rather in the United States are countless, more or less cohesive, more or less powerful, interest groups (or organized elites) whose concern over public policy is partial. That is, they are interested in only a single policy area, or, at best, a very narrow set of areas. In short, we are a pluralistic society of minorities rather than a society bifurcated by two groups—*a* majority and *a* minority. Hardly an issue exists that splits the nation into only two groups. The closest we come to that situation is during a Presidential election, but even that event illustrates the nature of our loosely organized coalitions of interests. Our political fights tend to be highly fragmented because of the complex social structure and the intricate formal structure of the political system. As suggested in Chapter 9, fights become isolated. They are made insular by the fact that they involve only small numbers of groups and are contained within the boundaries of countless units of government, forcing the struggle to be handled within its confines. Majorities, even on particular issues on the local level, are, as E. E. Schattschneider has said, very difficult to mobilize.[22] They are still more problematic at the national level.

PROPOSITION 1-2. *The goals of one set of leaders or minorities can usually be blocked by the actions of another set of leaders or minorities.*[23]

The American polity is characterized, as stated many times heretofore, by a decentralized power structure, with countless points of access to decision-makers, whether public or private. The resources of power are multiple, and not necessarily accumulative, and points of access and many opportunities are afforded small groups or minorities to block the goals of others. To overcome a minority entrenched in official offices or strategic private roles thus requires considerable organization, skill, and resources on the part of various other minorities. However, this combination or coalition of interests is seldom forthcoming, for it is easier to conduct a defensive political action than an offensive one designed to change or reform.

Let us illustrate the above proposition. The role of the committees, committee chairmen, and the seniority rule in Congress are all such as to afford the conservative minority groups plenty of power to resist, sidetrack, or prevent legislation they do not like. And they have so used these positions and rules. Likewise, it is also possible for the President to veto legislation he does not approve, and be fairly sure that Congress cannot override him. The Supreme Court also provides a safeguard for certain ideas or goals that may win favor in the other branches of government. States rights are still another means of coping with changes that some groups do not want to see adopted. We could endlessly catalogue such resources of defense or veto; these few should be sufficient to illustrate the thesis that minorities can block the goals of other minorities.

PROPOSITION 1-3. *For a public policy to be adopted and implemented requires the assent of several minorities.*

It follows from previous propositions that for a public goal to be adopted as public policy the assent of several minorities is required. To be sure, there is no guarantee that assent will be sufficient, but it is a necessary condition of action. Nor does the fact that several minorities may assent mean that an automatic majority is mobilized for the action; several minorities may still, and generally do, consist of less than a majority of the qualified citizens. Actually, the consent of those opposed seems more necessary than that of those who favor the policy. No large minority can be pushed too far under the American system, although they can be pushed, as many minorities well know from personal experience. Nevertheless, the bargaining process is such, in matters of nominations and preparing programs for legislation, that concessions must be made to the minority adversely affected in order to reduce his opposition or maximize his support. Thus, we frequently see such practices as "balancing the ticket" at conventions in order to appease those groups who have lost the major place on the ticket. We also witness Presidents watering down proposals in order to appease minorities who might oppose the proposals in extreme forms. Each of these efforts at compromise is a means of winning the assent of the minorities. Bargaining is the process by which such compromises are generally made and by which they are enacted into law.

Assent must also be understood as a kind of minimum agreement, and not as an enthusiastic support for a proposal. Indeed, a minority may well assent to a proposal simply because it is the least of evils or a means of forestalling some more disagreeable proposal. Because there frequently are many alternatives, men must and do have tables of preferences, whether explicit or implicit. In politics this means we would rather have our second preference realized than a third or fourth, assuming that we cannot have our first. Not being able to realize first preferences very often, we assent to the lesser valued preferences because this is a means of acquiring the acquiescence of others whose preferences differ from our own. In accepting a lesser value or preference, we are often able to convince others to adopt the proposal. An excellent example of this sometimes happens in national party conventions when the two major candidates and their followers are unable to win the nomination for themselves, but are in a position to prevent the other from getting the prize. Traditionally, the way out of such an impasse has been for a "darkhorse," or another candidate who is not so offensive to the front-runners, to be given the nomination. In a positive sense, neither of the leaders nor their supporters gets what they want, but both have realized their goal of preventing the other from winning. This has been accomplished, of course, at the cost of a nomination to a third person who is at best only their second preference.

PROPOSITION 1-4. *The need for widespread acceptance among the politically active often produces irrational agreement through logrolling.*[24]

With many groups and individuals having diverging preferences, and with bargaining as the technique of attaining agreements, the results are seldom apt to please everyone. Everyone may receive some portion of what he wants, but no one gets very much of what he had hoped for. In the legislature, this kind of agreed solution is called "logrolling."

The most frequent illustration of such can be found in the appropriations process in Congress.[25] Each member of Congress is generally anxious to get appropriations, or "pork barrel," for his district, and so trades votes with others interested in the same end for their districts. While many of these members are also interested in the costs of taxation and deficit financing, such considerations do not seem to play much of a role in determining the outcomes of pork-barrel legislation. The immediacy of the pork barrel for the individual district as against the diffused costs to the nation are easy to resolve in favor of the district. Thus, a result is produced that few members, as a whole, actually want, namely, an enlarged debt. In this sense, the result may be considered an irrational social product of rational action at the individual level.

PROPOSITION 1-5. *Seldom will all the affected groups be completely satisfied with the outcome of any given political struggle.*

Given the fact that most groups and individuals, most of the time, must accept something less than or other than they would prefer in the way of public goals or shares of the public values and costs, each will be somewhat less than completely satisfied with the outcomes.[26] And while the fact that each actor is less than fully satisfied does not mean that all share equally in values and costs, it does mean that they get less or pay more than hoped for. During given periods, various groups profit more than during others, but some of this may be evened out over the long run.

Thus, the upper classes, who profited a good deal from the Republican Administrations of the 1920's, were in turn the scapegoats of the 1930's. To be sure, few of the wealthy became poor and fewer of the poor became wealthy during these years; but, in political terms, each group was treated differently than it had expected. The upper classes were the butt of many reformers and the symbolic target of reforms; the poor had their position improved though hardly enough to offer a challenge to the wealthy. Nevertheless, the position of the working man was improved as contrasted with his past. The government did pay attention to him and was not obedient to the wealthy, as during the 1920's. Today, working-men's organizations wield great power, whereas before they were weak or even outlawed. And no Republican Congress or President would dare return to the old days in restricting the power of unions. Nor would a Democratic Congress or President dare nationalize industry or commerce. Each will accept restrictions, but that is all. As a result, each major segment of society and the polity receives less than hoped for and more than the opposition would like.

PROPOSITION 1-6. *The time span required to win acceptance of new goals or means is likely to number in the years and even decades.*

One of the major characteristics of group action is the slowness with which they act, particularly if they are large and complex groups. A political system the size and complexity of ours is no exception. There are many possible explanations for this state of affairs. First, decision-making in so large and complex a system—given the best intentions of all—is likely to be time-consuming because many people must be consulted and complex rules followed. Secondly, men differ as to the goals that ought to be pursued and therefore contend with one another in battles that often take a long time to become resolved. Thirdly, new goals are likely to be resisted because they upset the accepted ways of doing things; they infringe, or are thought to infringe, on the privileges of the status quo. And finally, many persons prefer present certainties to the uncertain benefits of the future. Indifference on the part of others may also act as an obstacle to change in the sense that support cannot be readily mobilized by those in favor of the change. On the other hand, indifference may at times facilitate some changes by the mere fact that indifferents are not opposing the alterations.[27] More often, however, the indifference found in society does act as an obstacle to new goals. New goals require organization for which apathy does not provide much support. Most crucial to the explanation of the long time span is the conscious opposition of those who benefit by existing goals and practices. They are the ones who have good reason to resist, delay, or prevent.

A good example of this slowness of decision-making can be found in the case of child labor legislation. We still have no Constitutional amendment on the problem, although other means are used to prevent such practices. Or take the efforts of many state governors and others to institute administrative changes in the interests of more rational procedures and controls. Seldom do these changes become accepted in fewer than decades of effort. On the national level, the Hoover Commission recommendations have not been accepted in great number, nor to any great extent by Congress or the President, although they have been advocated for over a decade. No, the citizen who starts out expecting to reform the political system or to pursue new goals is not likely to see many if any of them realized in his own lifetime.

P R O P O S I T I O N 1-7. *Responsibility for political action is difficult to locate in terms of persons, parties, and structures.*

A persistent and valid criticism on the part of many Americans concerning their government refers to the impossibility of discovering or assessing responsibility for actions. Seldom do we know who is to blame or to be credited with all the actions performed by the government and polity.

The reasons for this are not hard to find. Indeed, how could it be otherwise in a highly differentiated system where many people are but partially responsible for the outcomes the entire system renders? Even the most powerful official, such as the President, cannot really be held responsible for controlling the behavior of all the people who comprise the bureaucracy he heads, or for Americans in other capacities whose actions may embarrass him. No one official, in short, has *the* responsibility for very many acts. Usually, several units of government, branches, and officials must share some kind of control, and, in so doing, are not in control of one another. Lines of authority are neither hierarchical, nor nice and neat for all to see. If civil rights are not honored as they should be, whose fault is this: the Congress? the President? the states? the courts? or the people? Who would pretend to know? And, how would he make such judgments?

As far as responsibility is concerned, Americans must, therefore, view an uncertain political world. Where everyone shares responsibility to some extent, no one can accurately estimate to what degree each is responsible.

PROPOSITION 1-8. *The American political system has been extraordinarily wasteful in the use of its resources and implementation of goals.*

We hardly need provide documentation of the wastefulness of our society and polity in the use of resources. Some is wasted by poor societal management, such as the natural resources of forest, minerals, and the like. Other waste comes from refusal to use resources—for example, women, the Negro, the elderly, the disabled—in ways that would mean fuller use of their potentials. Moreover, we have a notoriously wasteful government that has not always practiced good management principles. If the government, for example, contracts at cost-plus to private concerns, the latter in turn encourage waste because it is more profitable. There is waste also through corruption and deviance as when contracts are let out for public projects to fill the pockets of official and favored concerns, or when patterns of evasion mean government spending for nothing.

The explanation of all this wasteful action is not be found solely in the political system. We are a wasteful nation because we have had much to squander, and little encouragement of parsimony has ever been instilled in Americans, subsequent to the thrifty era of Puritans. Even Ben Franklin typifies the age of aspiration for affluence and show. Our belief system sanctions profligacy in that it believes and advocates bigness, constant change, conspicuous consumption, and display of generosity.

Consequences for Public Policies

The above set of propositions had to do with the processes of competition and bargaining and their general consequences for the polity and the participants concerned. Nothing was said with regard to the types of policies one might expect from the polity itself. We may well ask what kinds of policies or public goals and means will result from allocative processes of the types we have described. Such is our question. Again we will list and briefly discuss a number of propositions that have fairly wide acceptance among political scientists and other students of politics.

PROPOSITION 2-1. *Public policies are seldom purely intellectual creations in which tidy, logically consistent, and empirically derived generalizations form the basis of the policies.*

Those who believe that policy ought to be derived from a set of rigidly defined ideological premises, and should consist of logically related courses of action, are bound to be upset and frustrated by the American polity.

Seldom, if ever, does it produce legislation and policy so characterized.[28] Public policy, within given areas as well as among several areas, is likely rather to be inconsistent, somewhat ambiguous, and often changing or unstable. It tends to be a product of compromise in which all interested groups and persons get something, but not all they might prefer. In addition, many policies appear to be the responses to crisis in which insufficient time is allowed to determine better means to the objectives.

A few illustrations should suffice. Monetary and fiscal policy is, according to all economists and businessmen, a pot-pourri of *ad hoc* legislation. Many of the elements, indeed, are in complete contradiction to each other. The Treasury Department, for example, may be in favor of low interest rates, while higher interest rates are being advocated and administered by the Federal Reserve Board. It is conceivable that the President may favor still another interest rate. His budget may and usually does contain contradictory fiscal policies. Each is in response to political pressures; each is an attempt to deal with that pressure. Besides various units at any given level of government pursuing incompatible preferences, so too may this be the case as between the three levels of government. The national government may favor one set of tax measures; the states and local governments, another. The same may be said for most policy areas in which all have some jurisdiction. Likewise, different units of government at the same level enact different legislation. Thus, the fifty states do not all have the same types of marriage and divorce laws; property laws; traffic regulations; sanitation laws; educational policies; nor tax policies.

American policy then differs from place to place as well as through time. It is seldom consistent and orderly. Yet, no polity ever produces completely logical sets of policies. In fact, democracies such as the United States may well have more stable policies over the long run. But since we live in the short run, public policy is apt to appear very disorganized.

PROPOSITION 2-2. *Public policies tend to be empirical and pragmatic rather than messianic and universalistic.*

We often forget how mundane most of our policy-making is in the sense that great and passionate appeals are seldom the product of the political processes. Ringing declarations are rarely enacted as such into law. Contrast this situation with that of the newly-developing areas where, as Lucian W. Pye said, "Political associations or groups cannot be oriented to a distinct political arena but tend to be oriented to some aspect of the communal framework of politics. In reflecting the communal base of politics, political parties tend to represent *total ways of life*." [29] Pye continues by saying, "In non-Western societies the intensity and breadth of political discussion has little relationship to political decision-making." [30] Peasants and villagers, he says, often speak about world affairs far beyond their control, while ignoring the immediate political problems over which they might effect changes. Discussion is regarded as more rewarding than implementation.

If the newly-developing states have this approach to politics, consider the case of totalitarian societies with their grandiose, messianic appeals for collective behavior. In such societies, policies are likely to be expansionist and global in orientation, rather than propagating the simple maintenance of the system and the status quo. Ideology assumes enormous significance and policy is expected to reflect the ideology. Accordingly, one finds ideological debates rather than debates over more mundane affairs of state as tend to dominate democratic political discussion. In the case of the United States, we could maintain like Daniel Boorstin that our belief system is so given that discussion over general principles is hardly required.[31] In totalitarian states, ideology is not given in the same sense; thus, it must constantly be asserted and reaffirmed. And all practical courses of action must be derived from it and constantly justified in its terms. The American democracy, as we have seen, also reaffirms its beliefs. But much more of the activity of politics is concerned with facing concrete empirical problems of a conventional sort such as devising an acceptable tax law, zoning a city, increasing the staff of a public institution, or allocating funds to various projects.

PROPOSITION 2-3. *Policy alternatives are not likely to be very divergent, if indeed there are alternatives.*

One of the more frustrating experiences for the ideological critic of American politics is the fact that clear-cut and diametrically opposed policy alternatives are not presented at very many elections. Such types of alternatives are offered occasionally. For the most part, however, voters are either confronted with very moderate and closely related alternatives, or with policies that are so vague as to render distinction impossible. Choice is restricted in both cases.

Schattschneider pointed this out quite effectively in his *Party Government*.[32] According to his analysis—one shared by many others—moderation in policy alternatives is a consequence of the competitive two-party system, operating within a heterogeneous population. The problem of both parties is one of mobilizing a majority from a great variety of interests. The only way in which so disparate a collection of interests and persons can be held together is to give some recognition to all. This, of course, means compromise, and compromise in turn means a watering down of alternatives and even escapism from having to confront alternatives. According to Schattschneider:

> It should be said at once that the reciprocal tendency of the parties toward moderation is only a tendency; it does not mean that the parties are identical. *Sufficient differences remain* and are likely to continue in the future to make the contest interesting and worth while. The processes by which the best offer of a party to the competing interests and the public is determined are not remarkably unlike the processes by which prices are made in a free market. In the course of the bidding, one of the competitors is apt sooner or later to make an offer that cannot be matched by the other, but the margin of difference is likely to be relatively slight. *The fact that the process ends with a narrow margin of difference does not prove that the competitors are corrupt or that the process is meaningless. It proves merely that competition is keen and the competitors are skillful.* The parties do not disagree for the sake of disagreeing as the members of a debating society might. They compete for power and make the best bids for support that they are able to offer under the circumstances. Moreover, if both parties estimate public opinion accurately and respond to it with equal zeal, who is injured? [Italics mine.] [33]

Of course, clear-cut alternatives are sometimes offered the people in direct form, as, for example, referenda. In legislative debates, too, such alternatives often appear, but generally they are not very different in the sense of affording totally distinct policies. Americans are seldom given the opportunity to express a preference for socialist- or communist-type policies and systems. Alternatives tend to be more concerned with means than ends, the ends being assumed as given. No political system, of course, ever affords regular opportunities to consider completely opposed sets of alternatives. Stability probably could not be maintained under such conditions because society would be continually subject to radical change. Even more crucial is the fact that no society sees all the alternatives, nor, indeed, desires to do so; the United States is no exception to this rule.

PROPOSITION 2-4. *Bargainers frequently become more concerned with maximizing their budgets than with maximizing their capabilities for goal-attainment.*

Both politicians and administrators tend to assume that their competitors for scarce resources are more interested in getting more of the current total budget than was the case in the previous budget. A common rule of thumb is to ask, or demand, a larger share than you expect to get; the larger amount being used for bargaining purposes. Because Congressmen expect these tactics from administrators, they often advocate "across the board" cuts in budgetary requests. The bureaucrats, of course, recognize this and attempt to compensate for the expected cut-back. Bargaining encourages the practice of maximizing one's own share because opportunities are provided to share in the decision-making processes and thereby make one's position known. Furthermore, the rewards offered by our polity and society for maximizing budgets are greater than the rewards for maximizing one's capacity given the resources. Bureaucrats and the clients of governmental agencies and programs tend to honor the leader who gets them more in the way of appropriations than they do the economizer who is achieving more diffused and indirect benefits.

14

The Allocation of Public Offices

Who is to govern and who does govern are key questions in both political life and political science. They are particularly important in view of the generally agreed upon fact that the number of decision-makers is considerably fewer than the total adult population. Among the many resources of power, one of the more important is possessing or control of the more than 500,000 elective public offices. Yet, in the quest to identify power-holders, many political scientists have, during recent years, tended to forget the politicians, and have concentrated rather upon other citizens who are presumed to make the major decisions. That decision-makers include others than the office-holders hardly requires emphasis. But it does seem necessary to recall that there are elective officials and that they are entrusted with public responsibilities for decision-making. We want to know who these people are. In order to identify them, we will advance a number of generalizations, most of which are well-known and substantiated findings in political science. These generalizations are of two types: first, those having to do with the direct outcomes of elections in which we relate outcomes to party affiliations; and secondly, those having to do with more indirect outcomes in the sense of identifying which social-economic groups benefit. Before we consider the empirical findings, let us take a look at the electoral process itself.

THE ELECTORAL PROCESS

Authoritative decisions in all societies are made not by the entire population in consultation, but usually by a small number. Accorded authority to make decisions, these people commit the resources of society

309

to the attainment of societal goals. In the process they also allocate benefits and burdens among the membership. Just how these authorities are
selected is, of course, a major characteristic of different political systems.
In some they are self-selected through competition, often violent, as in the
dictatorial states. In others, they receive their positions through inheritance,
as in kingdoms. In still others, they are accorded positions as a result of
electoral competition. This, of course, is the major, although hardly the
only, way in democracies such as the United States. Indeed, the choice of
rulers via election is, as Clokie had stated, ". . . a revolutionary change
in the conduct of public affairs." [1] This revolution in the means of selecting
leaders, is, moreover, a comparatively recent one, dating primarily from
the nineteenth century and the advent of democracy. Whatever the origins
of the electoral process, it is fairly unique in world history.

The electoral process has many variations among the democracies and
even in the United States. But regardless of these variations, there are
certain major characteristics that ought to be mentioned. In the first place,
an election is an *institutionalized form of competition* for public office.
That is, individuals and parties compete for the votes of the electorate in
accordance with agreed upon rules. It is, as Clokie put it so well, ". . .
the rationalized mathematics of collectivized individualism." [2] By counting
votes and determining which candidate has the greatest number, we elect
a man to office and authorize him to use the powers of his office to fulfill
his legal obligations. We also authorize him to use certain rights, and
collect certain perquisites of his office.

As an institutionalized process, elections are highly regulated by
formalized norms. Everything, from the length of terms, to the date of
the elections, to the manner in which candidates may be nominated, votes
counted, and the victor announced, are legally prescribed in great detail.
Unlike some countries, the United States holds elections on specified
dates, meaning that terms of office are not variable. In the case of the
Presidency and some state governors, the maximum number of terms any
given individual may serve is specified.

In addition to the highly formalized affairs, elections in the United
States are also characterized by a particular kind of payoff. An election is
really a "zero-sum" game in that only one candidate can win.[3] Offices are
not shared. Single member constituencies and plurality votes determine the
nature of the payoff. Of course, a plurality, in effect, does mean a majority
since only two parties have a chance of winning.

One last point should be made before we consider the outcomes of
elections. When Americans troop to the polls to allocate public offices,
they also allocate a number of other values and resources: power, prestige,
duties, rights, and even income (salaries). Gaining public office is a means

to these other values, thus making the control of office extremely important to the individual candidates as well as to the nation.

We have spoken of elections as institutionalized competition, and used the analogy of games thereby suggesting that elections are chiefly characterized by competition. But although an election is a formal provision for competition, there is no automatic guarantee that competition will necessarily take place, or do so in the forms of which the civics text are fond of proclaiming. Political scientists have long known that the forms and extent of competition are variable, but little work has actually been done to accurately determine the latter. Lest we create the impression that competition is widespread and that allocation does take place according to a purely competitive norm, let us enter a few facts and generalizations on the extent of political competition in elections.

EXTENT OF COMPETITION: SOME FINDINGS

Many of us assume that every office is subject to competition, not only in the primary elections but in the general elections as well. We assume that our two-party system is everywhere operative and effectively so. But when we look closely at the situation in specific areas of the country, we discover that the two-party system is largely a myth. Not only are many states and localities either purely one-party, or are dominated by one party, but often the opposition is in no position to wage an effective campaign and win office except under unusual circumstances. What then is the situation?

Before we can classify the various types of two-party situations, it will first be necessary to employ a few definitions and enter a few assumptions. Let us begin with definitions, which, it might be added, are those of Austin Ranney and Willmoore Kendall who pioneered in this venture.[4] The basis of their classification of party system rests on the number of parties that have a chance of winning an election. The determination of this prediction is based, in turn, on the past behavior of voters, namely, who won in those elections. Thus, the student looks at past voting trends to see which party wins the most elections. In some states and districts we find that only the Democrats have a probable chance, while in others only the Republicans. And in some, both parties compete on a fairly even basis, alternating more or less frequently in winning. According to Ranney and Kendall, we have three types of party systems in the United States:

> The two-party type.
> The modified one-party type.
> The one-party type.

The two-party system is one in which only two parties have shared the winning of most elections and offices; the winning party has gained a majority of votes or offices or both; and each party has won a substantial number of offices and elections. The national party system is of this type. The modified one-party system, on the other hand, is one in which one party has won most or all of the offices and elections; and, while the second party has not won many of either, it has received a sizable vote or percentage in each election. The one-party system, as suggested by the label, is one in which one party wins all or nearly all the elections and receives most of the votes. With these definitions, we may now proceed to see how they are applied to the data of elections themselves.

The problem, now, is to give specific operational definitions to the above criteria. Ranney and Kendall did so by studying voting for three offices during the period of 1914 to 1954. The offices were the most important ones of the Presidency, senator, and governor. Secondly, the authors decided to classify states according to the number of elections won during that period and the size of the majority vote, or, conversely, the size of the minority party vote. If the second party had won more than 25 per cent of the elections, it was classified as a two-party state; if it won less than 25 per cent, it was further investigated, and placed under the modified one-party system according to the percentages of the votes that were cast for the second party. If a state were one in which the second party won over 30 per cent of the vote in over 70 per cent of the elections studied, and won over 40 per cent of the vote in over 30 per cent of the elections, it was classified as a modified one-party state. If the state did not fulfill these two sets of criteria, it was regarded as a one-party state. When all the tabulations had been completed for the period 1914-1954, it was found that, on the national level, we have a two-party system, with the Republicans having won 59 per cent of the time, or on thirteen occasions, while the Democrats have won nine times or 41 per cent. If we add the years since 1954, we find that the Republicans have won the Presidency fourteen times, the Democrats ten. No third party has ever won. At best, third parties have won over 10 per cent of the popular vote in but three elections (those of 1892, 1912, and 1924). But what of the situation in the several states?

Of the forty-nine states classified by Ranney and Kendall, some twenty-seven are of the two-party type, twelve are modified one-party, and ten are of the purely one-party type. A more detailed presentation of their figures may be seen in Tables 6-1,[5] 6-2,[6] and 6-3.[7]

Table 6-1—The Two-Party States.

State	TOTAL OF ALL ELECTIONS			Per Cent of Second-Party Wins
	Rep. Wins	Demo. Wins	Third-Party Wins	
Arizona	12	33	0	26.7
California	24	11	1	33.3*
Colorado	23	22	0	48.9
Connecticut	31	16	0	34.0
Delaware	22	12	0	35.3
Idaho	28	18	0	39.1
Illinois	21	15	0	41.7
Indiana	21	13	0	38.2
Maryland	12	23	0	34.3
Massachusetts	26	19	0	42.2
Michigan	30	15	0	33.3
Minnesota	28	9	4	37.8*
Missouri	13	22	0	37.1
Montana	9	25	0	26.5
Nebraska	33	13	1	29.8*
Nevada	12	26	0	31.6
New Jersey	25	14	0	35.9
New Mexico	14	31	0	31.8
New York	17	24	0	41.5
Ohio	24	23	0	48.9
Rhode Island	17	28	0	37.8
Utah	13	21	0	38.2
Washington	15	19	0	44.1
West Virginia	12	22	0	35.3
Wisconsin	32	7	6	28.9*
Wyoming	16	21	0	43.2

* Second-party and third-party victories combined to make a total opposition percentage.

Table 6-2—The Modified One-Party States.

State	TOTAL OF ALL ELECTIONS			Per Cent of Second-Party Wins	Per Cent of Elections with Second-Party Vote over 30%	Per Cent of Elections with Second-Party Vote over 40%
	Rep. Wins	Demo. Wins	Third-Party Wins			
Iowa	36	10	0	21.7	89.1	71.7
Kansas	38	7	0	15.5	97.8	68.9
Kentucky	8	28	0	22.2	100.0	94.4
Maine	41	4	0	8.9	91.1	55.5
New Hampshire	40	6	0	13.0	100.0	86.9
North Carolina	1	35	0	2.8	77.8	30.7
North Dakota	37	8	0	17.8	75.5	57.8
Oklahoma	6	29	0	17.1	94.3	77.1
Oregon	27	8	1*	25.0	89.1	56.8
Pennsylvania	28	8	0	22.2	91.7	66.7
South Dakota	36	9	0	20.0	97.8	73.3
Tennessee	4	42	0	8.7	71.7	32.6

* Second- and third-party victories combined to make a total-opposition percentage.

Table 6-3—The One-Party States.

State	TOTAL OF ALL ELECTIONS			Per Cent of Second-Party Wins	Per Cent of Elections with Second-Party Vote over 30%	Per Cent of Elections with Second-Party Vote over 40%
	Rep. Wins	Demo. Wins	Third-Party Wins			
Alabama	0	34	1*	2.8	11.4	5.7
Arkansas	0	45	0	0.0	13.3	2.2
Florida	2	33	1	8.3	13.9	5.5
Georgia	0	45	0	0.0	2.2	2.2
Louisiana	0	33	1*	2.9	8.8	5.9
Mississippi	0	33	1*	2.9	2.9	2.9
South Carolina	0	33	1*	2.9	5.9	5.9
Texas	2	43	0	4.4	15.5	6.7
Vermont	45	0	0	0.0	55.5	20.0
Virginia	2	35	0	5.4	40.5	10.8

* Third-party victories considered as second-party (that is, opposition) victories.

Another indicator of competition, or the lack thereof, may be seen in the size of electoral victories. If they are consistently large, we may conclude that the opposition party has little likelihood of winning. Cortez A. M. Ewing has studied the results of many Congressional elections—10,572, in fact—during the period 1896 to 1946, and computed the size of majorities.[8] Table 6-4 [9] contains his results. Ewing's figures suggest that there are many one-party Congressional areas throughout the United States.

Table 6-4—Sectional Distribution of Congressional Pluralities by Percentages in Sectional Categories.

Plurality, per cent	West	East	South	Border	Middle West	U.S.	U.S. less South
Over 50	13.3	10.3	71.8	4.8	7.8	25.5	9.2
40-50	5.5	8.0	4.8	1.9	5.2	5.6	5.9
30-40	9.4	12.3	5.8	9.5	9.3	8.8	9.9
20-30	17.3	18.0	5.5	11.5	16.3	13.6	16.5
10-20	25.5	23.6	6.3	26.5	25.1	20.0	24.8
0-10	29.0	27.8	5.9	50.8	36.2	26.5	33.7

Tables 6-1 through 6-4 give some intimation of the extent and type of competition to be expected in the various states and elections. They suggest, first, that many elections are rather meaningless because the second party does not have much of a chance to win the election. They suggest, secondly, that whatever competition does take place in the one-party districts and modified one-party areas does so in the primaries rather than in the general elections. Fortunately, a number of political scientists have thought about this matter and have done considerable statistical analysis to measure the extent of competition in our primary elections.

In addition to checking the size of pluralities, Ewing also studied the results of primary elections in the Southern states for all offices during the span 1900 to 1948. He concluded that, while large percentages of them went unopposed in both parties, still more, as might be expected, went unopposed in the Republican party primaries. This is so because the Republicans as a minority party have little opportunity to win and therefore offer little incentive to aspirants for office. Ewing's conclusions are in keeping with those of V. O. Key, Jr., who studied primary competition with respect to state legislative posts.[10] Table 6-5 [11] presents some of Ewing's data.

Table 6-5—Percentages of Unopposed Nominations in Southern Primaries.

Type of Office	DEMOCRATS			REPUBLICANS *		
	Total Races	Unop-posed	Per Cent Unopposed	Total Races	Unop-posed	Per Cent Unopposed
Statewide	944	248	26.3	160	63	39.8
Intermediate	1,235	465	37.6	199	72	36.2
Local	1,293	704	54.4	12	11	91.7
Total	3,472	1,417	40.8	371	145	39.1

* Most of the data are from Oklahoma, a Democratic modified one-party state.

Another study was done by Julius Turner,[12] in connection with an attempt to determine the effectiveness of primaries in providing competition in one-party areas. It indicated that, even in such districts where victory is assured for one party, there is still startlingly little competition in the primaries of that party. Turner analyzed primaries in "safe" Congressional districts to see just how many contests there were; his results are found in Table 6-6.[13]

Table 6-6—Proportion of Safe Districts in Which Two or More Candidates Ran in Primaries of the Dominant Party.

Section	Number of Elections in Safe Districts	Number of Primaries Contested	Percentage
South	395	227	57.5
Northeast	222	66	29.7
Border	62	43	69.4
Central	207	95	45.9
West	79	52	65.8
Total	965	483	50.1

Each of the above-mentioned studies strongly suggests that, while we have many elections in the sense of being legally provided for, we do not have as many contests or competition as the civics book ideal would wish. Voters are not afforded alternatives in many elections, even in the primaries of the stronger party of modified one-party areas and the one-party districts. Nor are candidates in excess supply in many areas or for many offices.

SOME DIRECT OUTCOMES

Our primary purpose is of course not in describing the electoral processes, but in being able to determine the results or consequences; that is now our problem. At this point, we are not interested in all the conceivable consequences, but only in those having to do directly with the allocation of authority and power. We want to know, in other words, who wins American elections. Fortunately, as political scientists have been attuned to such considerations, ample data exists on which to base most of our generalizations. We will proceed by stating the generalizations, and then offer or refer to whatever data seems appropriate.

PROPOSITION 1-1. *Elections tend to be won by either Republicans or Democrats.*

This fairly obvious proposition is implicit in much of what has already been said in the present chapter. So complete is the monopoly of the two-party system, that third parties have almost no chance of winning an election in the United States. None has ever won a Presidential election; none has even come close, either in electoral or popular votes. Third parties may influence the outcome of the Presidential election, but the last time that happened was in 1912. On three previous occasions, outcomes were effected, as in 1844, 1848, and 1884, but in no case have they ever received over 16.5 per cent of the popular vote, which they did in 1924. In 1952, for example, third parties totaled only .055 per cent of the popular vote. In the House of Representatives, since 1855, when Republicans and Democrats became the two major parties, we have had but 392 third-party Congressmen. On the Senate side, during the same period, we have had only 98 Senators of other than the Republican or Democratic parties. In no case since 1855 has any party except the Democratic or the Republican held a majority. The greatest number of Congressmen ever elected in one Congress from third parties was 43 in 1857; and the greatest number of third-party Senators elected in one election was eight, which occurred in 1857, 1861, and 1899. The situation has not been vastly different on the state or local levels, although third parties have managed to do somewhat better during various periods in certain states. Thus, the Farmer-Labor Party could win in Minnesota; the Progressives, for a time in Wisconsin; the Non-Partisan League in North Dakota; and the American Labor and Liberal Party in New York. Socialist parties have won in local elections, such as those in Milwaukee, Wisconsin, and Bridgeport, Connecticut. But the role of minor parties has not been significant in terms of winning many elections in American history, and seems to be decreasing in terms of effectiveness.

PROPOSITION 1-2. *Incumbents appear to have a much better chance of winning than do their opponents.*

As the data on this proposition are extremely scanty, the qualifications must be many and explicit. About all we know is confined to the Presidency, primary elections in certain states, and by inference from other types of studies of certain offices, such as the Congressional. Given these limitations, however, the proposition does seem to have considerable validity for the offices and elections thus far investigated.

In the case of the Presidency, only eight Presidents have been defeated in their bid for a second term. And of those eight, only two are of the twentieth century (Taft in 1912 and Hoover in 1932). To be defeated, an incumbent President must either do an extraordinarily poor job, or be the victim of forces beyond his control. Given the advantages that a modern President has for guaranteeing his own reelection, there does not seem to be much incentive for an opponent for the second time around.

Various studies have been made by Julius Turner [14] and Cortez A. M. Ewing,[15] as well as V. O. Key,[16] on primary elections and incumbency. In the studies of the former two scholars, the incumbent won 90 per cent of the time in the primary elections analyzed. Turner considered safe districts in Congressional races, while Ewing studied primary elections for all offices, local, state, and national, during the years 1900 to 1948, analyzing 3,081 contests in which an incumbent was involved. The incumbents won over 90 per cent of all these contests. Of course, there are many variations around this figure depending on such variables as the type of office, primary, year, and number of opponents. Even so, Ewing concluded that the incumbent had hardly any trouble winning additional terms.

A recent study of U.S. Senators by Donald Matthews has also thrown light on the matter of incumbency and success at the polls.[17] Analyzing the electoral situation of 180 Senators during the post-World War II decade, Matthews found a number of interesting correlations. We need

not review all the variables associated with defeat or victory and incumbency, but simply include his gross figures in the form of a graph on
political longevity in the Senate. Figure 6-1 [18] summarizes the situation, but
does not indicate the correlates nor reasons why certain Senators win
reelection while others do not. For this additional data, the reader is
referred to Matthews' study.

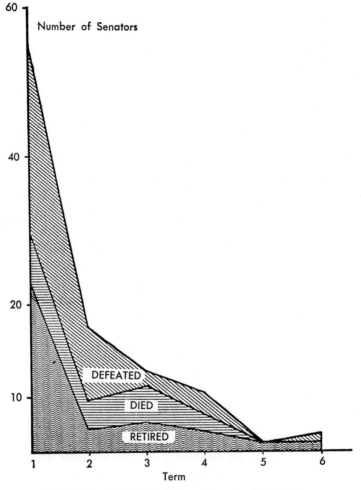

Figure 6-1.   Length of Service and Mortality (1947-1957).

As Figure 6-1 shows, the most dangerous election for the Senator is
his second one, or the attempt to gain reelection at the end of his first
term. Of the 180 Senators studied, 55 served for one term or less. Of
course, we must also observe that 125 were reelected, a total of 69 per

cent, so that even at the most insecure time, incumbency is of great importance. After the second term, incumbency becomes still more crucial in determining the electoral chances of aspirants to the Senate. Note the sharp drop in the number of defeated incumbents at the second term (10). Thereafter, an incumbent becomes extraordinarily difficult to unseat. Were it otherwise, the curve would slope upward and to the right.

Studies of the House of Representatives suggest that, while there is a biennial turnover of about 20 per cent, not all these Congressmen are defeated; some do not run for re-election, strange as that may seem.[19] Some notion of the situation can be gathered by looking at a table that shows the number of Congressmen who have served one or more consecutive terms. For purposes of illustration, we may use the Eighty-sixth Congress. Table 6-7 [20] lists the number and percentage of the total membership who have served one or more consecutive terms.

Table 6-7—Number and Percentage of Consecutive Terms Served by Members of the Eighty-sixth Congress.

Number of Terms	Number of Members	Percentage of Members	Accumulative Percentage
15+	12	3.0	
14	6	1.5	4.5
13	7	1.6	6.1
12	12	3.0	9.1
11	16	4.0	13.1
10	11	2.5	15.6
9	23	5.0	20.6
8	18	4.0	24.6
7	33	7.6	32.2
6	30	6.9	39.0
5	37	8.5	47.6
4	61	14.0	61.6
3	42	9.7	71.3
2	43	10.0	81.3
1	81	18.7	100.0
	432	100.0	

Reference to Table 6-7 quickly indicates the extent of experience in the House of Representatives during the Eighty-sixth Congress. Some 81.3 per cent of the membership had served two or more terms. While the table is based on the data of a single Congress, the Eighty-sixth was hardly unusual or abnormal. Service in the House is not as insecure as either we or the Congressmen are prone to believe. Put another way, incumbency is apparently a powerful advantage for the Congressman once he is past the first term or bid for his first reelection. Of course, incumbency, as in the instance of U. S. Senators, is more beneficial to more first termers than not.

Even though the danger time is the bid for a second term, more Congressmen are re-elected than are defeated.

PROPOSITION 1-3. *The major party, with but three exceptions since 1888 (1948, 1952, and 1956), which has controlled the House in the off-year elections preceding a Presidential election, has always elected its nominee for the President.*

Winning control of the House in the off-year elections is looked to by many observers, particularly those of the party that wins, as a harbinger of good things to come in the following Presidential election. And they have good reason to, for on some fourteen occasions the out-party, which managed to win control of the House or Senate, did go on to win the Presidency. On five occasions, however, the President managed to lose the midterm elections of Congress, while his party went on to win the Presidency in spite of the loss. The most recent such elections were the Republican win of the Congress in 1946 and the Truman victory of 1948, and Eisenhower's victory in 1956 after losing the 1954 Congressional elections. In 1958, however, the Democrats retained control of the Congress and went on to win the Presidency in 1960, thus conforming with the proposition.

PROPOSITION 1-4. *The party that controls the Presidency generally wins the House of Representatives.*

With House elections coinciding every four years with the Presidential elections, it would appear that a rather strong relationship might develop between the results of both. Such has been the case during most of American history. Ordinarily, a winning President carries with him a majority into the House. Indeed, correlations of Presidential and Congressional voting demonstrate a significant, if not a perfect, relationship. Thus, when President Eisenhower failed to bring in a Republican majority in the House during his own reelection in 1956, the result was regarded as most remarkable or amazing. It was the only time in the twentieth century that the winning candidate for the Presidency did not carry the House.

The effects of the central importance of the Presidency in deciding on the control of government is exerted through the coattails of the President. And, according to some observers such as Louis Bean, the President's broad coattails support about twenty Congressmen at each Presidential election.[21] It has also been claimed that, even when a President loses a midterm election, things could have been worse without his being in office. Whatever the explanation of the high correlation between control of the Presidency and the House, it is a fact of politics.

PROPOSITION 1-5. *With the exception of two Congressional elections (1878 and 1934), the party that controls the Presidency has lost seats in the off years.*

According to one count, the average number of seats lost by the party in control of the Presidency since 1900 has been forty-five.[22] And in several elections (1870, 1882, 1894, 1910, 1918, 1930, 1946, and 1954), the loss has been great enough to throw control of the House to the opposition party. The only exception to this tendency was the election of 1934 when Franklin D. Roosevelt's popularity was on the ascent and he was able to win a larger majority in the House of Representatives.

An explanation is not too difficult to produce for the generalization. Off-year Congressional elections are run without the direct pulling power of the winning Presidential candidate. At this time, Congressional candidates must fend largely for themselves, whereas during the Presidential elections a number will ride in on the coattails of the winner. Aiding this drop in the President's Congressional delegation at the off-year elections is a normal disillusionment with the performance of the President himself. A two-year period of time and many decisions is enough to make enemies for the President and his party. Consequently, the politicians who suffer most immediately are those who associate themselves with the President or his party. Thus, some of the freshmen Congressmen elected two years before are likely to be casualties. And so the generalization is confirmed.

PROPOSITION 1-6. *In the struggle for control of Congress, the Democratic party has a major advantage in having a greater number of "safe" districts.*

Let us begin with the House of Representatives. There, approximately 250 seats are generally regarded as "safe," that is, one-party districts in which the incumbent must rarely worry about reelection.[23] Of these 250 seats, about 100 are safe for the Democrats because of the South. Indeed, in many of these districts Republican opposition is simply not to be found. Added to this total is another thirty or so seats for the Democrats from the Border states. From other sections of the nation, another 50 seats may be regarded as safe for Democrats. This being the case, the Republican party is sorely beset in most Congressional elections. For not only do they have a much smaller number of sure seats, but many seats they may acquire are attained with very small margins. The proportions of "safe," "fighting," and "doubtful" districts, of course, vary from election to election, but generally, the Democrats have been the more fortunate during recent years.[24]

Let us now consider the Senate. A somewhat similar tale of dismay for Republicans must again be registered, for the number of safe Senate seats among Democrats is greater than among Republicans. Professor Key, in analyzing Senatorial elections for the 1920-1956 period, including some 600 elections, concluded that slightly more than one-half of the Democratic winners polled over 60 per cent of the popular vote, while only a bit over one-third of the Republicans did the same.[25] A more detailed enumeration of his results may be seen in Table 6-8.[26]

Table 6-8—Sure and Close Senate Races: Distribution of Senatorial Elections, 1920-1956, According to Democratic Percentage of Two-Party Vote.*

Democratic Percentage of Vote	Number of Elections	Per Cent of Elections	DISTRIBUTION OF WINNING PARTY	
			Per Cent of Republicans	Per Cent of Democrats
0-9	5	0.8	1.9	
10-19	6	1.0	2.3	
20-29	28	4.7	10.7	
30-39	51	8.5	19.5	
40-44	69	11.5	26.3	
45-49	103	17.2	39.3	
50-54	89	14.8		26.3
55-59	72	12.0		21.3
60-69	56	9.3		16.6
70-79	27	4.5		8.0
80-89	25	4.2		7.4
90-100	69	11.5		20.4
Total	600	100.0		100.0

* Includes only elections for a full six-year term; excludes eight elections at which independent or third-party candidates won.

SOME INDIRECT OUTCOMES

In the previous section we dealt with the outcomes of elections as they effected the candidates or who wins the contest. To this end, a number of propositions were enumerated. But while of great interest to politician and voter alike, they are not the only types of outcomes or consequences of significance. Other consequences of a less direct type also concern the allocation of power in American society. In addition to effecting the allocation of office and power, these outcomes of necessity effect the demands or goals selected and the means used for their implementation. Most, if not all, of these consequences are well-established generalizations of political science, subject to little dispute. They are products of our formal structure of the polity and, more particularly, of the electoral system. The order in which these propositions are listed is of no great import.

PROPOSITION 2-1. *Single-member plurality constituencies lead to disproportionate representation in legislatures.*

Because we tend to elect most of our officials from single-member plurality districts, we tend to give greater representation in the legislatures to the winning party than is justified by the popular vote.[27] The reason for this is quite simple: the winner takes all regardless of his plurality. If a candidate wins by one vote he wins the seat, while the loser gets none. Thus, a party winning, say, 55 per cent of the popular vote, wins, say, 60 per cent of the seats in Congress or the state legislature. If we had proportional representation, the situation would be such that each of the contending parties would receive the same percentage of seats in the legislature as it did of popular votes in the election.

One consequence of an overrepresentation in legislatures is that the Republican party tends to benefit in the case of the state legislatures, while the Democratic party has been benefiting during the past twenty-five to thirty years in the Congress.

PROPOSITION 2-2. *The less populated areas of the nation, including rural and small towns, tend to be overrepresented in state legislatures, Congress, and party conventions.*

This generalization is one of the oldest and best substantiated of propositions about American politics. The reasons why this proposition is true are several, but the major single reason stems from the fact that we have a formal political structure that divides power along geographic, as well as population, lines. Thus, while urban districts tend to be somewhat more adequately represented in the lower houses of our legislatures, the rural areas gain in power in the upper houses where equality in numbers of representatives is practiced. Accordingly, the State of Nevada, for example, has two Senators, just as does the State of New York. Within the several states the same principle tends to apply regarding state legislatures. Representation in the lower houses is likewise unfair. The failure of the state legislatures to reapportion and redistrict as the population increases and shifts has meant that the rural areas have managed to continue holding a disproportionate amount of power. As a result, some Congressmen represent more than one million citizens while others represent only 350,000. This elementary account is, of course, readily familiar to political scientists and politicians alike. The actual measurement of relative power potential, however, cannot be advanced with such simple facts. More precise estimates of the relative advantages that some states have has been provided by Robert Dahl in the form of a rank ordering of states on the

basis of a ratio or formula that Dahl calls an "index of advantage." [28]
The index is calculated by comparing actual representation with propor-
tionate representation. Accordingly, it is possible to calculate the exact
position of each of the states in the United States Senate. We need not
include Dahl's table of findings, since they are somewhat dated (1952), but
he indicates that states like Nevada, for example, had almost fifteen times
the "advantage" in the Senate as New York. Other states ranking high on
the Dahl "index of advantage" included Wyoming, Vermont, Delaware,
and New Mexico. States ranking at the bottom included the large states
of the East and Middle West and West (New York, California, Pennsylvania, Illinois, Ohio, and Michigan).[29]

Dahl's findings give precise measurements of the inequalities in representation that result from presumably equal representation; but what is
left out are the inequities within the states, even as represented in the
Senate. Not all groups within each state, as Dahl says, are equally represented; there are minorities within minorities.[30] The Southern states, for
example, are a minority in the Senate, but with considerable power or
advantage because all rank high on Dahl's list (mostly within the top
half), but the Negroes who reside in these same states can hardly be said
to enjoy any of that advantage. The following propositions, from Dahl,
are intended to illustrate who gains and loses from the principle of equal
representation in the upper house of the Congress.

PROPOSITION 2-3. *Various racial and ethnic minority groups,
including the Negro and Mexican-American, are less well represented than their numbers in the population would require.*[31]

PROPOSITION 2-4. *Among the occupational groups that tend
to be underrepresented are sharecroppers, migrant workers, wage
earners, and coal miners.*[32]

PROPOSITION 2-5. *Among the occupational groups overrepresented are the farmers, wool growers, and silver producers.*[33]

The above propositions may appear to be a miscellaneous listing of
some groups differentially affected by the electoral system; they are.
They have been included only because they illustrate some of the differences we wish to establish and because the data for these propositions have
been neatly collected and calculated by Professor Dahl. The methods used
by Dahl can be used by the reader himself to determine the situation of
almost any groups he may be interested in assessing. The support for
these propositions was attained by looking at the case of minorities within

minority states as defined by equal representation in the Senate. Negroes living in the Southern states, for example, do not receive the same attention as do whites from their equal representation in the U.S. Senate. Dahl devised a means of determining the power position or relative advantage of these groups by dividing the percentage of states in which these groups (mentioned in above propositions) are found, by the percentage of total votes cast in the 1952 Congressional elections. The result was a "relative advantage" for each group. Table 6-9 [34] contains Dahl's figures and results.

Table 6-9—Relative Advantages of Selected Groups in the Senate.

Number of States	Percentage of States	Percentage of Total Voters *	Relative Advantage †	Group	Percentage of Group in These States ‡
9+ D.C.	18.8	7.8	2.4	Negroes	50.0
11	22.8	13.2	1.7	Sharecroppers	68.0
8	16.7	12.5	1.3	Migrant workers	33.0
12	25.0	51.0	0.49	Wage earners	53.7
2	4.2	9.4	0.45	Coal miners	58.8
8	16.7	9.2	1.8	Farmers	35.4
7	14.6	6.2	2.4	Wool growers	57.6
6	12.5	5.0	2.5	Cotton farmers	67.0
4	8.3	1.9	4.4	Silver producers	84.4

* Votes cast for U.S. House of Representatives, November, 1952.
† Column 2 divded by column 3.
‡ Sources: Census: Vital Statistics and Census of Agriculture; Bureau of Mines, *Mineral Year Book;* 1950 Census: Characteristics of the Population.

Under the system of equal representation in the Senate, we find that the wool growers, cotton farmers, and silver producers are the best off, while the wage earners, coal miners, migrant workers, sharecroppers, and Negroes are worse off. There does not seem to be any good reason why we should penalize these groups. To be sure, equal representation does not cause the discrepancy, but it does institutionalize the situation.

PROPOSITION 2-6. *Elective public officials tend to be selected from a limited number of occupational groups with law, business, and agriculture most frequently represented.*

Data on the above proposition is rather uneven in that not all offices have been studied, nor are trend data readily available. Yet, on the basis of the research that has been conducted, the generalization appears sound. Donald Matthews has done an admirable job of assembling scattered materials on the entire area of social backgrounds of political leaders; we will rely heavily on his study.[35] Table 6-10,[36] taken from Matthews' work, summarizes the situation with respect to a selected list of elective officials.

Table 6-10—Occupational Class of American Elective Public Officials (in Percentages).

Occupational Class	President Vice President Cabinet * 1877-1934	U.S. Senators 1949-51	U.S. Representatives 1949-51	State Governors 1930-40	State Legislators † 1925-35	Labor Force 1940
Professionals	74	69	69	60	36	7
Lawyers	70	57	56	52	28	
Others	4	12	13	8	8	
Proprietors & officials	21	24	22	25	25	8
Farmers	2	7	4	11	22	11
Low-salaried workers	1	0	1	1	4	17
Wage earners	2	0	2	1	3	40
Servants	0	0	0	0	0	11
Farm laborers	0	0	0	0	0	7
Unknown or unclassified	0	0	2	3	10	0
	100	100	100	101	100	101
	(n = 176)	(n = 109)	(n = 435)	(n = 170)	(n = 12,689)	

* Occupations in this column are those for which Presidents, Vice Presidents, and cabinet officers were trained.
† Figures for the lower houses of thirteen selected states and the upper houses of twelve. The states are Arkansas, California (lower house only), Illinois, Indiana, Iowa, Louisiana, Maine, Minnesota, Mississippi, New Jersey, New York, Pennsylvania, and Washington.

It should be clear from Table 6-10 that the lawyers are, as Matthews put it, the "High Priests of American Politics." [37] Equally clear is the fact that proprietors and officials, or businessmen, rank second in terms of numbers in public office. Of course, it must also be recognized that local offices were not included in the tabulation. Had they been, the rankings might be somewhat different. Statistics on the matter are difficult to come by, but isolated studies have suggested that a wider distribution of occupations is to be found and that the businessmen might well vie with the lawyer for top ranking. William Form and Delbert Miller, sociologists, in investigating the occupational backgrounds of five city councils, of which three were American, concluded that four-fifths of the councilmen and mayors were from proprietary, managerial, and professional backgrounds.[38]

The situation on the local level more than likely varies considerably. In rural areas, for example, the number of farmers in public office is considerable. In many state legislatures, as Table 6-10 indicates, farmers hold third place. It seem highly probable that they would be numerous in township and county offices of the rural governments.

From this data, inadequate though it may be, we can provisionally conclude that many occupations are not represented, as such. We may also conclude that there is far greater access to the avenues of recruitment for public office by lawyers, businessmen, and farmers, with considerable variation in their ranking for various offices and levels of government.

15

The Allocation of Income and Benefits

The role of the political system in influencing the distribution and redistribution of income and other benefits among citizens has long been appreciated by both citizen and political scientist. Much of the struggle in politics, in fact, is a product of conflicting demands over the distribution patterns. And, as the polity comes to play a still greater role, we can rest assured that the struggle will include more persons and groups, and produce more competition and conflict. It is most imperative, therefore, that we get some clear notion of the actual patterns of distribution of income and other benefits resulting from governmental action.

Determining who gets how much of the benefits provided by the government is no easy task. Indeed, it is doubtful whether we can actually trace the ultimate receivers in any very precise sense. At best, we can merely suggest which groups appear to be getting certain types and shares. We can do this in part by analyzing the budgets of the various governments. In our case, we will concentrate on the national government, but mention will also be made of the situation at the state and local levels, for they too allocate benefits. The emphasis, however, will be on the national level as a case study.

Who gets how much depends in the first place on how much there is to allocate in actual hard cash, borrowed money through deficit spending, and other governmental powers and privileges. The political system, itself, directly generates but a small share of the national income; that is the function of the economy. But the polity does play an important role in shaping the conditions that either facilitate or discourage the economic system from producing still more national income or product.[1] Part of the allocative conflict is based on differences over the sorts of policies that the government ought to pursue with regard to the development of resources and increasing the national income or product. Some members of the system feel that the government ought to assume a relatively passive role, while others advocate more aggressive participation and guidance. What course the government will take depends, to a considerable extent, upon the allocation of authority and power as described in Chapter 14. But it also depends upon shifts of active demands and events that were not anticipated at election time.

TYPES OF BENEFITS

A catalogue of the benefits that the political system and government provide and allocate among the citizenry would not be infinite, but very long indeed, and somewhat useless for our purposes. Yet, it might be useful to provide some general categories of benefits distributed in order to better appreciate the role of the polity and government in this regard.

Four major types of benefits may be easily discerned: the more obvious, perhaps, is that of *services* to the public; but a second type, *facilities,* is also prominent. A third kind consists of *positions* or jobs. And, still a fourth—payments or *money income*—is also provided by government to citizens. Let us consider each briefly.

Services

In speaking of governmental services, we mean such items as mail; police and fire protection; administration of elections; research and reporting in fields such as agriculture, business, weather, and medicine; national defense; and the administration of many programs of social welfare. Such services have been on the increase during the past century. Some are paid for by the users, but some are given free of charge or for token fees. Many are financed out of the general receipts of the government, such as police and fire protection and national defense, but others come from special funds. Thus, some services provided the veterans are so financed from earmarked funds. Regardless of the means of financing, governmental services are numerous and are on the increase in terms of numbers, types, and persons covered.

Facilities

Closely related to services are those activities and resources provided by government that we will term "facilities." The distinction is simply one of convenience. Examples of facilities are such items as land, communications, transportation, and energy such as electricity, education, and recreation. Most of these examples suggest generalized resources that can be used by nearly everyone in the community in order to conduct a social life. Most, if not all, such resources are basic to everyone and could not or would not easily be furnished by the private economy. Parks and other recresational facilities, for example, probably would not be provided for under the aegis of the profit-motive since profits from such are not likely to be forthcoming. Other facilities, such as highways, parks, and airports, are better provided when administered by a central authority rather than by competitors, even if the latter were available. At one time, many of our roads were toll roads under private ownership. Today, governments control, finance, and administer almost all roads and high-ways. Just as the services provided by the government have been multiply-ing, so have the facilities. Moreover, they are likely to continue doing so, as evidenced by recent figures relating per capita expenditures on public works. The average growth rate of public works expenditures during the period 1915–40 was 4.5 per cent, with a sharp down turn during World War II, but an even sharper increase in rates since that time.[2] In 1960, the federal government, alone, spent over $5 billion on civil public works, while the state and local governments devoted over $20 billion to highways, their major public works. Total expenditures on facilities are rising just as per capita costs are also rising, but they have not yet reached the height they did in 1940. Total public works expenditures have lagged behind the growth of total national output. Regardless, the role of the various governments in providing facilities is considerable, and appears to be increasing in significance.

Jobs and Income

Under this heading, we have in mind governmental employment. The political system employs about eight million persons, if we include the armed services. Of these eight million about 2.5 million are in the employment of the federal government as civilians, while the remainder are employees of the states and local units. Each fiscal year, a total of about $30 billion goes into salaries and wages for these civilian government workers.

These many jobs range from the highest prestige positions, such as those appointed by the President, to the lowliest garbage collector hired by the city manager. Regardless of their status, they are jobs and provide an income to someone. As such, these jobs are sought after and, according to some research, social status for governmental work has been increasing. Because of this increasing status, and the increased activity of the govern-ment, the total number of governmental employees now makes up about

12 per cent of the total labor force, or triple the percentage at the turn of the century. As a consequence we must regard jobs and income as a primary value being allocated by the polity and government.

Money Income

Periodically, the government mails checks to many Americans. For some, these checks are wages and salaries as noted above; for others, the checks represent payments on the part of society to people who are suffering personal hardship and disability. The injured, the orphaned, the blind, the unemployed, the farmer, the war casualties, all are types of persons who receive income or benefits from the government.

We need not detail the number of persons receiving money income from the government nor the amounts at this point, but a few statistics will help to illustrate the enormous significance of government in the distribution of income.[3] Nearly one person in five over sixty-five years of age receives old-age assistance; but the proportions vary greatly from state to state. The average monthly payment to the aged needy is estimated at $61. In 1958, about 2.5 million needy old people, 2.6 million dependent children and the adults who cared for them, over 108,000 blind, and 300,000 needy disabled persons received assistance benefits. Nearly 2.8 million veterans were receiving compensations, pensions, or retirement pay. And another million persons received checks as survivors of deceased veterans. In addition to these incomes, various economic groups received governmental payments. Farmers, for example, are a prime recipient of government income. During 1957, price support of various commodities gave the average owner of a small farm $109, of a medium-sized farm $482, and of a large farm $1,993. Some of the larger farms received payments mounting into tens of thousands of dollars. Businessmen, too, in spite of their preference for limited government, have been the beneficiaries of governmental largess. Lucrative payments have been made not only for the fulfillment of contracts, especially in national defense and public works, but also to the various carriers (railroads, airlines, ships), to shipbuilders, and for the financing of investment. Indeed, there is hardly a group that has not been a beneficiary of government income, even though it is difficult to estimate the amounts or ultimate incidence.

BENEFICIARIES

Everyone, from the child to the aged, benefits in some way or at some time from the allocation of money, goods, and services by the polity and government. As observed many times by many scholars and others, the number of citizens and government officials and employees benefiting has steadily increased throughout the history of the country. So common-place an assertion explains very little, however, for it does not tell us who gets how much, nor why such patterns of distribution exist in the first place.

Casual observation would suggest that not only are outcomes unequal, but different benefits are allocated among unequally sized groups. In short, some benefits are widely distributed, while others are distributed to select numbers. Examples of diffused benefits include such expenditures as those for national defense, highways, parks, conservation, recreation, schools, and so forth. Illustrations of more narrowly directed benefits include such programs as tariffs protecting specific industries, farm programs, veterans' benefits, and subsidies for shipbuilders and other industries. In pointing out the more or less direct beneficiaries of govern-mental spending according to the size of the groups, we do not mean to say that these monies go directly to such groups and end there. No, such incomes may also benefit others less directly concerned, as a tariff may directly benefit a manufacturer and indirectly aid the workers in the industry. Nevertheless, it is desirable to attempt to trace the incidence of income.

Another word of caution: the recipients of governmental payments are not members of a single group, but of multiple groups both receiving income and making payments to the government. Thus, a single citizen may receive income from the government as a farmer, a veteran, and a conservationist. Moreover, he may pay money to the government in the form of several types of taxes, for services rendered by the government, and in the form of a loan or the purchase of a bond. Such a citizen is then involved in many programs or transactions of the government, both as recipient and supporter. How his financial position vis-à-vis the govern-ment finally stands at the end of a fiscal year is problematic and would be hazardous to guess at. Whether we could, in practice, actually determine how much a given person benefited or lost in relationship to the govern-ment is highly doubtful. For many of the services provided by the govern-ment are not easy to measure insofar as the individual citizen is concerned. We do not know in money terms, for example, what police protection is worth to individual citizens. Likewise, we do not know how much in money terms national defense is worth to the individual, although we do know how much is spent each year for the nation. For heuristic purposes, at least, it is desirable to think of the individual as involved in a set of input-output relationships with the government, that is, as paying into the government various costs and, in return, receiving certain benefits. Yet we do not know what might be the worth of such exchanges in particular instances, although many of the exchanges can be easily determined. Such exchanges include taxes, fees, fines, loans from the individual citizen; and services and various benefit payments he might receive from the government. The most vague or indeterminate figures are those pertaining to the diffused or generalized services of the government that go out to many or most people as citizens. However diffused these benefits, they are a form of income to the citizen.

WAYS OF INFLUENCING BENEFITS

The manner and processes by which income is generated and distributed in the economic system are fairly well known and appreciated. Less well known are the ways in which the polity affects these same matters. The present section is thus devoted to a brief summary of political action in determining the level of benefits and their allocation among the citizenry.[4]

Basically, there are two master processes or ways of shaping income distribution: first, the more direct way, the government simply distributes income among citizens by grants of money such as subsidies and by social benefits to specific groups such as the help to aged, soldiers' pensions, and school lunches. These kinds of incomes need not include direct money payments alone, but innumerable grants of kind. Thus, hospital care, free school lunches, police protection, fire protection, and the like. The second way in which government influences benefits, particularly income, is through its power to help shape or determine the rules of the game by which the economic system operates. This way is much more indirect in that the government does not actually hand out checks or services, but stipulates rules that have differential consequences for the income-making power of the persons and groups constituting the economy. The government may decide, for example, that an eight-hour day is the maximum work day, that one must be at least a certain age to work full time, and that a minimum wage be made mandatory. In turn, each of these rules then influences how much the worker and the owners will ultimately receive from the economy. Here, government, and not the workings of the free market, has determined the outcomes of the productive system. Of the two ways of effecting income through the political system, the latter is the more important, but also the more difficult to analyze in full.

Economists study the impact of these political decisions on economic matters when they deal with fiscal and monetary policies. We cannot go into all these matters, partly due to lack of competence, but also due to the magnitude of the task. The interested reader can find many good texts on the role of the government in economic life, most of them dealing in detail with precisely such matters as these. What we will do is somewhat different: we will look at the actual distribution of income by the government to specific groups in society—as a case study of outcomes. This we will do by inspecting a sample budget of the national government. Our conclusions, therefore, will be time-bound. But since many governmental expenditures are fairly stable with respect to both their over-all size and distribution, the generalizations should not be very misleading.

NATIONAL INCOME
AND GOVERNMENTAL REVENUES

Before any study of the distribution of benefits by the government can be conducted, we need to know the net national income from whence is drawn most of the revenues used by governments. Naturally, the national income of a society places a limitation on the amount a government may theoretically use as funds for distribution. But while the national income is the ultimate limitation, the effective limitations are much less. In the United States, the governments have typically taken about one-fourth of the national income, which many citizens feel to be too large a portion. Whatever the actual percentage going into taxes, this percentage is a product of the political values and norms of the society and of the problems confronting the nation. In America, as we have seen, governmental action is so restricted that only a portion of income actually goes into public programs. In 1957, for example, the net national income was $403 billion dollars, while total governmental expenditures, at all levels, was $112 billion. (See Figure 6-2.⁵) For the year 1957, then, governments had a total of $112 billion to allocate among various and often competing groups and persons. Of this total, the national government had the responsibility of controlling about $80 billion, the remainder being handled by the states and local units. Each of these levels of government and units, thereof, had to resolve the principles on which the allocation of these payments to the public were to be handled. In short, who was to benefit, how much, and in what ways were the major questions before politicians and others.

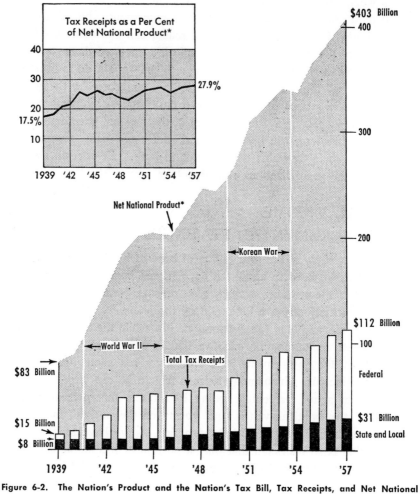

Figure 6-2.   The Nation's Product and the Nation's Tax Bill, Tax Receipts, and Net National
Product (1939-1957).

* Gross national product less capital consumption allowances.

THE ALLOCATION OF INCOME

The problem now is to account for the distribution of government payments to the public. Granted the usual strictures about case studies, we
will analyze a single case—the proposed national budget of 1960—to see
if we can gain some idea of who is getting how much of this. Before we
begin, it should be said that tracing the ultimate recipients of these funds
is probably impossible. Nevertheless, we can gain a better understanding
of income allocation by the government if we make some effort. To be

sure, the budget categories are not precisely suited for our needs, but they are indicators, and we will use them as given by the budget-makers. The reader should also be aware of the fact that the final expenditures of the government are as yet not known for 1960. Thus, we will actually be using the proposals of the President and his advisers, rather than the final figures of the government. In spite of these qualifications, however, our analysis should not be very much off from the expected patterns of income allocation.

Budget categories for payments to the public are based on programs and expenditures by each branch and agency of the government. We will use the program figures since they give a more accurate indication of the beneficiary. Departmental and agency expenditures in themselves do not afford such accurate designations, although they could be so used. Now to begin: the President's Budget Message and Summary Budget Statements use three major categories when analyzing programs.[6] The first, called "Protection," deals with national security; the second category is termed "Civil Benefits;" and the third is "Interest and General Government." Under each of these major categories are a number of sub-categories that spell out somewhat more precisely what the expenditures are to be used for in the way of programs. Thus, we find such functions as "international affairs and finances," "commerce and housing," "agriculture and agricultural resources," "natural resources," "labor and welfare," and "veterans' benefits."

Determining who gets how much of the federal payments to the public can probably never be fully nor accurately accounted for given the budgetary practices of the federal government and the technical problems of tracing the ultimate beneficiaries of governmental spending. How is one to analyze and stipulate, for example, the allocation of "major national security" expenditures? In some sense, all who approve of such expenditures receive benefits; but how are they to assess these benefits? And, among those who receive actual money income from the government, it is still difficult to determine how much various areas and various occupations, such as worker, clerk, manager, and stock-holder, receive. Even when the budget states that so much went into housing, we still do not know whether, and to what extent, unions, contractors, finance companies, and home owners benefit. In spite of these problems, however, certain generalizations can be made, and in some cases we can fairly accurately specify the beneficiaries. Let us try by viewing each program individually.

Major National Security

As is apparent from Figure 6-2, about 60 per cent of the annual federal budget goes into national security, expenditures for which have varied considerably since the end of World War II. Immediately after the war, for example, expenditures were about $11 to $14 billion. With the Korean War, however, costs jumped to over $40 billion, and have remained there since. In terms of proportions of the total budget, the percentages have varied in recent years, from 59 per cent in 1960 to 71 per cent in 1954. Defense requirements change rapidly so that the internal structure of the budget also changes rapidly, and various branches of the armed services benefit differently, as do various industries in the nation.

The question as to who gets what from national defense expenditures becomes acute whenever someone is adversely affected by a proposed budget cut. Among the first affected by any general cuts or redistribution of expenditures within the military are the military services themselves. During the past decade a continuous struggle has been waged by the three armed services over their respective shares of the defense monies. At stake are such matters as the ability of the services to fight various types of war, their comparative prestige, and the amount of employment within the military at different ranks. Shares of income are the major index of most of these matters. During most of the past ten years, it would appear that the Air Force has been the chief beneficiary of defense monies. In 1958, for example, the Air Force received $18.9 million; the Navy $10.9 million; while the Army got but $9.0 million.[7] In 1959, the estimates had each service getting slightly more, but in the same relative positions, vis-à-vis one another. The seriousness with which the services regard the struggles over budgets is well symbolized by the fact that two Army Chiefs of Staff—Ridgway and Taylor—have resigned in recent years over the "down-grading of the Army."

The services, of course, are not the only ones concerned with what the military budgets look like in money terms. Likewise interested are the politicians who represent districts with military installations or defense plants. Many of these politicians are Congressmen and Senators who must pass upon the budgets. They do not like the loss of either a military installation or a defense plant or contract. And in this opposition they are supported by constituents, especially by workers and businessmen. All bemoan taxes, to be sure, but none wants his own area to suffer the loss of a single federal dollar. Thus the flowing rationalizations in the home town about the necessity of defense expenditures. Leadership in these struggles is offered not only by politicians but also by businessmen who stand to profit. In such struggles, trade unions too are economically motivated and on the side of the business firms. Defense contracts and installations are lucrative enterprises and defense goals are morally unassailable. Reductions in national security budgets, therefore, are not likely prospects so long as defense seems vital. Patriotism and economic motives ensure that everyone will get something from defense.

A few figures on contracts can provide a more concrete picture of why business is sensitive to military expenditures. Table 6-11 [8] shows the total amounts spent with business firms in the United States and whether these contracts were negotiated or competitive.

Table 6-11—Net Value of Military Procurement with Business Firms in the United States, 1952-1958 (in Millions of Dollars).

Year	Negotiated	Competitive	Total
1952	$37,003	$4,479	$41,482
1953	24,733	3,089	27,822
1954	9,659	1,789	11,448
1955	12,544	2,386	14,930
1956	14,935	2,815	17,750
1957	15,812	3,321	19,133
1958	18,712	3,115	21,827

Clearly, very large sums are involved in contracting with private business firms. Furthermore, these firms are in the advantageous position of not having to compete for contracts, as shown by the large amounts under negotiated contracts in Table 6-11. Another fact of great significance in the allocation of these funds is the prominence of the large firm in securing these contracts. Little more than one-seventh of the money goes to plants employing fewer than 500 employees. It is rather the big manufacturing and construction companies who do most of the dollar volume work of the Defense Department.

Another facet of defense expenditures is of particular interest to the politician and political scientist: namely, the distribution of defense spending among the various states and Congressional districts. The fifty states do not share equally in these monies, and the fact that they do not is of considerable concern to their representatives in Congress. Those who have large manufacturing concerns and acquire lucrative contracts want to keep them, while those states that do not want a greater share. To some extent, however, the "have-nots" with respect to defense contracts are "have's" with respect to the location of defense installations. Some of the more rural states, for example, are ideal locations for Army posts,

Air Force bases, and the like. With regard to over-all defense spending among the several states, the leading states include California, New York, and Texas, with California far in the lead having both defense plants and military installations in abundance. States that do rather badly include North Dakota, West Virginia, Wyoming, Vermont, and Nevada.

Veterans' Services and Benefits

The power of the veterans as an interest group can hardly be denied in view of their success at the counters of government. In 1960, 7 per cent of the national government's budget was proposed for veterans' benefits and services. These various benefits are distributed in a number of ways. In the 1960 budget, they took the forms of programs in the following areas:

1. Education and training.
2. Readjustment benefits.
3. Compensation and pensions.
4. Insurance and indemnities.
5. Hospitals and medical care.
6. Various other services and costs of administration.

Of the above programs, by far the largest cost has been that of compensation and pensions, with hospitals and medical care in second place.

That so much money should be spent on veterans and their families is certainly understandable; we have been through three major wars during the past forty-five years. As a result, veterans and their families represent about one-half of the population. Moreover, many veterans are in politics, and several powerful organizations, such as the American Legion and the Veterans of Foreign Wars, exert considerable pressure on government for the interests of their members. Besides being large and well-represented, the veterans also have the unique identity of having served their nation under its most trying conditions. For these reasons, they are a highly successful group in American politics.

We can get a somewhat clearer idea of their success from the costs of such programs to the taxpayer. According to the President's Commission on Veterans' Pensions, reporting in 1956, federal benefits to veterans alone cost $27 per person in the United States, or about $95 per average family.[9] In fact, the costs of providing for the veteran is becoming more expensive than the actual waging of the wars. This has been true of the Civil War, the Spanish-American War, World War I, and will shortly be true of World War II. Already, the Korean War is costing more for veterans' benefits than did the war itself. Obviously, in the future, the cost of the aftermath of these wars will continue to mount until the last veteran and his family have deceased.

We can see, then, that in purely economic terms the veterans do "all right" in the political system. It must also be remembered, however, that the costs many of them paid during and after their services can hardly be reimbursed.

Labor and Welfare

Under the generalized label of "labor and welfare" used by the budget makers is a potpourri of programs designed to distribute income and benefits to a great variety of people, some of whom are workers, but many of whom are not. In 1960, a total of a little over $4 billion was allocated by the federal government for programs of a great variety. Among these programs were the following:

1.   Administration of Labor-Management Act of 1947 and other laws providing services to workers and unions.
2.   Federal-State Employment Offices.
3.   Workmen's Compensation.
4.   Unemployment Insurance.
5.   Old-Age and Survivors' Insurance.
6.   Aid to Dependent Children.
7.   Vocational Rehabilitation.
8.   Aid for the Blind, Deaf, and Disabled.
9.   Public Health Service.
10.   Federal Aid to Education.

In addition to the above illustrations of programs designed, primarily, to assist the lower income groups are many similar programs at the state and local levels. In many instances these programs are jointly operated or financed.

Some notion of the extent of coverage of welfare benefits and the amounts received by the public can be gained from the following figures:[10] under the Social Security Act, some 90 per cent or more of all wage and salary earners and self-employed are eligible for pensions, and 11 million already receive them. And while the individual helps to finance his own pension, employers also contribute, so that the government acts as a redistribution agent. From a total of $23 billion in the trust fund in 1958, a total of $8.5 billion was distributed. The maximum a worker could receive in that year was $127.00 per month, while the smallest amount was $33.00. The average was around $66.00.

Among the other programs under the Social Security Act are those providing aid to four special groups of the needy: the blind, dependent children, the totally disabled, and those not covered under regular old-age insurance. Nearly one in five persons receives old-age assistance, although the rate varies greatly among the states;[11] the average monthly payment is currently about $61.00. In 1958, approximately 2.5 million aged needy, 2.6 million dependent children and the adults who care for them, 108,000 blind, and 300,000 needy disabled received assistance payments.

The above miscellaneous figures, to be sure, do not provide anything resembling the meaning or significance of the monies allocated to welfare programs. Indeed, nothing less than a full-scale analysis could possibly do so, or trace the ultimate beneficiaries. Nevertheless, these few bits of data do suggest that welfare is a considerable item in the nation's budget, and that it is likely to increase as the character of the population changes and our social values adjust to newer realities.

Agriculture and Agricultural Resources

Although most people have heard of the farm problem, only one in eight persons currently lives on a farm. In recent years, however, the productivity of the farmers has gone up by enormous amounts. And the result has been a major social and political problem. For while per capita income over-all in the United States has increased, farm income per capita has decreased. Yet since agriculture was once the major source of liveli-hood, and because farm values have long prevailed, the farmer has fought a fairly hard and successful political campaign to maintain his income. He has, in other words, politicized his demands. As one result of this, the government now operates many services for the farmer, distributing a good deal of income to him. Among the services provided are the programs of education and research, soil conservation, marketing services, agricultural credit, rural electrification, and home finance assistance. The biggest income source provided by the government comes under the well-known price-support programs. In 1957, for example, the government spent a total of $7,338,000,000 to buy up surplus commodities. Yet, because crops are not covered by parity—although this varies as the governmental policies regarding agriculture change—most farmers do not benefit from these purchases. What seems apparent is that, while some farmers have benefited considerably from political action, the over-all position of the farmer as a political group has been weakening. The reasons for this are not hard to find. The proportion of farmers in the population is rapidly decreasing; the strength of the urban citizen in number and representation is increasing. Diminishing in appeal is the old farm or rural set of values. For these reasons, we may predict that, while agriculture will continue to be a powerful interest for some time to come, its days as a powerhouse are numbered.

Business Services and Benefits

Businessmen are likely to be more sensitive to the controls exercised over them and the taxes they pay than to the benefits that they receive and have received for a very long time. Governments in the United States have, however, been rather sensitive to the needs and demands of business for favorable conditions. As a result, the federal government provides many services primarily through the Department of Commerce, and the states through countless business bureaus and commercial and industrial boards. But even more important than these agencies are such basic protections and services as peace and order, protection of private property, a rational legal system, enforcement of contracts, rules of bankruptcy, patent rights, and, above all, a monetary system. And, today, the government attempts to maintain and foster an increasing national income through fiscal and monetary policies. All these benefits and services are of the sort that are taken for granted and therefore not considered as benefits by the recipients. Yet, they are just that. Indeed in many areas of the world these facilitating conditions are completely unknown to the private businessman.

But what of the income provided directly by the government? The tariff history of the nation should be enough to suggest that the government has greatly aided business by reducing the amount and severity of foreign competition, all of which has meant added income. Even more dramatic has been the history of subsidies provided the development of transportation and other industries, such as the postal subsidy for publishers. Tax reductions have also been given to industries that would expand, as during the Korean War. Stockpiling of scarce goods, too, has been financed by government. Today, some seventy-five different materials, worth $6.5 billion, are stockpiled. For the most part, these materials are strategic ores and minerals, thus benefiting the mining companies. Money-lending is also a service provided the businessman, although at present lending seems to have come to a halt. Small business, too, receives a hand from the government in the manner of technical services and lending facilities. Again, trying to determine how to measure these aids and benefits is difficult. But these qualitative materials should give some perspective to the important role that business plays as a beneficiary of governmental actions.

CONCLUSION

Determining the allocation of costs is much simpler than determining the allocation of benefits from the government and the political system. Nevertheless, we have shown some of the great variety of benefits the government provides and indicated a little how they are distributed and what the current trends in these areas suggest for the future.

16

The Allocation of Costs

A not uncommon expression among business-minded Americans is that everything has its costs, and so they do. Where the businessman is sometimes wrong, however, is in calculating *all* costs in terms of money. Many costs, essentially social and psychological in nature, are simply not susceptible to monetary treatment. The polity, like the economy, has to confront the problems of both these economic and noneconomic costs in its efforts to mobilize resources for the attainment of system goals. Thus, the people and their leaders must devise ways of determining how much they are to spend, and how to allocate the burdens among the citizenry. This aspect of the problem is of course the more conscious and rational; other costs, too, are distributed, but often unknowingly or unintentionally. In this chapter, we will attempt to answer a series of questions that runs somewhat as follows:

> Who pays?
> How much?
> In what forms?
> How?
> With what consequences?

When we have answered these questions, we should have a reasonably good idea of the types of costs of American democracy at the midpoint of the twentieth century. Although some historical data will be presented, we will be primarily concerned with today's problems and solutions.

The discussion will proceed by considering, first, the economic costs of the system, and secondly, the less easily measured, but just as tangible, costs where more social and psychological considerations are at stake.

343

ECONOMIC COSTS

Of all the costs, taxation is undoubtedly the most talked about. The sensitivity of Americans on this matter is quite understandable, for we are a materially-oriented people and, to a great extent, antigovernment. Thus, the payment of money to the government for public expenditures whose benefits are not easily comprehended seldom seems very just. We are sensitive, then, to the fact that the costs are more visible and painful than are the returns. Yet, the political system must function, and the government must employ men and women and provide for the common welfare, all of which costs money and for which someone must pay. It is for this reason that determining who will pay how much, by what means, and when, become major issues or sources of contention. Battles over the distribution of income to the public are always accompanied by battles over who is to pay for these programs. They may often not be the same persons. And with the services of the government increasing, and the costs of inflation slowly mounting, we may expect that future struggles over the allocation of costs will increase even more in number and intensity.

In assessing the economic costs of the political system, we need to look primarily at governmental budgets, but also at some private ones that support partisan political action, namely, budgets of political parties and interest groups. To be sure, these latter costs are rather miniscule when compared to those of the governments, proper. Nevertheless, we will look at both.

We will begin with the costs of the federal government. Here, we should note that both the total costs and per capita costs or taxes have risen considerably during the past fifty years.[1] In fact, they have risen greatly during the past ten years. In 1946, for example, net national income or the value of output was slightly under $200 billion, with about $44 billion of this total being taken in the form of taxation at all levels of government, and $33 billion of that tax bill being federal. In 1959, net national output had risen to $438 billion plus, of which $106 plus billion went went into taxes. The federal government's share was about $73 billion. In terms of percentages, this means that in 1946 the total tax bill was 22 per cent of the net national product, while in 1959, the percentage had increased to 24.3 per cent.[2] Certainly the tax burden is not insignificant when citizens pay out about one-fourth of their income for the support of governmental activities, some of which various individuals surely do not approve. But it must also be emphasized that taxes do not "go down the drain." Indeed, they are used for a whole host of goal-attainment efforts, as well as to allocate values and redistribute income more in accordance with basic democratic beliefs. Now, we should like to investigate the matter of incidence of taxation—one of the knottiest problems in economics—in order to determine somewhat more accurately *who* pays *what* amounts of the tax bill.

The Distribution of the Tax Burden

Estimating the tax burden paid by given individuals and groups, such as income levels, families, occupational groups, regions, and races or ethnic groups, is extraordinarily difficult. In fact, the problem of the incidence of taxation is one of the most difficult fields in economics.[3] For while much is known in terms of principles, and although much data has been collected, it deals largely with incidence according to income levels. Inferences, however, can be made about other groups from these income figures.

Having already presented figures on the total tax burden of the nation, we now want to know how this burden is distributed, or who pays how much of it. Our base figure will be taken from the year 1958, purely for reasons of convenience, in that studies have already been made of tax incidence during that year. To be sure, tax burdens do vary somewhat each year, but not so much as to invalidate our figures. In any case, we can get a fairly good notion of how the taxes were allocated for a single year.

The total tax bill for the year 1958 was $110,775,000 including social insurance payments, or, if we deduct them, a total of $95,654,000. During that same year, a total of 54.3 million families paid this bill. Not all these family units, however, paid the same amounts into the public coffers. Before we can determine how much each did, we need to know something about the incomes acquired by these families. Table 6-12 [4] contains the breakdown.

Table 6-12—Distribution of Families and Unattached Individuals by Income Class (Calendar Year 1958).

Family Personal Income Class	Number of Families and Unattached Individuals (Millions)	Per Cent Distribution
Under $2,000	7.6	14
$ 2,000-3,999	12.1	22
4,000-5,999	13.6	25
6,000-7,999	9.2	17
8,000-9,999	5.0	9
10,000-14,999	4.3	8
15,000 and over	2.5	5
Total	54.3	100

Now we may proceed to see how much these various families—by income per year—pay to support the activities of the government and the polity. Should we want to compute the average tax burden, that would be simple enough, but not particularly enlightening since there are no average tax burdens in practice. We can calculate the average taxes according to or for each income level, however, and that will bring us a bit closer to reality. Table 6-13 [5] presents these various averages.

Table 6-13—Average Tax Burden per Family by Level of Income (1958).

Total Income † per Family	AVERAGE TAX BURDEN PER FAMILY *		
	Total	Federal	State and Local
$ 1,454	$ 412	$ 229	183
3,751	986	595	391
5,934	1,535	972	563
8,160	2,097	1,407	690
10,250	2,454	1,656	798
13,868	3,332	2,382	950
32,284	11,576	9,615	1,961

* Includes social insurance taxes.
† Total income corresponding to net national product. Income figures are averages for income classes shown in Table 6-12.

Table 6-13 indicates that the average tax burden—as a percentage of total income—varies but slightly from one income bracket to another. The lowest bracket pays somewhat less than a third of its income in taxes, while the top bracket listed pays slightly more than a third. And, as is quite apparent, the federal government gets the lion's share of taxation.

The above mentioned averages will become more meaningful if we go on to a consideration of the amounts of money that each of the income levels contributes both in total amounts to the Treasury Departments, and the proportions or percentages of the total tax sums. In absolute amounts, the higher income levels—$15,000 or more—pay a larger amount than any other level. That is, those persons earning more than $15,000 pay more money into the government, as an income group, than do any of the other income groups.[6] In 1958, for example, this income bracket, made up of 5 per cent of the total number of unattached individuals and families, paid a total of $28,940,000 in taxes, or 26.1 per cent of the tax bill.[7] Those who earned between $4,000 and $6,000 per annum paid the second largest contribution, or about 18.8 per cent; while the $6,000 to $8,000 category paid about 17.4 per cent of the total revenues. In third place came the $10,000 to $15,000 income group who provided 12.9 per cent. In the lowest position are those who also earn the least: 2.8 per cent of the taxes were paid by those earning under $2,000 per year. Table 6-14 summarizes these data.

Of course, these figures do not tell the whole story about taxation because they do not indicate the percentages of personal income that go into taxation. When we view the situation, not from the perspective of the polity, but from the individual income earner, we discover that while the $15,000 plus income earner again pays out most, (35.9 per cent) it is a good deal easier for him to do this than it is for the person who earns but under $2,000 to pay out out some 28.3 per cent of his income, which he did in 1958. Obviously, the marginal utility of the dollar is greater for the person with fewer of them. We might also note that the federal tax program is more progressive than that of the state and local governments. Property and sales taxes are the chief reasons for this difference.[8]

Some Propositions on the Distribution of Taxation

The time has now come to state the major conclusions that flow from our data. These conclusions—stated in the form of propositions—are based upon the year 1958. But variations in taxation are hardly so unstable that we cannot assume some usefulness for other years. The propositions are based, more specifically, on Table 6-14,[9] which is a recombining of some of the data from previous tables.

Table 6-14—The Distribution of the Total Tax Burden by Income Class (1958).

Family Personal Income Class	Number of Families and Unattached Individuals (Millions)	Per Cent Distribution	Total Taxes Paid * (Millions)	Per Cent of Total Tax Receipts	Per Cent of Family Income
Under $2,000	7.6	14	$ 3,132	2.8	28.3
$ 2.000-3,999	12.1	22	11,925	10.8	26.3
4,000-5,999	13.6	25	20,873	18.8	25.7
6,000-7,999	9.2	17	19,297	17.4	25.7
8,000-9,999	5.0	9	12,270	11.1	23.9
10,000-14,999	4.3	8	14,329	12.9	24.0
15,000 and over	2.5	5	28,940	26.1	35.9
Totals	54.3	100	$110,775	100.0	

* Includes social insurance.

PROPOSITION 1. *The distribution of the total tax bill in the United States is approximately proportional to the income classes up to the $15,000-a-year salary class.*

The range is from 28.3 per cent for those families making under $2,000, to 24.0 per cent for those making $10,000 to $14,999 per annum.

This range, of course, illustrates a certain amount of regressive taxation, largely as a result of state and local taxes and the social insurance system. Nevertheless, the range is not great. But as stated before, 28 per cent of the income of a low-income family is a much greater burden than is 24 per cent of a higher income.

PROPOSITION 2. *The middle level income groups ($4,000 to $9,999) constituting 27.8 million families or 51 per cent of the population, pay 47.3 per cent of the nation's taxes.*

The middle class—primarily lower and middle classes—make the largest contribution in absolute amounts to the financing of government. In this sense, the middle class is the financial backbone of the government. Perhaps it is for this reason that they are frequently conservative in fiscal and monetary matters.

PROPOSITION 3. *The second largest contributor to the national tax receipts are families making $10,000 or more per annum.*

This group, making up 6.8 million or a total of 13 per cent of the population, pays 39 per cent of the tax bill, but they do so with an income of over $42 billion. They, too, are likely to worry about taxes. Still, they are more able to pay than are the lower and middle classes for whom the marginal utility or worth of an extra dollar is considerably greater. Furthermore, it is generally agreed among economists that the higher one goes in income level, the greater the number and types of deductions that can be made from taxes. As a result, determining the incidence of taxation at the higher levels, especially in the $50,000 class and above, is very difficult, and many unique cases result from any effort to calculate their contributions to the nation's coffers.

PROPOSITION 4. *The lowest income levels (under $4,000) pay the smallest amount into the treasury.*

This group, making up 6.8 million or a total of 13 per cent of the population, pays a total of about $15 billion in taxes, that is, 13.6 per cent of the tax burden. But as stated in Proposition 1, the burden on the individual family is the second highest in the class system, with 28.3 per cent for those under $2,000 and 26.3 per cent of the salary for those between $2,000 and $3,999 going into taxation. Only those with incomes over $15,000 pay a larger percentage of family income (35.9 per cent).

These figures do not tell the whole story about the burdens of taxation. Nor do they further identify people who earn the various levels of income. Concerning the latter, we need not present detailed information, except to say that the lower income groups tend to be workers, rural, Negro, Catholic, or Southern. The higher income levels, that is, from $4,000 upward, tend to be drawn from other social groups including the urban, suburban, white-collar and managerial, white, and Protestant, and from persons from other sections of the country than the South and the northern New England states. While these classifications are useful, they must not be assumed to be exclusive. A Southern white manager, for example, may earn in the tens of thousands of dollars. Nevertheless, income distribution is highly unequal among these different general groups as are the tax burdens, and such information as we have presented shows some of the results.

COSTS OF NONGOVERNMENTAL ORGANIZATIONS IN POLITICS

Financing the authoritative expenditures of the government is, of course, the major cost exacted in the polity, but it is not the only one. Other costs are incurred by private or quasi-public positions and organizations, as, for example, those costs that sustain party activities to elect officials, and interest group lobbying. Clearly, these are necessary costs of the polity even if they are *voluntary* expenditures of private individuals and organizations. That such costs are incurred in attempting to realize private goals does not prevent them from being included in the action that constitutes the political system. Such efforts at realizing one's goals are also efforts at specifying the societal goals. An interest group or a political party spending money to attain their own goals is still an expenditure in political action whether the action pays off or not. Consequently, we must consider such costs, just as the action, itself, as an element in the polity.

Because many organizations and private citizens conceal their political actions and costs, the availability of data on these costs leaves something to be desired. Unusually intense efforts and large expenditures on the part of some are often viewed with suspicion if not with actual condemnation. Nevertheless, there has been a good deal of research on these costs. We will look, first, at the costs incurred by political parties, then, at those sustained by interest groups.

Parties must finance their own activities because the government does not, except to pay for the administration of the actual elections. Unlike the taxation discussed above, party expenditures are largely voluntary, although there may be cases of compulsory spending levied by bosses, machines, unions, or business groups. Whether compulsory or not, the amounts spent by parties and individual campaigners is, in absolute figures, large, although rather small when averaged out according to the population of the nation, or when compared with the amounts taken in by the government as taxes. One estimate, and unquestionably the most authoritative we have, claims that, during the Presidential election year of 1952, the total financial outlay for campaigning alone came to around $140 million.[10] In addition to this sum, one ought also to include the amounts of voluntary services and goods provided by many party workers and others. Estimating these goods and services is, however, all but impossible. If we average the $140 million spent in 1952 among the total population, it turns out that the per capita expenditure was about 90 cents, a rather insignificant amount. The investigators in the study of these costs concluded that of the total, about 14 per cent was spent at the national level, 48 per cent at the state level, and the remaining 38 per cent at the local level.[11]

Just as the question of distribution of costs was raised in the matter of taxation, so it must now be faced with political contributions to parties and campaigners. Here again data is meager and somewhat unreliable. But an estimate by the Survey Research Center has about 4 per cent of the people contributing in 1952 and approximately 10 per cent in 1956, or a total of three million in 1952 and eight million in 1956.[12] These figures probably underestimate the number of givers because they refer only to the general elections in November and not to the primaries and other elections that may have occurred during the remainder of the year. Nevertheless, the percentage of citizens who finance electoral activities of the parties is very small indeed when compared to all who must pay taxes.

Who are the people who pay these costs? One estimate—and few of them are reliable—relating contributions or costs to annual family income, may be found in Table 6-15.[13]

Table 6-15—Percentage of Contributors According to Annual Family Income.

Annual Family Income	1952	1956
Less than $3,000	2	2
$3,000-4,999	3	6
$5,000-7,499	7	12
$7,500-9,999	14	17
$10,000 and over	17	31

Table 6-15 does not tell the whole story about contributions in that it leaves out the relative size of the contributions from individual gift-givers. Much of what we know about this problem, however, tells us that parties rely to a heavy degree on a relatively small number of givers who offer large sums. In the 1952 Presidential election, the Republican party got 68 per cent of its funds in the form of gifts of $500 or more; 20 per cent were in the range of $100 to $499; and only 12 per cent were in amounts of $100 or less.[14] The Democratic party during the same year acquired 19 per cent of its sums in gifts of less than $100; some 18 per cent in the category of $100 to $499; and 63 per cent from the givers of $500 and more.[15] While these proportions vary with party, election years, and type of elections, they do suggest that a relatively few of the more wealthy citizens tend to pay most of the campaign costs of the parties.

Because campaign financing is voluntary, motives of giving take on considerable significance. But they are very dangerous to assume and even more dangerous to correlate with outcomes of the allocation process. Contributors who have been queried on their motives tend to claim, in so far as they know them, that they give because they wish to influence governmental policies; because they have personal identifications with party or candidate, have a sense of duty or responsibility, are looking for governmental or private privileges, or wish entree into office or decision-making centers.

Whatever the motive, and the first two mentioned predominate, the costs of campaigning are borne by a few people in the United States. Indeed, most citizens do not want to contribute at all for they see little benefit either for themselves or the nation from such contributions. For the average American, the costs of selecting public officials and policies do not seem to be the most legitimate kind of activity. Selfish motives are frequently attributed to those who do contribute, and cynicism is not unusual concerning the benefits that are presumed to flow from having made a major donation. A Gallup Poll, in 1956, reported that persons in half of our families would not be willing to contribute even the lowly sum of $5.00 to the party of their choice if asked; 15 per cent were undecided. This leaves about one-third of the families willing to pay at least $5.00 to a political party. In another Gallup Poll, in 1958, it was concluded that only 23 per cent would contribute. Such is the view of politics; we might have expected as much in light of the belief system discussed in Chapter 5.

While electoral activity and attempts to elect certain persons and parties to public office constitute one type of political action and costs, another consists of actions designed to influence public officials and policies between elections. A more common label for this enterprise is lobbying. The actors involved are interest groups. As in the case of party contributions, determining the amounts spent and sources of these expenditures is most difficult. All we can do is offer some of the more authoritative estimates, a few relevant facts, and many more inferences.

The number of interest groups operating politically in the United States is very large. Whatever the precise number at any given moment of time, they would seem to add up to the tens of thousands, although all are not active every waking moment. Each of these active interest groups spends money—often a great deal, in fact—to influence societal goals through political action. According to one governmental source, the total spending by groups registered under the Regulation of Lobbying Act, which relates only to the lobbying of Congress, was nearly $4 million for the year 1960. Yearly totals may be seen in Table 6-16.[16]

Table 6-16—Total Spending Reported by Groups under the Regulation of Lobbying Act for Each Full Year since the Law's Enactment.

Year	Spending	Year	Spending
1947	$5,191,856	1954	$4,286,158
1948	6,763,480	1955	4,365,843
1949	7,969,710	1956	3,957,120
1950	10,303,204	1957	3,818,177
1951	8,771,097	1958	4,132,719
1952	4,823,981	1959	4,101,287
1953	4,445,841	1960	3,854,374

The amounts reported in Table 6-16 cannot be regarded as too reliable because interest groups are given the option, under the Act, of deciding what is to be included as lobbying expenses. As no interest group likes to be known—given American attitudes—as a heavy spender in politics, we may deduce that the expenses reported are significantly underestimated.

But what is the distribution of lobbying costs? Who pays how much? Taking the year 1959, and classifying the various lobbies or interest groups according to their occupational interests, we find some interesting facts. In Table 6-17 [17] you will observe the number of groups reporting and the amounts reported. These figures are not entirely accurate because all the groups had not reported their full year's expenditures. Most, however, did, and generally, of those who did not, the figures or amounts include the first three quarters of the year.

Table 6-17 is self-explanatory. Nevertheless, it should also be said that these expenditures vary greatly from year to year for individual groups as well as in absolute totals for all groups; a major condition being the kind of issues that arise in Congress. While some years a group may be unaffected by very many significant pieces of legislation, the next year

Table 6-17—Lobbying Expenditures by Various Groups in Congress (1959).

Category	Number Reporting	Amount Reported
Business	149	$1,609,187.87
Employee and Labor	34	1,206,860.38
Citizen	48	501,849.38
Professional	16	340,022.94
Farm	20	312,615.18
Military and Veterans	8	130,751.81
Total	275	$4,101,287.56

crucial legislation affecting their interests may be at stake. Undoubtedly, there are many other factors involved including the perceptions of the interest group leaders themselves, but we know little about such matters. Until we do, we must be content with the kind of data set forth in Table 6-17. At any rate, the costs of nongovernmental organization in the political system are substantial. Were we to include data on the local and state levels, these figures would go much higher. Little is known, however, about interest groups at the state capitals and local seats of government. Indeed, only twenty-nine states require registration of lobbyists, and, of these states, many are very vague as to what constitutes a lobby or expenditure. The *Book of States* (1948–49) claims that on the basis of their sampling of expense statements among states where registration is required, they "do not disclose large expenditures." [18] One example from 1954–55 has lobbyists in Kentucky reporting expenses of $55,984; while in Massachusetts, some 291 lobbyists reported $283,121 for 1952.[19] In 1951, Nebraska reported expenses on the part of 69 lobbyists at $116,800.[20] These few examples give some idea of the great variations at the state level. It is best, then, given the unreliable data, not to make any total estimates for states. There is no sense in attempting one at the local level, for there is nothing to go by or report.

SOCIO-PSYCHOLOGICAL COSTS

The nature of socio-psychological costs, if they may be called that, is somewhat different from those just discussed. Earlier, we indicated that, while these socio-psychological costs are just as tangible as the economic, they are less susceptible to measurement—monetary or otherwise. Furthermore, these costs are not entirely intended, but often are a resultant of the structure of the polity and our political culture.

In dealing with the economic costs of democracy in America, we attempted to detail both the total costs for the system and their distribution among the membership. And, despite some problems, we were able to give a reasonably accurate account of the incidence of these burdens. The problem of measuring and locating the incidence of socio-psychological costs is, however, somewhat more demanding. We shall not be as success-ful in our empirical endeavors. Part of the reason for this stems from the fact that an equivalent of money in the polity has yet to be found. But an important part of the explanation also has to do with the infinitely greater difficulty in distinguishing between the *over-all* costs incurred by the system, and the *distribution* of various costs among the people. It is relatively easy, for example, to specify how much various individuals and groups pay in the way of taxes. As all citizens pay some, it is mostly a question of figuring how much. But in the case of socio-psychological costs, it is both a matter of determining what kinds of costs are incurred, and how much by given individuals and groups. For while some persons pay one cost, others pay different types. We might note, for example, that the middle class—because it provides so many public and party officials—pays more of the costs of time and effort than do the upper and lower classes. The lower class, on the other hand, pays greater costs in the sense that it has less representation and influence, and less a sense of efficacy. Identifying the incidence of different costs among members is not the most challenging task, however; more difficult is that of assessing these costs from the point of view of the system. Admittedly, this aspect of the job is likely to be a good deal more normative and qualitative. Be that as it may, we will face up to the demand.

Before we can go on to sustaining the above contentions, it will first be necessary to delineate types of socio-psychological costs. The following list will serve our purpose; no priorities should be attached to their position in the listing:

1. Political indifference.
2. Political inefficacy.
3. Political intolerance.
4. Political corruption.

Political Indifference

One of the most commonplace observations and laments among many political scientists has to do with the political apathy or indifference of the American people. Even while the definitions of participation on which this lament are based are somewhat narrow or restrictive, there is no question as to the extent of indifference as defined. Countless studies have proven that Americans do not participate heavily in voting, party work, and political communications; do not consume political information and events; and do not contribute to party activity. Far more time, energy, and resources are devoted to private life.

If we are of the opinion that widespread and fairly intense involvement or participation in democratic processes is a good thing—as surely our value system requires us to—then we must view the facts of limited participation as a cost to the system and perhaps to some individual citizens who do not participate. On the other hand, for various aspects of political life and for the individual citizen, limited participation can have desirable consequences. Some of these we have discussed in earlier chapters.[21] Nonetheless, *given* our value system, restricted participation is a bad thing, and a cost.

What then are the facts concerning political participation? Let us look, first, at the most visible and most researched area of behavior: voting. Although problems of definition and measures present themselves in determining the levels of voting, such problems are not insurmountable nor of prime importance to us. Rather, we will report voting for a select number of offices and types of elections, both national and local, and from primaries and general elections. The obvious place to begin is with the Presidential elections.

Voting in Presidential elections generally appears to be higher than for any other office or type of election, that is, more people vote, and a greater percentage, vote at this time than at any other. We can see the situation very easily in Figure 6-3,[22] which shows both the total numbers voting and the percentages for elections since 1896.

As Figure 6-3 indicates, about 60 per cent of the electorate has voted in Presidential elections for the past few decades. To be sure, this is lower than during the 1896–1908 period, but then, of course, the enfranchised population was smaller. Since 1908 the size of the electorate has been increasing considerably and continuously, while the percentage voting has remained fairly stable, ranging from about 50 to 61 per cent in 1920 and 1956.

Voting in state and local elections varies greatly, but its incidence is generally less than during Presidential elections. The variations are dependent upon such factors as the office, issues, candidates, timing of the election, and traditions of the constituencies. While over-all statistics on the level of state voting are not available, it is clear, on the basis of what is known, that fewer voters turn out for elections when they occur

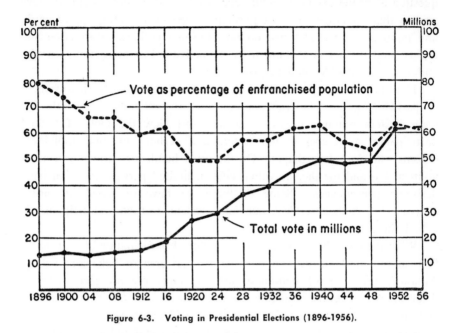

Figure 6-3.   Voting in Presidential Elections (1896-1956).

during the off-Presidential years. Moreover, there has been a pronounced effort by many states to isolate their politics and elections from national politics and elections.[23] In short, it is the drawing power of the Presidential contest that brings larger numbers of voters to the polls. Governors, Senators, Congressmen, and other lesser luminaries simply cannot match the glamour and excitement of the drive for the White House.

Local elections appear to pull still fewer voters. Indeed, it is not uncommon for local elections to attract less than a third of the qualified voters, sometimes amounting to but 10 per cent. Of state and local elections, the primaries—outside of the South—attract fewer voters than do the general elections. V. O. Key, Jr., who studied the results of 176 gubernatorial primaries in fifteen different states over the period of 1926–1952, concluded that "in about three-fourths of the primaries held . . . less than 35 per cent of the potential electorate voted on the nomination of gubernatorial candidates. On the other hand, in three-fourths of the general elections in the same states more than 50 per cent of the potential electorate went to the polls."[24] Furthermore, the primaries of the weaker party tend to draw still fewer voters than those of the majority party. Such, in brief, is the situation in state and local election participation.

Electoral participation is measured by counting the number of votes and comparing them to the potential electorate; this is rather easily done because the figures are legally collected and public. Less easily gathered information pertains to other forms of political activity such as contributing to parties, writing letters to government officials, and reading and discussing politics. Pollsters and social scientists have traditionally ignored these areas, but since World War II there has been a noticeable increase in gathering data on just such behavior. One such study—and well suited to our purposes—was done by Julian Woodward and Elmo Roper in 1950.[25] Using questionnaires on a national sample of 8,000 persons, they managed to learn much about types and extent of political participation in the United States. Questions were asked about political activities, and a scoring system or index was constructed so that each respondent not only told of the specific activities in which he engaged in, but a composite score could be devised that summarized all his actions and allowed comparisons with others. Table 6-18,[26] constructed from the "activity scores" of the various types of participation, shows the distribution of political activity in a scale ranging from the "very active" to the "very inactive." The greater the number of activities, the higher the score in the left column of the table.

Table 6-18—Distribution of Political Activity Scores.

Score of Respondent	Per Cent of Total Sample Who Make the Score	Cumulative Per Cent	
12	0.1	0.1	
11	0.3	0.4	
10	0.7	1.1	
			Very Active (10.3)
9	1.2	2.3	
8	1.6	3.9	
7	2.4	6.3	
6	4.0	10.3	
5	6.5	16.8	Active (16.8)
4	10.3	27.1	
3	15.6	42.7	Inactive (34.6)
2	19.0	61.7	
1	19.1	80.8	Very Inactive (38.3)
0	19.2	100.0	
	100.0		

The situation portrayed in Table 6-18 is so striking as not to require any belaboring of the obvious; as measured by Woodward and Roper's criteria, we are not a political people. But while political indifference is widespread, it is not equally distributed among the many subgroups of society. Certain groups are more active than others; certain groups are characterized by greater apathy or indifference. Who are these groups? For the answer, we again resort to Woodward and Roper and to a table they prepared correlating demographic characteristics and the amount of political activity. See Table 6-19.[27]

Table 6-19—Amount of Political Activity Exhibited by Various Subgroups in the Population.*

Subgroups	Very Active	Fairly Active	Fairly Inactive	Very Inactive
"A" economic level	36	33	23	8
Executives	34	29	28	9
Professional	31	32	25	12
Stockholders	28	30	30	12
College educated	24	28	30	18
"B" economic level	24	26	34	16
Republicans	15	21	39	25
Men	13	19	36	32
People over 50 years of age	12	17	34	37
"C" economic level	11	19	38	32
White people	11	17	36	36
Farmers	11	14	35	40
Independents in politics	10	21	37	32
Total adult population	10	21	37	32
High school education	9	17	40	34
Democrats	9	15	37	39
Nonstockholders	8	15	37	40
Women	8	14	33	45
People 21 to 34 years of age	8	14	32	46
Laboring people	6	14	37	43
Housewives	6	14	34	46
Grade school education	5	11	33	51
Negroes	5	10	25	60
"D" economic level	3	9	31	57

* In the total sample 4 per cent are "A" economic level, 10 per cent are "B," 52 per cent are "C," and 34 per cent are "D."

Clearly, the less-educated, the lower income, the younger, and the Negroes are among the politically indifferent. Clearly, it is these groups and others listed in Table 6-19 who pay the brunt of the costs of non-participation in the polity. They lose both the opportunity to participate in decision-making and the opportunity to become leaders themselves. They also lose the psychic values of participation, whatever they might be for the individual—accomplishment, comradeship, patriotism, or pleasure. To be sure, however, these same groups also share less of the responsibilities, and devote fewer energies and time to making the system function.

By way of explanation for at least some of the inactive members, and a cost in its own right, is the "sense of political efficacy." Let us see what happens in the United States with this cost.

Political Inefficacy

The reader is no doubt familiar with persons and expressions of futility where politics is the subject-matter. Such persons appear to feel that little they do will have any perceptible effect or influence on their polity and government. Much as we may regret the presence of such persons and feelings in our society, they are a much larger number than is generally supposed. Before looking into that matter, however, perhaps we ought to define the sense of political inefficacy a bit more precisely in order to facilitate measurement. The Survey Research Center of the University of Michigan made an attempt as a part of their national study of voting behavior in the 1952 Presidential election to get at the matter of inefficacy, and came up with some very interesting facts. Political efficacy was defined in terms of certain responses to a set of five questions in their questionnaire. The questions, requiring only an "agree" or "disagree" answer, were as follows:[28]

1. "I don't think public officials care much what people like me think."
2. "The way people vote is the main thing that decides how things are run in this country."
3. "Voting is the only way that people like me can have any say about how the government runs things."
4. "People like me don't have any say about what the government does."
5. "Sometimes politics and government seem so complicated that a person like me can't really understand what's going on."

If the respondent answered with an agreement to Item 2 and with a disagreement to Items 1, 3, 4, and 5, he was coded or described as "efficacious." Contrary answers, of course, were coded as representing a "low" sense of efficacy. The results of the analysis are quite interesting for they enable us to know which Americans score high, low, and medium in their sense of political efficacy, as well as to predict and understand their electoral participation in politics. Table 6-20,[29] taken from the study, indicates the demographic correlates of political efficacy.

If we assume that the test used by Campbell and his associates is a valid one, then a number of propositions can be derived from the findings

Table 6-20—Some Demographic Correlates of Sense of Political Efficacy.

	DEGREE OF POLITICAL EFFICACY					
Demographic Variables	High	Medium	Low	Not Ascer- tained	Total	Number of Cases
Sex						
Male	35	47	17	1	100	738
Female	20	55	23	2	100	876
Race						
White	28	53	18	1	100	1,453
Negro	14	36	48	2	100	157
Age						
21-34 yrs.	27	55	17	1	100	485
35-44 yrs.	31	52	17		100	381
45-54 yrs.	30	52	17	1	100	284
55 and over	22	48	28	2	100	442
Education						
Grade School	15	49	34	2	100	660
High School	30	56	13	1	100	712
College	50	44	6		100	238
Income						
Under $2,000	11	49	38	2	100	315
$2,000-2,999	19	54	25	2	100	255
$3,000-3,999	25	57	17	1	100	364
$4,000-4,999	33	51	16		100	233
$5,000 and over	43	46	10	1	100	415
Occupation of head						
Professional & Managerial	41	50	8	1	100	333
Other White Collar	39	46	14	1	100	155
Skilled & Semiskilled	25	57	17	1	100	462
Unskilled	15	47	37	1	100	174
Farm Operators	13	55	31	1	100	178
Region						
Northeast	30	53	15	2	100	390
Midwest	30	50	19	1	100	580
South	18	49	32	1	100	440
Far West	30	56	12	2	100	204
Type of Community						
Metropolitan	33	50	15	2	100	438
Cities & Towns	27	51	21	1	100	928
Open Country	16	55	28	1	100	248

concerning the incidence of inefficacy as a cost. For convenience they are listed as follows:

1. Women are inclined to feel somewhat less efficacious than men.
2. Negroes feel much less efficacious than whites.
3. The lower one's educational attainments, the greater the sense of inefficacy.
4. The lower one's income, the greater the sense of inefficacy.

5. The lower the status of one's work, the greater the sense of inefficacy.

6. Regionally, the South has the lowest sense of efficacy.

7. The sense of inefficacy decreases directly with population density.

For most citizens, voting and elections are hardly the major sources of contact with the governmental system. Each day countless citizens have dealings with officials of the government in one way or another. Thus, if we want to understand another aspect of the sense of inefficacy, or, contrariwise, the sense of efficacy, we might look at the citizen's evaluation of his dealings with public officials. Morris Janowitz and his colleagues did precisely this in a study of the public's perspectives of administration in the city of Detroit.[30] They attempted to discover how the public looked at governmental agencies during the year 1953–54. This unique study, fascinating with respect to a number of problems, was especially fascinating on the matter of efficacy. One of the questions asked of Detroit respondents was as follows:

> In general, if you had a problem to take up with a government bureau, would you do it yourself or do you think you would be better off if you got the help of some person or organization?[31]

The answers indicated that only 16 per cent would approach such an agency without aid. Moreover, the authors added that many of these people were quite truculent rather than self-confident. Some 75 per cent felt that they would need some kind of help. The vast majority would turn to private persons for advice and assistance. Attitudes toward access in government agencies are summarized in Table 6-21.[32]

Table 6-21—Attitudes Concerning Access to Government Agencies.

	Number	Per Cent
Would do it himself	123	16
Would try to do it himself; then get outside help	60	8
Would get help of an outsider	453	59
Depends	87	11
Not ascertained	41	5
Total	764	100

Table 6-21 seems to confirm the notion that many citizens do not feel particularly self-confident nor politically efficacious when dealing with governmental agencies. The authors also tell us that it was the lower classes that felt the least confident, and were likely to believe that political pull was a requirement to get anything done. According to the lower class, favoritism is a distinctly powerful advantage.

Political Intolerance

Americans like to think of themselves as being a tolerant people. Whether they are or not is dependent, of course, upon one's criteria of tolerance and this is largely a matter of personal preferences. However, a number of astute and sensitive commentators have noted, throughout American history, a considerable amount of intolerance in politics. Alexis Tocqueville in the late 1820's saw and wrote of the dangers of a "tyrannical" majority in the United States. Lord Bryce, in the latter part of the century, thought that Tocqueville's fears were less well-grounded, but agreed that majority opinion might tyrannize in the smaller localities. During our own time, Louis Hartz has said that the dangers are not in majority rule but in unanimity. No doubt, tolerance and intolerance do vary markedly over the years depending on various social, economic, and political conditions. Hartz, of course, was writing at a time when intolerance was particularly marked—the early 1950's—when the fear of communism was very widespread and intense. Yet one thing does seem clear in the history of tolerance: we have not been particularly sympathetic or tolerant of radical ideas or organizations. Where the left is concerned, we have an entire history of repressive legislation, vigilante activities, and a generally hostile set of attitudes. An illustration of this intolerance may be seen in Table 6-22,[33] a summary of the attitudes of a national sample of adult Americans in 1954, made by Samuel Stouffer, concerning their views on the liberties that should be accorded certain unpopular groups in our midst.

Table 6-22—Attitudes toward Civil Liberties (1954) (in Per Cent).

	COMMUNISTS			ATHEISTS			SOCIALISTS		
	Yes	No	No Answer	Yes	No	No Answer	Yes	No	No Answer
Should be allowed to speak	27	68	5	37	60	3	58	31	11
Book should be allowed in library	27	66	7	35	60	5	52	35	13
Should be allowed to teach	6	89	5	12	84	4	54	33	13

Professor Stouffer's study surely does not reflect much liberalism among Americans. However, there are important differences among various groups in the nation concerning their liberalism or belief in civil liberties. Thus, leaders are more tolerant than followers; urban people more tolerant than rural and small town citizens; the better educated more tolerant than the less educated; and the Northeast more tolerant than the South. Then, too, the figures do reflect a specific time in our history when intolerance was more widespread. Nevertheless, the Stouffer study strongly suggests, as do the historical inquiries, that many of us have an easily reached potential for intolerance in the political sphere, as well as in racial, religious, and ethnic spheres. Fortunately for the polity, many of these predispositions to intolerance are seldom mobilized and given concrete behavioral expression. Many of the people who would be regarded as intolerant according to Table 6-22 will not implement their attitudes. Thus, the number of actual demands that certain books be excluded from the library shelves is relatively miniscule. In addition, the more liberal leaders often act as a brake on the less tolerant.

Nevertheless, many forms of political intolerance are demonstrated daily in the United States. Economic sanctions and social ostracism are common weapons employed against the deviant. And these sanctions are effective for they probably prevent many persons from giving expression to their convictions for fear of the consequences. In many one-party areas of the nation, even being a member of the opposite party is something akin to sin, or at best a kind of oddity.

The point of all this assessment is to suggest that the polity suffers or pays a cost for intolerance of deviant political beliefs and attitudes. Seldom do citizens having divergent beliefs feel secure enough to express them publicly; many others are even afraid to entertain a different view as it would bother their political conscience. Thus, in structuring the range of alternatives so narrowly, we lose vitality as a nation. The cost of change, therefore, in terms of the numbers of citizens hurt in the process, is very high.

Political Corruption

Among the more common complaints about American government and politicians is that so much corruption is involved—a complaint that is not without some foundation in fact. For, to some extent, American politics has been characterized by unethical behavior. The question is how much and by how many? These questions, of course, presuppose definitions of the ethical.

We can define political corruption in simple terms as that behavior which either transgresses political norms, or takes advantage of their peculiar form of statement. We are not speaking of violation of such laws as traffic regulation or stealing from a private business; we are speaking rather of violation by those in positions of power, or in the performance of public duty, such as the acceptance of bribes by governmental officials, using government information for private profit, stuffing ballot boxes, and cheating the government of revenues or taxes. Corruption, then, includes the actions of both the official and citizen. We need not detail our discussion any further as that was done, in part, in Chapter 8 where we spoke of deviance. Here, we wish only to speak of one form of deviance: corruption as a cost to the political system and society.

Measuring the extent of corruption and its incidence is one of the more demanding tasks we have raised in the book. Due to its very nature as an essentially covert activity, it is difficult to detect and count. Moreover, as only a small portion of the behavior is ever detected and made public, the inferences about distribution and extent are, of necessity, extremely tenuous.

The costs of corruption are manifested in two ways: first, by financial costs to the citizenry, and secondly, the moral undermining of the rules by which the system is to work. Measuring the former is almost impossible and the latter, indeed, is impossible. This much can be said, however; corruption in both senses has been with us from the first days of the nation, waxing and waning ever since, with the periods of 1870–1900 and 1920–1930 being probably the worst at the national level. At the state and local levels, corruption has been a more or less permanent feature of American politics, particularly in the larger metropolitan areas like New York, Chicago, and Boston or with established rural machines, as in many states of the South. Among the branches of government, corruption has also flourished at various times in the legislative and administrative agencies. Seldom, however, has it thrived among the chief executives or courts at the national or state levels. At the local level, to be sure, corrupt practices have been conspicuous among licensing agencies, the police, and even among mayors. But no President has ever been personally tainted with evil-doing, although some of their Cabinet members and other assistants have been so implicated and found guilty. How much money corrupt government and politics has cost defies calculation, but the moral costs—while not susceptible to quantitative measure—are high, in the sense that public support for government and the leaders is reduced. There is some evidence of the cost on the consequences for support.

A national survey, based on a sample of 2,560 adult persons, questioned these individuals as to their political attitudes about the rating of politicians and governmental performances.[34] Among other results, it was found that 48 per cent of the respondents agreed to the proposition,

"It has been said that it is almost impossible for a man to stay honest if he goes into politics." When the 10 per cent who were undecided are eliminated from the poll, the result is 53 per cent agreeing with the generalization. To another question, regarding satisfaction with governmental performance, some 32 per cent said they were not satisfied with local politicians and their work.

Another investigation of citizen attitudes toward government has been referred to in earlier chapters: the so-called "Detroit Area" study conducted by Janowitz, Wright, and Delany.[35] Two of their tables are of interest to us: Table 6-23 [36] contains their results on the question, "How many of the higher government officials would you say are probably dishonest and corrupt—many of them, just a few, or none at all?"

Table 6-23—Attitudes Concerning Morality in Administration.

	Number	Per Cent
Many of them	96	13
Just a few of them	543	71
None of them	50	7
No opinion; not ascertained	75	9
Total	764	100

Table 6-23 actually suggests that respect for governmental leaders is higher, at least in the Detroit area, than has been commonly thought to be the case. Yet, in studies of this type, the crucial determinant of attitudes is the question asked. With different questions one is likely to get different answers. For example, the same study also made the following inquiry:

Some people think political pull plays an important part in whether the government will help a private citizen with some problems that he has; other people don't think so. In your opinion, does political pull play an important part in whether the government will help a private citizen? Table 6-24 summarizes the findings.[37]

Table 6-24—Attitudes on Political Pull.

	Number	Per Cent
Yes, it plays an important part	311	41
Yes, it plays some part	215	28
Depends	27	4
No	113	15
No opinion; not ascertained	98	13
Total	764	100

Table 6-24 indicates that 69 per cent of the respondents believed that pull does affect governmental decisions. The investigators also said that spontaneous remarks on the part of the interviewees would suggest that they take favoritism for granted, and that even those who denied pull did so with some hesitation. Furthermore, favoritism was tied up by the interviewees with *personal* connections, not with party identification or membership. According to some respondents, the practice is less one of outright dishonesty or corruption as it is of "expediting action." Whatever the connotations of pull, the fact remains that a very large number of citizens do appear to have doubts about the fairness of government actions.

Unfortunately, we have no good data on the attitudes of earlier generations of citizens. We do known, however, that the prestige of the government employment and employees has risen, at least since 1929.[38] Moreover, scholars and some politicians seem to be widely agreed that the amount of corruption which now exists in the United States is considerably less than it was, say, at the turn of the century, and during the 1920's. In large part this is due to the more effective implementation of civil service rules for government employment, and to broadened public welfare programs, which have reduced the relative dependence of citizens on patronage benefits. Nevertheless, the moral strength of the nation as reflected in politics is not as high as it could be; too many factors operate to reduce political morality. Among them are unreasonable dual standards, the impersonality of our system, a complex system of responsibility, a value system in which "success" and material rewards are rated very high, and a tradition of antigovernment.

In short, we do pay a price for a lower level of political morality even though it is difficult to measure. Evidences can be found in the attitudes toward government, which we just reviewed, in the unattractiveness of political careers, in a certain amount of cheating the government by citizen and official alike, and, of course, in reduced participation.

Part Seven

Political Change

THE end of our inquiry is now in sight. But important problems still remain to be discussed. That they come last must not be construed to mean that they are any less important. In fact, for many political scientists and others, the problems we are about to review are the *most* important. Without entering that debate, let us merely recognize that no analysis of American politics can be considered complete without accounting for history or change. Likewise, no analysis can be considered complete that does not account for the stability displayed in many areas of our political life. Our problem, then, is one of describing and explaining our political system when the *time dimension* is the focus of attention. For while we have by no means ignored processes and events acting through time in any chapter, we have tended to explain the functioning of the system at given moments, or as a product of the coterminus interaction of variables during relatively short spans of time. Time, in short, has not been the central focus of our investigation, but it has been a focus. Now it will become the major one. To this end, we will attempt to communicate some feeling and information for the ways in which the polity, its inputs and outputs, have responded during the past one hundred and seventy-five years to the passage of time and its events.

Chapter 17 on stability and change will show some of the trends with respect to each of the components of our analytical scheme. Little attention will be paid to the means of change, nor to the ways by which the system has been maintained. We looked at some of these ways in Part Four when discussing integration and system maintenance. At that time, socialization and political control were pointed out as the "master" processes, but accompanied by many others. It was also indicated that both these processes, as well as the allocation outcomes, were responsible, in part, for providing some of the impetus to change. By and large, however, these sets of processes work to maintain rather than to alter the polity. Thus, if we are to explain the stability of various elements in the polity, we need to use the analysis of Part Four. But should we wish to explain the changes that occur and have occurred, we must rely on explanations that go beyond the failures of socialization and control. In short, we need to use new variables.

In the next chapter we will describe our system as it has been affected through time. Some elements have changed enormously; others have changed but little; and some are difficult to assess. We will describe and try to account for both the stable and the unstable. Now, Chapter 17.

17

Changes in the American Polity

All things must come to pass, even in the United States of America. Lest we be accused of an apocalyptic vision, we mean only to suggest that our society and political system have changed, are changing, and will continue to change. Saying as much, however, is nothing more than a beginning; for our purposes, we must know political change in far greater detail, and be able to explain it. The first step in doing so is to realize the variety of forms change can take—*changes* rather than change is our subject. Secondly, we must provide a thread of consistency to the kinds of explanations possible. We need, in short, to find answers to questions such as the following:

1. What changes exist?
2. Through what processes?
3. The directions of the changes?
4. The rates of changes?
5. The scope or amplitude of the changes?
6. Reasons for the changes?

A THEORETICAL NOTE

Change is undoubtedly the least known area of the social sciences, whether in political behavior, social systems, or personalities.[1] Yet no student can remain satisfied without some knowledge of the many and vast changes that surround and include him. Fortunately, we need not describe nor explain all change, but only the major political aspects. In developing a theory, however, we need to begin somewhere, and, in this case, that somewhere will be in identifying the elements of the system, that is, the objects that are susceptible to changes. In this effort, our scheme of interpretation ought to be useful. Rather than proceed in an *ad hoc,* unsystematic way, we can simply follow the outline of the system of analysis employed throughout the book. The purposes, and it is hoped, the products, of doing this are several. Simplicity is the first, as just pointed out. Secondly, our conceptual scheme allows us to make distinctions in the levels of change, that is whether the changes are structural, or simply changes of particular roles, or of the personnel occupying the roles. Of course, change at any one of these levels may well affect the others, particularly if it is a fundamental structural one. Thirdly, the scheme enables distinctions concerning the various phases of change from the inputs, to the internal system processes, to outputs and feedback. Indeed, changes in the inputs are among the more common sources of change as they register environmental conditions having some autonomy. Distinguishing the nature of the input will also help to trace its consequences for appropriate functional responses on the part of the polity. Demands and expectations that emerge, rise, and fall, for example, will raise questions of the satisfactions produced by the responses of the polity. Of a different sort are the possible changes in the nature or rates of resource inputs, which may call into question the adaptive capacities of the polity to digest or handle new ratios of supply and demand, and to turn them effectively to goal implementation. Questions as to the sources of supply of resources are, of course, also appropriate: economic and technological change, population trends, and the like. These are to be contrasted with the sources of demand inputs more likely to be found in attitudinal and socio-psychological data, as people react to the threats and promise of their environment. Finally, support inputs, again of the socio-psychological dimension, but the reverse in "direction," may have their most obvious consequences in the release of more resources to the polity, such as the surge of patriotic support during wartime inspiring the contribution of much time and money to the service of the country. Each input, then, may have distinct consequences, either for the functioning of the system, for the other types of inputs, or for the very structure of the system, and then, ultimately, for its outputs. The nature of those outputs, of course, may cover a broad range of possibilities—symbolic laws or ceremonies, attention and information, services, monetary benefits, regulation, or outright extraction of costs. Moreover, knowing the nature of the provocation —its increase, decrease, addition, or removal—can help indicate the kind of outputs most likely to satisfy the need. Further investigation can show whether the polity has done so or not; whether the input persists, decreases, or generates further inputs. The interaction of the phases thus serves to guide inquiry.

In addition to locating and following through the processes of change through the framework offered here, it is of course important to find indicators of the dimensions of change—both objective (rates, scope or amplitude, and direction) and subjective (deliberate, unintended, and the like). This we will proceed to after presenting the framework once more in simplified diagrammatic terms, with some relevant types of change, or questions about change, added parenthetically. (See Figure 7-1.) In Figure

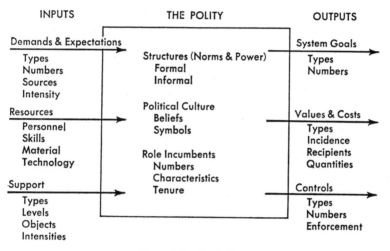

Figure 7-1. The Polity.

7-1, each of the illustrated major elements in the scheme will become the focal point of our interpretation of change. As we discuss each element, we will attempt to answer the questions as to what—if anything—has changed, through what processes, the rates of change, the scope, and the reasons. But before considering the empirical aspects of our problem, it may help to set things straight if we deal a bit more in the abstract about the nature of political change.

DIMENSIONS

Change in the polity takes place through a variety of ways or processes, some of which are highly rational and intended, as in the creation of a new administrative agency. Others, however, are quite nonrational, unintended, and uncontrolled in any meaningful sense.[2] What seems to happen most often is that we institute change in a deliberate sense, but fail to anticipate all the consequences such may have for the system. As a result, the latter are often not subject to rational direction, although we may sooner or later gain control, or increasing amounts of it, over selected phases. Thus, in the socialization process, many changes are brought about in the youth who are its subjects that may later have unintended consequences. In trying to create citizens who will support the system we may, in fact, be creating rebels. Or, we may attempt to institute laws, bureaucracies, and controls to make some men free, but dictate to many others in the process whom we did not intend to control or coerce. Intended and unintended changes effected by humans are not, however, the sole means or processes of action. There is also the character of deliberate change in terms of its peacefulness or violence, and of nondeliberate change (unintended consequences) in terms of its speed, scope, and depth.

Although most deliberate change probably assumes essentially peaceful and piecemeal forms, violence may at times be either a by-product or the vehicle of some of the changes that occur. In democracies, the hope is that violence will be minimized. But the fact remains that violence has played, and will probably continue to play, an important part as it did in the creation of the system, and in efforts to preserve either all or parts of the system from internal or external enemies. Thus, wars and military operations are examples of collective legalized violence by the polity. Our political changes, too, have often been accompanied by rebellions, strikes, demonstrations, and many more individualized forms of coercion. By and large, however, our polity has minimized brute force as an agent of change.

Violence may thus be one outcome or means of deliberate change involving the polity. Usually it is likely to be related most directly to the demand input—either as a means of expressing demands or of provoking resistance to demands. In the form of legalized violence, it represents a response of the polity to threats that appear crucial enough to be handled by force. As Clausewitz put it, "War is merely policy carried on by other means." But the question as to *why* a policy of force is used also brings into question the pattern of control involving decisions over the use of such force in the polity. One theory concerning this question is that crucial military influence over the "power elite" causes a "definition of the situation" resulting in militaristic policies. Other theories have claimed that armaments races, and ultimately armed aggression, are sponsored by munitions makers. But as discussed earlier, such theories before being accepted must be tested empirically.

To be sure, most change in the polity is the product of human agents, since the polity itself is a social entity. Yet not all change comes about by deliberate, intended means. There are two major kinds of nondeliberate change that pose special problems for the polity, one of which has been labeled by Robert Merton as the unanticipated consequences of social change,[3] referring to the effects of known changes in unknown ways— latent functions. Or, as John Dewey pointed out in his classic work, *The Public and Its Problems,* it is the *indirect* consequences of acts that call a (political) public into being. Yet, as Dewey went on to say, it takes more than the formation of a public to discern the sources of those consequences. Both these and other writers have pointed to the necessary role of the polity in managing the problems of indirect social change by having available the concentrated means of remedial action, whether for prevention, compensation, or control. A typical case of such indirect consequences at work is the problem of air or water pollution by industrial waste, which is likely to have its effects on users of water or air who have no direct access to the source of the ill. Thus, we see legislation for the control of air and water pollution becoming the object of political demand. Moreover, unanticipated consequences may stem from deliberate changes in the polity itself. Note the impact of national welfare programs on city political machines. Welfare benefits to the needy have been attributed as one of the causes of the decline in influence of the boss and his machine, no longer the sole or largest source of such benefits. Although it was never the intended purpose of welfare legislation to bring this about, the machines thereby lost a powerful means of control over loyalty, service, and votes.

The other major kind of unintended change is that stemming from developments, whether human or material, in the environment of the polity. Most significant for the American polity have been such demographic trends as the occupation and development of frontier lands, the increase in density of population, and the shift to cities, and now to the suburbs. Add to this the enormous strides in technology, particularly in production, transportation, and communication. Each of these developments, and others, has had unintended consequences for political activity and political structures, even before they became the subject of political decisions. The style of campaigns, for example, has been revolutionized by the use of radio, television, and airplane, as well as by the attempts of candidates to cover ever-greater proportions of an ever-larger populace. From the more distant socio-political environment, the polity may also be changed by the actions of other nations. In recent times, the policies and behavior of the Soviet Union have unquestionably been of tremendous significance in accounting for a number of political changes in the United

States. Our values, norms, and policies, all have been effected as a result of the Cold War.

The *direction* of political change will be used to mean such things as the values, norms, or goals toward which we are moving; the type of structure that has been developing in the system; and whether the inputs and outputs have been increasing, decreasing, or remaining constant through time. In some cases we can describe the direction in quantitative terms; in others, only through qualitative assessment. An instance of the former will be the assertion that political structures are becoming more highly differentiated; a measure of that claim will be in terms of the number of units of the system.

This, of course, raises the question of the *rates* of changes. Ideally, rates require mathematical expression. But since the social sciences leave much to be desired along those lines, we will have to be content with some rather simple numerical indices and many qualitative statements of the type that says "the change came quickly or very slowly." Nevertheless, we can measure a great many of the elements of change, and will do so.

The *scope* of change, another interesting facet of the entire problem of change, deals with the number of persons involved or effected, the number and kinds of units of the system, and the degree to which a change has occurred, that is, whether there has been addition or subtraction of elements, some alteration, or entire substitution. Thus, whereas the election of 1952 changed the personnel of high public office completely, it had little effect on foreign policy, some on domestic economic policy, and almost none on the more basic political values, norms, and the structure of the polity. Each of these assertions refers to the scope of change or potential change. Obviously, where little has altered, nothing can be said about the direction, type, or rates of change, for there is no problem. If there has been an alteration, however, the questions of direction, rates, scope, and processes become immediately relevant. And, of necessity, the question of explaining each of these facets is also raised. But, in a sense, it is also raised where there has been no change, for we should also like to know why change has not occurred, especially if we had intended one to follow certain actions.

Change, in terms of explanation, is a most challenging task. But while it has prompted many theories from the grandiose to the particular, from the metaphysical to the empirical, few have attempted to account for change in terms of a variety of possible dimensions. We recognize that at the very beginning. Yet, we need not despair, for some matters can be adequately accounted for with limited theories. Our preference will be for a theory that can be used empirically even when it cannot be fully or accurately checked, as under experimental conditions.

There is, finally, an aspect of change in the American polity involving a normative paradox. Certainly there are few, if any, peoples who have dedicated themselves so fully to a belief in progress and in deliberate change as have the Americans. Yet, from subscribing to such a blanket norm, the paradoxes abound. All Americans, for example, appear to take pride—at least they are subjected to constant publicity—over the technological advance affecting their modes of life. Yet, at the same time, there are costs involved too, and along with general pride have come particular discontents. Thus automation, a natural development in mass production, is seen as a direct threat to many. It is at such times that resistance to change, often a product of direct threat, or what is perceived as such, comes into being.

In short, while changes may result from internal events such as deliberate planning, social strains may also arise from conflicts in or within persons and groups that constitute the system. Reformism and resistance reflect demands for benefits or for mitigating the costs involved in change. Within the political system, expectations are created that stimulate members to demand more or different policies regarding the structure of the system. Indeed, many amendments to the Constitution have come about precisely because of political dissatisfactions with the existing situation. Frequently, these dissatisfactions are products of the allocation of income and other values or costs. Unless some people are disturbed by the present order, change cannot come about. In a society that generates high expectations, and therefore many frustrations for many people, deprivations and privileges are its major source.

In a sense, we may be said to have even built change into our polity by institutionalizing the possibility for it through free elections, free speech, association, and the other civil liberties. What is amazing about America is that, even with deliberate change highly approved of, with progress as a value, and with political opportunities for change, there has been so much institutional stability during these past two hundred and fifty years. To be sure, change has occurred in many areas, but fundamental substitutions or reversals in the major aspects of the polity have been kept to a minimum. Perhaps having escape values and opportunities to be heard tend to mitigate dissatisfaction with the system itself, and to divert attack onto the participants or segments within it. All of which leads us to the *elements* of political change in America. We begin the interpretation by looking at our political culture.

POLITICAL CULTURE: VALUES AND NORMS

If an index of political culture is the content of public statements about America's values, norms, and beliefs, it seems reasonable to conclude that they have not changed significantly during the history of the nation. Presidents are still giving voice to essentially the same themes that were expounded by the writers of the Declaration of Independence and the Constitution. Presidents are still quoting the better-known phrases and ideas of Washington, Jefferson, Lincoln, and Wilson. Public speakers on symbolic occasions still invoke past traditions and the continuity of our values.[4] Indeed, several very profound students of America's intellectual and cultural development have emphasized the absence of major change at this level. Louis Hartz, Daniel Boorstin, Henry Steele Commager, Ralph Barton Perry, and Robert McCloskey, all have claimed the American tradition to be essentially seamless and continuous.

Of course, the study of beliefs cannot be restricted to public pronouncements by high-ranking officials, or to the scholarly output of historians who may simply echo one another's conceptions. But it is remarkable that leaders should give voice to the same ideas and ideals, and use the same symbols for so long a time. Even if these beliefs are not their own, it is still remarkable that they should anticipate the public's need or desire to hear them over any other beliefs. Moreover, granted the possibility of the historian's unconscious perpetuation of stereotypes, it is not probable that their contentions have all been wrong.

Given all these qualifications, it is therefore necessary to look at other evidence concerning changes in the belief system. Historians have a tendency to consider only what the officials and writers say, rather than the expressions of the many. Unfortunately, as public opinion polls were not invented until quite recently, we have no reliable way of measuring changes in the value and normative attitude areas. About the best source of data on these matters, however, comes from the social scientists, not the historians. One social scientist who has seen fit to consider the problem is the late Clyde Kluckhohn, the anthropologist. Collecting as many sources as possible that might reflect light on the problem of changing values, he concluded that while there have been some changes in emphasis, there have been no sharp variations.[5] There is, for example, perhaps a greater emphasis on personal security than was the case in the nineteenth century; conversely, there has been a reduction of faith in "rugged individualism." In more recent periods, too, there has been more willingness to accept a strong government and greater regulation of behavior.

Some Changes of Political Norms

While our political *values* have changed relatively little during the past two hundred-odd years, such has not been the case respecting political *norms*. Changes in this area have been more numerous and frequent, and probably more marked in quality than have the value movements. We should not be surprised, however; the closer we get to daily behavioral patterns, the greater the variations to be expected.

A change in norms, or rules of conduct, is more crucial for the operation of the political system, or society generally, than are changes in the general ends giving such conduct worth or meaning. This is due to the chain of interaction or interrelationship of the conduct that the norms attempt to guide. For while a variety of norms can be logically consistent with the same general value, they may diverge considerably in terms of how the resultant behavior affects the structure of the system. Thus, it is appropriate to inquire whether our norms have changed more than the value system. In most of these changes of norms, we will contend that the changes appear to have been in the direction of greater consistency with the values. But this contention is not our major point. Rather, the major point is that many norms of American political behavior *have* changed.

As general areas in which these developments have come about, we shall discuss, first, the behavior of citizens, especially in the matter of participation and loyalty; secondly, the role of the partisan politician and the voter; and thirdly, the role of the government employee and public official. The discussion will proceed in that order.

In charting changes in citizen participation—electoral and other—one may start with the most obvious proposition that such participation has increased proportionately over the decades since the inception of the republic. This is attested to by conventional histories of the franchise, using as evidence voting totals compared to population figures, and the legal changes admitting successively more citizens to the polls.

The general norm, that it is a good thing to have widespread participation, has been at least an outcome, if not a cause, of mounting turnout percentages. Some have attributed this increase to the influence of egalitarian frontier conditions, others to the necessities of party competition for voter support, and still others to the fight of various status and minority groups for political influence through the weapon of the ballot.

More difficult to establish are the more qualitative factors of the changing *content* of norms of political participation. Unlike turnout figures, evidence for this cannot easily be summarized statistically. At best, content analysis of types of prescriptive statements in politics would serve this purpose—trends, for example, in the nature of campaign promises as the explicit criteria of how the victorious candidate "ought to behave." With regard to trends in the norms of citizen participation, content analyses of themes in textbooks concerning citizenship would be a good indicator. In the absence of well-substantiated trends, a few impressionistic hypotheses will have to serve as illustrations.

The role of the politician or partisan seeking office and acting in office, once elected, has shown some interesting changes. In an earlier year, partisanship was a far more raucous and emotive activity than it is today. The language of campaigning used by Lincoln and Douglas in their famous debates was rife with verbal symbols no longer considered as acceptable in modern society.[6] Nor would the types of accusations once made be acceptable today on radio, television, or any other media of expression. Law suits would be more frequent, and the voters would be appalled at the language of the nineteenth century. The following public advertisement from the year 1847 in the state of Oregon serves as an eloquent and amusing reminder.[7]

TO THE WORLD ! !

J. Quinn Thornton

Having resorted to low, cowardly and dishonorable means, for the purpose of injuring my character and standing, and having refused honorable satisfaction, which I have demanded, I avail myself of this opportunity of publishing to the world as a reclaimless liar, an infamous scoundrel, a black-hearted villain, an arrant coward, a worthless vagabond, and an imported miscreant, a disgrace to the profession and a dishonor to his country.

JAMES W. NESMITH

Oregon City, June 7, 1847.

Politics is today much less dominated by violence, mudslinging, accusation, and emotion. It is far more rationalized and bureaucratized at all phases of government, including electoral campaigns. To some critics it is also, for those reasons, less exciting and rewarding; the point is, politics is not as rough as it was a century ago.

One can probably link this fact to general theories of the increasing bureaucratization of society, particularly where accompanied by a technology that has made political contacts increasingly impersonal. In recent campaigns, it has become more apparent that campaign strategies change in view of the changing nature of the audience. Where a speech on the stump could be fitted to the particular fears, prejudices, and emotional style of a locality, the address over the mass media must minimize special appeals in favor of a common denominator, likely to be more respectable and more generalized. The greater impersonality of the contact thus tends toward increasing generalization of appeals, greater conformity to norms of respectability, as well as more likelihood of dealing with national and international problems. Thus, another generalization—that there is, as there ought to be, increasing interest in national and international problems and less to special or local interests—may also be explained by the newer modes of political communication. Content analysis of mass media could demonstrate this, particularly if accompanied by opinion studies on the levels of interest, attitude, and information concerning these problems.

Partisanship among the voters is probably also less approved of than in the nineteenth century, if the figures on the growing numbers of independents is a valid criteria.[8] Increasingly, the claim of being an independent appears to be a socially approved claim, whereas being a partisan, at least a strong one, is becoming less widely touted. Indeed, a recent President rested a good deal of his appeal on the claim that he was above the battle, and nonpartisan. Among the voters themselves, the practice of splitting tickets is highly sanctioned as demonstrated by the great number of this type of ballot. The responses of voters in a national sample survey to questions as to their actions regarding a vote for a candidate of their party of whom they disapproved, and whether they thought they ought to vote for Congressmen and Presidents of the same party, shed light on the quality of nonpartisanship.[9] In answer to the first question, only 22 per cent thought they would vote for a man of their party of whom they disapproved; while 53 per cent said they probably would vote for the opposition candidate; and, 23 per cent said they would not vote at all. In answer to the question of whether a voter should support the same party for both the Presidency and Congress, the response was somewhat more favorable toward parties, with 40 per cent saying they agreed, while 50 per cent disagreed, and said or believed that ticket-splitting was in order.[10] Party loyalty, as a political norm, is somewhat more tenuous in the America of today. Larger numbers of citizens appear to be less proud of their party affiliations or identifications than was the case in the nineteenth century. The popular public course of action is to declare oneself "independent."

Another area in which the norms of politics have changed rather sharply is that centering about the acceptability of corruption. In the late nineteenth century, corruption was a commonplace of public life. Today, it has either taken on more subtle forms, or been reduced.[11] If the forms are more subtle, we may interpret this to mean that present-day norms are more stringent or that the old forms are inappropriate to success in contemporary politics. In any case, a number of laws governing such conduct are now on the books, and they may, in a sense, be regarded as indicators of the "public conscience." The Hatch Act (1940), Federal Corrupt Practices Act (1925), Federal Regulation of Lobbying Act (1946), and conflict of interest laws, as well as Congressional investigations into such conflicts, are all indicators of a changing morality. Where money is concerned, the rules are becoming more elaborate as if money itself were the major clue to moral evasion. Admittedly, these laws and public opinion are hardly as effective as their sponsors and others might prefer. But they are evidence of changing moral expectations and norms.

In addition to the formal steps taken to regulate campaigning, a number of proposals are submitted each year in Congress to further amend or improve the moral status of politics. Indeed, hardly a year passes in which codes of ethics for administrators and others are not suggested, adopted, or discussed. Many groups, such as the Honest Ballot Association and the Fair Campaign Practices Committee, Inc., operate to improve standards. In other words, Americans are constantly subjected to moralistic preaching about politics.

The last area of changing political norms concerns public employees directly, and somewhat more indirectly, the politicians. In addition to the codes spoken of above, the criteria for employment have also changed sharply during the last one hundred years. Until the passage of the Civil Service Act in 1883, the bulk of government employees were chosen on the basis of political considerations. Today, about 84 per cent of the government employees are selected on the basis of civil service examination. (See Figure 7-2.[12]) It is universalistic rather than particularistic norms that dominate selection processes.

POLITICAL STRUCTURE

Our country has the oldest democratic political system in the world, and perhaps in history. This fact alone should suggest that in terms of basic legal structures there have been relatively few changes, and most of them gradual. Most other countries have, during the same stretch of time, gone through several political reorganizations and experienced varying types of rule ranging from monarchy to democracy to dictatorships. Even stable Great Britain has altered the role of the monarchy from one of great legal power and responsibility to one of little more than integrative significance.

However, there have been changes in our basic political structure, and we would be remiss not to see them. The Constitution has had some

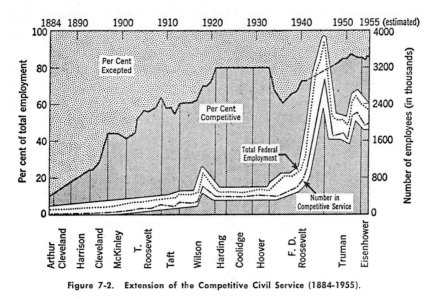

Figure 7-2. Extension of the Competitive Civil Service (1884-1955).

(Solid line is for the several years of World War II during which exact figures on the number in competitive service were not made available.)

twenty-two amendments, most of which have had something to do with the structure of the polity or government, and with the allocation of formal power. In several instances the changes have been slight, and of no fundamental importance. And in at least one case, the Eighteenth Amendment, the relationship to structural change has been totally absent. But the first ten amendments were fundamental changes because they defined the role of government toward the private sphere of the citizen. Likewise, the direct election of Senators, the Seventeenth Amendment, was of considerable significance in altering certain power relationships among the citizens and their states. While federalism and the separation of powers have not been changed in the sense of being abolished, crucial changes in both Constitutional and judicial interpretation have altered the meaning and political import of both principles. Major shifts in the powers of the various levels of the government and the responsibilities of each have both been sharply altered. The power of the national government has been limited by the first eleven amendments, the Thirteenth, and the Twenty-first. Conversely, the power of the national government has been increased through the adoption of the Thirteenth through Sixteenth Amendments, as well as the Eighteenth and Nineteenth. Powers of the state governments have been effected and limited by the Thirteenth through Fifteenth, and the Nineteenth Amendments. In addition, such amendments as the Twentieth and

Twenty-second also have affected the processes of politics, although they do not represent basic structural changes. However, they have had an impact on the distribution of power.

Twenty-three amendments over a period of almost 175 years averages one amendment every thirteen years! What is even more amazing is that but twenty-three amendments should have been adopted from more than 4,484 proposals laid before Congress from 1789 to 1962.[13] To be sure, formal procedural requirements have had much to do with this low acceptance rate, but it is still a reflection of the stability of the system. Of course, history does not unfold in a nice even series or curve. What has happened rather is that amendments have come in clusters ranging from two to ten within very short but erratic spans of time. Table 7-1,[14] a chronology of the amendments, shows both characteristics, all of which gives further rise to inquiry about the conditions that produce the demands and facilitate their acceptance. Only a complete history could answer these problems, however, and that we cannot provide.

Table 7-1—The Clustering of Constitutional Amendments.

1789	I-X	Period of
	XI-XII	initial adoption
1810		
1830		
1850		
1870	XIII-XV	Post-Civil War
		Abolitionist reforms
1890		
1910	XVI-XIX	Populist-Progressive
		reform era
1930	XX-XXI	New Deal
1950	XXII	Post-New Deal "reaction"
1960	XXIII	

Further change in the structure of the polity, again less than fundamental, can be found in its increasing size and complexity. Whether measured in terms of the geographical area encompassed, or in terms of the numbers of people included, the system has obviously increased in size. What is amazing is that a system could grow so much with so few fundamental changes. In addition to the manifest increase in size, the polity has also grown increasingly more differentiated or complex. The multiplication of governmental units, officials, bureaucracies, and laws has seen little let-up. Growth, if uneven, has been continuous. Many results or consequences have stemmed from this increased size and differentiation, such as longer time spans in the decision-making processes, less visibility in the same processes, greater inefficiencies, and the difficulty of imputing responsibility. But happier consequences, such as increased social welfare programs, have also been derived, and will be referred to later on.

The extent of differentiation and bureaucratization is so apparent as not to require elaboration. To many citizens, the increase has been enormous and frightening. They have noted that not only has the number of governmental bureaucracies increased, but that the rate of employment by the government is greater than the growth in the population, as Figure 7-3 [15] makes eminently clear.

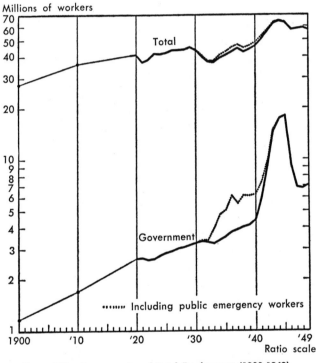

Figure 7-3. Government and Total Employment (1900-1949).

That the major outlines of the structure of the American polity have not been drastically altered should not blind us to the possibility of structural changes within the levels of the system itself. The structure of local units of government, for example, has been subject to a fairly wide range of change, particularly during the present century. Various types of government, including the "weak mayor-strong council," "strong mayor-weak council," "council manager," and "commission" types of government have been experimented with frequently. We have also experimented with the total number of such governments by devising new ones and recombining or integrating existing structures. The latter has been the practice, especially with school districts.[16] But while there have been structural changes at the local level, we must remember that these changes have not been drastic nor have they included the abandonment of democratic forms. Always we have experimented within the democratic forms or structures.

One of the most baffling phenomena to foreigners was our Civil War, for not even then did so terrible a struggle produce any major formal structural changes in the polity. The nation kept the same system after the war as before, except that the power position of the sections of the nation was altered for a considerable time, as was the legal status of a substantial minority, the Negro—a change in the legal norms of participation, discussed earlier. That a nation can maintain its system so long without drastic change surely demands a reason or explanation. Given the logical possibility for so many demands that the polity be changed, it is indeed remarkable that so little change has actually taken place. Why?

There would seem to be at least two major reasons: the first has to do with the success that the system has enjoyed in meeting its demands and problems, whether they have stemmed from within or without the society. Change, in most societies, is likely to come about (both consciously and unconsciously) because the systems do not meet significant demands made upon them. In the United States, the polity has been able to satisfy the functional needs of integration, goal attainment, and adaptation with considerable success. Likewise, the allocation of both values and costs has generally been regarded as satisfactory. To be sure, there have always been Americans who have not felt that they were receiving their just shares nor being treated as equals. But seldom has there been a large enough group so prevented from being heard and given recognition that it would choose to change the system. Even the Negroes who have been most mistreated, and for longer than anyone else, have not generally revolted nor advocated serious changes of a structural nature in the polity that has been so instrumental in holding them down. Perhaps one reason why they have been so reluctant to do so is that they have also been able to use that same polity for their own advancement. Witness the use of the freedoms guaranteed by it to employ the judicial process for their grievances. The system, in short, has sufficient access points, and hopes are always great enough to maintain belief in the ideal that within the system one can still gain his rightful position.

On the matter of citizens eventually getting what they want, Robert A. Dahl has developed some interesting evidence. He says that even in the case of the Supreme Court, which has prevented action for the realization of some group goals—eighty-one laws have been held unconstitutional— the aims of the legislation in almost one-third of these cases were subsequently realized by other means; in one-fifth of the cases, this action took place within four years.[17] In a few cases, four, some twenty years were required for action. In the remaining cases a considerable number involved temporary legislation, and a large number were essentially trivial. On the basis of the evidence, Dahl has concluded that, "There is, I believe, no case on record where a persistent law-making majority has not, sooner or later, achieved its purposes." [18]

If we have been blessed with a minimum of internal social strains and political conflict, we have also been spared the demands that many foreign countries have experienced from their neighbors, or the external environment. Our isolation during most of our history has, as pointed out in Chapter 2, enabled us to concentrate our national resources and energies on meeting internal problems and mastering the physical environment. It is interesting to note that during crises arising out of foreign affairs we generate not only cohesion, under some conditions, but a great deal of bickering, as well, in domestic politics. To be sure, if the crisis is a sharply felt one among the people, they will unite and forget differences; but if the threat is not felt as crucial, it frequently leads to argumentation, recrimination, dislike, distrust, and other discordant behavior.[19] Occasionally these threats have led to extreme forms of behavior in our foreign policies when we in turn have threatened and engaged in warfare. Seldom, however, have external threats led to major revisions of the structure of the polity. The only instances when such shifts or changes might have been made were during such times as the Civil War and the two World Wars. During these periods, the President, in fact, did act as a dictator, even though the formal structure of the polity and government were not significantly altered after the conclusion of hostilities. This is primarily due to the willingness of those directly concerned to revert once more to the traditional and legally based political structure, and the impossibility of their maintaining support otherwise, given powerful norms to the contrary.

SHIFTING POWER PATTERNS

There has been no major American theorist comparable to Marx in projecting a philosophy of history based on stages in the exercise of power. And this perhaps is appropriate, in view of the relatively short history of this nation. There are in fact many reasons why the Marxist formulation fails to explain the changing patterns of power in America—

the frontier as an escape value from the class struggle, the recourse of the politically strong farmer to an antibusiness vote, the extremely rapid bureaucratization of economic power and the consequent expansion of the new middle class, and especially the growth of the managerial and technologically skilled groups. Elite theories of power in America, therefore, quickly outgrew the Marxian mold, and seldom posited any inevitable trends toward the concentration of power, let alone any ultimate revolution.[20]

Looking over the history of the American polity, there are several distinct types of *explanations* of power, though few deal further with whether and why power changes. Let us note some major themes, and possible ways to interpret trends.

Social Classes and Political Power

Not until Jackson's Administrations did the political power of the upper class appear to be challenged. It was the age of Jackson that stood for the emergence of the artisan and wage earner into political considerations, his famous battle with the Bank depicted as being waged in the interests of the lower class.[21] However, the question must be raised as to evidence of the *means* by which this power of the lower classes was exercised. Did they now have sufficient access to the franchise and a "balance of power" through the vote? Did they dominate at least one of the parties and thus win power in their own right? Did the party and governmental leadership come from their ranks? What once had appeared as a clear-cut case of the lower classes finally achieving political goals, however briefly, now appears to require reservations as to the means and degree that this was so.[22] To establish with some certainty that there was a transition of power, there should be a further examination of voting patterns by classes (and turnout), social backgrounds of the party and elected officials, and further analysis of legislative and executive policies in terms of outcomes for the various socio-economic groups. For while the means have been made available in this republic for the transition of power from the control of one social group to another, whether such transitions do in reality take place, or how effectively, must also be determined. Certainly one can hardly question that the use of the franchise has made gains for the Negro, particularly in the North. But this has been accomplished primarily in terms of recognition by non-Negro party elites, to a much smaller extent in terms of actual government programs benefiting the Negro as a distinct social group (apart, say, from other low status minorities), and still less in terms of their having general access to actual positions of power. Later reform movements and the New Deal also require such analysis. In the case of the New Deal, the beginning of the national spending programs for welfare certainly did attest to benefits on the part of some of the lower and working classes. And voting studies have supported the thesis of a relative concentration of lower-class votes for Roosevelt, and of upper- and upper-middle-class votes for the Republican candidates.[23] At least in the New Deal years, the lower classes were one of the ascendant groups. But, as Samuel Lubell and more recent studies have demonstrated,[24] the distinctness of the pattern has already faded. To trace power patterns simply by the results of election day may be a laborious and, in the end, a thankless task!

Thus far, the question of changes in power patterns has been discussed in terms of a possible class struggle thesis, however refined and pacified by the democratic battle of the ballot. Much more compelling, however, are the theories of political change in terms of shifting group access to power. The word "group" is here used loosely, for one of the best formulations of this view has referred to alliances of sectional interests as the means of gaining national power in this country. Arthur Holcombe, in his classic work, saw economic interests as the basis of this sectional pattern of politics.[25] Shifts in party alignments, thus, might come about with changes in economic demands, with an external situation affecting the economy, and with technological shifts, in each case creating an advantage or disadvantage for the party of each section.

Locus of Power in the Government

Two factors must be considered concerning the locus of formal power in the government: first, the shifts in power among the three levels of government, and secondly, shifts in power among the branches of government at each level. The noteworthy changes have been easy to detect; at the level of government, the shifts have gradually but consistently favored the national government, with the most dramatic shifts and rate of change taking place during the twentieth century. Both the state and local levels, as stated above, have grown in power, absolutely, but not relatively compared to the national level. No documentation is really necessary to sustain the point.

Another equally evident shift in the locus of power has occurred with respect to the increasing powers and importance of the executive branch at each level. The judiciary and legislatures in particular have not been able to maintain their nineteenth century position of leadership. Overshadowing them are the President and the governors, who have grown immensely in power and status.[26] The developments at the local level are much more difficult to interpret, but it is probably safe to say that local "legislatures" have managed to hang on longer than the state legislature or Congress as a powerful branch. Of course, in many cities and counties and other local units, the board or council is also an executive or serves executive functions, and thus has formal direction of the bureaucracy.

One other shift must be included in our analysis: namely, the increase in the power of the administrative branch of the government. Today, the administrators make many decisions, which would have appalled citizens of an earlier generation, simply because Congress and state legislatures have granted them the power to use their superior resources to make such decisions.[27] Many critics of bureaucracy have been greatly worried by this power. Whether they should or not is based, of course, on personal preferences. The fact still remains, however, that their power has increased noticeably.

Changes in Leadership

Many facets of leadership could be analyzed in a full-length study of leaders, including their personalities, types of behavior, resources, and social backgrounds. We will make no such attempt to be exhaustive; rather, we will be content with some simple observations on the kinds of changes in leadership.

Politicians and many political scientists have long been convinced that insecurity of tenure is a major characteristic of elective public office.[28] Actually, we have had relatively few studies that could clear up the matter once and for all. Nevertheless, a few well-substantiated propositions can be made on the matter of security of tenure. In the first place, it would seem to be true that the United States has had a greater turnover in political leadership than have the traditional "gemeinschaft" societies where leadership is an ascriptive rather than achieved role. Even among the democracies of the world, however, the United States has had a greater turnover than many other countries, at least among the top leaders. This is ensured in part because we have had a tradition of but two terms for the President, and now, of course, a Constitutional amendment to prohibit third terms such as Franklin D. Roosevelt had. Accordingly, with the single exception of Roosevelt, none of our Presidents has served longer than eight years in office. In fact, of thirty-three Presidents, only fourteen have been elected to two terms. Moreover, once a President leaves office, it is rare for him to continue on as national leader, although he may remain in the public spotlight.

The situation at the governor's level is not greatly different, for many states—twenty-one—have restrictions on the number of terms that may be served. The restriction usually is one of not permitting the governor to succeed himself, as it is in fifteen states. In six states, two consecutive terms is the limitation.

The case of Congressmen and Senators is rather different from the President and Governors, primarily because there are no restrictions on terms of service. As a result, the turnover among legislators at the national level is very much lower than that of the chief executives. Congress experiences on the average only a 20 per cent turnover every other year, and about 80 per cent of the members have served two or more terms.[29] In the Eighty-sixth Congress, almost 62 per cent have served at least four terms, or the equivalent of the President's two terms. Many Congressmen currently serving have served under four Presidents, and a few have been in office since the time of President Wilson.

State legislators are not so fortunate, as demonstrated in several studies of tenure.[30] Over half of the state legislators are new at each session, with the lower house having a greater proportion of new members.[31] Of course, variations are to be found among the states, according to a number of variables including type of constituency, length of term, salaries, and, as just stated, the house. But whether trend or case studies have been made, they all seem to confirm the generalization that the turnover of state legislators is considerable.

Leadership stability among other state officials and local governments is simply unknown. Yet, impression seems to suggest that at these levels, too, insecurity or instability is predominant, although there are likely to be many variations depending on the office, state, and locality. What seems to be the case is that, while there is considerable turnover in individual offices, the turnover results from many politicians moving on to other offices in the polity. The few studies we have of career patterns indicate that most politicians have served in several offices during the course of a political career.[32]

What may we conclude on the basis of this extremely scanty data about the stability of American political leadership? The first conclusion is obvious: we need much more data on the question. That which now exists is limited and likely to be misleading because it is partial and unrepresentative. More substantive conclusions are still possible, however. We may conclude, for example, that we have considerable mobility *into,* *within,* and *out of* the political system so far as leaders are concerned. Each year, large numbers of new leaders come into state legislatures, and every even-numbered year about eighty-five new Congressmen appear on the scene. How many new local and state officials show up is still undetermined. But the fact that new faces do appear in public office must not be construed to mean that these men are without political experience. Many of the new Congressmen and Governors have served in other offices. And, it is possible and has happened that Presidents may be elected who have never served in previous offices, and who may not have ever dreamed of being a politician, let alone President. Top leadership is hardly as stable as it is in Great Britain, although more so than in France under the Third and Fourth Republics.[33] We may tentatively conclude then that leadership is not highly stable in terms of continuity in the United States; few of us live under the same set of individual officials—local, state, or national—for extended periods of time.

Party Control of Government

While instability may exist so far as individual leaders are concerned, the situation need not be the same when viewed from the perspective of party or group control. For while individual leaders may come and go, a single party may dominate for long periods of time, as is patently the case in the one-party areas of the nation. We will not look into every possible case or indicator, but will instead take a few samples from the political universe. Let us begin with the Presidency.

The first fact worthy of note is that, while we have a four-year term for the President, and restrict the number of terms to two, there have been but fifteen party changes out of the forty-three elections. Party control, apparently, has operated in cycles of something like twenty-five years. After Washington and John Adams, the Democratic-Republicans (forerunners of today's Democrats), held the Presidency for twenty-eight years; then, after the Whigs and Democrats alternately held control until 1861, a Republican tide came into being, lasting twenty-four years. Cleveland interrupted their control on two separate occasions, and Wilson did the same in two consecutive terms. Otherwise, the Republicans dominated from 1861 until 1932 when the Democrats came back for twenty years. Obviously party trends on the national level are of long duration; we have no erratic curve of party alterations or changes, but long periods of one-party control.

Although the situation in Congress is not so easily characterized, even there party control has not shifted with each election. Figure 7-4 [34] quickly indicates the nature of the changes in control. Control of the House, for example, has roughly paralleled that of the Presidency, as one might expect, given the propositions in Chapter 14 as to the relationship between Congressional victories and presidential wins. As shown in Figure 7-4, party control does not change in the House after each election. Rather, changes occur on the average of about every third Congress. Of course, an average does not really clarify the situation. The figure seems to show that control of the House is interrupted only once in a while when the opposition party wins a single election. Thus, the Republicans have controlled the House but twice since 1931. The same is true of the Senate; the Republican party came into the majority during the same years in both Houses (1946–47 and 1952–53). Much more apparent in Figure 7-4 is the fact that control of Congress proceeds in cycles of roughly the same duration, coinciding with the Presidency. In neither the Presidency nor the Congress, are erratic shifts commonplace.

If the party control at the national level is highly stable, the situation

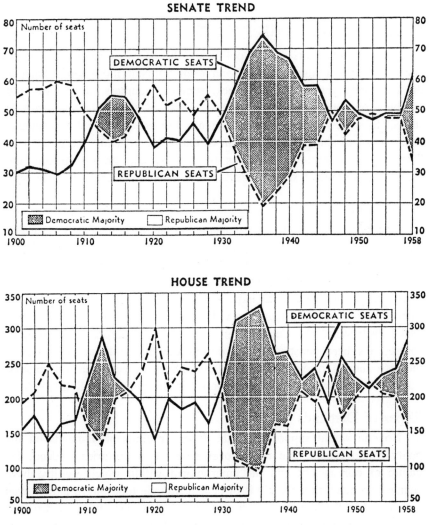

Figure 7-4. Shifting Political Patterns of Congress (1900-1958).

in many, but not all, states and localities is even more markedly stabilized. We need only recall our discussions of the number of one-party and modified one-party states to realize that shifts in control are almost impossible by definition. Ten one-party and twelve modified one-party states mean that shifting control is not a feature of these areas. Hardly a Southerner has known a state or local Republican office-holder; hardly a New Englander nor many Midwesterners have known a Democratic office-holder. In short, political changes in the United States are neither precipitous nor frequent.[35] More shifts seem to occur among personalities than between the parties.

VARIATIONS IN THE INPUTS

Because the inputs of the polity are the focus of so many factors, one might expect many changes and even frequent movements. Such is the case with respect to the types, sources, numbers, intensities, and numbers of people making demands. Each of these characteristics is subject to somewhat different movements, but not to radically distinctive changes nor to changes independent of one another. Thus, the number of demands made and the numbers of persons and groups making the demands have tended to vary together. Let us consider each characteristic.

Number of Demands

A number of facts strike the imagination almost immediately regarding the volume of demands made throughout the history of the nation. Every elementary text tells the reader that the functions of the government are more numerous today than ever before, and so they are. What we need, however, are more accurate indicators of the demands themselves. One such indicator and one that is readily used is the number of bills introduced each year into Congress and the state legislatures. The rise, of course, has been most dramatic during the twentieth century. Today, the introduction of more than 18,000 bills is expected each Congress. Table 7-2 [36] shows the steady increase for the period 1943 to 1960.

Types of Demands

No one would suppose that the types or kinds of demands on the polity would remain a constant over nearly two centuries. Indeed, the nature of our society and the environment within which we live have changed so much that the kinds of demands made today were hardly even anticipated in the late nineteenth century.[37] But while many new demands do exist, the American society has not changed so much that all the

Table 7-2—Measures Introduced into Congress (1943-1960)
(Excludes Simple and Concurrent Resolutions).

Item	78th Congress	79th Congress	80th Congress	81st Congress	82d Congress
Period of session	1943-44	1945-46	1947-48	1949-50	1951-52
Measures introduced	8,334	10,330	10,797	14,988	12,730
Bills	7,845	9,748	10,108	14,219	12,062
Joint resolutions	489	582	689	769	668

	83d Congress	84th Congress	85th Congress	86th Congress
Period of session	1953-54	1955-56	1957-58	1959-60
Measures introduced	14,952	17,687	19,112	18,261
Bills	14,181	16,782	18,205	17,230
Joint resolutions	771	905	907	1,031

contemporary demands are totally different. Many are simply new forms of the old. Accordingly, we still demand police and fire protection and national defense just as did the Founding Fathers and their contemporaries. Today, however, new technological developments such as nuclear energy have brought in their wake new demands for control of armaments and protection from radiation fallout.

Proceeding in an *ad hoc* fashion will tell us little about the changes in types of demands. A more direct indicator of these changes can be devised by recording the inauguration of new governmental services and agencies that symbolize changes in types of demands. The following listing of the advent of the various Departments of the federal government may be used as a beginning in such an enterprise:

Department of State, 1789
Treasury Department, 1789
Department of Justice, 1789
Department of the Navy, 1789
Department of War, 1789
Post Office Department, 1829
(previously a branch of the Treasury Department)
Department of the Interior, 1849

Department of Agriculture, 1862
Department of Commerce and Labor, 1903
Department of Labor, 1913
Department of Defense, 1947 (consolidation of the Departments of War and the Navy)
Department of Health, Education, and Welfare, 1953

As the above list suggests, the order in which various problems and demands confront the nation determines the order in which they are accorded recognition in political activity and in the governmental structure. Basic problems of defense, foreign relations, internal order, and justice were provided for from the very beginning. Later, as society changed, new problems of the development of the national resources and problems of specific groups such as the farmer, businessman, and the worker were confronted and dealt with. Most recently, problems such as health, education, and welfare, stemming from life in an urbanized and industrialized society, have been sufficiently pressing to demand and receive recognition. No doubt, the future will see some of the services of the Health, Education, and Welfare Department split off and new departments created.[38]

Another indicator of national problems and their political recognition can be gained by a glance at the dates of origin of the many regulatory or independent agencies that abound in Washington, D.C. Although the following list is an abbreviated one, it is sufficient to suggest the changing nature of demands made on the polity:

Civil Service Commission, 1883
Interstate Commerce Commission, 1887
Federal Reserve System, 1913
Federal Trade Commission, 1914
Farm Credit Administration, 1916
Tariff Commission, 1916
Federal Power Commission, 1930
Veterans' Administration, 1930
Tennessee Valley Authority, 1933
Federal Communications Commission, 1934

Securities and Exchange Commission, 1934
National Labor Relations Board, 1935
Civil Aeronautics Board, 1940
Atomic Energy Commission, 1946
Federal Mediation and Conciliation Service, 1947
Housing and Home Finance Agency, 1947
Selective Service System, 1948
Small Business Administration, 1953
U.S. Information Agency, 1953

Though there are changes in the types of demand as represented by the above listing, it should also be noted that the general problems of the regulation of the economy continue, but appear to require more specialized treatment; therefore, the added differentiation and proliferation of agencies. Problems of housing and atomic energy, for example, are now matters that confront general groups rather than isolated individuals, and demand the exercise of controls beyond the resources of more particularized or localized units than the national government. Likewise, problems of the interdependence of the economy now face a nation and not individuals. Regulation of these areas of interdependence has, in short, become a necessity.

An exhaustive study of the growth of governmental services and regulation would, of course, have to include the developments at the state and local levels as well. The trends would indicate conflicting tendencies, that is, an increase in the number of services performed, but also transfer of some from one level of government to another.

Growth in Volume of Resources

Just as demands have grown rapidly and continuously throughout the history of the nation, so too have the resources available to meet these demands. This seems to be the case regardless of the indicator used to measure the growth or changes. Fortunately, an imaginative and thorough study, from which we shall borrow, has been made on the matter of resources. According to Solomon Fabricant, if one measures the number of workers employed by the government, the purchases made, and capital assets owned by government, he will have some fairly accurate measures of changes in the volume of resources used by the government. After computing these various indices (Table 7-3),[39] Fabricant concluded that if one included national defense, the rise in resources from 1900 to 1949 was more than 500 per cent. "The rise in government input," said Fabricant, "was more than twice the rise in the nation's total input." [40]

Table 7-3—Growth in Volume of Resources Used by Government (1900-1949).

		Percentage Change over Period Shown	Annual Average Percentage Rate of Change
All functions			
Number of workers	(1900-49)	509	3.8
Purchases, in constant prices	(1903-49)	1,156	5.6
Excluding National Defense			
Number of workers	(1900-49)	357	3.1
Purchases, in constant prices	(1903-49)	453	3.8
Capital assets, in constant prices *	(1902-46)	326	3.4
Total			3.4†

* Includes land; excludes roads, streets, and related assets, and assets of defense corporations.
† This is an arithmetic mean, weights being payrolls, expenditures, and imputed net rent (at 4 per cent of book value) on capital assets at the opening of the century. An harmonic mean, with weights based on values in 1946 or 1949, also yields an estimate of 3.4 per cent.

Variations in Support

Unfortunately, we cannot be so precise about changes in the levels of support for the polity or of its various elements. Indicators have not been developed, partially because support has been assumed, but also because the construction of indicators and measurements of support is an extremely difficult task. We are not totally at a loss, however; we can make some qualitative assertions. In the first place, the general level of support for the system has long remained at a high level as testified to by the relative lack of revolts and demonstrations. Moreover, public opinion polls, too, have tended to give evidence of high levels of support for the major political institutions and practices. And as we have cited elsewhere, many foreign commentators have noted the patriotism of the nation. A somewhat more precise index of satisfaction or support may be had in the emigration figures, that is, the numbers of American citizens who leave the country and become citizens elsewhere. American governmental agencies do not, apparently, keep such figures, but it is possible to get them from other nations. When it is remembered that the largest percentage go to Canada and that that number is not high, the numbers of people emigrating do not seem large. In 1958, for example, some 10,846 people migrated across the border.[41] During an earlier period (1947–51), only 40,169 took up permanent residence in Canada. Thus, we may conclude that the numbers of Americans voluntarily migrating is a very small fraction indeed of the total population. Compare these figures with the reverse flow of immigrants: during 1947–51, some 147,391 Canadians took up permanent residence in the United States.[42] If it be assumed that emigration is a good index of support, we must conclude that satisfaction with the polity and society is at an unusually high level.

Another indicator of the resources used by the government is, of course, that most unwelcome one—taxes. The tax burden has increased, although hardly as much as many disgruntled citizens would like to believe. In absolute amounts, the tax load has, as Figure 7-5 [43] suggests, multiplied many-fold, in fact some twelve times from 1933 to 1953. But

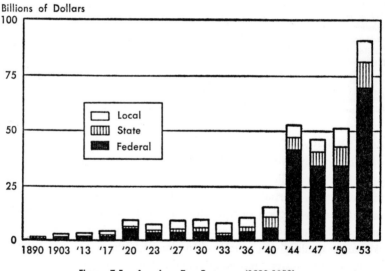

Figure 7-5. American Tax Revenues (1890-1953).

it must also be understood that such a figure can be misleading. For example, the figure does not show the actual burden on each taxpayer. In order to do this, one would have to take into account such factors as population and income increases. Should this be done, the actual increase in tax burdens would be somewhat under fourfold.[44] Nevertheless, taxes have increased.

GROWTH IN THE VOLUME OF OUTPUT

Here, we are interested in knowing what has happened to the polity's capacity to generate power, decisions, and services. We want to know what has happened to all the resources and demands, plus the support that has gone into the system in increasing amounts during the past several decades. A number of indices are available for measuring this output. In the first place, the power of the nation seems to have increased in that the United States is today the leader of the free world nations; this has come about since World War I, when the United States was still a lesser power. It is also evident that the polity has produced a greater number, variety, and quality of services for the citizenry. Once again, according to Solomon Fabricant, we may recall that government employment went up about sixfold during the 1900–1949 period. And if we assume that productivity per man remained the same, government output would also have gone up 500 per cent.[45] This, says Fabricant, is probably a conservative estimate since productivity has also increased with increased use of better technology. The output of the polity has also been increased in the sense that many more public enterprises are government-operated today than was the case in 1900. In fact, in 1949 there were 5.6 times as many such enterprises including water works, electric power, port facilities, incinerators, street railways, and the like.[46] Adequate data on the productivity of these enterprises is hard to come by, so our assessment of their role in the production of power and services is bound to be somewhat suspect. Nevertheless, even if average productivity per man or unit of production has decreased, the greater increases in government ownership and management of productive facilities are likely to augment the total output.

Just as the polity produces facilities and services for its members, so it also produces greater numbers of controls over them. The individual citizen of today is likely to be affected by the government to a far greater extent than ever before. The number of areas in his life controlled by the government is greater and the number of laws affecting him has increased. The number of administrators, police, and other officials who control him has also multiplied by large percentages. In short, the productivity of the polity in both services and controls has expanded enormously during the history of the nation. And it is likely to continue to do so.

Notes

CHAPTER 1

1. The literature on structural-functional analysis is extensive. For general background, see Marion J. Levy, *The Structure of Society* (Princeton, N.J.: Princeton University Press, 1952), chaps. i-v; Robert K. Merton, *Social Theory and Social Structure* (New York: The Free Press of Glencoe, 1957), chap. i.

2. L. J. Henderson, *Pareto's General Sociology* (Cambridge, Mass.: Harvard University Press, 1935), p. 11.

3. The most relevant works of Talcott Parsons, with respect to our problems, include the following: *The Social System* (New York: The Free Press of Glencoe, 1951); *Toward a General Theory of Action*, edited with Edward A. Shils (Cambridge, Mass.: Harvard University Press, 1952); *Working Papers on the Theory of Action*, with Robert F. Bales and Edward A. Shils (New York: The Free Press of Glencoe, 1953); *Economy and Society*, with Neil J. Smelser (New York: The Free Press of Glencoe, 1956); *Structure and Process in Modern Societies* (New York: The Free Press of Glencoe, 1960).

4. Parsons *et al., Working Papers,* pp. 181-190.

5. Parsons and Smelser, *op. cit.,* pp. 47-48.

6. Cf. David Easton, "An Approach to the Analysis of Political Systems," *World Politics,* IX (April, 1957), 383-400.

7. S. F. Nadel, *The Theory of Social Structure* (London: Cohen & West, Ltd., 1957), chap. i.

8. Gabriel Almond, "Comparative Political Systems," *Journal of Politics,* XVIII (August, 1956), 391-409.

9. Charles E. Merriam, "Political Power," in Harold D. Lasswell, C. E. Merriam, and T. V. Smith, *A Study of Power* (New York: The Free Press of Glencoe, 1950), p. 103.

10. *Ibid.*

11. Max Weber, *The Theory of Social and Economic Organization,* trans. and ed. by A. M. Henderson and Talcott Parsons (New York: The Free Press of Glencoe, 1947), pp. 324-363.

CHAPTER 2

1. Except for a few students of international relations, concern over the physical environment of political behavior is not very conspicuous. See, however, Harold and Margaret Sprout (eds.), "The Geography of Conflict," *Conflict Resolution,* IV (March, 1960).

2. David Potter, *People of Plenty* (Chicago: The University of Chicago Press, 1954), especially chaps. iii, v, and vii. In earlier times, both Tocqueville and Bryce made much of America's unique abundance.

3. For some curious reason, the dominant theory of American politics—group theory—has not emphasized the relationships of resources and political behavior.

4. See Louis Hartz, *The Liberal Tradition in America* (New York: Harcourt, Brace, and World, 1955); Edward A. Shils, *The Torment of Secrecy* (New York: The Free Press of Glencoe, 1956).

5. Oscar Handlin has, perhaps, during recent years, done the most to describe problems faced by immigrants. See *The Uprooted* (Boston: Little, Brown and Co., 1951); *Race and Nationality in American Life* (Boston: Little, Brown and Co., 1957); and, *The Newcomers* (Cambridge, Mass.: Harvard University Press, 1959).

6. V. O. Key, Jr., *Politics, Parties and Pressure Groups* (New York: Thomas Y. Crowell Co., 1958), p. 584.

7. The above figures are taken from the *Statistical Abstract of the United States, 1961* (Washington, D.C.: U.S. Department of Commerce, Bureau of the Census, 1961), p. 23.

8. Charles R. Adrian, *State and Local Governments* (New York: McGraw-Hill Book Co., Inc., 1960), pp. 16-17; 20-22.

9. *Statistical Abstract of the United States, 1961* (Washington, D.C.: U.S. Department of Commerce, Bureau of the Census, 1961), p. 5.

10. For an able short summary, see Gordon E. Baker, *Rural versus Urban Political Power* (New York: Doubleday & Co., Inc., 1954).

11. See Max Weber's monumental studies in the sociology of religion, the most relevant of which is *The Protestant Ethic and the Spirit of Capitalism,* trans. Talcott Parsons (New York: Charles Scribner's Sons, 1930).

12. An excellent summary and introduction of materials is Merle Fainsod, Lincoln Gordon, and Joseph C. Palamountain, Jr., *Government and the American Economy* (3rd ed.; New York: W. W. Norton & Co., 1959).

13. Daniel Bell has written one of the most sensitive and stimulating essays in recent years on the matter. See "Work and Its Discontents," in *The End of Ideology* (New York: The Free Press of Glencoe, 1960), chap. xii.

14. These figures come from Fainsod, *op. cit.,* chap. i.

15. Rockefeller Brothers Fund, Special Studies Project Report IV, *The Challenge to America: Its Economic and Social Aspects* (New York: Doubleday & Co., Inc., 1958), p. 322.

16. A number of excellent textbooks on social stratification may be consulted. Among the better are Bernard Barber, *Social Stratification* (Harcourt, Brace and World, 1957); Reinhard Bendix and Seymour M. Lipset, *Class, Status and Power* (New York: The Free Press of Glencoe, 1953); John F. Cuber and William F. Kenkel, *Social Stratification in the United States* (New York: Appleton-Century-Crofts, Inc., 1954); Joseph A. Kahl, *The American Class Structure* (New York: Holt, Rinehart & Winston, 1957); and Leonard Reissman, *Class in American Society* (New York: The Free Press of Glencoe, 1959).

17. One of the few comparative studies of social mobility is that of Seymour M. Lipset and Reinhard Bendix, *Social Mobility in Industrial Society* (Berkeley: University of California Press, 1959). The authors question the Horatio Alger myth, but do so only with the United States and European countries. Social mobility in pre- or non-industrial societies is not considered.

18. Talcott Parsons, "A Revised Analytical Approach to the Theory of Social Stratification," *Essays in Sociological Theory* (New York: The Free Press of Glencoe, 1954), pp. 415-417.

19. *Capitalism, Socialism, and Democracy* (New York: Harper & Brothers, 1947), p. 67.

20. See footnote 16, above, for references.

21. Arthur N. Holcombe, *The Middle Class in American Politics* (Cambridge, Mass.: Harvard University Press, 1940), pp. 265-66.

22. Arthur F. Bentley, *The Process*

of Government (Evanston, Ill.: The Principia Press of Illinois, Inc., 1949).

23. David Truman, *The Governmental Process* (New York: Alfred A. Knopf, 1951).

24. Nearly all of the voting studies confirm the proposition. However, the most complete theoretical treatment of class and voting behavior is to be found in Angus Campbell *et al.*, *The American Voter* (New York: John Wiley & Sons, Inc., 1960), chap. xiii.

25. Julian L. Woodward and Elmo Roper, "Political Activity of American Citizens," *American Political Science Review,* XLIV (Dec., 1950), 872–85; Robert E. Lane, *Political Life* (New York: The Free Press of Glencoe, 1959), chaps. xiv and xxi.

26. An excellent inventory of propositions on voting behavior may be found in Bernard Berelson *et al.*, *Voting* (Chicago: The University of Chicago Press, 1954), pp. 327-47.

27. See Talcott Parsons, "Age and Sex in the Social Structure of the United States," *American Sociological Review,* VII (Oct., 1942), 604–16. Also, reprinted in author's *Essays in Sociological Theory* (New York: The Free Press of Glencoe, 1954), pp. 89-103. A more complete analysis of the American family is in Talcott Parsons and Robert F. Bales, *Family: Socialization and Interaction Process* (New York: The Free Press of Glencoe, 1955), chap. i.

28. Exceptions among political scientists include Charles E. Merriam, *The Making of Citizens* Series (Chicago: The University of Chicago Press, 1931); and V. O. Key, Jr., *Politics, Parties, and Pressure Groups* (2nd ed.; New York: Thomas Y. Crowell Co., 1948), chap. xxi.

29. Seymour Martin Lipset, "Some Social Requisites of Democracy: Economic Development and Political Legitimacy," *American Political Science Review,* LIII (March, 1959), 69-105. Reprinted in the author's *Political Man* (New York: Doubleday & Co., Inc., 1960), pp. 45-96.

30. These figures are derived from the *Statistical Abstract of the United States, 1961* (Washington, D.C.: U.S. Department of Commerce, Bureau of the Census, 1961), p. 44.

31. Donald Matthews, *Social Backgrounds of Political Decision-Makers* (New York: Doubleday & Co., Inc., 1954), pp. 26-27.

32. For a most interesting study of the internal political life of a church, see Paul M. Harrison, *Authority and Power in the Free Church Tradition* (Princeton, N.J.: Princeton University Press, 1959). Tocqueville noted that the lower-class membership of the Catholic Church tended to make Catholics more "democratic and republican." See *Democracy in America,* I, chap. xvii.

33. A good description of church activities in politics is contained in Luke Eugene Ebersole, *Church Lobbying in the Nation's Capital* (New York: The Macmillan Co., 1951).

CHAPTER 3

1. Perhaps the best recent efforts at analyzing political systems in terms of role structures are Gabriel Almond, "Comparative Political Systems," *Journal of Politics,* XVIII (August, 1956), 391-409; and Lucian W. Pye, "The Non-Western Political Process," *Journal of Politics,* XX (August, 1958), 468-86.

2. *The Sociology of Georg Simmel,* trans. and ed. by Kurt H. Wolff (New York: The Free Press of Glencoe, 1950), pp. 3-25.

3. A. R. Radcliffe-Brown, "Preface" to M. Fortes and E. E. Evans-Pritchard, *African Political Systems* (London: Oxford University Press, 1955), p. xxi.

4. William Goodman, *The Two-Party System in the United States* (2nd ed.; Princeton, N.J.: D. Van Nostrand Co., Inc., 1960), p. 574.

5. *Elective Offices of State and Local Governments* (Washington, D.C.: U.S. Department of Commerce, Bureau of the Census, 1957).

6. *Statistical Abstract of the United*

States, 1961 (Washington, D.C.: U.S. Department of Commerce, Bureau of the Census, 1961), p. 394.

7. Almond, *op. cit.,* p. 398.

8. *Ibid.,* p. 404.

9. Pye, *op. cit.,* p. 480.

10. Robert K. Merton, "Manifest and Latent Functions," in *Social Theory and Social Structure* (New York: The Free Press of Glencoe, 1957), pp. 72-82.

11. Almond, *op. cit.,* p. 399, uses the term "manifest" to convey much the same idea as "visible" and "observable."

12. Edward Shils, *The Torment of Secrecy* (New York: The Free Press of Glencoe, 1956).

13. *Ibid.,* p. 39.

14. David Truman, *The Governmental Process* (New York: Alfred A. Knopf, 1951), p. 264.

15. Alfred de Grazia, *The American Way of Government* (New York: John Wiley & Sons, Inc., 1957), p. 783.

16. *Governments in the United States* (Washington, D.C.: U.S. Department of Commerce, Bureau of the Census, 1957), p. 29.

17. *Ibid.,* p. 29.

18. *Ibid.*

19. Taken from Alfred de Grazia, *The Elements of Political Science* (New York: Alfred A. Knopf, 1952), p. 466.

20. Pye, *op. cit.,* pp. 468-86.

CHAPTER 4

1. The research and scholarly debate on community power structures is increasing at a rapid rate. A fairly complete bibliography of research in this area is included in Morris Janowitz (ed.), *Community Political Systems* (New York: The Free Press of Glencoe, 1961), pp. 251-56. For critical reviews of the research, see such items as Robert A. Dahl, "A Critique of the Ruling Elite Model," *American Political Science Review,* LII (June, 1958), 463-69; Nelson W. Polsby, "Three Problems in the Analysis of Community Power," *American Sociological Review,* XXIV (Dec., 1959), 796-803; Raymond E. Wolfinger, "Reputation and Reality in the Study of 'Community Power,'" *American Sociological Review,* XXV (Oct., 1960), 636-44.

2. Something along these lines is done in a highly sophisticated manner by Robert A. Dahl, *A Preface to Democratic Theory* (Chicago: The University of Chicago Press, 1956).

3. See V. O. Key, Jr., *Southern Politics* (New York: Alfred A. Knopf, 1950), Part V, for a thorough and eloquent documentation on restrictions of voting in that section of the nation.

4. Gordon E. Baker, *Rural versus Urban Political Power* (New York: Doubleday & Co., Inc., 1955), pp. 12-15.

5. Speech by Senator Paul H. Douglas, *Congressional Record,* March 26 and 29, 1956, pp. 5543-45.

6. The classic work on personality and political behavior is Harold Lasswell, *Psychopathology and Politics* (Chicago: The University of Chicago Press, 1930).

7. The most complete summary of the data is found in Robert Lane, *Political Life* (New York: The Free Press of Glencoe, 1959).

8. Anthony Downs, *An Economic Theory of Democracy* (New York: Harper & Brothers, 1957), Part III.

9. Joseph A. Schumpeter, *Capitalism, Socialism, and Democracy* (2nd ed.; New York: Harper & Brothers, 1947), pp. 258-64; 291-92.

10. V. O. Key, Jr., *Politics, Parties, and Pressure Groups* (New York: Thomas Y. Crowell Co., 1958), pp. 626-28.

11. For a spirited critique of various schools of thought on "the public interest," see Glendon Schubert, *The Public Interest* (New York: The Free Press of Glencoe, 1960).

12. See Julian L. Woodward and Elmo Roper, "Political Activity of American Citizens," *American Political Science Review,* XLIV (Dec., 1950), 872-85. The findings of Woodward and Roper on the national scene are corroborated on the local levels by nearly all of the community studies dealing with political affairs.

13. There is some debate on the rule. For an able summary, see Austin Ranney and Wilmoore Kendall, *Democracy and the American Party System* (Harcourt, Brace & World, 1956), chap. i.

14. Dahl, *op. cit.,* pp. 124-32.

15. Arthur F. Bentley, *The Process of Government* (reissue; Evanston, Ill.: The Principia Press of Illinois, 1949).

16. David Truman, *The Governmental Process* (New York: Alfred A. Knopf, 1951).

17. It should also be pointed out that others have assisted in the development of group theory: E. Pendleton Herring, *Group Representation before Congress* (Baltimore: Johns Hopkins Press, 1929); E. E. Schattschneider, *Politics, Pressures and the Tariff* (Englewood Cliffs, N.J.: Prentice-Hall, Inc., 1935); Earl Latham, *The Group Basis of Politics: A Study in Basing-Point Legislation* (Ithaca, N.Y.: Cornell University Press, 1952).

18. Recent critiques of group theory include Peter H. Odegard, "The Group Basis of Politics: A New Name for an Old Myth," *Western Political Quarterly,* XI (Sept., 1958), 689-702; Stanley Rothman, "Systematic Political Theory: Observations on the Group Approach," *American Political Science Review,* LIV (March, 1960), 15-33; and the symposium "Bentley Revisited" including papers by R. E. Dowling, "Pressure Group Theory: Its Methodological Range"; Myron Q. Hale, "The Cosmology of Arthur F. Bentley"; and Robert T. Golembiewski, "The Group Basis of Politics," all appearing in *American Political Science Review,* LIV (Dec., 1960), 944-71.

19. An exception is E. E. Schattschneider, *op. cit.*

20. Merle Fainsod, "Some Reflections on the Nature of the Regulatory Process," in C. J. Friedrich and Edward S. Mason (eds.), *Public Policy* (Cambridge, Mass.: Harvard University Press, 1940), pp. 297-323.

21. Clear recognition of the power of governmental officials is found in various places in the book. See Truman, *op. cit.,* pp. 332-49; 446-56; and 484-85.

22. See Harold H. Sprout, "Pressure Groups and Foreign Policies," *Annals of the American Academy of Political and Social Science,* CLXXIX (May, 1935), 114-23; Margaret Hardy, *The Influence of Organized Labor on the Foreign Policy of the United States* (Liège: Vaillant, 1936); John W. Masland, "Pressure Groups and American Foreign Policy Preceding Pearl Harbor," *Public Opinion Quarterly,* VI (Spring, 1942), 115-22; Fred W. Riggs, *Pressures on Congress: A Study of the Repeal of Chinese Exclusion* (New York: King's Crown Press, 1950); Roscoe Baker, *The American Legion and American Foreign Policy* (New York: Bookman, 1954); Bernard C. Cohen, *The Political Process and Foreign Policy: The Making of the Japanese Peace Settlement* (Princeton, N.J.: Princeton University Press, 1957); and, Bernard C. Cohen, *The Influence of Non-Governmental Groups on Foreign Policy-Making,* "Studies in Citizen Participation in International Relations," II (Boston: World Peace Foundation, 1959).

23. With respect to military policymaking and interest group activity, see Samuel P. Huntington, *The Common Defense* (New York: Columbia University Press, 1961); and Morris Janowitz, *The Professional Soldier* (New York: The Free Press of Glencoe, 1960), Part VII.

24. Truman, *op. cit.,* pp. 264-70; 506-508.

25. The theory of bargaining is not highly developed; it remains mostly at the implicit level. As the Table of Contents suggests, the book deals primarily with "The Tactics of Influence" among interest groups.

26. Hale, *op. cit.,* p. 960.

27. C. Wright Mills, *The Power Elite* (New York: Oxford University Press, 1956).

28. The other major figure is Floyd Hunter, *Community Power Structure* (Chapel Hill: University of North Carolina Press, 1953); *Top Leadership, U.S.A.* (Chapel Hill: University of North Carolina Press, 1959). Earlier,

more generalized statements are, of course, to be found in Pareto, Mosca, Michels, and Burnham.

29. Daniel Bell, "Is There a Ruling Class in America? The Power Elite Reconsidered," *American Journal of Sociology,* LXIV (Nov., 1958), 238-58. Reprinted in the author's *The End of Ideology* (New York: The Free Press of Glencoe, 1960), pp. 43-67. Further citations are to the latter volume.

30. *Ibid.,* p. 47.

31. *Loc. cit.*

32. Talcott Parsons, "The Distribution of Power in American Society," *World Politics,* X (Oct., 1957), 123-43. Reprinted in the author's *Structure and Process in Modern Societies* (New York: The Free Press of Glencoe, 1960), pp. 199-225.

33. Bell, *op. cit.,* pp. 49-50; 64-67.

34. Mills, *op. cit.,* p. 12.

35. Cited by Bell, *op. cit.,* p. 49.

36. Mills would probably have contended that policy advisers structure the issues for the elite. But in doing so, he would have had to admit more persons into the elite.

37. Perhaps, Mills might have argued that socialization and selective recruitment provide the unity of perspectives. See pp. 63-68; 106-107; 128-29; 180-81; 193; 248; 295.

38. We may now add Edward Banfield, *Political Influence* (New York: The Free Press of Glencoe, 1961), and Robert A. Dahl, *Who Governs?* (New Haven, Conn.: Yale University Press, 1961).

39. Bernard Barber, *Social Stratification* (New York: Harcourt, Brace & World, 1957), p. 235.

40. Bell, *op. cit.,* pp. 50-52; 58.

41. See Janowitz, *op. cit.,* Part VI. Autobiographies of Generals Gavin, Taylor, and Ridgway also provide interesting accounts of schisms within the military establishment.

42. Floyd Hunter, *Community Power Structure, op. cit.*

43. Robert O. Schulze, "The Bifurcation of Power in a Satellite City," in Morris Janowitz, *Community Political*

Systems (New York: The Free Press of Glencoe, 1961), pp. 19-80.

44. Harry Scoble, "Leadership Hierarchies and Political Issues in a New England Town," *ibid.,* pp. 117-45.

45. William Form and Delbert Miller, *Industry, Labor, and Community* (New York: Harper & Brothers, 1960), p. 444.

46. Mills, *op. cit.,* chap. xii.

CHAPTER 5

1. See Daniel J. Boorstin, *The Genius of American Politics* (Chicago: The University of Chicago Press, 1953), Introduction; and Louis Hartz, *The Liberal Tradition in America* (New York: Harcourt, Brace & World, 1955).

2. Even a partial listing of writers on America would have to include the names of Brogan, Bryce, Commager, Hartz, Hofstadter, Laski, Lerner, Myrdal, Parrington, Riesman, and Tocqueville.

3. The increasing use of public opinion polls will one day make these problems of the distribution of beliefs and attitudes much easier to handle. For some of the possibilities, see Hadley Cantril and Mildred Strunk (eds.), *Public Opinion 1935–1946* (Princeton, N.J.: Princeton University Press, 1951).

4. See the brilliant new book of Lee Benson, *The Concept of Jacksonian Democracy* (Princeton, N.J.: Princeton University Press, 1961), pp. 272-77; Robin M. Williams, Jr., *American Society* (New York: Alfred A. Knopf, 1960), especially chap. xi and pp. 544-61; and Hartz, *op. cit.,* p. 11.

5. For some novel and interesting observations on Locke and liberalism, generally, see Sheldon S. Wolin, *Politics and Vision* (Boston: Little, Brown and Co., 1960), chap. ix.

6. Hartz, *op. cit.*

7. William C. Mitchell, "The Ambivalent Social Status of the American Politician," *Western Political Quarterly,* XII (Sept., 1959), 683-98.

8. Robert Lynd, "Power in American

Society as Resource and Problem," in Arthur Kornhauser (ed.), *Problems of Power in American Society* (Detroit: Wayne State University Press, 1957), p. 9.

9. David Riesman, *The Lonely Crowd* (New Haven, Conn.: Yale University Press, 1950), pp. 199-209.

10. Alexis de Tocqueville, *Democracy in America* (New York: Vintage Books, 1954), II, 3-8.

11. On the extent of charisma during one election, see James C. Davies, "Charisma in the 1952 Campaign," *American Political Science Review*, XLVIII (Dec., 1954), 1083-1102. Reprinted in Heinz Eulau *et al.* (eds.), *Political Behavior* (New York: The Free Press of Glencoe, 1956), pp. 193-204.

12. D. W. Brogan, *Citizenship Today: England, France, the United States* (Chapel Hill: University of North Carolina Press, 1960).

13. Edward Shils, *The Torment of Secrecy* (New York: The Free Press of Glencoe, 1956), chap. ii.

14. See James M. Burns, *The Lion and the Fox* (New York: Harcourt, Brace & World, 1956).

15. Gabriel A. Almond, "Comparative Political Systems," *Journal of Politics*, XVIII (August, 1956), 398-99.

16. Riesman, *op. cit.*, pp. 212-15.

17. James A. Farley, *Behind the Ballots* (New York: Harcourt, Brace & World, 1938), p. 113.

18. Gabriel A. Almond, *The American People and Foreign Policy* (New York: Harcourt, Brace & World, 1950), p. 52; Geoffrey Gorer, *The American People: A Study in National Character* (New York: W. W. Norton & Co., Inc., 1948), pp. 50-69; George Kennan, *American Diplomacy 1900–1950* (New York: Mentor Books, 1954), pp. 93-101; Ralph Barton Perry, *Puritanism and Democracy* (New York: The Vanguard Press, 1944).

19. On vigilante movements, see Wayne Gard, *Frontier Justice* (Norman: University of Oklahoma Press, 1949); Nathaniel P. Langford, *Vigilante Days and Ways* (Chicago: A. C. McClurg & Co., 1927); William J. McConnell, *Frontier Law: A Story of Vigilante Days* (Chicago: World Book Co., 1924).

20. Almond, *op cit.*, pp. 69-86.

21. Maurice Klain, " 'Politics'—Still a Dirty Word," *Antioch Review*, XVI (Winter, 1955-56), 457-66.

22. In this respect, the uniqueness of America is striking when compared with underdeveloped countries. See Edward Banfield, *The Moral Basis of a Backward Society* (New York: The Free Press of Glencoe, 1958).

23. Frederick Jackson Turner, *The Frontier in American History* (New York: Holt, Rinehart & Winston, 1948). For an evaluation, see George R. Taylor (ed.), *The Turner Thesis* ("Problems in American Civilization" [New York: D. C. Heath & Co., 1956]); and Lee Benson, *Turner and Beard: American Historical Writing Reconsidered* (New York: The Free Press of Glencoe, 1960), Part II.

24. The wealth of research on underdeveloped areas is increasing at a very rapid rate. Given our concern, the most valuable of these studies include Gabriel Almond and James Coleman (eds.), *The Politics of Developing Areas* (Princeton, N.J.: Princeton University Press, 1961); Rupert Emerson, *From Empire to Nation* (Cambridge, Mass.: Harvard University Press, 1960); Daniel Lerner, *The Passing of Traditional Society* (New York: The Free Press of Glencoe, 1958); and Max Millikan and D. L. M. Blackner (eds.), *The Emerging Nations* (Boston: Little, Brown and Co., 1961).

CHAPTER 6

1. The following titles are hardly exhaustive but they are among the better volumes: Thurmond W. Arnold, *The Symbols of Government* (New Haven, Conn.: Yale University Press, 1935); Sebastian de Grazia, *The Political Community* (Chicago: The University of Chicago Press, 1948); Harold D. Lasswell, *Politics: Who Gets What, When,*

How (New York: McGraw-Hill Book Co., 1936); Harold D. Lasswell and Abraham Kaplan, *Power and Society* (New Haven, Conn.: Yale University Press, 1950); and Charles E. Merriam, *The Making of Citizens* (Chicago: The University of Chicago Press, 1931); *Political Power* (New York: McGraw-Hill Book Co., 1934); *Systematic Politics* (Chicago: The University of Chicago Press, 1945).

2. Leslie A. White, *The Science of Culture* (New York: Farrar, Straus & Co., 1949), p. 25.

3. See Talcott Parsons, " 'Voting' and the Equilibrium of the American Political System," in Eugene Burdick and Arthur J. Brodbeck (eds.), *American Voting Behavior* (New York: The Free Press of Glencoe, 1959), pp. 80-120.

4. Interestingly, the opposition to the remodeling of the Capitol in Washington, D.C., was overcome only recently (1959) after many years of intermittent struggle. See Ada Louise Huxtable's "Buildings That Are Symbols, Too," *New York Times Magazine,* April 5, 1959, p. 18; Alvin Shuster, "Lest Washington Be 'An Unplanned Cemetery,' " *New York Times Magazine,* Sept. 11, 1960, p. 46; and John K. Galbraith, "For Public *and* Potent Building," *New York Times Magazine,* Oct. 9, 1960, p. 34.

5. Charles E. Merriam, *Political Power,* p. 107.

6. *Ibid.,* p. 103.

7. The point has been made by T. V. Smith, *The Legislative Way of Life* (Chicago: The University of Chicago Press, 1940), p. 55; and, by Alfred de Grazia, *Public and Republic* (New York: Alfred A. Knopf, 1951), p. 170. Smith does suggest some of the meanings elections have for politicians. Among them are "an education in tolerance and generosity. . . ." Smith, *op. cit.,* p. 55.

8. E. Pendleton Herring, *The Politics of Democracy* (New York: W. W. Norton & Co., Inc., 1940), p. 229.

9. I am indebted to Eliot D. Chapple

and Carleton S. Coon, *Principles of Anthropology* (New York: Holt, Rinehart & Winston, 1942), for first calling my attention to such rites. See, chap. xx.

10. Arnold van Gennep, *The Rites of Passage,* trans. Monika B. Vizedom and Gabrielle L. Caffee (Chicago: The University of Chicago Press, 1960).

11. The ease with which this transformation takes place depends upon a number of other variables, including office, status of the politician, and his margin of victory.

12. See John McDiarmid, "Presidential Inaugural Addresses—A Study in Verbal Symbols," *Public Opinion Quarterly,* I (July, 1937), 79-82.

13. Jerry Voorhis, *Confessions of a Congressman* (New York: Doubleday & Co., Inc., 1947), p. 26.

14. *Ibid.,* p. 346.

15. *Ibid.*

16. *Ibid.,* p. 348.

17. Quoted in Richard Neuberger, *Adventures in Politics* (New York: Oxford University Press, 1952), p. 160.

18. Sebastian de Grazia, *op. cit.,* pp. 110-15; see, also, the same writer's "A Note on the Psychological Position of the Chief Executive," *Psychiatry,* VIII (August, 1945), 267-72; and Dorothea E. Johannsen, "Reactions to the Death of President Roosevelt," *Journal of Social and Abnormal Psychology,* XLI (1946), 218-22.

19. Carl Sandburg, *Abraham Lincoln: The War Years* (New York: Harcourt, Brace & World, 1939), IV, 296-413.

20. A miscellaneous pamphlet of the Immigration and Naturalization Service, dated 1940.

CHAPTER 7

1. Reinhold Niebuhr, *The Children of Light and The Children of Darkness* (New York: Charles Scribner's Sons, 1944), p. xiii.

2. For an excellent introduction to the study of socialization and bibliog-

raphy, see Frederick Elkin, *The Child and Society* (New York: Random House, 1960).

3. Charles E. Merriam was responsible for much of what has been done in political socialization. See the series he edited and for which he contributed a volume: *Studies in The Making of Citizens* (Chicago: University of Chicago Press, 1931); and his contribution to *Civic Education in the United States* ("Report of the Commission on Social Studies: American Historical Association," Part VI [New York: Charles Scribner's Sons, 1934]). Only recently have we seen a revival of interest in political socialization. Cf. David Easton, "The Perception of Authority and Political Change," in C. J. Friedrich (ed.), *Authority* (Cambridge, Mass.: Harvard University Press, 1958), pp. 170-96; David Easton and Robert D. Hess, "Youth and the Political System," in Seymour M. Lipset and Leo Lowenthal (eds.), *Culture and Social Character* (New York: The Free Press of Glencoe, 1961), pp. 226-51; Robert D. Hess and David Easton, "The Child's Image of the President," *Public Opinion Quarterly,* XXV (Winter, 1961), 632-44; Fred I. Greenstein, "The Benevolent Leader: Children's Images of Political Authority," *American Political Science Review,* LIV (Dec., 1960), 934-43; Lewis A. Froman, Jr., "Political Socialization," *Journal of Politics,* XXIII (May, 1961), pp. 341-52; Herbert Hyman, *Political Socialization* (New York: The Free Press of Glencoe, 1959); and Robert A. LeVine, "The Internalization of Political Values in Stateless Societies," *Human Organization,* XIX (Summer, 1960), 51-58.

4. Talcott Parsons, *The Social System* (New York: The Free Press of Glencoe, 1951), chap. vi.

5. Margaret Mead, *And Keep Your Powder Dry* (New York: W. Morrow and Co., 1942).

6. Robin Williams, Jr., *American Society* (New York: Alfred A. Knopf, 1960), pp. 415-67.

7. An excellent background for our discussion is contained in Williams, *ibid.,* chap. xi.

8. This is, of course, an observation of Tocqueville.

9. Dwight Waldo, *The Administrative State* (New York: Ronald Press, 1948), chaps. iii, v, and x.

10. Talcott Parsons, "The Motivation of Economic Activities," in author's *Essays in Sociological Theory* (New York: The Free Press of Glencoe, 1954), pp. 50-68.

11. Herbert Hyman, *Political Socialization* (New York: The Free Press of Glencoe, 1959), p. 69.

12. Paul F. Lazarsfeld *et al., The People's Choice* (New York: Columbia University Press, 1944), pp. 140-45; Angus Campbell *et al., The Voter Decides* (Evanston, Ill.: Row, Peterson and Co., 1954), pp. 97-107; 199-206; Bernard R. Berelson *et al., Voting* (Chicago: University of Chicago Press, 1954), pp. 88-92; Angus Campbell *et al., The American Voter* (New York: John Wiley & Sons, Inc., 1960), pp. 146-49.

13. Jean Piaget, *The Moral Judgment of the Child* (New York: Harcourt, Brace & World, 1952), pp. 19-49.

14. Mead, *op. cit.,* pp. 138-57.

15. *Ibid.*

16. Edward Flynn, *You're the Boss* (New York: Viking Press, 1947), p. 226.

17. Campbell, *op. cit.,* p. 148.

18. V. O. Key, Jr., *Politics, Parties, and Pressure Groups* (2nd ed.; New York: Thomas Y. Crowell Co., 1948), especially chap. xxi; and V. O. Key, Jr., *Public Opinion and American Democracy* (New York: Alfred A. Knopf, 1961), p. 315.

19. Cf. Donald Matthews, *The Social Backgrounds of Political Decision-Makers* (New York: Doubleday and Co., Inc., 1954), pp. 28-29.

20. William Form and Delbert Miller, *Industry, Labor, and Community* (New York: Harper & Brothers, 1960), p. 248.

21. *Ibid.,* p. 249.

22. For an excellent contemporary history, see Robert W. Iversen, *The Communists and the Schools* (New York: Harcourt, Brace & World, 1959).

23. Sister Francis Jerome Woods, *The American Family System* (New York: Harper & Brothers, 1960), pp. 108-110.

24. Erik H. Erikson, *Childhood and Society* (New York: W. W. Norton & Co., Inc., 1950), pp. 273-77.

25. V. O. Key, Jr., *op. cit.,* p. 234.

26. Campbell, *op. cit.,* p. 92.

27. Bessie J. Pierce, *Citizens' Organizations and the Civic Training of Youth* (New York: Charles Scribner's Sons, 1933).

28. For a representative statement, see Dayton D. McKean, *Party and Pressure Politics* (Boston, Mass.: Houghton Mifflin Co., 1949), p. 25.

29. David Truman, *The Governmental Process* (New York: Alfred A. Knopf, 1951), pp. 213-61.

30. An excellent reader in public opinion is Daniel Katz *et al.* (eds.), *Public Opinion and Propaganda* (New York: Holt, Rinehart & Winston, 1954). The primary professional publication is, of course, the *Public Opinion Quarterly.*

31. Raymond B. Nixon, "Concentration and Absenteeism in Daily Newspaper Ownership," in Bernard Berelson and Morris Janowitz (eds.), *Reader in Public Opinion and Communication* (New York: The Free Press of Glencoe, 1953), p. 194.

32. Clarence H. Schettler, *Public Opinion in American Society* (New York: Harper & Brothers, 1960), p. 228.

33. *Ibid.,* p. 229.

34. *Ibid.*

35. William Albig, *Modern Public Opinion* (New York: McGraw-Hill Book Co., Inc., 1956), pp. 373-74.

36. Undoubtedly, we know more about political socialization in totalitarian than in democratic societies. Hardly a volume on the former is without chapters on schools, propaganda, and indoctrination, while very few books on American *politics* treat the same institutions and phenomena.

37. Some highly imaginative and suggestive ideas on family authority are advanced by Eric Erikson, *op. cit.,* pp. 265-83: 288-95. Gabriel Almond's *The Appeals of Communism* (Princeton, N.J.: Princeton University Press, 1954) is also highly useful in this regard. A somewhat less directly related study, but germane nevertheless, is Kaspar D. Naegele, "Some Problems in the Study of Hostility and Aggression in Middle-Class American Families," *Canadian Journal of Economics and Political Science,* XVII (Feb., 1951), 65-75.

38. Louis Hartz, *The Liberal Tradition in America* (New York: Harcourt, Brace & World, 1955).

39. *Ibid.*

40. Raymond Mack, "Do We Really Believe in the Bill of Rights?" *Social Problems,* III (April, 1956), pp. 264-269.

41. *Ibid.,* p. 267.

42. Samuel A. Stouffer, *Communism, Conformity and Civil Liberties* (New York: Doubleday & Co., Inc., 1955).

43. Seymour Martin Lipset, *Political Man* (New York: Doubleday & Co., Inc., 1960), chaps. iv and v. The former treats working-class authoritarianism, while the latter considers the incidence of fascism among various classes here and abroad.

44. Edward Shils, "Authoritarianism: 'Right' and 'Left,'" in R. Christie and M. Jahoda (eds.), *Studies in the Scope and Method of "The Authoritarian Personality"* (New York: The Free Press of Glencoe, 1954), pp. 24-49.

45. National Opinion Research Center, *The Public Looks at Politics and Politicians,* Report No. 20, March, 1944.

46. National Opinion Research Center, "Jobs and Occupations: A Popular Evaluation," *Opinion News,* IX (Sept., 1947), 3-13. Reprinted in Reinhard Bendix and Seymour Martin Lipset (eds.), *Class, Status and Power* (New York: The Free Press of Glencoe,

1953), pp. 411-425. Further references will be to the latter source.

47. *Ibid.,* p. 412.

48. Julian L. Woodward and Elmo Roper, "Political Activity of American Citizens," *American Political Science Review,* XLIV (Dec., 1950), 872-85. Reprinted in Heinz Eulau *et al.* (eds.), *Political Behavior* (New York: The Free Press of Glencoe, 1956), p. 135. Further references will be to the latter source.

49. *Ibid.*

50. Morris Janowitz, Deil Wright, and William Delany, *Public Administration and the Public—Perspectives toward Government in a Metropolitan Community* (Ann Arbor, Mich.: Bureau of Government, Institute of Public Administration, University of Michigan, 1958).

51. *Ibid.,* p. 18.

52. *Ibid.*

53. *Ibid.*

54. *Ibid.,* pp. 17-18.

55. *Ibid.,* p. 20.

56. *Ibid.*

57. *Ibid.*

58. Campbell, *op. cit.,* chap. viii.

59. Herbert Hyman and Paul Sheatsley, "The Current Status of American Public Opinion," in Daniel Katz *et al.* (eds.), *Public Opinion and Propaganda* (New York: Holt, Rinehart and Winston, 1960), pp. 33-48.

60. *Ibid.,* p. 41.

61. See footnote 3, above, for references.

CHAPTER 8

1. David Easton, "An Approach to the Analysis of Political Systems," *World Politics,* IX (April, 1957), 383-400, makes control an important output or feedback.

2. E. H. Sutherland and D. R. Cressey, *Principles of Criminology* (5th ed.; Philadelphia: J. B. Lippincott Co., 1955), p. 330.

3. See footnote 19 in Chapter V.

4. Floyd Hunter, *Community Power Structure* (Chapel Hill: University of North Carolina Press, 1953).

5. William Form and Delbert Miller, *Industry, Labor, and Community* (New York: Harper & Brothers, 1960), report on many studies dealing with the political power of those with great economic resources.

6. Arthur J. Vidich and Joseph Bensman, *Small Town in Mass Society* (Princeton, N.J.: Princeton University Press, 1958), especially Part III.

7. A few studies suggest, however, that the power of "economic determinates" is much less than Hunter, the Lynds, and Mills believe to be the case. In particular, see Robert A. Dahl, *Who Governs?* (New Haven, Conn.: Yale University Press, 1960); Edward C. Banfield, *Political Influence* (New York: The Free Press of Glencoe, 1961); and Robert O. Schulze, "The Bifurcation of Power in a Satellite City," in Morris Janowitz (ed.), *Community Political Systems* (New York: The Free Press of Glencoe, 1961), pp. 19-80.

8. For a highly impassioned but suggestive treatment of the type of social control that dominates in the United States, see C. Wright Mills, *The Power Elite* (New York: Oxford University Press, 1956), chap. xiii.

9. F. H. Allport, "The J-Curve Hypothesis of Conforming Behavior," *Journal of Social Psychology,* V (1934), 141-83.

10. Talcott Parsons, *The Social System* (New York: The Free Press of Glencoe, 1951), pp. 251-56. An unusually clear theoretical discussion of the sources of deviance with respect to juvenile delinquency is contained in Richard A. Cloward and Lloyd E. Ohlin, *Delinquency and Opportunity* (New York: The Free Press of Glencoe, 1960), pp. 31-46.

11. See William S. White, *Citadel* (New York: Harper & Brothers, 1956); Donald Matthews, *U.S. Senators and Their World* (Chapel Hill: University of North Carolina Press, 1961);

Ralph K. Huitt, "The Morse Committee Assignment Controversy: A Case Study in Senate Norms," *American Political Science Review,* LI (June, 1957), 313-29, and "The Outsider in the Senate: An Alternative Role," *American Political Science Review,* LV (Sept., 1961), 566-75.

12. Illustrations in the area of voting are provided in Murray B. Levin, *The Alienated Voter* (New York: Holt, Rinehart & Winston, 1960). For a more general discussion of apathy and cynicism, see David Riesman and Nathan Glazer, "Criteria for Political Apathy," in Alvin W. Gouldner (ed.), *Studies in Leadership* (New York: Harper & Brothers, 1950), pp. 505-59.

13. Robert A. Dahl and Charles Lindblom, *Politics, Economics and Welfare* (New York: Harper & Brothers, 1953), pp. 107-110.

14. One of the most convincing and eloquent statements on the inequality in the administration of justice is the classic study of Gunnar Myrdal, *An American Dilemma* (New York: Harper & Brothers, 1944), especially chap. xi. Also, see William A. Westley, "Violence and the Police," *American Journal of Sociology,* LIX (July, 1953), 34-41 and; Edwin M. Lermert and Judy Roseburg, *The Administration of Justice to Minority Groups in Los Angeles County* (Berkeley: University of California Press, 1948).

15. Myrdal, *loc. cit.*

16. H. L. Searles, *Logic and Scientific Methods* (New York: The Ronald Press, 1948), pp. 46-49.

17. Robert K. Merton, "Social Structure and Anomie," *Social Theory and Social Structure* (New York: The Free Press of Glencoe, 1957), pp. 131-60.

18. *Ibid.,* p. 140.

19. *Ibid.,* p. 153.

20. See Morris Rosenberg, "The Meaning of Politics in Mass Society," *Public Opinion Quarterly,* XV (1951), 5-15.

21. This is suggested, but not claimed, by Robert E. Agger, Marshall N. Goldstein, and Stanley A. Pearl, "Political Cynicism: Measurement and Meaning," *Journal of Politics,* XXIII (Spring, 1961), 477-506.

22. Angus Campbell *et al., The Voter Decides* (Evanston, Ill.: Row, Peterson and Co., 1954), pp. 187-94.

23. On methods, see James L. McCamy, *Government Publicity* (Chicago: University of Chicago Press, 1939).

24. Alexis de Tocqueville, *Democracy in America* (New York: Vintage Books, 1954), II, 11-12.

25. *Ibid.*

26. Richard Hofstadter, "The Pseudo-Conservative Revolt," in Daniel Bell (ed.), *The New American Right* (New York: Criterion Books, 1955), pp. 33-55.

27. Talcott Parsons, "Social Strains in America," *ibid.,* pp. 117-40.

28. The term "garrison state" apparently was coined by Harold D. Lasswell, "The Garrison State," *American Journal of Sociology,* XLIV (Jan., 1941), 455-68. For implications in the American case, see Lasswell's *National Security and Individual Freedom* (New York: McGraw-Hill Book Co., Inc., 1950).

29. Mills, *op. cit.*

CHAPTER 9

1. Sheldon S. Wolin has recently written one of the more imaginative histories of political thought based, in part, upon the recognition of this point. See *Politics and Vision* (Boston: Little, Brown and Co., 1960).

2. David M. Potter, *People of Plenty* (Chicago: University of Chicago Press, 1954).

3. *Ibid.,* p. 118.

4. E. E. Schattschneider, *The Semi-Sovereign People* (New York: Holt, Rinehart & Winston, 1960), especially chaps. vi and viii.

5. Émile Durkheim, *The Division of Labor in Society,* trans. George Simpson (New York: The Free Press of Glencoe, 1949), p. 267.

6. According to Natalie Rogoff, the total amount—not rates—of vertical mobility had increased between 1910 and 1940, the time span she studied in one large urban center. See "Recent Trends in Urban Occupational Mobility," in Reinhard Bendix and Seymour Martin Lipset (eds.), *Class, Status and Power* (New York: The Free Press of Glencoe, 1953), pp. 442-53.

7. See *Schenck* v. *United States,* 249 U.S. 47 (1919), for the formulation of the "clear and present danger" rule in the famous dissent by Justices Brandeis and Holmes. For subsequent cases revolving around the affective content of speech and its potential for conflict, see *Cantwell* v. *Connecticut,* 310 U.S. 296 (1940); *Terminiello* v. *Chicago,* 337 U.S. 1 (1949); *Feiner* v. *New York,* 340 U.S. 315 (1951); and *Kunz* v. *New York,* 340 U.S. 290 (1951). But the question of conspiracy and *possible* long-run violence, or revolution, brings in another aspect of the legal proscription of speech and advocacy. Thus, the "bad tendency" and "remote possibility" rule of the cases of *Gitlow* v. *New York,* 268 U.S. 652 (1925); *Dennis* v. *United States,* 341 U.S. 494 (1951).

8. David Truman, *The Governmental Process* (New York: Alfred A. Knopf, 1951), pp. 483.

9. William C. Mitchell, "Reduction of Tension in Legislatures," *PROD,* II (Jan., 1959), 3-6.

10. Consult any introductory text for a discussion of the means of repression, their causes and functions. One such text is David Krech and Richard S. Crutchfield, *Elements of Psychology* (New York: Alfred A. Knopf, 1959), pp. 648; 659-60.

11. Bernard Berelson *et al., Voting* (Chicago: University of Chicago Press, 1954), pp. 101-109.

12. Such is the claim of Raymond Moley, *Twenty-Seven Masters of Politics* (New York: Funk & Wagnalls Co., 1949), p. 49.

13. E. E. Schattschneider, *Party Government* (New York: Holt, Rinehart & Winston, 1942), p. 115.

14. Harold Lasswell, *World Politics and Personal Insecurity* (New York: McGraw-Hill Book Co., Inc., 1935), p. 73.

15. Georg Simmel, *Conflict,* trans. Kurt H. Wolff (New York: The Free Press of Glencoe, 1955), p. 92.

16. See Glendon Schubert, *The Public Interest* (New York: The Free Press of Glencoe, 1960), for a stimulating analysis of various theories of the "public interest" and a useful bibliography.

17. V. O. Key, Jr., *American State Politics* (New York: Alfred A. Knopf, 1956), chap. ii.

18. See Talcott Parsons, " 'Voting' and the Equilibrium of the American Political System," in Eugene Burdick and Arthur J. Brodbeck (eds.), *American Voting Behavior* (New York: The Free Press of Glencoe, 1959), pp. 80-120.

19. Paul Lazarsfeld *et al., The People's Choice* (New York: Columbia University Press, 1944), pp. 37-39.

20. *Ibid.,* p. 37.

21. *Ibid.*

22. American Institute of Public Opinion, poll sent out January, 1961.

23. James Reston, "The Reassuring Civility of the Transition," *The New York Times,* Jan. 15, 1961.

24. Anthony Downs, *An Economic Theory of Democracy* (New York: Harper & Brothers, 1957), chap. viii.

25. Angus Campbell, *The Voter Decides* (Evanston, Ill.: Row, Peterson and Co., 1954), p. 35.

26. *Ibid.,* p. 38.

27. V. O. Key, Jr., "A Theory of Critical Election," *Journal of Politics,* XVII (Feb., 1955), 3-18.

28. For scattered bits of data, consult the following: Morris Janowitz *et al., Public Administration and the Public Perspectives toward Government in a Metropolitan Community* (Ann Arbor: University of Michigan, Michigan Governmental Studies, No. 36, 1958), chap. iii; Amos H. Hawley and Basil G. Zimmer, "Resistance to Unification in a Metropolitan Community," in Morris Janowitz (ed.), *Community Political*

Systems (New York: The Free Press of Glencoe, 1961), pp. 164-69; 174-81.

29. David H. Kurtzman, "Influence of Organizations of Local Government Officials," *Annals of the American Academy of Political and Social Sciences,* CXCV (Jan., 1938), 103.

30. Donald Matthews, *U.S. Senators and Their World* (Chapel Hill: University of North Carolina Press, 1961), p. 238.

31. *Ibid.,* p. 239.

32. Compiled from Joseph N. Kane, *Facts about Presidents* (New York: Permabooks, 1960), p. 409.

33. John Mason Brown, "The State Legislatures as Training for Further Public Service," *Annals of the American Academy of Political and Social Sciences,* CXCV (Jan., 1938), 178.

34. *Ibid.,* p. 179.

35. *Ibid.* Glendon Schubert informs us that of the 99 per cent of the justices who held political jobs before their appointment to the Supreme Court, 60 per cent had held federal offices, 35 per cent state offices, and the remaining 4 per cent were political-party officeholders, with the largest number in federal executive positions (34 per cent). *Constitutional Politics* (New York: Holt, Rinehart & Winston, 1960), p. 31. For the most complete study of the justices, see John R. Schmidhauser, "The Justices of the Supreme Court: A Collective Portrait," *Midwest Journal of Political Science,* III (1959), 1-57.

36. Brown, *op. cit.,* p. 179.

37. Alfred de Grazia, *The American Way of Government* (New York: John Wiley & Sons, Inc., 1957), p. 417.

CHAPTER 10

1. Other indicators such as public opinion polls might also be employed, but they, too, may be misleading in the sense that attitudes may not be the equivalents of actions.

2. *Statistical Abstract of the United States, 1961* (Washington, D.C.: Bureau of the Census, U.S. Department of Commerce), pp. 406-07.

3. Don Martindale, *American Social Structure* (New York: Appleton-Century-Crofts, Inc., 1960), p. 71.

4. *Ibid.,* pp. 73-74.

5. J. Frederic Dewhurst, *America's Needs and Resources* (New York: Twentieth Century Fund, 1955).

6. John Kenneth Galbraith, *The Affluent Society* (Boston: Houghton Mifflin Co., 1958).

7. AIPO, February 26, 1961.

8. G. D. Wiebe, "Responses to the Televised Kefauver Hearings: Some Social Psychological Implications," *Public Opinion Quarterly,* XVI (Summer, 1952), 179-200.

9. Robert E. Agger, Marshall N. Goldstein, and Stanley A. Pearl, "Political Cynicism: Measurement and Meaning," *Journal of Politics,* XXIII (1961), 477-506.

10. Angus Campbell *et al., The Voter Decides* (Evanston, Ill.: Row, Peterson and Co., 1954), pp. 187-93.

11. Murray B. Levin, *The Alienated Voter* (New York: Holt, Rinehart & Winston, 1960).

12. Morris Janowitz and Dwaine Marvick, *Competitive Pressure and Democratic Consent* (Ann Arbor, Mich.: Institute of Public Administration, 1956), pp. 30-39.

13. David Riesman and Nathan Glazer, "Criteria for Political Apathy," in Alvin Gouldner (ed.), *Studies in Leadership* (New York: Harper & Brothers, 1950), pp. 505-59.

14. Morris Rosenberg, "The Meaning of Politics in Mass Society," *Public Opinion Quarterly,* XV (1951),

15. C. Wright Mills, *The Power Elite* (New York: Oxford University Press, 1956).

16. Clinton Rossiter, *Constitutional Dictatorship* (Princeton, N.J.: Princeton University Press, 1948).

17. Julian L. Woodward and Elmo Roper, "Political Activity of American Citizens," *American Political Science Review,* XLIV (Dec., 1950), 872-85.

18. Alfred de Grazia, *The Elements of Political Science* (New York: Alfred A. Knopf, 1952), pp. 87-90.

19. *Statistical Abstract of the United States, 1961* (Washington, D.C.: Bureau of the Census, U.S. Department of Commerce), p. 359.

20. *Ibid.*, pp. 392, 421.

CHAPTER 11

1. See Robert F. Bales, *Interaction Process Analysis* (Reading, Mass.: Addison-Wesley, 1949), for problem-solving in small groups. For decision-making models in organizations, see James G. March and Herbert A. Simon, *Organizations* (New York: John Wiley & Sons, Inc., 1958), especially chap. vii.

2. Lawrence Chamberlain, *The President, Congress, and Legislation* (New York: Columbia University Press, 1946). It should be noted that Chamberlain did not include foreign policy measures and that he defined what "important" meant during the period studied.

3. Elizabeth McK. Scott and Belle Zeller, "State Agencies and Lawmaking," *Public Administration Review,* II (1942), 205-20. New York, of course, has a tradition of strong executive leadership.

4. *Congressional Quarterly Almanac* (Washington, D.C.: Congressional Quarterly, Inc., 1961), p. 91.

5. Richard E. Neustadt, "Presidency and Legislation: The Growth of Central Clearance," *American Political Science Review,* XLVIII (Sept., 1954), 641-71; and, "Presidency and Legislation: Planning the President's Program," *American Political Science Review,* XLIX (Dec., 1955), 980-1021.

6. The most thorough study of political strategy in the Congressional context is, undoubtedly, Bertram Gross, *The Legislative Struggle* (New York: McGraw-Hill Book Co., Inc., 1953). Cf. J. Leiper Freeman, *The Political Process* (New York: Random House, 1955).

7. Henry F. Pringle, *Theodore Roosevelt* (New York: Harcourt, Brace & World, 1931), p. 427.

8. Samuel Lubell, *The Future of American Politics* (New York: Harper & Brothers, 1951), p. 10.

9. The point is well made by Charles E. Lindblom, "Decision-Making in Taxation and Expenditures," in National Bureau of Economic Research, *Public Finances: Needs, Sources, and Utilization* (Princeton, N.J.: Princeton University Press, 1961).

10. But a casual reading of the *United States Government Organization Manual* (Washington, D.C.: Government Printing Office, 1961-62) suggests that many more government agencies are transferred to other agencies or departments than are abolished. See Appendix A of aforementioned document.

11. Charles L. Black, *The People and the Court* (New York: The Macmillan Co., 1960), chap. iii.

12. *Ibid.*, p. 65.

13. Warren C. Baum, *The French Economy and the State* (Princeton, N.J.: Princeton University Press, 1958), p. 132.

14. *Ibid.*

15. Edward C. Banfield, *The Moral Basis of a Backward Society* (New York: The Free Press of Glencoe, 1958), pp. 7-8.

16. Philip Selznick, *TVA and the Grass Roots* (Berkeley: University of California Press, 1953), especially Part III.

17. *Statistical Abstract of the United States, 1961* (Washington, D.C.: U.S. Department of Commerce, U.S. Government Printing Office, 1961), p. 422.

18. Bronislaw Malinowski, *Argonauts of the Western Pacific* (London: Routledge & Kegan Paul, 1922).

CHAPTER 12

1. Morris Janowitz *et al., Public Administration and the Public—Perspectives toward Government in a Metro-*

politan Community (Ann Arbor, Mich.: Bureau of Government, Institute of Public Administration, University of Michigan, 1958).

2. *Ibid.,* p. 32.

3. *Ibid.,* p. 33.

4. *Ibid.,* p. 36.

5. *Ibid.*

6. *Ibid.*

7. *Ibid.*

8. *Ibid.,* p. 37.

9. Scott Greer, "Dilemmas of Action Research on the 'Metropolitan Problem,'" in Morris Janowitz (ed.), *Community Political Systems* (New York: The Free Press of Glencoe, 1961), pp. 197-98.

10. *Ibid.*

11. *Ibid.*

12. Robert Lane, *Political Life* (New York: The Free Press of Glencoe, 1959), p. 157.

13. Most of Harold Lasswell's work is relevant to the study of political motivation. In particular, see his *Psychopathology and Politics* (Chicago: University of Chicago Press, 1930) and *Power and Personality* (New York: W. W. Norton & Co., Inc., 1948).

14. *Ibid.,* p. 38.

15. M. Brewster Smith, Jerome Bruner, and Robert White, *Opinions and Personality* (New York: John Wiley & Sons, Inc., 1956); see also Smith, "The Personal Setting of Public Opinions: A Study of Attitudes toward Russia," *Public Opinion Quarterly,* XI (1947), 516-23.

16. John Dollard, *Caste and Class in a Southern Town* (New Haven, Conn.: Yale University Press, 1937), especially chap. xv.

17. The figure represents the total number of bills introduced in the Eighty-Fifth Congress. See the *Congressional Record,* Sept. 12, 1958.

18. *Ibid.*

19. The problem is dealt with, at length, by the writer in "Politics as the Allocation of Values: A Critique," *Ethics,* LXXI (January, 1961), 78-89.

20. David Truman, *The Govern-*

mental Process (New York: Alfred A. Knopf, 1951), pp. 104-105.

21. *Ibid.*

22. *Ibid.*

23. Parsons makes the point in a brilliant essay, "The Role of Ideas in Social Action," in his *Essays in Sociological Theory* (New York: The Free Press of Glencoe, 1954), p. 23.

24. Robert A. Dahl, *A Preface to Democratic Theory* (Chicago: University of Chicago Press, 1956), p. 125-35.

25. *Ibid.,* p. 125.

26. Bertram M. Gross, *The Legislative Struggle* (New York: McGraw-Hill Book Co., Inc., 1953), p. 391.

27. Joseph Dineen, *The Purple Shamrock* (New York: W. W. Norton & Co., 1949).

CHAPTER 13

1. Robert A. Dahl and Charles Lindblom, *Politics, Economics and Welfare* (New York: Harper & Brothers, 1953), p. 93.

2. For a highly formalized, but lucid and perceptive, discussion of competition, see Georg Simmel, *Conflict,* trans. Kurt Wolff (New York: The Free Press of Glencoe, 1955), chap. ii.

3. Joseph A. Schumpeter tended to emphasize the competitive aspect of democracy, but the normative regulation is implicit and necessary in any definition of democracy. Cf. *Capitalism, Socialism and Democracy* (New York: Harper & Brothers, 1947), pp. 269-83.

4. Neil W. Chamberlain, *A General Theory of Economic Process* (New York: Harper & Brothers, 1955), pp. 275-81.

5. The concept "universalism" is defined by Talcott Parsons and Edward Shils as "the role expectation that, in qualifications for memberships and decisions for differential treatment, priority will be given to standards defined in completely generalized terms, independent of the particular relationship of the actor's own statuses (qualities or per-

formances, classificatory or relational) to those of the object." Cf. Parsons and Shils, *Toward a General Theory of Action* (Cambridge, Mass.: Harvard University Press, 1952), p. 82.

6. "Achievement" is contrasted by Parsons and Shils to "ascription" in the sense that the former norm gives ". . . priority to the objects' actual or expected performances, and to their attributes only as directly relevant to these performances . . . ," while ascription refers to priority being accorded the " 'objects' given attributes." *Ibid.*

7. The theory of deviance developed originally by Émile Durkheim, and extended and refined by Robert K. Merton, is apropos to our discussion. Cf. "Social Structure and Anomie," in *Social Theory and Social Structure* (New York: The Free Press of Glencoe, 1957), p. 136.

8. This is essentially the way in which Neil W. Chamberlain, *op. cit.,* pp. 74-99, defines bargaining.

9. The volume of literature on the theory of games is enormous and still expanding. The best introduction is that of R. Duncan Luce and Howard Raiffa, *Games and Decisions* (New York: John Wiley & Sons, Inc., 1957). Two other volumes—less technical—but more relevant to political behavior, are Anatol Rapoport, *Fights, Games, and Debates* (Ann Arbor: University of Michigan Press, 1960); and Thomas C. Schelling, *The Strategy of Conflict* (Cambridge, Mass.: Harvard University Press, 1960).

10. Dahl and Lindblom, *op. cit.,* pp. 325-26.

11. Floyd Hunter, *Top Leadership, U.S.A.* (Chapel Hill: University of North Carolina Press, 1959).

12 Dahl and Lindblom, *op. cit.,* pp. 326-33.

13. Chamberlain, *op. cit.,* p. 80.

14. Dahl and Lindblom, *op. cit.,* p. 326.

15. *Ibid.,* pp. 335-36.

16. Chamberlain, *op. cit.,* pp. 266-75.

17. *Ibid.,* p. 266.

18. *Ibid.,* pp. 266-67.

19. *Ibid.,* pp. 268-75.

20. Dahl and Lindblom, *op. cit.,* p. 336.

21. *Ibid.*

22. E. E. Schattschneider, *Party Government* (New York: Holt, Rinehart & Winston, 1942), p. 33.

23. Dahl and Lindblom, *op. cit.,* p. 336.

24. *Ibid.,* p. 339. Also see the unique demonstration of irrational outcomes in the legislative process by William H. Riker, "Voting Methods and Irrationality in Legislative Decisions," in John Walke and Heinz Eulau (eds.), *Legislative Behavior* (New York: The Free Press of Glencoe, 1959), pp. 97-108.

25. See Stephan K. Bailey and Howard D. Samuel, *Congress at Work* (New York: Holt, Rinehart & Winston, 1952) for case studies, of which chap. vii, "Pork," is the most relevant.

26. This is not to say that each bargainer receives the same amounts of satisfaction and dissatisfaction. Measurability and interpersonal comparability of "utilities" pose questions that have not been satisfactorily resolved. The welfare economists have, of necessity, been most concerned with these problems. For an excellent presentation of the issues, and one answer which requires traditional welfare economists to revise considerably their assumptions and language, see I. M. D. Little, *A Critique of Welfare Economics* (2nd ed.; London: Oxford University Press, 1957).

27. Bernard Berelson *et al., Voting* (Chicago: University of Chicago Press, 1954), pp. 314-15.

28. It should be added that no political system, including the totalitarian, has ever acted upon purely rational premises, nor produced logically consistent sets of public policies. Yet, political scientists are most apt to point this out with respect to the United States and frequently to bemoan the fact.

29. Lucian W. Pye, "The Non-Western Political Process," *Journal of Politics,* XX (Aug., 1958), 468-86.

Reprinted in James N. Rosenau (ed.), *International Politics and Foreign Policy* (New York: The Free Press of Glencoe, 1961), p. 287.

30. *Ibid.,* p. 290.

31. Daniel Boorstin, *The Genius of American Politics* (Chicago: University of Chicago Press, 1953), pp. 8-9.

32. Schattschneider, *op. cit.,* pp. 85-93.

33. *Ibid.,* p. 92.

CHAPTER 14

1. H. McD. Clokie, "The Modern Party State," *Canadian Journal of Economics and Political Science,* XV (May, 1949), 140.

2. *Ibid.,* p. 157.

3. Another way of putting the matter is that the sum of the "payoffs" is zero.

4. Austin Ranney and Willmoore Kendall, "The American Party Systems," *American Political Science Review,* XLVIII (June, 1954), 477-85. Revised and reprinted in Austin Ranney and Willmoore Kendall, *Democracy and the American Party System* (New York: Harcourt, Brace & World, 1956), chap. vii. Further citations are to the latter source. It should be added that the authors' scheme of classification has been criticized. See Joseph A. Schlesinger, "A Two-Dimensional Scheme for Classifying the States According to Degree of Inter-Party Competition," *American Political Science Review,* XLIV (Dec., 1955), 1120-28.

5. Ranney and Kendall, *op. cit.,* p. 162.

6. *Ibid.,* p. 164.

7. *Ibid.*

8. Cortez A. M. Ewing, "Primaries as Real Elections," *Southwestern Social Science Quarterly,* XXIX (March, 1949), 293-98.

9. *Ibid.,* p. 296.

10. V. O. Key concludes that "over the long run there seems to be associated with the primary a tendency for the district party cliques and leadership in the minority party to atrophy."

American State Politics (New York: Alfred A. Knopf, 1956), p. 195. For some refinements in definitions and measurements pertaining to "safe" and "competitive" districts, as well as further empirical data, see William H. Standing and James A. Robinson, "Inter-Party Competition and Primary Contesting: The Case of Indiana," *American Political Science Review,* LII (Dec., 1958), 1066-77.

11. Cortez A. M. Ewing, *Primary Elections in the South* (Norman, Okla.: University of Oklahoma Press, 1953), as summarized in Ranney and Kendall, *op. cit.,* p. 27.

12. Julius Turner, "Primary Elections as the Alternative to Party Competition in 'Safe' Districts," *Journal of Politics,* XV (May, 1953), 197-210.

13. *Ibid.,* p. 201.

14. Turner, *op. cit.,* pp. 208-209.

15. Ewing, *op. cit.,* pp. 59-73; 71.

16. V. O. Key, "The Direct Primary and Party Structure: A Study of State Legislative Nominations," *American Political Science Review,* LXVIII (March, 1954), 14-16. A later version of the article was printed as chap. vi of Key's *American State Politics.*

17. Donald Matthews, *U.S. Senators and Their World* (Chapel Hill: University of North Carolina, 1961).

18. *Ibid.,* p. 238.

19. *Ibid.*

20. Compiled from the *Official Congressional Directory* (Washington, D.C.: Government Printing Office, 1959).

21. Louis Bean, *The Mid-Term Battle* (Washington: Cantillon Books, 1950), chap. v. Cortez A. M. Ewing, *op. cit.,* disagrees and argues that "Presidential coattails" have little effect. Malcolm Moss assumes a moderate position —after exhaustive studies—in *Politics, Presidents and Coattails* (Baltimore: Johns Hopkins Press, 1952).

22. Ivan Hinderaker, *Party Politics* (New York: Holt, Rinehart & Winston, 1956), p. 431.

23. V. O. Key, Jr., *Politics, Parties, and Pressure Groups* (New York: Thomas Y. Crowell Co., 1958), p. 605.

24. *Congressional Quarterly,* XVIII (Mar. 20, 1959), 1.

25. Key, *op. cit.,* p. 594.

26. *Ibid.*

27. Perhaps the clearest exposition of the phenomenon is that of E. E. Schattschneider, *Party Government* (New York: Holt, Rinehart & Winston, 1942), pp. 69-84.

28. Robert A. Dahl, *A Preface to Democratic Theory* (Chicago: University of Chicago Press, 1956).

29. *Ibid.,* pp. 114-15.

30. *Ibid.,* p. 115.

31. *Ibid.*

32. *Ibid.,* p. 117.

33. *Ibid.*

34. *Ibid.*

35. Donald Matthews, *The Social Background of Political Decision-Makers* (New York: Doubleday & Co., Inc., 1954).

36. *Ibid.,* p. 30.

37. *Ibid.*

38. William Form and Delbert Miller, *Industry, Labor, and Community* (New York: Harper & Brothers, 1960), p. 162.

CHAPTER 15

1. The Keynesian revolution in economics has probably done most to acquaint us with the role of politics in economic performance, although the earlier German historical school and the American institutionalists also helped to prepare the way.

2. Rockefeller Brothers Fund, *Prospect for America* (New York: Doubleday & Co., 1961), p. 280.

3. These figures come from the *Statistical Abstract of the United States, 1961* (Washington, D.C.: Bureau of the Census, U.S. Department of Commerce), Sec. 10; and Rockefeller Brothers Fund, *ibid.,* pp. 293-96.

4. A number of useful, if somewhat uninspired, books summarize the state of knowledge with regard to political economy. Among the better ones are Merle Fainsod, Lincoln Gordon, and

Joseph C. Palamountain, Jr., *Government and the American Economy* (New York: W. W. Norton & Co., Inc., 1959); and a volume with a somewhat narrower focus, by Clair Wilcox, *Public Policies toward Business* (Homewood, Ill.: Richard D. Irwin, Inc., 1960).

5. *Facts and Figures on Government Finance, 1958–1959* (New York: Tax Foundation, Inc., 1958), p. 13.

6. *Budget of the United States Government for the Fiscal Year Ending June 30, 1960* (Washington, D.C.: U.S. Government Printing Office, 1959).

7. *Statistical Abstract of the United States, 1959* (Washington, D.C.: U.S. Department of Commerce, Bureau of the Census, 1959), p. 245.

8. *Ibid.*

9. U.S. President's Commission on Veteran's Pensions, *Veteran's Benefits in the United States* (Washington, D.C.: U.S. Government Printing Office, 1956), pp. 98-126.

10. Reported in Robert K. Carr, Marver H. Bernstein, and Donald H. Morrison, *American Democracy in Theory and Practice* (New York: Holt, Rinehart & Winston, 1960), p. 713.

11. *Ibid.*

12. Rockefeller Brothers Fund, Inc., *Prospects for America* (New York: Doubleday & Co., 1961), p. 295.

CHAPTER 16

1. *Allocation of the Tax Burden by Income Class* (New York: Tax Foundation, Inc., 1960), p. 18.

2. *Ibid.,* p. 19.

3. Most introductory texts in the field of public finance have extended sections on problems of shifting and incidence of taxation. A representative text is William J. Schultz and C. Lowell Harriss, *American Public Finance* (New York: Prentice-Hall, Inc., 1954), especially chaps. viii-ix.

4. Tax Foundation, Inc., *op. cit.,* p. 10.

5. *Ibid.,* p. 13.

6. *Ibid.,* p. 14.

7. *Ibid.,* p. 15.

8. Schultz and Harriss, *op. cit.,* pp. 249-64.

9. Tax Foundation, Inc., *op. cit.,* p. 17.

10. Alexander Heard, *The Costs of Democracy* (Chapel Hill: University of North Carolina Press, 1960), p. 7.

11. *Ibid.*

12. *Ibid.,* p. 40.

13. *Ibid.,* p. 44.

14. *Ibid.,* p. 51.

15. *Ibid.*

16. "1960 Lobby Spending," *Congressional Quarterly Almanac,* XVII (1960), 959.

17. *Ibid.,* p. 404.

18. *The Book of the States* (Chicago: Council of State Governments, 1949), p. 127.

19. *The Book of the States* (Chicago: Council of State Governments, 1955), p. 134.

20. *Ibid.*

21. See Bernard Berelson *et al., Voting* (Chicago: University of Chicago Press, 1954), pp. 313-23, for the argument about the desirable consequences for the polity of limited participation. For an explanation of the costs entailed by individuals when participating in politics, see Anthony Downs, *An Economic Theory of Democracy* (New York: Harper & Brothers, 1957), Part III.

22. V. O. Key, Jr., *Politics, Parties, and Pressure Groups* (New York: Thomas Y. Crowell, 1958), p. 624.

23. *Ibid.,* pp. 626-27.

24. *Ibid.,* p. 628.

25. Julian Woodward and Elmo Roper, "Political Activity of American Citizens," *American Political Science Review,* XLIV (Dec., 1950), 872-85. Reprinted in Heinz Eulau *et al.* (eds.), *Political Behavior* (New York: The Free Press of Glencoe, 1956), pp. 133-37. Further citations are to the latter volume.

26. *Ibid.,* p. 135.

27. *Ibid.,* p. 136.

28. Angus Campbell *et. al., The Voter Decides* (Evanston, Ill.: Row, Peterson and Co., 1954), pp. 187-88.

29. *Ibid.,* p. 191.

30. Morris Janowitz *et al., Public Administration and the Public—Perspectives toward Government in a Metropolitan Community* (Ann Arbor, Mich.: Bureau of Government, University of Michigan, 1958).

31. *Ibid.,* p. 53.

32. *Ibid.*

33. Samuel Stouffer, *Communism, Conformity, and Civil Liberties* (New York: Doubleday & Co., 1955). Table is reconstructed from data of Chapter 2. For some interesting remarks on the Stouffer study, see Nathan Glazer and Seymour Martin Lipset, "The Polls on Communism and Conformity," in Daniel Bell (ed.), *The New American Right* (New York: Criterion Books, 1955), pp. 141-65.

34. National Opinion Research Center, "The Public Looks at Politics and the Politician," *Public Opinion News,* XX (Mar., 1944).

35. Janowitz, *op. cit.*

36. *Ibid.,* p. 48.

37. *Ibid.*

38. Morris Janowitz and Deil Wright, "The Prestige of Public Employment. 1929-1954," *Public Administration Review,* XVI (Winter, 1956), 15-21.

CHAPTER 17

1. Alvin Boskoff, "Social Change: Major Problems in the Emergence of Theoretical and Research Foci," in Howard Becker and Alvin Boskoff (eds.), *Modern Sociological Theory* (New York: The Dryden Press, 1957), pp. 260-304; and Talcott Parsons, *The Social System* (New York: The Free Press of Glencoe, 1951), chap. xi. Parsons maintains that a theory of change is not yet possible; p. 486.

2. Population changes, from the point of view of the society, would appear to be the resultant of unintended and uncontrolled decisions, even though

intended by specific members of the society.

3. Robert Merton, "Manifest and Patent Functions," in *Social Theory and Social Structure* (New York: The Free Press of Glencoe, 1957), pp. 51; 61-62; 66.

4. See John McDiarmid, "Presidential Inaugural Addresses—A Study in Verbal Symbols," *Public Opinion Quarterly,* I (July, 1937), 79-82.

5. Clyde Kluckhohn, "The Evolution of Contemporary American Values," *Daedalus,* LXXXVII (Spring, 1958), 78-110.

6. Paul H. Douglas, "Is Campaign Oratory a Waste of Breath?" *The New York Times Magazine,* Oct. 19, 1958.

7. Cartoons of Lincoln were far more vicious than they are of present-day Presidents.

8. I am aware of the contention that the term "independent" is a slippery one and that any estimate of the trend of independent voting is likely to be little more than a guess. My point is that, regardless of the extent of independent voting, increasing social approval is being given the term. Cf. Samuel Eldersveld, "The Independent Vote: Measurement, Characteristics, and Implications for Party Strategy," *American Political Science Review,* XLVI (September, 1952), 732-53.

9. Angus Campbell *et al., The Voter Decides* (Evanston, Ill.: Row, Peterson and Co., 1954), pp. 94-97.

10. *Ibid.,* p. 95.

11. See George Graham, *Morality in American Politics* (New York: Random House, 1952).

12. Commission on Organization of the Executive Branch of Government, "Personnel and Civil Service," (Washington, D.C.: U.S. Government Printing Office, 1955), p. 6.

13. Everett S. Brown, *Proposed Amendments to the Constitution of the United States* (Ann Arbor, Mich.: George Wahr, 1953), p. 1.

14. Adapted from John H. Ferguson and Dean E. McHenry, *The American Federal Government* (6th ed.: New York: McGraw-Hill Book Co., Inc., 1961), p. 63.

15. Solomon Fabricant, *The Trend of Government Activity in the United States since 1900* (New York: National Bureau of Economic Research, Inc., 1952), p. 13.

16. The basic reference on special districts is J. C. Bollens, *Special District Governments in the United States* (Berkeley: University of California Press, 1957).

17. Robert A. Dahl, *A Preface to Democratic Theory* (Chicago: University of Chicago Press, 1956), p. 109.

18. *Ibid.,* p. 110.

19. The contrast in public opinion during World War II and the Korean War illustrates the differences.

20. To be sure, the trends are powerful. See James Burnham, *The Managerial Revolution* (New York: John Day Co., 1941); and C. Wright Mills, *The Power Elite* (New York: Oxford University Press, 1956).

21. This, of course, is the claim of Arthur Schlesinger, Jr., *The Age of Jackson* (Boston: Little, Brown & Co., 1946).

22. See Lee Benson, *The Concept of Jacksonian Democracy* (Princeton, N.J.: Princeton University Press, 1961).

23. For summary discussion, see Angus Campbell *et al., The American Voter* (New York: John Wiley & Sons, Inc., 1960), especially chaps. xii, xiii, and xiv.

24. Samuel Lubell, *The Future of American Politics* (New York: Harper & Brothers, 1952).

25. Arthur Holcombe, *The Political Parties of To-Day* (New York: Harper & Brothers, 1924). Wilfred E. Binkley also argues a similar position. See his *American Political Parties* (New York: Alfred A. Knopf, 1947).

26. Perhaps the authoritative volume on the growth of the Presidency is Edward S. Corwin, *The President* (New York: New York University Press, 1957). On the governors, see Leslie Lipson, *The American State Governor* (Chicago: University of Chicago Press,

1939), and C. B. Ransone, Jr., *The Office of Governor in the United States* (University, Ala.: University of Alabama Press, 1956).

27. For a somewhat polemical, but informative, statement on the proper role of bureaucracy, consult Charles S. Hyneman, *Bureaucracy in a Democracy* (New York: Harper & Brothers, 1950). Annotated bibliographies are provided with each chapter.

28. Charles S. Hyneman, "Tenure and Turnover of Legislative Personnel," *Annals,* CXCV (January, 1938), 21-31.

29. See page 371 above.

30. Hyneman, *op. cit.,* and Belle Zeller (ed.), *American State Legislatures* (New York: Thomas Y. Crowell Co., 1954), pp. 65-69.

31. *Ibid.,* p. 65.

32. One such study is that of Joseph A. Schlesinger, *How They Became Governor* (East Lansing: Michigan State University Press, 1958).

33. The evidence is scanty, but see Mattai Dogan, "Political Ascent in a Class Society: French Deputies 1870–1958," and W. L. Guttsman, "Changes in British Labour Leadership," both in Dwaine Marvick (ed.), *Political Decision-Makers* (New York: The Free Press of Glencoe, 1960).

34. From *The New York Times,* Nov. 9, 1958.

35. Such would seem to be implied by V. O. Key, Jr., in his "A Theory of Critical Elections," *Journal of Politics,* XVII (Feb., 1955), 3-18.

36. Table adapted from the *Statistical Abstract of the United States, 1961* (Washington, D.C.: U.S. Department of Commerce, Bureau of the Census, 1961), p. 356.

37. See the "Chatters-Hoover Inventory of Governmental Activities in the United States," cited in Alfred de Grazia, *The Elements of Political Science* (New York: Alfred A. Knopf, 1952), pp. 50-60.

38. A Department of Urban Affairs seems the next likely prospect for Cabinet rank.

39. Fabricant, *op. cit.,* p. 24.

40. *Ibid.,* p. 25.

41. *Canada 1959* (Ottawa: Dominion Bureau of Statistics, 1959), p. 19.

42. *The Encyclopedia Americana* (New York: Americana Corporation, 1959), p. 293.

43. William J. Schultz and C. Lowell Harriss, *American Public Finance* (New York: Prentice-Hall, Inc., 1954), p. 251.

44. *Ibid.,* p. 253.

45. Fabricant, *op. cit.,* p. 102.

46. *Ibid.,* p. 108.

A Selected Bibliography

This listing of books and articles is highly selective. To include all of the titles that have somehow influenced my thinking on American politics would not only be impossible, but unnecessary. I have tried, instead, to include only those items that have seemed most important and useful. They are categorized according to the major parts of the book.

CONCEPTUAL FRAMEWORK

Aberle, D. F., *et al.* "The Functional-Prerequisites of a Society," *Ethics,* LX (January, 1950), 100-111.

Almond, Gabriel A. "Comparative Political Systems," *The Journal of Politics,* XVIII (August, 1956), 391-409.

———, and Coleman, James S. (eds.). *The Politics of Developing Areas.* Princeton, N.J.: Princeton University Press, 1960.

Boulding, Kenneth. "General Systems Theory: The Skeleton of Science," *General Systems.* Ann Arbor, Mich.: Society for the Advancement of General Systems Theory, I (1956).

Dahl, Robert A., and Lindblom, C. E. *Politics, Economics and Welfare.* New York: Harper & Brothers, 1953.

Easton, David. "An Approach to the Analysis of Political Systems," *World Politics,* IX (April, 1957), 383-400.

———. *The Political System.* New York: Alfred A. Knopf, 1953.

Friedrich, Carl J. (ed.). *Authority.* Cambridge, Mass.: Harvard University Press, 1958.

Hall, A. D., and Flagen, R. E. "Definition of a System," *General Systems,* I (1956), 18-28.

Kaplan, Morton. *System and Process in International Politics.* New York: John Wiley & Sons, Inc., 1957.

Lasswell, Harold D., and Kaplan, A. *Power and Society.* New Haven, Conn.: Yale University Press, 1950.

Merriam, Charles E. *Systematic Politics.* Chicago: University of Chicago Press, 1945.

Nadel, S. F., *The Theory of Social Structure.* London: Cohen & West, Ltd., 1957.

Parsons, Talcott. *The Social System.* New York: The Free Press of Glencoe, 1951.

———. *Essays in Sociological Theory: Revised Edition.* New York: The Free Press of Glencoe, 1954.

———. *Structure and Process in Modern Societies.* New York: The Free Press of Glencoe, 1960.

———, and Shils, Edward A. (eds.).

Toward a General Theory of Action. Cambridge, Mass.: Harvard University Press, 1952.

——, and Smelser, Neil. *Economy and Society.* New York: The Free Press of Glencoe, 1956.

Rommetveit, Ragnar. *Social Norms and Roles.* Minneapolis: University of Minnesota Press, 1955.

Sjoberg, Gideon. "Contradictory Functional Requirements and Social Systems," *Journal of Conflict Resolution,* IV (June, 1960), 198-208.

von Bertalanffy, Ludwig. "General System Theory," *General Systems.* Ann Arbor, Mich.: Society for the Advancement of General Systems Theory, I (1956).

THE AMERICAN ENVIRONMENT
POLITICAL STRUCTURES

Adrian, Charles R. *State and Local Governments.* New York: McGraw-Hill Book Co., Inc., 1960.

Baker, Gordon E. *Rural versus Urban Political Power.* New York: Doubleday & Co., Inc., 1955.

Banfield, Edward C. *Political Influence.* New York: The Free Press of Glencoe, 1961.

Barber, Bernard. *Social Stratification.* New York: Harcourt, Brace & World, 1957.

Cohen, Bernard C. *The Influence of Non-Governmental Groups on Foreign Policy-Making.* Boston: World Peace Foundation, 1959.

Cuber, John F., and Kenkel, W. F. *Social Stratification in the United States.* New York: Appleton-Century-Crofts, Inc., 1954.

Dahl, Robert A. *A Preface to Democratic Theory.* Chicago: The University of Chicago Press, 1956.

——. *Who Governs?* New Haven, Conn.: Yale University Press, 1961.

Eulau, Heinz, *et al.* (eds.). *Political Behavior.* New York: The Free Press of Glencoe, 1956.

Form, William, and Miller, Delbert. *Industry, Labor, and Community.* New York: Harper & Brothers, 1960.

Galbraith, John K. *The Affluent Society.* Boston: Houghton Mifflin Co., 1958.

Handlin, Oscar. *Race and Nationality in American Life.* New York: Doubleday & Co., 1950.

Hunter, Floyd. *Top Leadership, U.S.A.* Chapel Hill: North Carolina University Press, 1959.

Kahl, Joseph A. *The American Class Structure.* New York: Holt, Rinehart & Winston, 1957.

Key, V. O., Jr. *American State Politics.* New York: Alfred A. Knopf, 1956.

Lerner, Max. *America as a Civilization.* New York: Simon and Schuster, 1957.

Lipset, Seymour Martin. *Political Man.* New York: Doubleday & Co., Inc., 1960.

Mills, C. Wright. *The Power Elite.* New York: Oxford University Press, 1956.

Potter, David M. *People of Plenty.* Chicago: The University of Chicago Press, 1954.

Reissman, Leonard. *Class in American Society.* New York: The Free Press of Glencoe, 1959.

Schattschneider, E. E. *Party Government.* New York: Holt, Rinehart & Winston, 1942.

——. *The Semi-sovereign People.* New York: Holt, Rinehart & Winston, 1960.

Williams, Robin M., Jr. *American Society.* New York: Alfred A. Knopf, 1960.

THE AMERICAN POLITICAL CULTURE

Almond, Gabriel A. *The American People and Foreign Policy.* New York: Harcourt, Brace & World, 1950.

Bell, Daniel (ed.). *The New American Right.* New York: Criterion Books, 1955.

Boorstin, Daniel J. *The Genius of American Politics.* Chicago: The University of Chicago Press, 1953.

Commager, Henry Steele. *The American Mind.* New Haven, Conn.: Yale University Press, 1950.

de Grazia, Sebastian. *The Political Community.* Chicago: The University of Chicago Press, 1948.

Edelman, Murray. "Symbols and Political Quiescence." *American Political Science Review,* LIV (1960), 695-704.

Gorer, Geoffrey. *The American People.* New York: W. W. Norton & Co., Inc., 1948.

Graham, George A. *Morality in American Politics.* New York: Random House, 1952.

Hartz, Louis. *The Liberal Tradition in America.* New York: Harcourt, Brace & World, 1955.

Herring, Pendleton. *The Politics of Democracy.* New York: W. W. Norton & Co., Inc., 1940.

Hilsman, Roger. "The Foreign Policy Consensus: An Interim Research Report," *Journal of Conflict Resolution,* III (December, 1959), 361-82.

Hofstadter, Richard. *The American Political Tradition.* New York: Alfred A. Knopf, Inc., 1948.

———. *The Age of Reform.* New York: Alfred A. Knopf, 1955.

Janowitz, Morris, *et al. Public Administration and the Public—Perspectives toward Government in a Metropolitan Community.* ("Michigan Govern- mental Studies, No. 36.") Ann Arbor, Mich.: Bureau of Government, University of Michigan, 1958.

Jones, Alfred W. *Life, Liberty, and Property.* Philadelphia: J. B. Lippincott Co., 1941.

Loewenstein, Karl. "The Influence of Symbols of Politics," in Roy V. Peel and Joseph S. Roucek (eds.), *Introduction to Politics.* New York: Thomas Y. Crowell Co., 1941, pp. 62-84.

Marshall, James. *Swords and Symbols.* New York: Oxford, 1939.

Morison, Elting E. (ed.). *The American Style.* New York: Harper & Brothers, 1958.

Oliver, Henry M., Jr. "Attitudes toward Market and Political Self-Interest," *Ethics,* LXV (April, 1955), 171-180.

Perry, Ralph B. *Puritanism and Democracy.* New York: The Vanguard Press, 1944.

Riesman, David. *The Lonely Crowd.* New Haven, Conn.: Yale University Press, 1950.

Shils, Edward A. *The Torment of Secrecy.* New York: The Free Press of Glencoe, 1956.

Smigel, Erwin O. "Public Attitudes toward Stealing as Related to the Size of the Victim Organization," *American Sociological Review,* XXI (1956), 320-27.

Warner, W. Lloyd. *The Living and the Dead.* New Haven, Conn.: Yale University Press, 1959.

POLITICAL PROCESSES:
INTEGRATIVE AND TENSION-MANAGEMENT

Berelson, Bernard, *et al. Voting.* Chicago: The University of Chicago Press, 1954.

Cohen, J., Robson, R.A.H., and Bates, A. *Parental Authority: The Community and the Law.* New Brunswick, N.J.: Rutgers University Press, 1958.

Diamond, Stanley. *Schools and Development of Good Citizens.* Detroit: Wayne State University Press, 1953.

Erikson, Erik H. *Childhood and So- ciety.* New York: W. W. Norton & Co., Inc., 1950.

Greenstein, Fred I. "The Benevolent Leader: Children's Images of Political Authority," *American Political Science Review,* LIV (December, 1960), 934-43.

Grodzins, Morton. *The Loyal and the Disloyal.* Chicago: The University of Chicago Press, 1956.

Hale, Robert L. "Force and the State:

A Comparison of 'Political' and 'Economic' Compulsion," *Columbia Law Review*, XXXV, No. 2 (February, 1935).

Hapgood, Norman. *Professional Patriots*. New York: Albert & Charles Boni, 1928.

Hess, Robert D., and Easton, David. "The Child's Image of the President," *Public Opinion Quarterly*, XXIV (Winter, 1960), 632-44.

Hollister, William W. *Government and the Acts of Obedience*. New York: King's Crown Press, 1948.

Horowitz, E. L. "Some Aspects of the Development of Patriotism in Children," *Sociometry*. III (August, 1940), 329-41.

Horowitz, Robert, and Tjerandsen, Carl (eds.). *Civic Education in the United States: A Directory of Organizations, 1954*. Chicago: The University of Chicago Press, 1954.

———. *1958–59 Supplement to Civic Education*. East Lansing, Mich.: Michigan State University School of Business and Public Service, Bureau of Social and Political Research, 1958.

Hunter, Earle L. *A Sociological Analysis of Certain Types of Patriotism*. New York: Maisel, 1932.

Hyman, Harold M. *To Try Men's Souls: Loyalty Tests in American History*. Berkeley: University of California Press, 1959.

Hyman, Herbert. *Political Socialization*. New York: The Free Press of Glencoe, 1958.

Iverson, Robert W. *The Communists and the Schools*. New York: Harcourt, Brace & World, 1959.

Landecker, Werner S. "Types of Integration and Their Measurement," *American Journal of Sociology*, LVI (January, 1956), 332-40.

Lane, Robert E. *Political Life*. New York: The Free Press of Glencoe, 1959.

Levin, Murray B. *The Alienated Voter*. New York: Holt, Rinehart & Winston, 1960.

McClosky, Herbert, and Dahlgren, Harold E. "Primary Group Influence on Party Loyalty," *American Political Science Review*, LIII (September, 1959), 757-76.

Merriam, Charles E. *The Making of Citizens*. Chicago: The University of Chicago Press, 1931.

———. *Civic Education in the United States*. New York: Charles Scribner's Sons, 1934.

Nietz, John. *Old Textbooks*. Pittsburgh: University of Pittsburgh Press, 1961.

Opie, Iona and Peter. *The Lore and Language of School Children*. London: Oxford University Press, 1959.

Piaget, Jean. *The Moral Judgment of the Child*. trans. Majorie Gabain. New York: The Free Press of Glencoe, 1948.

Pierce, Bessie L. *Civic Attitudes in American School Textbooks*. Chicago: The University of Chicago Press, 1930.

———. *Citizen's Organizations and the Civic Training of Youth*. New York: Charles Scribner's Sons, 1933.

Ross, E. A. *Social Control*. New York: The Macmillan Co., 1901.

Schaar, John H. *Loyalty in America*. Berkeley: University of California Press, 1957.

Stouffer, Samuel A. *Communism, Conformity, and Civil Liberties*. New York: Doubleday & Co., Inc., 1955.

Westley, W. A. "Violence and the Police," *American Journal of Sociology*, LIX (July, 1953), 34-41.

Wilson, H. E. *Education for Citizenship*. New York: McGraw-Hill Book Co., Inc., 1938.

POLITICAL PROCESSES: ADAPTATION AND GOAL-ATTAINMENT

Barnard, Chester I. *The Functions of the Executive*. Cambridge, Mass.: Harvard University Press, 1938.

———. *Organization and Management*. Cambridge, Mass.: Harvard University Press, 1952.

Blau, Peter M. *Bureaucracy in Modern Society.* New York: Random House, 1956.

Brownlow, Louis. *The President and the Presidency.* Chicago: Public Administration Service, 1949.

Doob, Leonard W. *The Plans of Men.* New Haven, Conn.: Yale University Press, 1940.

Gouldner, Alvin W. *Studies in Leadership.* New York: Harper & Brothers, 1950.

Herring, Pendleton. *Presidential Leadership.* New York: Holt, Rinehart & Winston, 1940.

Hyneman, Charles S. *Bureaucracy in a Democracy.* New York: Harper & Brothers, 1950.

Laski, Harold, Jr. *The American Presidency.* New York: Harper & Brothers, 1940.

Leighton, Alexander A. *The Governing of Men.* Princeton, N.J.: Princeton University Press, 1945.

Leiserson, Avery. *Administrative Regulation.* Chicago: The University of Chicago Press, 1942.

Mannheim, Karl. *Man and Society in an Age of Reconstruction.* New York: Harcourt, Brace & World, 1940.

————. *Freedom, Power, and Planning.* New York: Oxford University Press, Inc., 1950.

March, James G., and Simon, Herbert A. (with collaboration of Guetzkow, Harold). *Organization.* New York: John Wiley & Sons, Inc., 1958.

Neustadt, Richard E. *Presidential Power.* New York: John Wiley & Sons, Inc., 1960.

Redford, Emmett. *Administration of National Economic Control.* New York: The Macmillan Co., 1952.

Selznick, Philip. *TVA and the Grass Roots.* Berkeley: University of California Press, 1953.

Simon, Herbert A. *Administrative Behavior.* 2nd edition. New York: Macmillan Co., 1957.

————, Smithburg, Donald W., and Thompson, Victor A. *Public Administration.* New York: Alfred A. Knopf, 1954.

Weber, Max. *The Theory of Social and Economic Organization.* trans. Henderson, A. M., and Parsons, Talcott. New York: The Free Press of Glencoe, 1947.

POLITICAL PROCESSES:
THE ALLOCATION OF VALUES AND COSTS

Allocation of the Tax Burden by Income Class. New York: Tax Foundation, Inc., 1960.

Bentley, Arthur F. *The Process of Government.* Evanston, Ill.: The Principia Press of Illinois, Inc., 1949.

Brooks, Robert C. *Corruption in American Politics and Life.* New York: Dodd, Mead and Co., 1910.

Chamberlain, Neil W. *A General Theory of Economic Process.* New York: Harper & Brothers, 1955.

de Grazia, Alfred, and Gurr, Ted. *American Welfare.* New York: New York University Press, 1961.

Downs, Anthony. *An Economic Theory of Democracy.* New York: Harper & Brothers, 1957.

Fischer, John. "Unwritten Rules of American Politics," *Harper's Magazine* (November, 1948), 27-36.

Gross, Bertram. *The Legislative Struggle.* New York: McGraw-Hill Book Co., Inc., 1953.

Heard, Alexander. *The Costs of Democracy.* Chapel Hill: The University of North Carolina Press, 1960.

Huntington, Samuel P. "Strategy and the Political Process," *Foreign Affairs,* XXXVIII (January, 1960), 285-99.

Kendrick, M. Slade. *A Century and a Half of Federal Expenditures.* Occasional Paper 48. New York: National Bureau of Economic Research, Inc., 1955.

Key, V. O., Jr. "A Theory of Critical

Elections," *Journal of Politics,* XVII (Fall, 1955), 3-18.

———. *Politics, Parties, and Pressure Groups.* New York: Thomas Y. Crowell Co., 1958.

Matthews, Donald R. *The Social Background of Political Decision-Makers.* New York: Doubleday & Co., Inc., 1954.

Pen, J. "A General Theory of Bargaining," *American Economic Review,* XLII (March, 1952), 24-42.

Rapoport, Anatol. *Fights, Games, and Debates.* Ann Arbor, Mich.: The University of Michigan Press, 1960.

Schelling, Thomas C. *The Strategy of Conflict.* Cambridge, Mass.: Harvard University Press, 1960.

Shackle, G. L. S. *Expectation in Economics.* Cambridge: Cambridge University Press, 1949.

Schultz, William J., and Harriss, C. Lowell. *American Public Finance.* Englewood Cliffs, N.J.: Prentice-Hall, Inc., 1954.

Stevens, Carl M. "On the Theory of Negotiation," *Quarterly Journal of Economics,* LXXII (February, 1958), 77-97.

Truman, David B. *The Governmental Process.* New York: Alfred A. Knopf, 1960.

POLITICAL PROCESSES: STABILITY AND CHANGE

Barnett, H. G. *Innovation: The Basis of Cultural Change.* New York: McGraw-Hill Book Co., Inc., 1953.

Cadwallader, Mervyn L. "The Cybernetic Analysis of Change in Complex Social Organizations," *American Journal of Sociology,* LXV (September, 1959), 154-57.

Cancian, Franseca. "Functional Analysis of Change," *American Sociological Review,* XXV (December, 1960), 818-27.

Fabricant, Solomon. *The Trend of Government Activity in the United States since 1900.* New York: National Bureau of Economic Research, Inc., 1952.

Ford, Henry Jones. *The Rise and Growth of American Politics.* New York: The Macmillan Co., 1900.

Himes, Joseph S. *Social Planning in America.* (Doubleday Short Studies in Sociology.) New York: Doubleday & Co., Inc., 1954.

Merriam, Charles E. *The Role of Politics in Social Change.* New York: New York University Press, 1936.

Moore, Wilbert E. "A Reconsideration of Theories of Social Change," *American Sociological Review,* XXV (December, 1960), 810-18.

Washburne, Norman F. *Interpreting Social Change in America.* (Doubleday Short Studies in Sociology.) New York: Doubleday & Co., Inc., 1954.

Wilson, Godfrey, and Wilson, Monica. *The Analysis of Social Change.* Cambridge: Cambridge University Press, 1945.

Name Index

427

Subject Index